Shaping American Catholicism

Shaping American Catholicism

Maryland and New York, 1805–1915

Robert Emmett Curran

The Catholic University of America Press
Washington, D.C.

The paper used in this publication meets the minimum requirements of
American National Standards for Information Science—Permanence
of Paper for Printed Library Materials, ANSI Z39.48-1984.
∞

Library of Congress Cataloging-in-Publication Data
Curran, Robert Emmett.
Shaping American Catholicism : Maryland and New York, 1805–1915 / Robert
Emmett Curran.
p. cm.
Includes bibliographical references (p.) and index.
ISBN 978-0-8132-1967-7 (cloth : alk. paper) 1. Catholic Church—Maryland—
History. 2. Catholic Church—New York—History. 3. Catholic Church—
United States—History. 4. Maryland—Church history. 5. New York—Church
history. 6. United States—Church history. I. Title.
BX1415.M3C87 2012
282′.75209034—dc23 2011038268

Contents

Abbreviations

In the notes, the following abbreviations are used:

AAB	Archives of the Archdiocese of Baltimore
AAC	Archives of the Archdiocese of Cincinnati
AASMSU	Associated Archives of St. Mary's Seminary and University
AANY	Archives of the Archdiocese of New York
AASPOW	Archives of the Abbey of St. Paul Outside the Walls
ACSC	American Catholic Sermon Collection
ACUA	Archives of the Catholic University of America
ADR	Archives of the Diocese of Rochester
ADRi	Archives of the Diocese of Richmond
APF	*Archivo Di Propaganda Fide*
ARSI	*Archivum Romanum Societatis Jesu*
AUND	Archives of the University of Notre Dame
GULSC	Georgetown University Library Special Collections
GVA	Georgetown Visitation Archives
MD	*Marylandia*
MPA	Archives of the Maryland Province of the Society of Jesus
NARA	National Archives and Records Administration
NYPA	Archives of the New York Province
SAB	Sulpician Archives, Baltimore
WL	*Woodstock Letters*

Shaping American Catholicism

Introduction

As colonies in British America, Maryland and New York were starkly different in terms of their economy, the nature of their government, and their ethnic composition, to mention three. One thing they did have in common that distinguished them from all the other colonies established under British auspices, permanent or otherwise.[1] Each knew an interlude in which its government was headed by Catholics: Maryland for more or less a half century, New York for but a few years. Beyond this parallel in governance, Catholicism in Maryland and New York had very different histories in the Colonial and early national periods, with Maryland at the center of the Catholic experience and New York very much on the periphery. In the nineteenth century, that situation would radically change. Maryland and New York would be the two most important areas in the shaping of Catholicism in America, with the center of influence shifting steadily from the Chesapeake to New York in the course of that century. It was no coincidence that the first two sees to have a cardinal archbishop in the United States were New York and Baltimore, respectively. The three plenary councils during the century were held under the auspices and leadership of Baltimore prelates. Baltimore was the premier see, but New York by the latter half of the century became the most important one: the most populous, the wealthiest (in the commercial and financial capital of the country), the publishing home of Catholic America, the biggest contributor to Peter's Pence, and the Vatican's American banker. Significantly, it was the city that was the biggest beneficiary of the Irish immigration that transformed the Catholic community from the 1830s on.

1. Avalon, the short-lived settlement that Sir George Calvert initiated in 1621 on a peninsula of Newfoundland, was begun three years before Calvert converted to Catholicism.

Lord Baltimore's Colony

Despite the religious affiliation of its founder, Maryland was never a "Catholic" colony. Lord Baltimore's intention in making a second effort at colonization was primarily motivated by business aspirations, not religious concerns to establish a sanctuary for his persecuted Catholic brethren in England. The vast majority of those who crossed the Atlantic in 1633–34 to begin the colony were Anglicans. By 1641 perhaps a quarter of the settlers were Catholic, a demographic that would greatly worsen for them as the colony grew. From the mid-seventeenth century to the Revolution Catholics would constitute about twelve percent of the population. George Calvert himself, in a world in which religion was considered too central to the total life of a society to admit more than one faith, had no mind to establish Catholicism as the religion of the colony. No doubt sensitive to the demographics within his colonial enterprise, Calvert also had come to realize that to force allegiance to a particular religion was to undermine society itself, since those who feign religious beliefs for political or social ends cannot in the end be trusted. Still, more than prudence seems to have been at play in Lord Baltimore's fostering religious liberty in Maryland. For almost a century before the *Ark* and the *Dove* sailed for Maryland, English Catholics had been dissidents. They could not remember the time when Catholicism was the established religion of the realm. They had long since known a *de facto* separation of church and state. For Calvert, in organizing his colony in Maryland, practice would precede theory. Religion, in effect, was to be a private matter, not a state institution. In 1639 the first assembly of the colony decreed that "Holy Churches within this province shall have all her rights and liberties."[2] The ambiguity may have been deliberate; what was clear was that there was to be no established religion in Maryland.

The lord proprietor did transport three Jesuits on the initial voyage—to minister to the Catholic minority in the colony and to evangelize the natives—but the state would not subsidize their work. They would have to support themselves, so the original three Jesuits and those who followed took up land on the same terms as any settler did, largely through the headright sys-

2. *Archives of Maryland* (Baltimore: Maryland Historical Society, 1883–), 1:82–84, cited in James Hennesey, S.J., *American Catholics: A History of the Roman Catholic Community in the United States* (New York and Oxford: Oxford University Press, 1981), 41.

tem that awarded acres of land according to the number of persons brought into the colony. By grants from this system, acquisitions, and legacies, the Jesuits came eventually to possess six plantations in southern Maryland and on the Eastern Shore of the Chesapeake, more than 20,000 acres, worked at first by indentured labor, then, from the late seventeenth century on, by slaves.

The English Civil War had an unhinging effect on Maryland's governance for a decade and a half, beginning in 1645, when Virginia Puritans invaded the state and, with the help of some of Maryland's Protestant majority, seized power temporarily and plundered the Jesuit missions. The two leading Jesuits in Maryland, Andrew White and Thomas Copley, were taken back to England in chains; the rest fled into Virginia. Having returned to the colony in 1648, the Jesuits were forced to seek refuge in Virginia once more in 1655, when another Protestant uprising unseated the Calverts for another brief period. After thirty years of uneasy peace, in 1689, in one of the Colonial ripples of the Glorious Revolution in England, insurgents swept the proprietor out of power, Maryland became a royal colony, and its Catholic minority gradually found itself under the same penal laws they had fled England to escape. By 1718 Catholics could not vote, practice certain professions, bear arms, or worship publicly. They could be doubly taxed. To educate their children in a Catholic school was to risk disqualifying a child from any inheritance or worse. Despite these political and religious disabilities, the Catholic gentry managed to flourish economically. At his death in 1749 the Maryland Catholic Richard Bennett was reputed to be the richest man in America. A generation later, Charles Carroll of Carrollton enjoyed the same reputation.

Over this long penal era, with the exception of the brief presence of some Franciscan priests in the late seventeenth century, Jesuits were the official face of Catholicism. The Jesuit plantations continued to be the heart of the outcast Catholic community in Maryland. They served as liturgical centers for the Catholics in the area; from them Jesuits visited by horseback, circuit-rider style, those in outlying areas once a month, or more frequently where Mass, catechetical lessons, and the sacraments would be dispensed in chapels or Mass-houses of the Catholic gentry. They also began some short-lived schools at St. Mary's City and Newtown in St. Mary's County. At the beginning of the eighteenth century the Jesuits expanded their mission to the Eastern Shore, where they established two plantations, Bohemia and Tuckahoe, on the upper part of the peninsula. At Bohemia they also established an academy that, in the 1740s, educated Charles and John Carroll, among others. In

1764 Baltimore Town became a part of the Jesuits' ministry when they built an unimposing church there, St. Peter's, on a hill overlooking the harbor.

Moving Beyond Maryland

From Bohemia in the 1730s Jesuit missioners introduced Catholicism to Philadelphia, where they started their first urban parish for a polyglot congregation of English, Germans, and Irish. A decade later, German Jesuits acquired farmland in two areas of southeastern Pennsylvania—at Goshenhoppen and Conewago—to begin missions of ministry to the Rhineland and Palatinate immigrants in the region, as well as to Maryland Catholics who had migrated to Pennsylvania. By the eve of the American Revolution the Catholic population of Pennsylvania numbered about 7,000. Although they were effectively barred from holding office and could not bear arms, they enjoyed more civil rights than their fellow Maryland Catholics.

In New York the Catholic community originated in the 1670s under the convert proprietor James, Duke of York. In 1682 James appointed a Catholic, Thomas Dongan, governor of the colony. One of the first acts that the new governor successfully sponsored was a Charter of Liberties and Privileges that extended religious toleration to all Christians. Dongan, like Leonard Calvert fifty years earlier, brought Jesuits with him to New York, with the intention that they would serve as a counter to French Jesuit evangelization of the Iroquois. Jesuit superiors in Rome and London saw this opening as an opportunity to make the new colony its center in British America, from which its members could go out to "neighboring" colonies in Pennsylvania and Maryland to meet the spiritual needs of Catholics there (European appreciation of American geography was always limited, at best). When the governor managed to work out a peace accord with the natives, the Jesuits were free to concentrate their energies on New York City, where they began an elementary school funded by a glebe from Dongan. For five years the school prospered, attracting the children of Protestants and those of the relatively few Catholics in the city. That all ended in 1689 when, in New York's variant of the Glorious Revolution, Jacob Leisler overturned the government, drove out the Jesuits, and closed the school. Two years later Catholics in the colony formally lost the free exercise of their religion.

Revolution and Its Consequences

By 1776 Catholics constituted approximately one percent of the population in the thirteen colonies, with the vast majority of them in Maryland, where the relentless influx of dissenters and anti-papist laws marginalized them within the colony's southernmost counties and in a few pockets of the Eastern Shore. Two events in that decade—the suppression of the Society of Jesus and the American Revolution—had monumental consequences for the development of Roman Catholicism in the colonies soon to be states. Pope Clement XIV's worldwide suppression of the Society in 1773 effectively cut off the clergy in America (all Jesuits) from their source of authority in Rome. The rebellion of the colonists against Great Britain two years later severed their link with England, as well. The result was an utterly disorganized Catholic community in the revolting colonies. In the civil war that Americans fought against the British and each other, Catholics were also divided as a community, but leading Catholics in Maryland and elsewhere played significant roles in the events that led to revolution, independence, and the formation of the federal government. Most prominent was Charles Carroll of Carrollton, whose controversy with fellow Marylander Daniel Dulaney was his major contribution to the colonists' argument for self-government. Through his leadership in Maryland the Catholic gentry began to place its fortunes on the rising "Country" Party, which was laying the groundwork for revolution. When revolution came, Charles Carroll placed his life, honor, and considerable fortune behind the patriot cause. In 1776, as a delegate to the Continental Congress, he was among the signers of the Declaration of Independence. His cousin, the ex-Jesuit John Carroll, joined him in the delegation that the Continental Congress sent to Montreal to attempt to persuade the Canadians to join the fight for independence. John's brother Daniel later served as a delegate to the convention that framed the Constitution.

No one better realized how much the Revolution had changed the lot of Catholics than did John Carroll, whom the suppression of the Society of Jesus had serendipitously brought back to America in 1774. Religious freedom and the separation of church and state meant enormous opportunities for the growth and expansion of the Church in the new republic. That new situation plus the suppression of his religious order led Carroll to take the lead in reorganizing the official Church that the twenty-five clergy, all ex-Jesuits, represented. Even before the war's end, Carroll devised a plan to organize the priests into a representative body to administer the former property of the Jesuits in Maryland and Pennsylvania for the good of the Catholic community and to plan for the needs of a rapidly expanding Catholic population. The result was the Select Body of the Clergy, organized in three districts of Maryland, which eventually had the property incorporated by the state of Maryland in 1792, made the decision to found a college in 1786, and solicited Rome for a bishop in 1787. As James Hennesey has noted: "With no effective episcopal government for 150 years, colonial Catholicism everywhere developed independent ways."[3] John Carroll was acting in the spirit of that tradition in framing such republican-style governance for the Church.

Maryland and New York in the Early National Period

In the new republic Maryland became the site of the institutional nucleus of the hierarchical Church that came into being with John Carroll's elevation as bishop in 1789. Baltimore was named the first Catholic see in America. Within two decades Maryland counted within its borders the first three colleges founded for Catholics: Georgetown (1789), St. Mary's (1800), and Mount Saint Mary's (1808); the first seminary (1791); the first community of women religious: the Carmelites (1790); and the first Catholic school for girls: Georgetown Visitation (1799). During the early national period, Catholicism in the United States continued to be largely a Southern phenomenon. Into the 1820s the largest concentrations of Catholics were in Maryland, Kentucky, and Louisiana (added in 1803). The two greatest churchmen within American Catholicism in that period were southern bishops, John Carroll of Baltimore and John England of Charleston.

When the United States formally gained its independence with the Peace of Paris in 1783, there were approximately two hundred Catholics in New York City. A German Jesuit, Ferdinand Farmer (Steinmeyer), had, during the latter part of the Revolution, made the city one of his missions and organized the first permanent Catholic congregation there. In 1785 that congregation erected St. Peter's Church, a small-frame building near Wall Street. As early as 1810 New York, with its nearly 100,000 inhabitants, had become the largest city in the country. Baltimore could claim fewer than half that number

3. James Hennesey, "Catholicism in the English Colonies," in *Encyclopedia of the American Religious Experience*, ed. Charles H. Lippy and Peter W. Williams (New York: Charles Scribner's Sons, 1988), 1:354.

(46,555), Washington far fewer (15,000). Two years earlier Rome had made the city one of four new dioceses in the country, the first ones created since the establishment of the Baltimore diocese in 1789. Anthony Kohlmann, whom Carroll appointed to govern New York until a Rome-appointed bishop could arrive from Europe, saw in the city the Church's future in America. Its wealth and population made it the most fertile ground for Catholicism's growth and progress in the new republic. The New York Literary Institution, a school that Kohlmann had begun as soon as he had reached New York, was to him the key to the Church's recognition and growth. By 1813 it had become strictly a boarding school, with an ecumenical student body that counted the sons of prominent New Yorkers, including the son of the governor. Then Kohlmann received the shocking news from Jesuit officials that he would have to close the school. Superiors in Maryland had determined that the Jesuits needed to consolidate their resources. Faced with a choice of the New York Literary Institution or Georgetown College, they opted for the latter. Kohlmann claimed to be astonished by what he could see as the most shortsighted of decisions. How could they abandon New York, "the Emporium . . . of America," to bury themselves in Maryland, from which "even seculars flee into the wilderness of Kentucky?" "There is no man acquainted with the . . . State of N.Y. and Maryland that will not pronounce without hesitation that it would be fifty times more for the advantage of the Society to have a college at N.Y. than in any other part of the union."[4] Kohlmann's pleas failed to move the Chesapeake-based superiors, the Institution closed, and it was nearly three decades before another Catholic college opened in the city, and even longer before the Jesuits returned.

The Center Shifts

As late as 1840 the majority of Catholic episcopal sees were located in the South. By the fifth decade of the century, however, mass immigration was shifting the center of the Catholic Church in America from Southern plantations and farms to Northern cities. The most important city within this new immigrant Church was New York. Ironically, at the height of this shift, Rome in 1858 granted "prerogative of place" to the Archdiocese of Baltimore in an implicit recognition of its leadership within the American Church. That rec-

4. Anthony Kohlmann to Giovanni Grassi, White Marsh, May 23, 1815, Archives of the Maryland Province of the Society of Jesus (hereafter cited as MPA), 204-H-10.

ognition, Thomas Spalding points out, was one not based on history alone. In 1860 Baltimore, although half the size of New York in Catholic population, still had an edge in churches and priests and far more institutions and religious orders serving the multitudinous needs of its own immigrant community.[5] That would change dramatically over the next three decades.

What follows are a series of chapters on various matters that were integral to the Catholic experience in these two regions in nineteenth century America: church polity, slavery, religious culture, education and the intellectual life, and social justice. Chapter 1 examines a long-running controversy between the Archbishop of Baltimore and the Jesuits of the Maryland Province, with its implications for the model of ecclesial republicanism that John Carroll had been responsible for creating in the Select Body of the Clergy and its legal offshoot, the Corporation of the Roman Catholic Clergymen of Maryland. Chapters 2 and 5 explore Catholic slaveholding, the former focusing on the Maryland Jesuits' experience, the latter on the interaction of the Church in America and the Holy See on the contentious question. Chapter 3 reviews the way in which one Jesuit historian's concern about contemporary developments within the Society of Jesus in the eastern United States seriously affected his portrayal of that group's past. Chapter 4 attempts to put in context the wave of miraculous cures that swept through the Catholic community in the Chesapeake in the third and fourth decades of the nineteenth century as a precursor of the religious culture that came to dominate Catholic life in the late nineteenth century. Chapter 6 rehearses the brief, troubled life of the Maryland Province of the Society of Jesus, which reflected the shifting center of gravity within Catholic America from the Chesapeake region to New York. New stirrings of the republican tradition, now in a liberal framework, are the subject of Chapter 7, which traces the evolution of a group of dissenting priests in the Archdiocese of New York to chart their relationship to and impact upon the episcopal movement known as "Americanism" at the end of the century. Chapter 8 examines the controversy that swirled around one member of that New York group, the reformer Edward McGlynn, and the role that controversy played in the formation of episcopal blocs and the molding of their world views in fin-de-siècle Catholic America. Chapters 9 and 10 address the growth of the movement for universal parochial education and, in

5. Thomas W. Spalding, *The Premier See: A History of the Archdiocese of Baltimore, 1789–1989* (Baltimore and London: The Johns Hopkins University Press, 1989), 158–60.

particular, the role that New York prelates and laity played in making that goal the norm for American Catholics. Chapter 11 surveys the evolution of American Catholic thought on the socio-economic order in the nineteenth century. The final chapter reflects on the competition among ambitious parties in New York and Washington to develop a university that would be the intellectual center of a maturing American Catholic community.

Eight of the chapters have appeared in earlier versions elsewhere: "Ambrose Maréchal, The Jesuits, and the Demise of Ecclesial Republicanism in Maryland, 1818–1838," in *U.S. Catholic Historian* 26 (Spring 2008): 97–110; "'Splendid Poverty': Jesuit Slaveholding in Maryland, 1805–1838," in *Catholics in the Old South*, ed. Randall M. Miller and Jon L. Wakelyn (Macon: Mercer University Press, 1983), 125–46; "From Saints to Secessionists: The Past as Prologue," in *Studies in Catholic History in Honor of John Tracy Ellis*, ed. Nelson H. Minnich, et al. (Wilmington: Michael Glazier, 1985), 239–59, under the title "From Saints to Secessionists: Thomas Hughes and *The History of the Society of Jesus in North America*"; "'The Finger of God is Here': The Advent of the Miraculous in the Nineteenth Century American Catholic Community," in *The Catholic Historical Review* 73 (January 1987): 41–61; "Rome, the American Church, and Slavery," in *Building the Church in America: Studies in Honor of Monsignor Robert F. Trisco on the Occasion of his Seventieth Birthday*, ed. Joseph C. Linck, C.O., and Raymond Krupke (Washington, D.C.: The Catholic University of America Press, 1999), 30–49; "Prelude to Americanism: The *Accadémia* and Clerical Radicalism in the Late Nineteenth Century," in *Church History* 47 (March 1978): 48–65; "The McGlynn Affair and the Shaping of the New Conservatism in American Catholicism, 1886–1899," in *The Catholic Historical Review* 66 (April 1980): 184–204; and "Confronting the 'Social Question': American Catholic Thought and the Socio-Economic Order in the Nineteenth Century," in *U.S. Catholic Historian* 5 (1986): 165–93. Portions of "The Church in the Public Square: New York and the School Question in the 1890s" were originally published in "Conservative Thought and Strategy in the School Controversy, 1891–1893," *Notre Dame Journal of Education* 7 (Spring 1976): 44–62.

Part 1

The Chesapeake

Chapter 1

Ambrose Maréchal, the Jesuits, and the Demise of Ecclesial Republicanism in Maryland, 1818–1838

THIS OPENING ESSAY has the longest history of all the chapters in this volume. It originated as a research paper in a graduate history course I took in the early 1960s at Shrub Oak Seminary in Westchester, New York. The professor of the course, Francis X. Curran, S.J., had suggested the topic of the long-running dispute between the Archbishop of Baltimore, Ambrose Maréchal, and the Jesuits of the Maryland Mission of the Society of Jesus over the ownership of the vast property that the Jesuits held in the archdiocese. Father Curran had also introduced me to the source that was the richest repository of the materials documenting the controversy: the Roman Archives of the Society of Jesus. Curran had acquired a microfilm copy of the portion of the archives dealing with the Maryland Mission (later Maryland Province) of the Society, from the mission's origin in the seventeenth century to the 1890s. My subsequent research, mostly in the Maryland Mission's records within the Roman Archives, yielded a lengthy paper (in excess of 100 pages) that Curran assured me he could get into publication, most likely in *Historical Records and Studies*, a journal that frequently published master's theses or extended papers on American Catholic history. I accordingly submitted the manuscript to provincial officials for review by its appointed censors, as was the practice in the Society at that time. The response of the provincial censor was that the essay had historical merit but that its publication might stir up old grievances that were better left unstirred. So I simply filed it away among other unpublished manuscripts.

More than four decades later I happened by chance to learn that Chris Kauffman was in need of essays for an issue of the U.S. *Catholic Historian* on early American Catholic history that was to come out in the spring of 2008. I indicated that I could provide something about the Maréchal-Jesuit controversy. Being told that any piece would be needed within a week or ten days gave me momentary pause, but I agreed to deliver by the promised date. A week later I was able to make good on my promise. What had come forth from the original graduate paper was an essay that was one-third its former size and had been radically recast to reflect the larger issues at play in the dispute. The passage of four decades had given me a more mature prospectus that could situate the conflict within a much broader context. In the end I was grateful that the essay had not appeared in its original form, even if I still rejected the censor's reason for keeping it out of print.

The Corporation of the Roman Catholic Clergymen of Maryland

The letter from the Archbishop of Baltimore to the trustees of the Corporation of the Roman Catholic Clergymen of Maryland began innocently enough. "If Almighty God had listened to my prayers and granted me the grace of spending my days in the humble state of life I embraced from my youth," Ambrose Maréchal assured them, "I should never have troubled you with this letter." What followed touched off a conflict between the prelate and the Society of Jesus that would last more than a decade, reach into the highest quarters of ecclesiastical and secular government in Italy and the United States, and, in the process, emasculate the republican institution—the corporation—that lay at the heart of the dispute. The archbishop went on to inform them that, since he found himself "by a disposition of Divine Providence" to be the Archbishop of Baltimore, "charged with the administration of a vast diocese" that necessitated "considerable expenses" that he did not have the means to meet, he was consequently seeking the renewal of the $1,200 annual stipend that the corporation had granted to his predecessors for nearly the past twenty years.[1]

1. Maréchal to the Trustees and Representatives of the Corporation of the Clergy of Maryland, Baltimore, June 6, 1818, in *History of the Society of Jesus in North America*, by Thomas Hughes, S.J., Documents, vol. 1, part 2 (New York: Longmans, Green, 1910), 892.

The Corporation of the Roman Catholic Clergymen of Maryland had been established in 1792 to secure the extensive property held by individuals for the Society of Jesus, now suppressed by the papacy since 1773. Throughout the Colonial period, except for a handful of Franciscans in the late seventeenth century, the Jesuits had been the ministerial church in British America. Since there was originally no state support for religion under the rule of the Calverts, the Jesuits had to support themselves as everyone else did—through working plantations. Over the course of its first century in Maryland, the Society acquired land in various ways: through the headright system that Lord Baltimore established to award property to those who brought persons into the colony, through purchase, and through donations, such as the one of the huge plantation of White Marsh that John Carroll's uncle made to the Society in 1729. Because Maryland law forbade ecclesiastical entities from holding property, all the Jesuit lands were held by individual Jesuits or laymen in trust for the Society. When Pope Clement XIV suppressed the Society of Jesus in 1773, Rome instructed bishops throughout the Catholic world to take possession of all the property that had belonged to the Society. Since there was no bishop in British America south of Quebec, the "Jesuit" property in Maryland remained in the hands of former Jesuits or lay friends. Still there was fear that Rome, through its Congregation of the Propagation of the Faith, under whose jurisdiction mission countries, such as the United States (after 1776), fell, would take some action to seize the property. This was part of a larger concern that, with the Society no longer in existence, the lands would fall into the wrong hands or that the new state would confiscate them.

The securing of the estates was a principal reason for John Carroll's leadership in establishing, in 1783, the Select Body of the Clergy, organized into three districts encompassing Maryland and Pennsylvania, each of which would send two representatives to the appointed meetings of the group. The Select Body was the embodiment of Carroll's plan whereby all the priests in America would organize themselves as a republican body that would choose representatives to adopt "some system of administration" to provide a foundation for the support of the present clergy and for "the good of Religion."[2] The main function of the Select Body was the management of the estates that were to be the principal means of providing that support. Inherent in the rationale of the Select Body of the Clergy, out of which the corporation grew,

2. Hughes, *History of Society*, Documents, 2:644–45.

was the affirmation of a clear-cut separation of spiritual and temporal realms of the Church in Carroll's republican philosophy. Linked to this was Carroll's belief in the fundamental right to property that was intrinsic to citizenship in a republic, since possession of property was the surest safeguard of an independent citizenry. Accordingly the Select Body (and later the corporation) had complete control over the administration of the properties of the Church; no one, not the bishop nor Rome itself, could override that authority. It was a republican division of spiritual and temporal power that reflected the emerging American tradition (in the 1780s) of the separation of church and state. Nine years later, to secure legal protection of the property, the Select Body secured an act from the Maryland legislature that incorporated the property and established a civil corporation, the Corporation of the Roman Catholic Clergymen, as its legal holder.

In a sense, the entire republican polity that Carroll created in the Select Body and the Corporation of the Roman Catholic Clergymen was a provisional one; the groups acted, as it were, as agents or trustees for the suppressed Society of Jesus. At the meeting in 1783 in which they formed the Select Body, the attending clergy resolved to do all in their power to "promote and effect an absolute and entire restoration to the Society of Jesus . . . of all property belonging to it."[3] Should the Jesuits be restored (as many ex-Jesuits fully expected), Carroll and the others assumed that the Select Body of the Clergy would dissolve itself and control of the corporation fall to the provincial superior of the Jesuits. Indeed in 1805, when Rome granted ex-Jesuits in Maryland permission to join with the remnant of the Society of Jesus that had survived in Russia, although the Select Body continued to exist and added members over the next two decades—including Jesuits and non-Jesuits, both native-born and naturalized—it ceased meeting at established times to act as a deliberate body. A decade later, when Pope Pius VII approved the universal restoration of the Society, Carroll indicated that he soon expected the superior to take control of the corporation, according to the rules prescribed by the Jesuit Constitutions.[4] That did not happen, and the trustees continued to act as autonomous agents of the property that the corporation held.

3. Cited in Peter Guilday, *The Life and Times of John Carroll, Archbishop of Baltimore (1735–1815)* (New York: Encyclopedia Press, 1922), 1:529.

4. Carroll to Charles Plowden, Baltimore, March 20, 1815 in Hughes, *History of Society*, Documents, 2:855.

Archbishop Maréchal's Claim

From its beginning the Select Body had granted an annual stipend to Carroll, who in 1784 was named by Rome as superior of the American Mission and five years later as bishop. This was apparently initially given to Carroll, not as the Roman-appointed leader, but as the de facto superior of Jesuits who found their society now suppressed. Indeed the Select Body in the same year that Rome appointed Carroll superior specifically declared that it had no obligation to use the revenue of the estates to support any bishop as such.[5]

Archbishop Maréchal, in his appeal to the corporation in 1818, contended that his right to a stipend had three foundations: the numerous declarations of Archbishop Carroll that the annuity he enjoyed should extend to his successors; the agreement that Carroll and Robert Molyneux, the first Jesuit superior, after the Society's partial restoration in 1805, had signed, in which Molyneux had pledged that the stipend that Carroll annually received was a perpetual one, to extend to his successors; and the very act of incorporation of the Roman Catholic Clergymen of Maryland that expressly stated that the property should be used for the maintenance of the ministers of the "Roman Catholic Religion in Maryland," the chief of whom, he reminded them, was himself.[6] Within the month the trustees responded that, alive to "the embarrassment which the suspension of the yearly allowance formerly paid to your venerable Predecessors was likely to occasion," particularly in light of the financial straits the prelate was experiencing with the construction of the cathedral, they were appropriating for the next three years an annual sum of $560 for his use. By the end of that period, they expected that his financial condition would be such that he would no longer need their assistance.[7] The reduced sum of the stipend and its limitation to three years clearly showed that the trustees rejected the archbishop's claim that he had any right to the yearly support. His predecessors had received the stipend as former Jesuits and as members of the Select Body; Maréchal could claim neither status.

5. Resolution of the Chapter Meeting, October 11, 1784, in Hughes, *History of Society*, Documents, 2:622.

6. Maréchal to the Trustees and Representatives of the Corporation of the Clergy of Maryland, June 6, 1818, in "The Life of the Most Reverend Ambrose Maréchal Third Archbishop of Baltimore, 1768–1828," by Ronin John Murtha, O.S.B. (Ph.D. diss., The Catholic University of America, 1965), 252.

7. Fenwick to Maréchal, Georgetown, June 23, 1818, Archives of the Archdiocese of Baltimore (hereeafter AAB), 16-N-4, Associated Archives of St. Mary's Seminary and University (hereafter AASMSU).

When the corporation in 1820 donated the property of St. Peter's Church to the archbishop, the trustees felt they had satisfied any obligation they had toward aiding the prelate in meeting his expenses.

The archbishop did not agree. Once more, in April 1820, he appealed to the corporation for the granting, on a perpetual basis, of the full stipend that he was entitled to receive as the successor of John Carroll and Leonard Neale. The trustees' response to Maréchal made clear what they had only implied two years earlier: that there were no grounds for such a claim, and for them to admit one would do violence to the duty they had as trustees to administer the properties for the Society of Jesus.[8] The archbishop proceeded to take the step he had threatened to take when he made his first appeal to the trustees in 1818: to take his case to the Congregation of Propaganda Fide. In August 1820 he wrote the cardinal prefect of the congregation that the trustees of the corporation were unjustly denying him the stipend that his predecessors had enjoyed. The property that the corporation controlled, the prelate contended, had been intended for the use of the Church in America in general, not for the Society of Jesus alone. The Carroll-Molyneux agreement to make the stipend perpetual and inalienable was an implicit recognition of this reality. He was not asking for charity, he explained, only for what was his strict due. In particular he was asking the congregation, in order to satisfy his just claim, to assert its authority to convey to the archbishop one of the Jesuit plantations, that of White Marsh, just east of Washington. If there was any doubt about the intended use of the properties the Society had come by during the Colonial period, there was absolutely none about this particular tract. The historical record made it clear, he asserted, that the donor had intended the property for the general use of the Church, not of the Society of Jesus.[9] The archbishop had every confidence that the civil courts in Maryland would support his case and force the Jesuits to honor the practice of an annual stipend that they had begun with Maréchal's predecessors. But he had brought the matter to Rome, to avoid scandal and to secure justice from within, as it were.[10]

8. Peter Edelen to Maréchal, St. Thomas Manor, April 20, 1820, AAB 16-G-5, AASMSU.

9. In asking for White Marsh, the archbishop revealed his lack of knowledge about the state of this plantation. It was large, between three and four thousand acres, with more than sixty slaves. Of that enormous spread only some 400 acres were arable, and the plantation lacked the equipment for the slaves to farm them profitably. In addition the plantation had heavy debts and gave little or no promise of eliminating them.

10. Maréchal to Fontana, Baltimore, undated [August 19, 1820], *Archivo Propaganda Fide* (hereafter APF), Cong. Gen., vol. 927 (1822), ff. 290r–302r, in Murtha, "Life of Maréchal," 260.

Little action resulted from this petition aside from its being passed on by Propaganda to the superior general of the Society of Jesus in Rome. The archbishop's agent in Rome, Robert Gradwell, the rector of the English College, whom Maréchal had engaged to represent him against the lay trustees in Virginia and South Carolina who had taken their grievances to Rome, did pursue the matter with officials of the congregation, arguing that the recalcitrant action of the corporation was but a clerical variant of lay trusteeism. When Gradwell received no more satisfaction from Propaganda than Maréchal had received about his petition to that body, the archbishop decided in the fall of 1821 to make his *ad limina* visit to Rome, to defend his interests in person, including those *vis a vis* the Society of Jesus in his archdiocese.

Luigi Fortis and the Corporation

Meanwhile the superior general of the Society, Luigi Fortis, had been doing his own research on the history of the property and the stipend. He found no foundation for the archbishop's claim of jurisdiction over the corporation's property, he informed the prelate in a January 1822 letter. The Act of the Maryland legislature that Maréchal cited as one of his chief grounds seemed to the general to have no relevance to the matter, since it made no mention of any right of the bishop to the property involved. The Carroll-Molyneux agreement, he went on, had no canonical validity, since no local superior could grant such a perpetual stipend without the explicit approval of the superior general. If the archbishop did have proof that the Jesuit lands were intended for the general welfare of the Church in Maryland, he needed to produce it.[11]

In February 1822 the superior general offered a compromise under which he would tax the Maryland Mission to provide a stipend for the archbishop, if Maréchal would attest that he had no strict right to it.[12] The archbishop refused to waive the right he was convinced he had. Instead, pleading for relief for his impoverished state, which the hard times of the early twenties were worsening, he continued to press his case with Propaganda and renewed his threat to resign if help did not soon come through Rome.[13] In June Fortis informed Propa-

11. Fortis to Maréchal, Rome, January 20, 1822, AAB 22-D-14, copy, cited in Murtha, "Life of Maréchal," 257–58.

12. Fortis to Maréchal, February 4, 1822, AAB 22-D-15, AASMSU.

13. How grave was the archbishop's financial need was a question that loomed ever larger as the conflict continued through the decade. The Jesuits contended that he had ample resources at hand to support himself and his see. William Beschter, the Jesuit pastor of St. John's Church in

ganda that, given Maréchal's refusal, any possibility of the Jesuits and the archbishop settling the conflict on their own seemed hopeless. If the congregation found that the archbishop's claims were valid, the pope himself would need to order the Maryland Jesuits to turn over their property. When the congregation subsequently decided in favor of the archbishop, Pius VII issued a brief, *Ad Futuram Rei Memoriam*, in late July 1822 in which he pronounced that his predecessor, Pius VI, had put all of the properties under the "administration" of John Carroll in the bull that made him Bishop of Baltimore in 1789 and thus ordered the superior general of the Jesuits to command his subjects in Maryland to surrender by the end of the year the plantation of White Marsh to John Carroll's successor in order to provide him with the financial support he needed.[14]

Despite the superior general's disagreement with the pope's decision, he forwarded the brief (through Archbishop Maréchal, who was returning home to Baltimore) to the mission superior, Charles Neale, with the explicit command that he "in virtue of holy obedience [carry out] everything which is contained in the Apostolic Brief...without delay or excuse."[15] When Neale finally received the brief from the archbishop in November, he and his fel-

Baltimore, adjoining the cathedral, claimed that Maréchal had an annual income of more than $1,800. The archbishop himself insisted that his yearly personal income was a fraction of that—some $240, half of which went to Gradwell for his services in Rome. In his will he left approximately $6,000 to various beneficiaries, but a large amount of this sum seems to have come to him in the last few years of his life, probably after 1826. Certainly he could expect little support from the Catholic population itself. The early twenties were locust years for the United States economy. The Panic of 1819 had left widespread financial ruin: trade stagnated, the price of staples collapsed, real estate depreciated, rents shrunk precipitously (in Baltimore by almost 50 percent), businesses failed; in the large cities like Baltimore, there was broad unemployment. The archbishop confessed to a Roman friend in 1823 that he had "never seen anything as distressing" as what he had been witnessing in the region over the past several years. To alleviate his own poverty he inferred he had nowhere to turn except to Rome (Anthony Kohlmann to Fortis, December 5, 1823, *Marylandia* (hereafter MD) 2-I-67, *Archivum Romanum Societatis Jesu* (hereafter ARSI); Francis Dzierozynski to Fortis, Washington, D.C., February 10, 1828, *MD* 3-I-52, *ARSI*; James Whitfield to Gradwell, February 5, 1828, in Hughes, History of Society, Documents, 2:1105; Marèchal to Plessis, November 6, 1823, cited in *Records of the American Catholic Historical Society* 18: 451–52.

14. Hughes, *History of Society*, Documents, 1:476. That the bull of Pius VI had given the Bishop of Baltimore some right to the Jesuit property by placing it under his administration was a matter that the superior general had gone into extensive detail to refute in his correspondence with Propaganda in the weeks preceding the issuance of the brief in July 1822. The bottom line for the general was that the bull's reference to "administration" was simply the stock language of such documents and provided no evidence whatsoever of any "rights" being conferred (Fortis to Consalvi, June 1822, in *MD* 6 *ARSI*).

15. Fortis to Neale, July 30, 1822, Archives of the Maryland Province of the Society of Jesus (hereafter MPA), Georgetown University Library Special Collections (hereafter GULSC).

low trustees of the corporation (his brother, Francis, Benedict Fenwick, and Joseph Carbery) were not about to obey blindly. In a forty-four page reply to Fortis, Neale protested that "the Archbishop of Baltimore is not entitled, in strict justice (whatever his pretensions may be) to one inch of landed or other property now held for the Corporation of Clergy, for the Society in Maryland." In going into minute detail about the society's acquisition of property throughout the Colonial and early republic periods, Neale gave particular attention to the circumstances by which they came to possess White Marsh. James Carroll, he pointed out, had made no stipulation as to how the land was to be used. The fact that two relatives of Carroll were Jesuits argued that his intention had been to give the land for the use of the society to which they belonged, not for the use of the Church in general. A major contention of Neale's was that Propaganda had lacked the basic information to make a valid decision. He referred only briefly to the civil nature of the corporation. As trustees of the corporation, they would be violating the oath they had taken to fulfill their duties if they handed over any of its property to the archbishop.[16]

The incompatibility of the civil status of the trustees and their religious subordination as Jesuits and priests was a point Neale emphasized in a December letter to the archbishop. Neale and his confreres would violate their oath as trustees by jeopardizing the well-being of the corporation through the alienation of one of its most valuable properties. More importantly, they could not in good conscience hand over their property to the archbishop, because its incorporation by the state gave it a civil nature that a prelate could not touch.[17] Nor was this position peculiar to the trustees. Jesuits, both native- and foreign-born, shared the conviction that the papal command was a violation of the wall that should exist between the religious and civil spheres. Francis Dzierozynski, the Polish Jesuit whom Fortis had sent to the United States precisely to settle the conflict with the archbishop (the general would name him superior after Neale's death in 1823), wrote Fortis that, given the civil nature of the property and the strong feelings of the government about foreign intervention affecting the civil rights of Americans, it was impossible for the trustees to obey the brief.[18] Another immigrant Jesuit and former superior, Anthony Kohlmann,

16. Neale to Fortis, November 22, 1822, MD 6, ARSI. The lengthy letter bore the signature of Neale, but was actually the work of both Neale and the secretary of the corporation, Benedict Fenwick.

17. Neale to Maréchal, Mount Carmel, December 23, 1822, AAB 22B-V-2, AASMSU.

18. Dzierozynski to Fortis, December 28, 1822, MPA, GULSC. Whether the property was civil

seconded Dzierozynki's reasoning: "The [Maryland] Jesuits as Jesuits have no possessions; as members of the Corporation they are subject solely to the civil authority just as their lands are." Should Rome force the Jesuit trustees to hand over White Marsh, the United States government would clearly read it as foreign interference with the civil rights of American citizens.[19]

The United States Government and Papal Intervention

As the deadline for carrying out the pope's command approached in late December, the archbishop informed the prefect of Propaganda of Neale's continuing resistance and ingenuously advised that the congregation lay no canonical censures on the disobedient Jesuits, since they would likely reject them as well, given their convictions about their inalienable right to their own property; instead the congregation, along with the superior general of the Society, should make a joint declaration that expulsion from the Society of Jesus and incardination as lay priests within the archdiocese of Baltimore would be

or canonical in its character was central to the dispute. The Maryland Jesuits claimed that it was completely civil in character. The archbishop insisted that it was strictly ecclesiastical. Although the archbishop was essentially correct about the nature of the property, he failed to show that by the very fact that members of a religious order had acquired or inherited property, it automatically passed under the jurisdiction of the Church and became subject to its laws. As Lord Coke had defined the principle: "*Quidquid monachus acquirit, monasterio acquirit.*" That the United States legal system made no distinction between civil and ecclesiastical property did not change the status of the property in the eyes of the Church. In fact, in every country, it had been Jesuit policy to secure civil rights and titles to property as far as the laws permitted (Patrick J. Dignan, *A History of the Legal Incorporation of Catholic Church Property in the United States: 1784–1932* [Washington, D.C.: The Catholic University of America Press, 1933], 38). This did not undo its canonical status. As far back as 1641 the English provincial superior had seen that the property was clearly ecclesiastical (Edward Knott to Carlo Rosetti, November 17, 1641, in Hughes, *History of Society*, Documents, 2:1033). Fortis had no illusions about the matter. He bluntly told Dzierozynski that the "property (say what you like) is an ecclesiastical possession, and therefore subject to the jurisdiction of the Congregation of Bishops and Regulars" (Fortis to Dzierozynski, Rome, May 1, 1825, MPA, GULSC). The American Jesuits kept insisting that because the property was held by individuals in a civil organization, it had no ecclesiastical character, no matter how it was being used or by whom. If they alienated any part of the property to the archbishop, they would be violating their civil trust, and the government would likely seize the property. This fear flew in the face of the fact that they had regularly sold or given away property, including St. Peter's Church to the archbishop, without any reaction from the government. Of course none of these transactions had been occasioned by a Roman mandate. The archbishop himself was never able to refute their argument because it would have meant admitting that the property did belong to the Society of Jesus. He could have undermined the Jesuits' position only by undermining his own case.

19. Kohlmann to Fortis, December 6, 1822, MD 6, ARSI.

the fruit of continued resistance to the papal brief.[20] The trustees ignored the deadline and Propaganda ignored the archbishop's wild suggestion. But the Jesuits' warning, in response to the papal brief, that the United States government would never tolerate a foreign government forcing American citizens to give up property, had obviously gotten the congregation's attention. Cardinal Joseph Fesch in August 1823 strongly advised Archbishop Maréchal to provide official documentation that would refute the Jesuits' claim.[21] Such documentation would best come from the United States government itself, but, for some reason, more than a year elapsed before the archbishop sought assurance from the State Department that it would not object to the Jesuits' transferring property to him.

By then the Secretary of State had long known about the papal brief and was, according to various sources, disturbed by this threat to the civil rights of American citizens. A former Jesuit and present priest of the archdiocese, William Matthews, a nephew of the Neales and a member of the corporation, brought the document to John Quincy Adams, the Secretary, who became "very indignant" about this foreign imposition, but took no steps to lodge a protest with Rome.[22] Maréchal, very tardily learning that the Jesuits had sought to have the U.S. government intervene, wrote to the State Department in October 1824 to find out whether the government had become involved in the case. Daniel Brent, the chief clerk of the State Department and as a Catholic related to the Carrolls and a friend of the Neales and Fenwicks likely Matthews' connection at State, informed the archbishop that Adams had decided not to make a formal protest over the brief, but went on to warn him that any further attempts to have the Holy See dictate the civil actions of American citizens would bring a strong response from the government. "[T]he government of the United States," he concluded, "can never view with indifference any future appeals to such foreign states, touching the administration of temporal concerns under its jurisdiction."[23] The archbishop then secured testimony from several lawyers, including the future Chief Justice Roger Taney, who wrote that, in his opinion, there were no grounds for the government's

20. Maréchal to Consalvi, Baltimore, December 27, 1822, APF, Congr. Gen., vol. 932 (1824), ff. 356r–357v; 354r–355v, cited in Murtha, "Life of Maréchal," 268).

21. Fesch to Maréchal, Rome, August 27, 1823, AAB 17-F-10, cited in Murtha, "Life of Maréchal," 269–70.

22. Joseph Tristan to Fortis, May 28, 1823, cited in Hughes, *History of Society*, Documents, 2:1071.

23. Brent to Maréchal, October 24, 1824, in Hughes, *History of Society*, Documents, 2:1072.

interference in any transfer of property that should take place from the Jesuits to the archbishop.[24] In December the archbishop sent this opinion to Brent.

Four days earlier one of Maréchal's worst fears about the controversy was realized when the *Daily National Journal*, a Washington paper, published *Ad Futuram Rei Memoriam* (in Latin) together with a letter in which the writer promised that an English translation of the document would soon follow, so that everyone could see for themselves "how far foreigners, whether ecclesiastics or seculars, but especially the former, are desirous of having a share in the management of the concerns of this free country."[25] With the brief now public, the archbishop feared not only a revival of anti-popery, but further pressure being put upon the federal government to take action. Facing this dual threat, the archbishop began to express his willingness to receive a pension rather than property. White Marsh soon disappeared from any discussion of the terms of a resolution of the conflict.

Breaking the Autonomy of the Corporation

In the meantime there was a new superior of the Jesuits' American Mission. Charles Neale had died in April 1823, and Superior General Fortis named Francis Dzierozynski as Neale's successor the following fall. Fortis, who since 1822 had determined to reach an equitable settlement with the archbishop, had become convinced that a non-American local superior was the only hope he had of attaining that goal. No settlement was possible, Fortis realized, so long as the trustees of the corporation remained autonomous. (In a recent letter Anthony Kohlmann had referred to the corporation as "a state within a state.")[26] The general therefore charged the new superior with the obligation of having the trustees convey to the Society the property they legally held. Dzierozynski, once in office, made this transaction his top priority. In December 1823 he secured a major breakthrough when the trustees drew up a statement that admitted that all the property belonged to the Society and thus the local superior had sole authority over it. In writing they pledged that, although it was necessary to preserve the corporation, the superior would have ultimate control over the business of that body.[27] There was

24. Maréchal to Brent, Baltimore, December 8, 1824, AAB 22B-W-3, in Murtha, "Life of Maréchal," 277.

25. The letter was signed "Truth"; *Daily National Journal*, December 4, 1824.

26. Kohlmann to Fortis, Washington, D.C., June 20, 1823, MD 2-II-8, ARSI.

27. Declaration of Trustees, December 16, 1823, MD 6, ARSI.

one hitch, however. They could not sign the paper. Doing so, they contended, would involve turning the corporation over to a person (Dzierozynski) who was not a citizen of the United States and thus invalidate the corporation and leave the property open to confiscation, surely the last thing superiors of the order desired.[28] When the superior confided this predicament to Fortis, the superior general replied that he wanted nothing less than a formal renunciation, complete with signatures. If they had scruples about legal consequences, they could do it in secret and the document would never see public light.[29]

The new pontiff in 1824 had authorized Propaganda to work out a settlement of the conflict with the superior general of the Jesuits. Fortis told the congregation's officials that he was trying to get the property transferred from the corporation to the Society so that he himself might be able to carry out the brief. From what he had learned, however, he was not sure the Mission in Maryland could afford to surrender its White Marsh plantation without putting the entire Mission in financial ruin. They were willing, he reported, to pay the Archbishop $1,000 a year. In the summer of 1824 the archbishop learned from his agent that Propaganda had reaffirmed *Ad Futuram Rei Memoriam* and ordered the Jesuits to pay Maréchal $1,000 a year "with arrears" until they turned over White Marsh to him. Gradwell warned him not to expect anything to come of it. The agent thought it an empty gesture by a congregation that, with the deaths of Cardinal Consalvi and Pius VII, was coming more and more under the influence of the Jesuits. "Indeed the Society carries all before it here," he concluded.[30] Moved by this reading of the shifting Roman winds, as well as his growing fears of Washington's involvement in the affair, Ambrose Maréchal by the fall of 1824 informed Gradwell that he was ready to accept the annual pension and to leave it to his successors to work out the execution of the papal brief.[31] But the compromise worked out by Fortis failed when the Maryland Jesuits insisted that the archbishop count the $400 income he received from the property that had housed St. Peter's church as part of the annual stipend from the corporation.[32]

The archbishop was becoming sick of the entire affair. "The delay which

28. Peter Epinette to Fortis, December 19, 1823, MD 6, ARSI.

29. Fortis to Dzierozynski, September 6, 1825, MPA, GULSC.

30. Gradwell to Maréchal, Rome, August 5, 1824, AAB 17-F-10, AASMSU.

31. Maréchal to Gradwell, Baltimore, October 12, 1824, Archives of the English College, Baltimore Papers, 1–133.

32. Hughes, *History of Society*, Documents, 1:327.

I experience," he confessed to Gradwell in June of 1825, seven years after first approaching the trustees about a stipend, "has thrown me into extreme difficulties. There are days when my soul is sad unto death."[33] To Pope Leo XII he wrote that if aid did not come to him quickly, he would have to resign his see, since it would be impossible to administer it in his financial straits.[34] Propaganda actually sent the prelate $1,000 that summer to relieve him.[35]

In May 1825 the three trustees of the corporation—Francis Neale, Benedict Fenwick, and Peter Epinette—signed a formal document in which they solemnly declared that, as trustees, they held the property "*for the sole and exclusive use, benefit and advantage of the members of the Society of Jesus*... and that we shall in no wise... administer... any part or parts of the said property but with the full consent and approbation of the General."[36] That did not change their attitude toward any settlement with the archbishop. In August of that year they sent a formal petition to Propaganda in which they pleaded that abiding by the papal brief would bring economic and political disaster. The Mission was already so impoverished that the loss of White Marsh would force them to abandon the country, since the plantation provided, so they claimed, two-thirds of the Mission's revenue. To pay a pension in lieu of ceding property would only postpone slightly their economic collapse. And they reiterated the government's grave concern about Rome's intrusion. Even to pay the pension would be considered a violation of United States laws, in the government's eye, and the result would be federal confiscation of the funds as well as the loss of their citizenship.[37] The plea was one based mainly in fantasy.

Toward a Settlement

The archbishop himself was determined to make one last attempt to obtain satisfaction from Rome. In January 1826 he sent a long *discursus* on the controversy that matched the hyperbole of the Jesuits' letter. Maréchal's theme was the riches of the Jesuits and their gross exaggeration of their debts. He

33. Maréchal to Gradwell, June 14, 1825, in Hughes, "History of Society," Documents, 2:1086.

34. Maréchal to Leo XII, July 14, 1825, in Hughes, "History of Society," Documents, 2:1086.

35. Hughes, "History of Society," Documents, 2:1072.

36. Declaration of the Trustees of the Corporation of the Roman Catholic Clergymen, May 10, 1825, MD 6, ARSI.

37. Maryland Jesuits to Propaganda Fide, August 16. 1825, MD 6, ARSI.

included a mass of statistics to support his contention that the corporation possessed a much greater portfolio of land, slaves, and livestock than it was purporting to possess. In contrast Maréchal claimed to be so destitute that he could not even afford the postage for all the letters his position entailed him writing to persons at home and abroad. He thought there was little chance that the federal government would defend the Jesuits in their claims of foreign intrusion regarding White Marsh, but for prudence's sake he was willing to settle for $1,000 from the Jesuits, whether the source was the American mission or the Roman curia of the order. The time had come, he ended, for the "Sacred Congregation to pronounce whether or not the See of Baltimore will be fraudulently deprived of the funds, from which it has prospered since its foundation; . . . or whether [this See] will be blotted out from [the Catholic world.]"[38]

The Sacred Congregation in June 1826 decreed that if the Maryland Jesuits continued to defy all authority and gave the archbishop neither a pension nor a piece of property, then this obligation should fall upon the Society in Italy. The superior general, after praying over the matter for several days, agreed to pay the Archbishop of Baltimore $800 for the rest of his life. As he explained to Dzierozynski, "I was alive to the fact that a continuance of this controversy would become a matter of public scandal, since men of authority and judgment were not at all brought round by your reasoning. . . . I came to the conclusion that there was no settling the case except by settling with the claim, and by paying the money which you said you did not have."[39]

This final outcome left the archbishop feeling that his long struggle had hardly been worth the effort. Maréchal complained that this settlement would not give to him the funds that the Jesuits had failed to pay him these past eight years. Moreover, he thought $1,200 rather than $800 to be a fairer settlement. But he signed the agreement, with the provision that his successors would share the stipend.[40] The general agreed.

The archbishop lived to receive but two stipends from the Society. When James Whitfield succeeded him in 1828, the payments from Rome continued

38. Maréhal to Somaglia, Baltimore, January 15, 1826, APF, Congr. Gen., vol. 938 (1826), ff. 253r–263r.

39. Fortis to Dzyierozynski, in Hughes, *History of Society*, Documents, 1:558.

40. "De Mensa Episcopali Praesulis Balt.[is]," undated and in Maréchal's hand, probably 1827, Arch. Carroll Corresp. 1799–1815, Church Deeds 1824–1862, vol. 1:2, AAB, in Murtha, "Life of Maréchal," 285.

throughout his six-year tenure. When Samuel Eccleston became the Archbishop of Baltimore in 1834, he renewed the claim for the annual stipend. A new superior general, Jan Roothaan, informed William McSherry, the Maryland Provincial (the mission had been raised to a province in 1833) in 1835 that he should settle the matter, once and for all, with Eccleston. Perhaps unaware of the history of the controversy, he suggested that the new provincial make an end of it by giving the prelate a farm or the yearly revenue from a farm. "The one thing I desire," he concluded, "is that this business be settled between you, by mutual consent and with satisfaction; and that the Society here in Rome have nothing more to do with it."[41] Negotiations began, but it was not until another provincial replaced McSherry that prelate and province reached a settlement in July 1838. Eccleston agreed to receive $8,000 as an investment for the perpetual support of the See of Baltimore. Ironically the Maryland Jesuits were able to make this settlement because of the $115,000 they had secured from the mass sale of their plantation slaves, many of whom worked at White Marsh. Thus the plantation figured in the beginning and the end of the two-decade controversy.

The Impact of the Controversy

That a mass sale of slaves had enabled the province to settle the long-standing stipend claim had in large part been possible because of the changing nature of the corporation. Although it did not occur immediately, the trustees' renunciation of 1825 was the beginning of the loss of the autonomy that the members of the corporation had known since its establishment. Steadily the provincial superior came to control the body and the selection of its members. By 1838 there was no longer a Select Body, only trustees appointed by the Provincial of Maryland. The preservation of property and the slave economy that sustained it—the prime reasons for the creation of the corporation in the 1790s—were no longer the key to supporting the ministry of the Jesuits, which was increasingly centering no longer on the parishes in the traditional rural areas of Maryland, but on the emerging urban areas of Washington, Baltimore, and Philadelphia, with their promise of educational apostolates.

Thus ended the last remnant of republican government that Carroll had devised for the American clergy in the 1780s. Archbishop Maréchal's claims

41. Hughes, *History of Society*, Documents, 2:1117.

against the Jesuit property had been the key to ending this experiment in clerical republicanism. Ironically, at the very same time, the archbishop was responsible for the demise of the lay republicanism within American Catholicism that trusteeism represented. His opposition to the legal control that trustees enjoyed and to the prerogatives they claimed as a consequence led to a declaration by the Holy See in 1822 that the ultimate authority over the administration of property lay not with parish trustees, but with the bishop. In all things, trustees were to be the bishop's servants. Thus Ambrose Maréchal was key to the effective emasculation of the two major republican institutions established within the Church during the early national period: the corporation and the trustee system.

As these crucial events were unfolding in the 1820s, a new and more ambitious form of republican governance involving bishop, clergy, and laity was being introduced in the diocese of Charleston by Bishop John England, the Irish immigrant, who picked up the torch of ecclesial republicanism that John Carroll had first held aloft. England sought to build a Catholic community in his diocese in which bishop, priests, and laity worked together within the framework of a basic body of law that they had commonly adopted. The constitution that he drew up for Charleston was unique in the history of American Catholicism. It established vestries composed of elected laity and resident clergy for the governance of parishes and annual conventions of representatives from the laity and clergy for the governance of the diocese itself. Sadly, England's republican experiment had an even shorter life than Carroll's, effectively ending with the former's death in 1842.

Chapter 2

"Splendid Poverty"

Jesuit Slaveholding in Maryland, 1805–1838

IN THE FALL OF 1979 Stafford Poole, CM, approached me about joining him and Douglas Slawson in putting together a session on slaveholding by religious communities for the 1980 annual meeting of the American Historical Association. His intention was for Slawson and him to do a paper on Vincentian slaveholding in Missouri, and I would present one on Jesuit slaveholding in Maryland. Having agreed to participate, I turned again to the Roman Archives as the focus of my research. The microfilm reels of the Maryland Papers in the archives had by then completed an odyssey that had brought them from Shrub Oak, when that institution closed at the end of the 1960s, to New York City to be part of the archives of Woodstock College, which had recently moved there from Maryland, only to be transferred to Georgetown in 1974 when the Society closed Woodstock as a theologate. That happy (for me) development meant virtually unlimited access to the correspondence, reports, petitions, and other materials related to Jesuit slaveholding in Maryland, from the complete restoration of the Society there in 1815 to the aftermath of the mass sale of slaves in 1838.

Our AHA session took place in late December 1980, with Kenneth Stampp and Eugene Genovese as chair and commentator, respectively. A few months later Randall Miller asked if I would consider developing the paper into an essay for a book that he and Jon Waklyn were putting together on Catholics in the South in the antebellum period. The book was published by Mercer University Press in 1983 under the title *Catholics in the Old South: Essays on Church and Culture.*

"A Prodigious Number of Negroes"

In 1788 Patrick Smyth, an Irish Roman Catholic clergyman who had recently returned from a brief ministry in Maryland, published a pamphlet on *The Present State of the Catholic Mission, Conducted by the Ex-Jesuits in North-America.* Smyth's conclusion was that any impartial observer could readily see why the mission was languishing. The ex-Jesuits, Smyth reported, were

> superbly lodged on the banks of the Potomack, or basking in the luxuriant climes of the Eastern Shore.... They have a prodigious number of negroes and these sooty rogues will not work, unless they be goaded and whipped, and almost flayed alive.

"Oh God of Heaven!" he melodramatically exclaimed,

> and is it thus your widely extended vineyard is neglected?... Are your very ministers become taskmasters? they, who should cherish the hapless African in their bosoms, and share the sad burden of his afflictions?[1]

John Carroll, one of the ex-Jesuits and the superior of the Church's missions in America, responded to Smyth in a pamphlet of his own, exposing the falsehoods and distortions that Smyth was spreading.[2] But the accusations and insinuations of the Jesuits as "Lords of the Land" persisted. They reached a climax with the mass sale of their slaves in 1838.[3]

Jesuit landholdings in Maryland by the nineteenth century *were* extensive, though small when compared to the former estates of their brethren in Latin America. In 1824 they amounted to something more than 12,000 acres, most of which consisted of four large estates in the southern counties of Prince Georges, Charles, and St. Mary's and two smaller plantations on the Eastern Shore. In addition, the order possessed two farms totaling more than 1,700 acres in eastern Pennsylvania.[4] It had acquired these properties from Lord Baltimore according to the conditions of plantation issued by the proprietor

1. Patrick Smyth, *The Present State of the Catholic Mission, Conducted by the Ex-Jesuits in North-America* (Dublin: P. Byrne,1788), 17–18.

2. "Response to Patrick Smith," in *The John Carroll Papers*, ed. Thomas O'Brien Hanley, 3 vols. (Notre Dame: University of Notre Dame Press, 1976), 1:337–46.

3. In May 1839, for instance, an official of the Society for the Propagation of the Faith, who had been supporting the Maryland Jesuits for years, confided to the treasurer of the Maryland Province of the Society of Jesus that the SPF kept getting reports of the great wealth in land and slaves that the Maryland Jesuits possessed; Francis Vespre to Jan Roothaan, New York, May 30, 1839, MD 7-I-13, ARSI.

4. Thomas Hughes, S.J., *The History of the Society of Jesus in North America: Colonial and Federal Documents* (London: Longmans, Green, 1908), 1:379–80.

in 1636, by acquisitions, and by bequests from individual Catholics. From the beginning, the Jesuits depended upon their estates to support their ministries to settlers and indigenous Americans.

To work these lands, the Jesuits relied upon indentured servants, a practice they never completely abandoned. As this form of labor became increasingly difficult to secure and retain in Maryland, as elsewhere in the Chesapeake region, the Jesuit missionaries, like their secular fellow planters, turned to slave labor. Although there is explicit evidence of Jesuits' slaves only from 1711 on, it is highly probable that they were working the plantations for at least a generation by that time.[5] By 1765 there were 192 such slaves.[6]

The Corporation and the Maryland Mission

At the suppression of the Society of Jesus by Pope Clement XIV in 1773 every bishop in the world was instructed to take possession of the order's property within his jurisdiction. Since no bishop in British America was closer than Quebec, the order was never carried out in Maryland.[7] The lands there remained in the control of the ex-Jesuits. To protect the property, they organized, in 1783, the Select Body of the Clergy, and nine years later received legal recognition from the state of Maryland as the Corporation of the Roman Catholic Clergymen (see chapter 1). The charter empowered three to five trustees, elected by the members of the Select Body, to administer the property. With this authority the trustees appointed the managers of the several plantations, distributed the revenue accruing from them, approved expenditures, and oversaw the general business of the estates.

In 1805 five of the former Jesuits in Maryland received permission to affiliate with the Russian Province of the Society of Jesus, which Catherine the

5. Hughes, *History of Society*, Documents, 1:222. Andrew White, the first Jesuit in Maryland, brought two mulattoes to Maryland, in 1633 and 1635, but there is no evidence they were slaves; see Peter Finn, "The Slaves of the Jesuits in Maryland" (master's thesis, Georgetown University, 1974), 6; Whittington B. Johnson, "The Origins and Nature of African Slavery in Seventeenth-Century Maryland," *Maryland Historical Magazine* 73 (1978): 236–45. Joseph Zwinge, S.J., speculated from ex-slave reminiscences that two servants working on the plantation at St. Inigoes in 1644 were slaves; "The Jesuit Farms in Maryland," *Woodstock Letters* 41(April 1912): 204.

6. Zwinge, "Jesuit Farms," 204.

7. Richard Challoner, the vicar apostolic of the London District, to whom fell the task of carrying out the Holy See's orders regarding Jesuit property in territory controlled by Great Britain, ruled out any American confiscation as being impractical (Hughes, "History: Text III" [unpublished redaction of 1933], 209, in Georgetown University Libraries Special Collections [hereafter GULSC].

Great had protected from suppression. John Carroll, now bishop of Baltimore and head of the corporation, signed an agreement with Robert Molyneux, the Jesuit superior, allowing the society to reenter into possession of its old estates. The corporation, however, continued to be the legal owner and to control the operation of the land. Membership in the Select Body was limited to Jesuits after 1816, but the Jesuit superior, as noted in chapter 1, had no direct authority over the corporation.

In the first three decades after the restoration of the Society in the United States, a majority of those in the Maryland mission were foreigners.[8] With two exceptions, all of the mission superiors during that period were foreign-born. Since only citizens could be members of the Select Body, the foreign superiors had no legal authority over the property.[9] Persistent tensions continued between the native Jesuits and their foreign brethren. The American Jesuits tended to regard the immigrants—particularly those from Russia, Italy, and Belgium—as "ignorant monarchists" who appreciated neither the republican traditions of this country nor the peculiar position of the Society of Jesus in Maryland as a large landowner. Superiors like Giovanni Grassi and Anthony Kohlmann were criticized for incurring large debts to promote what the indigenous Jesuits regarded as unrealistic plans for their colleges in Georgetown, New York, and Washington. Francis Dzierozynski, the superior from 1823 to 1830, struck many as a good religious who was more fit to "be governed than to govern."[10] The trustees of the corporation particularly resented the financial burdens placed upon the mission by the superiors' admission of novices from Ireland, Belgium, and elsewhere in Europe.

Many of the Jesuits from continental Europe, if not openly antidemocratic, were critical of American institutions and values. Dzierozenski wrote a young Maryland Jesuit in Rome that he hoped that the Marylanders studying there would shed their republican spirit.[11] Men like Dzierozynski, a native of Pol-

8. The catalogue of the mission in 1819, for instance, showed that of the 53 members, only 19 were Americans. Irish (16), Belgians (8), Germans (4), and French (3) Jesuits made up most of the foreign majority.

9. The corporation's trustees, for instance, acknowledged in 1817 that with the death of Archbishop Leonard Neale, an ex-Jesuit, spiritual jurisdiction of the estates had now passed to the superior of the mission. It was understood that the trustees retained temporal jurisdiction (GULSC, Maryland Province Archives [hereafter MPA], Corporation Minutes, October 11, 1817).

10. George Ironside to Aloysius Fortis, Washington, D.C., October 10, 1825, MD 3 I 31, ARSI.

11. Peter Kenney to John McElroy, Tullahey, June 28, 1822, MPA, GULSC. Kenney reported in 1833 that a story was making the rounds in Ireland that during the War of 1812 one of the foreign

ish Russia, and Stephen Dubuisson, who had left Sainte-Domingue with his parents during the revolution there, found the American Jesuits too independent, too materialistic, and too little observant of the rules of religious life. To Dzierozynski, Dubuisson, and others, the American Jesuits were too much the children of their culture.

The State of the Plantations

These factions and the poor financial condition of the mission caused the general of the Society, Thaddeus Brzozowski, to send an Irish Jesuit, Peter Kenney, as his special visitor in 1820. One of Kenney's assignments was to examine the state of the farms. He found "splendid poverty . . . so much apparent wealth & real poverty. . . . Complaints of bad management, unprofitable contracts, useless & expensive experiments & speculations" greeted Kenney on every plantation with the exception of the one at Newtown.[12]

Adam Marshall, the Jesuit charged with overseeing the plantations for the corporation, described them as "immense tracts of land resembling rather an Indian hunting ground than lands inhabited by men acquainted with the arts of civilized life."[13] Marshall reported to the superior general that St. Inigoes, St. Thomas, White Marsh, Bohemia, and St. Joseph's were all "in wretched condition." The dwellings for the slaves were "almost universally unfit for human beings to live in." Even the best farm within the mission, Conewago in Pennsylvania, was in debt. Everywhere accounts were incorrectly kept, if at all. In only two places could he reckon with any reasonable certainty the annual revenues and expenses. None of the estates were fulfilling the purpose for which they had been created—that of supporting the apostolic work of the mission. The tobacco the Potomac plantations grew was of an inferior quality.[14] White Marsh, potentially the most valuable property they possessed, had a debt in excess of $6,000, despite the large revenues it had brought in for

Jesuits in Maryland "sallied out of the house & abused a number of American soldiers who were drawing cannon through our grounds, Calling them rebels to their King, & wishing that the fate of rebels might attend them." John England, Bishop of Charleston, was the bearer of the tale and his source, according to Kenney, was Benedict Fenwick, the former Maryland Jesuit and then Bishop of Boston (Kenney to Stephen Dubuisson, Dublin, October 28, 1833, MPA, GULSC).

12. Kenney, "Temporalities," 1820, MPA X-T-1, GULSC.

13. Adam Marshall to Enoch Fenwick, August 14, 1820, MPA 205-G6, GULSC.

14. Marshall to Luigi Fortis, Georgetown, February 6, 1821, MD 2-II; Marshall to Fortis, March 5, 1821, MD 2-I-32, ARSI.

the past several years.[15] The general debt of the mission was nearly $32,000.[16]

Nor did Marshall think improvement a possibility. "We have no men capable of managing a farm."[17] During the Colonial period Jesuit brothers had been assigned this responsibility wherever possible, but their numbers were few so that priests, with the occasional assistance of lay overseers, most often served as managers. With the restoration of the Society in 1805, Jesuit brothers slowly were given charge of the farms by the corporation. By 1820 brothers managed five of the six plantations in Maryland, with the exception of St. Joseph's at Tuckahoe in Talbot County. Two years later four of them had either been removed or demoted to the status of assistant manager under a priest, the apparent victims of Kenney's and Marshall's devastating reports.[18]

One aspect of the brothers' management that disturbed Kenney was their arbitrary treatment of the slaves. He had found general disaffection among the blacks. In some places the weekly ration of meat was only a pound and a quarter ("often this has not been sound"); pregnant women were being whipped; the behavior of the slaves was scandalous; and their practice of religion was virtually nonexistent. At the conclusion of his visit in 1820, Kenney instructed the mission consulters to issue regulations concerning the treatment of slaves with which the local procurators would have to comply strictly. "Great zeal, piety, prudence & charity with a regular system," he concluded, "are requisite to check the evils attendant on the possession of slaves."[19]

The Maryland Jesuits, one should note, did make conscientious, if not consistent, attempts, by word and example, to shape among their fellow Catholic slaveholders an appropriate Christian attitude toward the treatment of their human property.[20] As early as the 1760s a Maryland Jesuit chastised his congregation for regarding their slaves as "inferior species."[21] John Lewis, the last superior of the mission before the Jesuits' suppression, reminded his hearers of Saint Paul's warning that "he who takes no care of his dome-

15. Marshall to Fortis, White Marsh, February 5, 1822, MD 2-II-26, ARSI.

16. Charles Neale to Fortis, Portobacco, November 27, 1822, MD 6-II-1, ARSI.

17. Marshall to Fortis, February 5, 1822, MD 2-II, ARSI.

18. Joseph Heard remained in charge of Bohemia, which Marshall had found recovering under Heard's careful management (Marshall to Fortis, March 5, 1821, MD 2 II-6, ARSI).

19. Kenney, "Temporalities," 1820, MPA X-T-1, GULSC.

20. See Peter Finn, "The Slaves of the Jesuits," 45–74; Thomas Murphy, S.J., *Jesuit Slaveholding in Maryland, 1717–1838* (New York and London: Routledge, 2001), chap. 4.

21. The hand seems to be that of John Boone; the date 1765–1770, American Catholic Sermon Collection (hereafter ACSC), GULSC.

sticks is worse than an infidel and has denyed his faith." He urged them to regard their slaves as "Brothers in Jesus Christ."[22] The slaves, in the Jesuits' eyes, had certain basic rights: adequate food, clothing, shelter; proper care when they were old or sick; a Christian marriage in which the spouses were not separated.[23]

By the 1820s the living conditions for the slaves on most of the plantations were less than adequate. The hard times of the early years of that decade were partly responsible. By 1823 the novice Jesuits at White Marsh subsisted on a diet of little more than bread and water before the corporation closed the novitiate. Two years later the local superior had to sell a portion of the estate to buy winter clothing for the blacks.[24] The high percentage of slaves either too young or too old to work also compounded the pressures upon the estates to provide for all those dependent upon them. Thus, in 1820, only fourteen of the sixty-one slaves at St. Inigoes were working the land; twenty-three were under fourteen years of age.[25] At White Marsh a higher proportion was working: thirty-two out of sixty-eight. Twenty-six were under fourteen, and fourteen were over forty-five.[26] These exceptionally high percentages of underage or superannuated slaves may have been due to the general good care the blacks received. At any rate, by the early 1830s the material condition of the slaves seems to have improved significantly as conscientious priests like Joseph Carbery, Ignatius Combs, and Peter Havermans were assigned to St. Inigoes, St. Thomas, and Newtown respectively.

An immigrant Jesuit, Fidèle de Grivel, reported to Rome in 1831 that St. Thomas remained somewhat in a "delapidated state" but improvements were taking place, and all, including the slaves, had plenty to eat. Indeed, in their enjoyment of the rudiments of life, de Grivel thought that the blacks were "Lords" in comparison to the peasants of his native France.[27] White Marsh

22. John Lewis, before 1761, ACSC, GULSC.

23. Finn, "The Slaves of the Jesuits," 50–51; Brother Joseph Mobberly's Diary, 1820, 142–43, GULSC.

24. Dzierozynski to Fortis, Georgetown, January 29, 1825, MD 3-I-19, ARSI.

25. Census of 1820, Prince Georges County, Maryland, National Archives and Records Administration (hereafter NARA).

26. Census of 1820.

27. De Grivel to Jan Roothaan, Georgetown, January 26, 1831, MD 4-II-9, ARSI. According to de Grivel, forty of the sixty slaves were female. Peter Kenney echoed de Grivel's conviction about the relative position of the slaves in comparing the latter with the peasants in Ireland; Kenney to McElroy, March 30, 1822, McElroy Papers, MPA, 206-Z-10a, GULSC.

was still struggling to meet its basic needs, although by 1832 Father Samuel Mudd had paid off all its debts.[28] The most thriving plantation was St. Inigoes, where Carbery had instituted a system of dividing the estate into several farms. One farm he rented out to a white farmer. Another he worked himself with approximately half of the active slaves. The other five tracts of land he assigned to slave families at the annual charge of $1.25 an acre. These last families were responsible for providing for all their needs. By the mid-1830s, Carbery was claiming success for this free-enterprise project. The debt was paid off, the blacks had an incentive to produce for themselves, and their economic improvement led them to better moral and spiritual lives, as well.[29]

The Jesuits' slaves on most of the estates were routinely able to earn money, either by doing extra work for their owners or by selling products they had made, produce they had raised in their own gardens, or seafood they had gotten from the river. Joseph Mobberly, a Jesuit brother manager, estimated that the average family at St. Inigoes was able to earn from eighty to 100 dollars a year.[30] Carbery's experiment was the first attempt to increase productivity by giving at least some of the blacks the incentive of working their own fields exclusively.

The moral and spiritual condition of the slaves also was a concern in these years. Despite catechesis and required attendance at Mass, Kenney found their lives a moral wasteland and a scandalous reproach to the Society. At Bohemia he encountered illegitimacy: a *ménage à trois* involving a slave, a free black, and an abandoned married woman; another slave living with a prostitute; still another's house serving as a "tavern for selling whiskey &c to ours & our neighbour's servants." Except for an old woman, none had been to the sacraments for twelve years[31]—all this among a slave population of seven. Bohemia's slaves were particularly notorious, but Kenney received similar complaints at all the plantations in Maryland.[32]

Some Jesuits attributed this moral anarchy to the Society's own failure to discipline the slaves. To William Beschter in Baltimore the proverb "he is

28. De Grivel to Nicholas Sewall, White Marsh, May 30, 1832, MPA 4-5-6, GULSC.

29. De Grivel, "*Memoire Sur la Congregation Prov. du Maryland commences le 3 Mai le 8 Juillet 1835*" [1835] MD 5-I-21, ARSI; Carbery to Stephen Dubuisson, St. Inigoes, April 25, 1838, MPA, GULSC.

30. Mobberly Diary, 1:132–33, GULSC.

31. Kenney, "Temporalities," 1820, MPA X-T-1, GULSC; "Observations made by R. F. Visitor at the Residence of St. Francis Xavier Bohemia Cecil Co., Mar., June 1831," MPA, X-P-5, GULSC.

32. "Memorial Left with the Superior of the Mission, S.J. in Missouri by the Rev. F. Peter Kenney, Visitor of the Society in the United States, N. Amer. 1832," MPA, X-S-1, GULSC.

as bad as a priest's slave" was all too warranted. "Our slaves corrupt... with impunity," he wrote. Neither their moral offenses nor their laziness was punished. It was no surprise to Beschter that the farms languished, given this moral climate.[33] Brother Mobberly, who managed St. Inigoes from 1806 to 1820, shared Beschter's conviction that a lack of discipline lay at the root of the growing corruption and discontent among the slaves. "The better a Negro is treated," Mobberly wrote in his diary, "the worse he becomes."[34] Mobberly's own attempts to discipline his slaves had just the opposite effect. By the time Kenney visited the plantation in 1820, the blacks compiled a litany of complaints to cite against the brother. Kenney listened (as he had elsewhere), and the corporation removed Mobberly within a month.[35]

Seeking Change

Mobberly, a Maryland native, had given much thought to the place of "the peculiar institution" within the mission. He wrote a long tract in 1823 justifying slavery as a necessary good that provided for the forty percent of the human family that was "deficient in point of intellect... & know not how to take care of themselves."[36] Despite this pro-slavery position, long experience on the Jesuit plantations had convinced him that the present slave economy based on the raising of tobacco and corn was unprofitable and was destroying the soil. Furthermore, abolitionist activity in Maryland among the Quakers and Methodists was causing the slaves to grow more restive. Fears of insurrection were growing. In 1814 an abortive uprising had occurred within sight of St. Inigoes. As early as 1815 Mobberly was urging that the mission rid itself of its slaves and entrust the land to tenant farmers and the production of wheat.[37]

The corporation was actually ahead of Mobberly. In the fall of 1814, the trustees raised the issue of not only changing from slave to free labor but also of freeing the slaves themselves. The following June they resolved "to dispose for a limited time of the greatest part of the blacks on the different plantations."

33. Beschter to ?, Georgetown, March 27, 1829, *MD* 3-IV-18, *ARSI*.

34. Mobberly Diary, 1:143, GULSC.

35. Corporation Minutes, April 20, 1820, MPA, GULSC; Kenney, "Temporalities," 1820, MPA X-T-1, GULSC. As Finn notes, the slave of the Jesuits had the unique opportunity of voicing his complaints and problems to a superior higher than his local master; Finn, "The Slaves of the Jesuits," 81.

36. Mobberly Diary, 2:1–87, GULSC.

37. Mobberly Diary, 1:74–77, 139–41, GULSC; Mobberly to Giovanni Grassi, St. Inigoes, February 15, 1815, MPA 204-K-3, GULSC.

They intended to set a term of service for each black on their estates, after which he or she would be free. As John Carroll, one of the trustees, explained,

> since the great stir raised in Engld, about Slavery, my Brethren being anxious to suppress censure, which some are always glad to affix to the priesthood, have begun some years ago, and gradually proceeding to emancipate the old population on their estates.[38]

Such deferred emancipation was a policy of the corporation that predated the restoration of the mission in 1805.[39] Probably more common was the practice of allowing the slaves to purchase their freedom through their earnings. In 1801 the corporation censured Peter Brosius of Conewago for manumitting a slave on that estate. Such a precedent, the trustees noted, would prove "not a little injurious to that subordination, which ought to be preserved among the other slaves belonging to the Corporation." They advised Brosius to have the slave purchase his freedom, at least on a *post factum* basis.[40]

During the 1790s, when the Abolition Society in Maryland was fostering many slave petitions for freedom in the courts, several blacks on the estates at White Marsh and St. Thomas adopted this strategy of suing for their freedom through the aid of sympathetic lawyers. None apparently was successful, although one of the cases remained in the courts until 1811.[41]

The resolution passed by the corporation in 1814 was never carried out. At a meeting six years later the trustees repealed it with the explanation that "mature reflection" had convinced them that such a plan was "prejudicial."[42] By 1820 two things had happened: Kenney had been appointed visitor, and Ambrose Maréchal, Carroll's successor as archbishop of Baltimore, had initiated his claims against the Jesuit estates. Kenney agreed to support the Jesuits' desire to "part with the slaves" on the two conditions that the change be well planned and that they were certain that it would be for the better.[43] The archbishop's threats to go to court with his claim may also have caused the trustees to delay any mass sale of slaves.

38. Corporation Minutes, June 14, 1814, MPA, GULSC; John Carroll to John Troy [1815] in *Carroll Papers*, 3:313.

39. John Carroll to Francis Neale, Baltimore, October 3, 1805, MPA 203-T-8, GULSC.

40. Corporation Minutes, Newtown, 1801, MPA, GULSC.

41. Proceedings of Representatives, Select Body of the Clergy, St. Thomas, June 3, 1795, MPA, GULSC; see Jeffrey Brackett, *The Negro in Maryland: A Study of the Institution of Slavery* (Baltimore: Johns Hopkins University Press, 1889), 54–155.

42. Minutes of Corporation, St. Thomas, August 22, 1820, MPA, GULSC.

43. Kenney to Louis De Barth, April 24, 1820, MPA 205-H-3, GULSC.

As the debts of the mission grew in 1822, the trustees mortgaged White Marsh and its blacks.[44] A month later they authorized the agent, Adam Marshall, to sell as many as thirty slaves from that plantation, if he judged it could survive without their labor.[45] For whatever reason, no sales ensued.

As noted in chapter 1, in July 1823 the Holy See ruled in favor of the archbishop's claim and ordered the Maryland Jesuits to surrender White Marsh with all its slaves and equipment to Maréchal, but they refused to do so on the grounds that the incorporation of their property in Maryland gave it a civil character that a bishop could not touch. In that same summer the superior general, Aloysius Fortis, appointed another foreign superior, Francis Dzierozynski, to resolve the controversy and to break the power of the corporation as an independent authority. To Fortis the real cause of their impoverished state was that they loved property too much and obedience not enough. "Let them renounce the property," he exhorted Dzierozynski, and God would bless their work.[46] Within two years the trustees reluctantly renounced any right to administer the property without the consent of the superior general.

A New Impetus to End the Maryland Tradition

In the fall of 1830 Peter Kenney returned to America as visitor. A decade earlier he had been forced to cut short his first visit in order to attend the General Congregation in Rome that the Society had called upon the death of its superior general. Now a new general, Jan Roothaan, had instructed Kenney to make a thorough investigation of the question of whether or not to sell the plantations. Kenney found them in much better condition than they had been in 1820. Almost all were debt-free. Only St. Joseph's seemed a bad investment for the future.[47] But the estates were still not supplying revenue to the general fund of the mission to support the training of Jesuits or Georgetown College. Indeed, regarding the financing of education, a traditional major apostolic activity for Jesuits, Kenney concluded that the mission was "as perfectly destitute of means, as if it had not one acre of landed property."[48]

Before the visitor could complete his investigation of the estates, Father

44. Corporation Minutes, St. Thomas Manor, October 16, 1822, MPA, GULSC.

45. Corporation Minutes, St. Thomas Manor, November 20, 1822.

46. Fortis to Dzierozynski, Rome, March 25, 1824, MPA 500 39b, GULSC.

47. Kenney to McElroy, St. Joseph's, July 2, 1832, MPA, GULSC.

48. "Instructions given by Revd. F. Kenney to Revd. F. McSherry Procurator" [1833] MPA X-M-2, GULSC.

General Roothaan ordered that the Maryland Jesuits not sell, but continue their efforts to improve them.[49] The premature decision apparently was the result of the intervention of the former superior, Dzierozynski, who had informed the general in January 1831 that, contrary to reports, the farms were producing and the mission debts were practically gone.[50]

The superior general had said nothing about the slaves. A year later, in August 1832, Kenney's four appointed advisors in Maryland urged him to make clear to Roothaan "the State of public feeling on the subject of slavery & the other disadvantages of the system." Four of the five wanted Roothaan's permission to liberate in a gradual manner the mission from its slaves and to substitute free laborers in their place. Three of them, Fidèle de Grivel, Thomas Mulledy, and William McSherry, strongly supported the proposal. Dzierozynski was equally opposed to it; Stephen Dubuisson favored it with great reservations.[51]

In 1820 Kenney had already been of the mind that ridding the estates of the slaves would remove "an immense burden" from the mission and "the odium" that the survival of slavery on the Jesuit estates in Maryland cast upon the whole Society.[52] The thrust for change, however, now came from a new breed of American Jesuits with no particular loyalty to the Maryland tradition. Mulledy and McSherry were among six young Jesuits that Kenney had sent to Rome in 1820 for their philosophical and theological training. By 1830 Mulledy was already rector of Georgetown and McSherry the assistant to the mission superior. To some of the older Jesuits in Maryland they seemed all too ambitious. One had the impression that they were trying to take over the mission with "grand plans of selling the farms . . . putting the money in a bank . . . and manumitting the slaves, at least after some years of service."[53]

Mulledy and McSherry both came from northwestern Virginia, an area in which slaveholding was not so deeply implanted. Although the sons of slaveholders (McSherry himself had been raised on a large estate near Martinsburg with more than a score of slaves), both were convinced that the problems that plagued the Society in Maryland—pressing debts, lack of funds,

49. Kenney to Dubuisson, July 20, 1831; MPA 210-T-8, Kenney to McElroy, August 4, 1831, MPA 210-T-E, GULSC.

50. Dzierozynski to Roothaan, January 28, 1831, MD 4-I-5, ARSI.

51. August 28, 1832, MD 4-I-23, ARSI.

52. Kenney, "Temporalities," 1820, MPA X-T-1, GULSC.

53. Beschter to Roothaan, February 15, 1830, MD 3-IV-23, ARSI.

struggling colleges, corrupt slaves—stemmed from the attempt of the Maryland Jesuits to be both priests and planters.[54] Of the two, Mulledy proved the more aggressive in urging the Society to abandon the "Maryland Way" that had prevailed since the 1630s. Shortly after he had returned from Rome in 1829 he petitioned Roothaan to reopen the question of selling the farms and slaves. By 1833 he was telling the superior general that it was impossible to maintain both the estates and the colleges at Georgetown and Frederick. "We can not have both flourishing colleges and flourishing missions," Mulledy warned Roothaan.[55]

In that year the Maryland mission was raised to the level of a province and McSherry named the first provincial superior. He made his headquarters at St. Thomas Manor, where he had the opportunity to study closely the workings of that plantation, as well as those at St. Inigoes and Newtown. He is "verifying what I foresaw many years ago," Mulledy reported to Roothaan in March 1835, "that these farms were a curse on the Society in this region. The negroes behave abominably on many of them & the priests allow them to destroy soul and body. They are neither farmers nor priests, nor religious—but some bad combination of all."[56]

The Decision to Sell

In 1830 Mulledy had suggested to the superior general that the slaves be sold on the basis of deferred emancipation in order that they might be prepared for their eventual freedom during their stipulated years of future service. The longer the Society kept the slaves, he went on, the more it would run the risk of being forced to sell some as their numbers grew or became more restless under the influence of abolitionists. "Wouldn't it be necessary to separate families?" he conjectured. "And isn't this a hideous thing in America?"[57]

The Maryland Jesuits had long been sensitive to the changing climate concerning slavery.[58] By the 1830s Jesuits like Mulledy and McSherry were

54. Mulledy to Roothaan, Georgetown, January 7, 1830, *MD* 3-IV-20, *ARSI*. This concept of the hyphenated priest first appears in a letter from Richard McSherry to his Jesuit brother. It was a theme that both William McSherry and Mulledy repeated often in the next several years.

55. Mulledy to Roothaan, Georgetown, October 28, 1833, *MD* 5-III-4, *ARSI*.

56. March 8, 1835, *MD* 5-III-6, *ARSI*.

57. Mulledy to Roothaan, January 7, 1830, *MD* 3-IV-20, *ARSI*.

58. This heightened concern among Jesuits survived John Carroll. Two years after his death in 1815, the corporation sold five troublesome blacks at the Bohemia estate to a slave trader with the understanding that he would transport them to Louisiana. A local magistrate, a Methodist

becoming increasingly uncomfortable about their status as slaveowners. At the same time, new legislation in Maryland, triggered by the rampant fears among whites concerning the growing free black population, made it more difficult to pursue a policy of deferred emancipation.[59] Thus the declining status of the free black in Maryland was making emancipation less acceptable as a goal, while persistent financial pressures were making a mass sale more thinkable. Should the latter occur, it would almost certainly involve the removal of the slaves to the Deep South, since the plantations in the Chesapeake region were, on the whole, too small to absorb the nearly three hundred blacks on the Jesuit estates. Since the typical Maryland slaveholder had one slave and ninety percent held fewer than fifteen, the possibilities for a local sale of nearly three hundred slaves without breaking up families were clearly extremely limited.

In 1835 the Maryland Province held its first congregation. Out of the deliberations of the ten delegates came requests to the superior general to allow them to reduce the number of country missions, to sell the slaves and some of the lands, and to work the remainder with tenant labor. This would enable the province, so the delegates reasoned, to focus its limited resources on establishing colleges and a mission band in cities like Baltimore, Philadelphia, and Richmond.[60] Mulledy, McSherry, James Ryder, and George Fenwick (all Roman-trained) were persuaded that the future of the Society in America lay in rapidly growing urban centers rather than the stagnant rural areas of southern Maryland and the Eastern Shore.[61] These four were joined by Stephen Gabaria, who had been in the United States less than two years, and Francis Vespre to form the majority that supported the *postulatum* to sell the slaves.

Aloysius Young, the provincial's assistant from an old Maryland family related to the Carrolls, wanted Roothaan to know that Mulledy, the domi-

opposed to slavery, intercepted the stage carrying the blacks out of the state and charged the Jesuit superior at Bohemia with kidnapping. The charge was dropped, but the corporation bought back the blacks to avoid scandal (Mobberly Diary 1:111–17, GULSC).

59. Ira Berlin, *Slaves Without Masters: The Free Negro in the Antebellum South* (New York: Pantheon Books, 1974), observes that "nowhere was the sense of crisis greater than in Maryland" (210ff).

60. *Acta Primae Congregationis, Provinciae Marylandiae Societatis Jesu*, 1835, MPA, GULSC.

61. Even Augustine Bally, a Jesuit missioner in rural Pennsylvania who was so successful during his long tenure at the province's church/farm in Goshenhoppen that the village was renamed for him, had to admit that Catholicism was advancing much more rapidly in the cities than in the country places; Bally to Roothaan, Goshenhoppen, January 31, 1842, *MD* 7-VII-3, ARSI.

nant force in the congregation, and his supporters were biased against the rural tradition. Young claimed that Vespre, the province procurator, had succumbed to Mulledy's pressure but personally opposed the plan. He urged the superior general not to abandon the lands and institutions in Maryland, where Catholicism and the Society had flourished for over two hundred years, simply to appease the empty fears about an imminent division of the Union and a possible civil war (two reasons that had been given in the congregation for selling the slaves).[62]

Young spoke for other native Marylanders who remained committed to the estates. Most of the local superiors opposed the sale. They pointed to the profits they were beginning to realize at Newtown and St. Inigoes, and contended that the blacks on their plantations, far from being corrupt, were leading truly edifying lives in the practice of religion and in their general behavior. They were skeptical about the superior opportunities to be found in the cities. At least one local superior of an estate, Ignatius Combs at White Marsh, opposed slavery in principle, and much more the slave trading that such a sale would involve.

One delegate to the congregation pleaded that the general consult the opinion of some of the older men in the province who knew much more about slaveholding than most of those who were supporting the sale.[63] To Roothaan's query about seeking such wider advice, McSherry airily replied that he already knew what these older Jesuits thought and what weight to give to their opinion.[64]

It was the Europeans who were most vocal in opposing the sale. With the exception of Young, all those who had voted against the measure in the congregation were Europeans. Dzierozynski, the former superior, had wrestled as early as 1822 with the morality of selling the blacks in order to relieve the mission's financial pressures. By 1831 he was convinced that selling the lands and "our blacks" was "a dangerous . . . unjust" scheme.

> Lands are a patrimony from our Fathers . . . by what right can they be alienated? I consider the blacks under this respect only, that they are our sons, whose care and salvation has been entrusted to us by Divine Providence and are always happy under our Fathers.[65]

62. Young to Roothaan, Georgetown, October 1835, MD 5-II-2, ARSI.
63. Dubuisson Memorial, 1836, MD 5-II-4, ARSI.
64. McSherry to Roothaan, Georgetown, August 30, 1836 MD 5-II-3, ARSI.
65. Dzierozynski to Fortis, Georgetown, April 12, 1822, MD 2-I-51, ARSI.

Peter Kolchin has pointed to the similarity in viewpoints that Russian noblemen and Southern planters exhibited toward serfs and slaves, respectively.[66] What is striking about the arguments used by the European Jesuits in Maryland is the manner in which they tend to imagine the master-slave relationship as an idealized master-serf relationship. They tended to see the slaves as innocent and pious, gathering as families to recite their rosaries, working hard when treated properly, bringing consolation to the missionary by their staunch faith despite their lowly position. In the Europeans' view the lot of the country slaves was a blessed one compared to that of the corrupt, impoverished free blacks in the cities.[67]

The European Jesuits regarded the estates not only as a sacred trust, but as a refuge from the cities and as a guarantee of their status in society. As Fidèle de Grivel observed to Roothaan in 1835, "The Protestants have, up to now, appreciated us only because of our large estates; if we sell them, they will consider us no better than Methodist preachers who crisscross the country to accumulate money."[68]

To Jesuits like Dubuisson and de Grivel a bond existed between the Society and its blacks that could be broken only for the most extreme reasons, such as incorrigibility, but not need of money. They argued that selling them would lead to the slaves' physical and moral ruin, and would give great scandal to Protestants and Catholics alike. Dubuisson informed Roothaan while in Rome in 1836:

> There is in general a great repugnance among the blacks of Maryland to being sold south. Without doubt [our slaves]... would despair when they should be dragged from their ancient manors and churches. Isn't the very idea of being forced to go with new masters a cruel one?

66. Peter Kolchin, "In Defense of Servitude: American Proslavery and Russian Proserfdom Arguments, 1760–1860," *American Historical Review* 85 (October 1980): 809–27.

67. *Memoire du Pere Stephen Langaudelle Dubuisson de la Campagnie de Jesus, missionarie aux Etats unis d'lAmerique Septentrionale, Mai 1836, MD* 5-IX-7, ARSI. Dubuisson told of blacks with Protestant masters who had stoically suffered whipping for converting to the Catholic faith. Giovanni Grassi, born in Parma and educated in Polish Russia, had written in 1818 about "the very great consolation which the negroes bring to the missionary; for among them, although they are poor slaves and so abject in the eyes of the world, are found chosen souls filled with such beautiful sentiments of true piety, that they move one to tears"; Grassi, *Notizie varie sullo stato presente della repubblica degli Stati Uniti dell' America settentrionale scritte al principio del 1818* (Milano: 1819).

68. De Grivel, *Memoire Sur La Congregation* [1835], MD 5-I-21, ARSI.

What it meant, Dubuisson concluded, was that in a state in which selling slaves south was virtually unknown (less than two percent of sales), the Maryland Jesuits would be collaborating with planters from the deep South to parlay the labor of their blacks into immediate financial gain. The abolitionists, he warned, would not miss the meaning.[69] Peter Havermans tried to explain to Roothaan what it meant for a slave to be sold south:

> As far as I can determine, they are to be sold to non-Catholics . . . in a non-Catholic area, more than a thousand miles away, which will surely give many an occasion of criticizing us. For no one does this sort of thing except evil persons, such as slave traders who care about nothing but money, or those who by necessity are so pressed by debts that they are forced into such a sale. . . . I tell you this will be a tragic and disgraceful affair . . . especially since some of the slaves have been my personal responsibility.[70]

The Sale of 1838

Selling slaves was not new to the Maryland Jesuits. But the sales had usually taken place to keep families together or to punish refractory slaves, such as at Newtown in 1774 or at Bohemia in 1832. In 1835, however, McSherry began to sell blacks to meet financial needs. Fourteen were sold from St. Thomas, then eleven from St. Inigoes.[71] The latter were sold to Henry Johnson, the ex-governor of Louisiana, and Thomas Jameson, a Catholic planter from the same state. McSherry claimed, against the objections of Dubuisson and others, that it was not possible to sell them to neighbors, and that Johnson had promised to provide for their religious needs in the same manner the Jesuits themselves had cared for them.[72]

In October 1836 Superior General Roothaan finally approved the sale of the slaves, provided that their religious needs be met, that families not be separated, especially spouses, and that the money be invested for the support

69. Dubuisson Memorial, *MD* 5-II-4, *ARSI*. The one European to support the sale, Gabaria, was merely concerned about the persons to whom they would be sold. He judged the sale itself would cause little stir; Gabaria to Roothaan, Georgetown, January 20, 1837, *MD* 5-III-13, *ARSI*.

70. Havermans to Roothaan, Newtown, October 20, 1838, *MD* 7-I-9, *ARSI*.

71. De Grivel claimed that one of the slaves sold at St. Thomas was actually exchanged for a horse, and that the trade had given great offense to the Catholics in the area. "They were saying," he reported to the general's assistant, "even priests engage in the business of human flesh." "After a month," he added, "the horse died and the Catholics rejoiced"; de Grivel to Aloysius Landes, October 24, 1835, *MD* 5-II-1, *ARSI*.

72. McSherry to Roothaan, Georgetown, August 30, 1838, *MD* 5-II-3, *ARSI*.

of Jesuits in training.[73] The Panic of 1837, with its deflationary effects upon the economy, delayed its execution. "We could not at the present time," McSherry wrote Roothaan in May 1837, "obtain one tenth part of what we could have obtained last year for them."[74] The onset of the cancer that would within two years claim his life forced McSherry to ask to be replaced as provincial. In October 1837 the superior general appointed Mulledy to succeed him.

Mulledy wasted little time making the final sale. In June of 1838 he agreed to sell 272 slaves from the four estates in southern Maryland to Johnson and a partner for $115,000. The pair made a down payment of $25,000 and were given ten years to complete the transaction. Eight thousand dollars went to the settlement of the archbishop's claims against the estates, and $17,000 was applied to the $30,000 debt Georgetown College had incurred through Mulledy's ambitious building campaign when he had been rector. The remaining $90,000 was to be invested for the support of the Jesuits in formation. "All the Catholics who live near our estates, with no exceptions," Mulledy assured Roothaan, "approve the sale. They say it should have been done twenty years ago. "He admitted that the Jesuit superiors on the plantations were quite upset "because they no longer will be great lords." He hoped, however, that this would make them better Jesuits.[75]

Rumors of a mass sale had been circulating among the slaves since at least 1832. To give the local superiors no chance to encourage their blacks to escape, Mulledy arrived without notice, accompanied by Johnson and a sheriff. Thomas Lilly, stationed at St. Thomas Manor, was outraged. "They were dragged off by force to the ship and led off to Louisiana. The danger to their souls is certain," he wrote to Roothaan. "The buyers have promised they will be treated in a Christian fashion. But given the laws and customs of that region it will be very difficult to keep them." Lilly, a native of Pennsylvania, did not believe the superior general could have permitted such a scandal had he been properly informed, or had he consulted more of the members of the province. The majority, he reported, were appalled.[76]

One is tempted to wonder whether the sale would have happened had the corporation still been a semiautonomous body. Carbery, Combs, Dubuisson, Dzierozynski, and de Grivel all had the seniority that had normally

73. Roothaan to McSherry, October 27, 1836, MPA F-3-A[2]-F5-E, GULSC.

74. Georgetown, May 13, 1837, MD 5-I-39, ARSI.

75. Mulledy to Roothaan, Fredericktown, August 9, 1838, MD 7-I-5, ARSI.

76. Lilly to Roothaan, St. Thomas Manor, July 2, 1838, MD 7-II-1, ARSI.

meant membership on the corporation before it became subservient to the provincial.

The main body of the slaves was sent in a second ship in November 1838. This time there were runaways at White Marsh and St. Inigoes. Joseph Carbery at the latter plantation and (apparently) Ignatius Combs at the former warned their blacks to hide in the woods. At least nine did so at White Marsh and two at St. Inigoes. There is reason to believe that some escaped at St. Thomas, as well.[77] Most of these seem to have returned eventually to the farms.[78] By late November the only blacks who remained, except the elderly and runaways, were those who were married to spouses on other plantations or to free blacks. Mulledy wrote John McElroy on November 11, 1838, that Johnson had left behind these slaves in order to attempt to purchase their spouses as well.[79] It would seem at this point that Mulledy was already resigned to shipping them with or without their spouses. Four days later he was again at Newtown rounding up the remaining slaves. The Dutch Jesuit Peter Havermans, who was as disturbed as Lilly about the sale, recorded a particularly pathetic scene in which the slaves submitted to their fate with "heroic courage and Christian resignation."[80] At the end of November a third ship carried the last of the slaves south. The available evidence suggests that, despite the elaborate instructions of Superior General Roothaan, families were separated.[81]

77. Zwinge, "Jesuit Farms," 195; in the census of 1840 fourteen slaves were listed for St. Inigoes, six at White Marsh, and seventeen at St. Thomas.

78. The census of 1840 listed fourteen slaves at St. Inigoes, six at White Marsh, and seventeen at St. Thomas, many of whom were not elderly; NARA, Census of 1840, Charles, Counties of Charles, Prince Georges, and St. Mary's.

79. Mulledy to McElroy, Georgetown, November 11, 1838, MPA 212-M-16, GULSC.

80. According to Havermans, one old woman sought his blessing on her knees and begged to know what she had done to deserve this. "All the others came to me seeking rosaries. . . . If ever any one had reason to despair, it was I," he told Roothaan; Newtown, October 20, 1838, MD 7-I-9, *ARSI*.

81. According to Fidèle de Grivel, all the blacks married to spouses not belonging to the Society were sold to their spouses' masters or to those nearby. Some children, however, had been separated; de Grivel to Charles C. Lancaster, Georgetown, May 4, 1839, MPA 212-G-9, GULSC). But de Grivel, who was at Georgetown, seems to have underreported the fragmentation of families that the sale had incurred. The sale records indicate that at least some of the couples were separated; Newtown Account Book, MPA 112-W-O, GULSC. Some complex situations could exist. One father at White Marsh reportedly escaped to Baltimore with his three children. The wife was nonetheless willing to leave without him because the husband was living with another woman; de Grivel to C. C. Lancaster, Georgetown, November 11, 1838, MPA 212-M-5a, GULSC.

"The Stock of Slave Traders Who Value Nothing Except Money"

The scale of the sale created something of a sensation within the Catholic community along the East Coast of the country. Benedict Fenwick, the Bishop of Boston, thought it "extraordinary news. Poor Negroes! I pity them," he wrote his brother in September 1838. The bishop supposed that the antislavery party was ultimately responsible for forcing the Maryland Jesuits to resort to such an extreme measure.[82] Many others, however, did not share the bishop's judgment about where the blame lay. Stephen Dubuisson wrote the general from his parish in Alexandria that the sale had badly affected the Society's reputation, both in Washington and Virginia.[83] Havermans told Roothaan that Catholics and Protestants alike were scandalized. What Mulledy had done, Havermans charged, was "the stock of slave traders who value nothing except money," or the desperate recourse of those overwhelmed by debts.[84]

Dubuisson and Havermans' readings of the reaction were undoubtedly colored by their own convictions about the immorality of the sale. There is strong evidence, however, that other people were highly disturbed by what had happened; that some took their complaints to the Archbishop of Baltimore, Samuel Eccleston, and that Eccleston carried their charges to Roothaan. Eccleston had proposed to McSherry, in 1837, that the Province sell both its land and slaves in order to concentrate on urban missions and colleges, which he promised to help them found.[85] At that time he already knew about the slaves McSherry had sold to Louisiana. Although the complete Eccleston-Roothaan correspondence has apparently not survived, it would seem that the core of the charges he brought to the general was the separation of families.[86]

In the late fall Roothaan began a correspondence with the former provincial superior, McSherry, about the scandal Mulledy had created with the sale

82. Benedict Fenwick to George Fenwick, Boston, September 1, 1838, MPA 212-N-2, GULSC.

83. Dubuisson to Roothaan, Alexandria, June 24, 1839, MD 7-I-14, ARSI.

84. Havermans to Roothaan, Newtown, October 20, 1838, MD 7-I-9, ARSI.

85. McSherry to Roothaan, Georgetown, March 13, 1837, MD 5-II-5, ARSI.

86. The Jesuit historian Thomas Hughes, who knew intimately the Roman Archives, wrote in 1907 that "it was Eccleston . . . who . . . when people threw up their hands highly scandalized, . . . ran forward and denounced Mulledy to the General"; Hughes to E. I. Devitt, Rome, January 29, 1907, GUA, GULSC.

of the slaves.[87] Roothaan evidently was ready to remove Mulledy as provincial, but McSherry counseled delay.[88] By August, however, Roothaan became convinced that there no longer could be any doubt about what had happened and that greater scandal would be given if nothing were done. The general ordered McSherry to inform Mulledy to resign as provincial, at least until he could clear himself of the charges, which the general doubted he could. If he refused, he was to be dismissed. Roothaan conlcuded: "In some way it must be understood even in America, that men of the Society, unless they are motivated by the spirit of the society... and the observance of the Rules, not only will not be a great help, but will make for great ruin!"[89]

By this time, however, Mulledy was already on his way to Rome. In late June Eccleston and McSherry had persuaded him that, for his own sake, he had to step down as provincial superior and take his case to Roothaan himself. Within the week Mulledy was on his way to the Eternal City. Eccleston urged Roothaan not to dismiss Mulledy from the Society. The latter was in shock. He wrote in his diary: "No Mass (unwell). *Ave Crux. Spes Unica* [hail the cross, our only hope]."[90]

Peter Havermans congratulated the general for taking such decisive action. What Mulledy had done, Havermans pointed out, was "a sad example that many can follow: but decent men had now seen in Mulledy's removal

87. In the Roothaan-McSherry corresponse, there is never any explicit identification of the "scandal" Mulledy had given. However in a letter to a Maryland Jesuit at the end of 1839, the superior general admitted that the scandal was connected to the sale of the slaves; Roothaan to Francis Vespre, December 31, 1831, 169, Register of Responses of the Superior General, ARSI.

88. Roothaan to McSherry, Rome, February 14, 1839, MPA 500-84b, GULSC.

89. Roothaan to McSherry, Rome, August 3, 1839, MPA, 500-84c, GULSC. It is clear from Roothaan's letter that Eccleston's testimony had been crucial. In December 1839 Pope Gregory XVI issued an apostolic letter in which he denounced the slave trade in which blacks "as if they were not men, but mere animals, howsoever reduced into slavery, are... contrary to the laws of justice and humanity bought [and] sold." He condemned any ecclesiastic or lay person who "shall presume to defend that very trade in negroes as lawful under any pretext or studied excuse"; Pope Gregory XVI, *In Supremo Apostolatus fastigio*, English translation in *Letters to the Honorable John Forsyth on the Subject of Domestic Slavery*, by John England (Baltimore: John Murphy, 1840). Benedict Fenwick later thought that the Maryland Jesuits might have had advanced notice of this papal letter and thus accelerated their efforts to sell their slaves before it was promulgated; Fenwick to Eccleston, Boston, March 11, 1840, Eccleston Papers, AAB 24-U-1, AASMUS. There is no evidence that Mulledy or any of the Maryland Jesuits knew that such a letter was coming. But it is quite likely that Roothaan was aware of it.

90. Eccleston to Roothaan, Georgetown, June 27, 1839, MD 7-I-15, ARSI; Mulledy Diary, June 27, 1839, GUA, GULSC.

that the Society did not approve of such things. They would see it even more clearly, Havermans suggested, should Mulledy not return from Europe.[91]

Children of Their Culture

Four years later, in 1843, Mulledy was allowed home through the intercession of Bishop Fenwick, who needed a president for the new school he was founding in Worcester. In the year of his return, the debating society at Georgetown College invited him to give a public address. In his remarks Mulledy contrasted the peaceful liberty that American enjoyed with the conscription that was becoming the curse of Europe. The worst feature of conscription, he told them, was the cruel way in which it separated parents from children, wives from husbands. Prize liberty, he instructed them, and work to make right what is wrong in America. But be cautious, he warned, for "if special care be not taken in eradicating the vice you will root out the virtue too."[92] Mulledy would seem to have had more than conscription in mind.

Thus ended the Society's history in Maryland as a large slaveholder. The change to exclusive tenant farming eventually proved a profitable one by the late 1840s, as sharecropping was gradually introduced. Ironically, the Society abandoned its slave labor at the very time the estates were beginning to produce. In Carbery, Combs, Havermans, and Lilly, the Society finally had a set of effective managers. Had the alliance between the European Jesuits and these local managers had its way, there might well have been increasing efforts to make the Jesuits' estates models of Christian slavery, such as Christian evangelists like Charles Colcock Jones were attempting to create elsewhere in the South. Most Maryland Jesuits, including those on the farms, seemed to have perceived by the 1830s that slavery's days in Maryland were numbered. They might then have begun consciously to prepare the slaves for freedom, as Carbery was in effect doing at St. Inigoes. But few seemed prepared to go against the prevailing climate. For much of their history Maryland Jesuits had been outcasts, if not outlaws, but still very much the children of their culture who wanted to prove that they belonged. This tradition, economic expediency, and the urban vision of a younger American generation of Jesuits prevailed. The sale of 1838 with all its consequences was part of the price of progress and a morality play worthy of Harriet Beecher Stowe.

91. Havermans to Roothaan, Frederick, February 14, 1840, MD 7 VI 7, ARSI.

92. Address to the Philodemic Society (1843), Mulledy Papers, GUA, GULSC.

Chapter 3

From Saints to Secessionists

Reading the Past as Prologue

I FIRST ENCOUNTERED Thomas Hughes' *History of the Society of Jesus in North America* in my research for the paper dealing with the Maréchal-Jesuit dispute. The Jesuit slaveholding paper and a project study of the Maryland Catholic community from the overthrow of the Calverts in 1689 to the American Revolution took me deeper into the volumes that Hughes had produced about the Jesuit experience in British America and the early national period, including an unpublished manuscript that carried the history of the Society of Jesus in North America from the Revolution through the 1830s, a document that I had come upon in the Special Collections Division of Georgetown's Lauinger Library. When, in the early 1980s, I was invited to contribute a piece to a *festschrift* for John Tracy Ellis, it occurred to me that the Hughes corpus, despite its apparently terminal particularity, constituted a significant story about the powerful tendency to project one's current preoccupations and presumptions upon our interpretation of the past. Subsequent examination of Hughes' other writings and correspondence confirmed my suspicion of the ideological war that he came to wage on liberalism in the course of compiling the five volumes.

The resulting essay, under the title "From Saints to Secessionists: Thomas Hughes and *The History of the Society of Jesus in North America*," first appeared in *Studies in Catholic History in Honor of John Tracy Ellis*, ed. Nelson Minnich, et al. (Wilmington: Michael Glazier, 1985), 239–59.

Seeking the Story

"I miss the story," a historian commented in 1913 about the latest volume of Thomas Hughes' *History of the Society of Jesus in North America.*[1] Many readers have had the same frustrating experience in trying to use, much less read through, the four volumes of text and documents that Hughes published on the North American Jesuits of the Colonial and Federal periods. Hughes himself confessed to his editor that there was "no story," but "odds & ends scraped up everywhere; I had no narratives to give, except in the Canadian section," where Hughes contended that he had no intention of "repeating ten-times told tales."[2]

In an age in which even "Popes admit everyone into the private archives of the Holy See," Hughes prided himself on being a modern scientific historian who mined the field for original sources and respected their integrity too much to force them into patterns simply for the sake of a narrative.[3] Nor did he hesitate to include the unpleasant. "I should like it to be seen," he once wrote, "that I never omit anything because I may not happen to like it."[4] "To allow of tampering . . . with these Documents," he protested when some Jesuits were expressing concern about his publishing the records of the acrimonious dispute between the Society and the Archbishop of Baltimore, Ambrose Maréchal, "would be like permitting each story of a house as it rises to have its bearings knocked out, columns dispensed with, arches kicked away—& there would be no reason for going to other stories at all."[5] What those documents in their totality would reveal to the discerning reader, Hughes was confident, was "the circumstances, . . . [the] environment, and habits of

1. William Poland, S.J., to Edward Devitt, S.J., St. Louis, May 19, 1913, GUA, GULSC.

2. Thomas Hughes, S.J. to Devitt, Rome, July 21, 1918, GUA, GULSC.

3. Thomas Hughes, S.J., *The History of the Society of Jesus in North America: Colonial and Federal, Text* [hereafter cited as *History of Society, Text*] (London: Longman's Green, 1907), 1:25.

4. Hughes to Devitt, Rome, April 19, 1913, GUA, GULSC.

5. Hughes to Devitt, Rome, June 26, 1906, GUA, GULSC. Hughes felt that John Gilmary Shea, "to please his patrons," had sanitized his histories. "I have pleased no one," Hughes wrote after publishing the fourth volume, "neither Cath. nor Prot., neither South nor North, neither inside nor outside, but only the truth, and *ruat coelum*"; Hughes to Devitt, Rome, July 21, 1918, GUA, GULSC. The critical reception of Hughes' first two volumes was much more positive than he implies here. The initial volume won Columbia University's Loubat Prize in 1907 and was widely and favorably reviewed. When the companion volume of documents was largely ignored, Hughes became convinced that there was a boycott of his work, especially in Maryland, because of his treatment of the Maréchal affair; Hughes to Devitt, Rome, April 6, 1908, GUA, GULSC.

thought" that had prevailed in the world the American Jesuits worked in from the seventeenth to the nineteenth centuries.[6]

Discerning readers might protest that any such patterns were hopelessly buried in the sheer weight of Hughes' poorly organized material and convoluted prose. An irrepressible bent for polemics and digressions only further obscured his subject. But from the beginning there were larger themes present. Hughes himself confessed that he realized the full implications of those themes only after he had completed the fourth volume. He subsequently incorporated them more explicitly into a fifth volume of *The History* that was never published. That volume in its two redactions, like its predecessors, told more about Roman perceptions of the Society and Church in Rome and America in the early twentieth century than it did about Society and Church a hundred years earlier.

Thomas Hughes and the History of the Society of Jesus in North America

Born and raised in Liverpool, Thomas Hughes upon his graduation from Stonyhurst College entered the English Province of the Society of Jesus in 1866. During his novitiate he volunteered to transfer to the Missouri Province in order to work with indigenous Americans in the West. The pages of his histories were the closest he came to realizing this ambition as his intellectual promise quickly caught the eye of superiors. Once he completed his studies he was assigned to teach, first at the Jesuit novitiate at Florissant, Missouri, and then at St. Louis University. At St. Louis he was particularly remembered for having begun a prestigious lecture series in the 1880s that helped to lay the groundwork for graduate studies in that institution.[7]

In 1894 he was called to Rome to work with a team of Jesuit historians preparing to write the history of the Society. The following year he was charged with doing the history of the Jesuits in North America in the nineteenth century. Hughes accordingly concentrated his research on that more recent history, with particular attention upon the long controversy the Jesuits in the Maryland Mission had had with Archbishop Maréchal over their property. The General of the order, Father Luis Martín, wanted that delicate mat-

6. Hughes, *History of Society*, *Text*, 1:79.

7. William B. Faherty, S.J., *Better the Dream: St. Louis University and Community, 1818–1968* (St. Louis: St. Louis University Press, 1968), 175–79.

ter to be "altogether exhausted."[8] Apparently sometime in the latter 1890s Hughes was told that he was now to do the early history of the Maryland Mission as well, beginning in the seventeenth century. According to Hughes, Martín indicated that "the old history should be treated as a mere preliminary to the nineteenth century."[9]

With one assistant in Rome and two in America, Hughes accelerated his research on two continents. By 1906 he had two volumes ready for the publisher, Longmans, Green and Co. of London, one a collection of documents and the other a text. In his preface to the text Hughes presented the two volumes as companion pieces, but acknowledged that the documents went beyond the matter treated in the text. In fact fewer than two hundred of the six hundred pages of the volume of documents dealt with the history of the Jesuit mission in the seventeenth century. Most of the volume concerned Jesuit property and the Maréchal controversy.

Revisiting the Maréchal Controversy

Father General Martín's interest in the old property fight was in large portion a practical one. The Jesuit generals had long wanted the Maryland Jesuits to free themselves from the farms and country parishes in southern Maryland and on the Eastern Shore. Martín particularly wanted Hughes to ascertain whether the lands were held in fee simple or in trust. If the latter, he intended to press the Archbishop of Baltimore to take over the parishes and at least some of the land. Ironically that had been the basic issue of the controversy—whether the lands belonged to the Society or were merely held for "the Church."[10]

Hughes saw more in the question than a matter of title or settlement of property. Having lived in Maryland (he was in the first class at Woodstock College, the theologate in Baltimore County that the Jesuits opened in 1869), he knew the stories that still circulated among clergy and laity about Jesuits retaining property that belonged to the diocese. As he got deeper into the research of the early nineteenth century, he became more convinced that the

8. Thomas Hughes, S.J., "Reminiscences," *Woodstock Letters* 51 (1922): 181.

9. The Colonial history of the Maryland Mission was originally to have formed part of the history of the English Province, but the Jesuit doing that history found Maryland "a very jejeune subject." Hughes confessed that he himself might have been "the origin of that impression (Hughes, "Reminiscences," 182).

10. Hughes, "Reminiscences," 180–81.

Jesuit reputation had been unjustly damaged by the affair. When some Jesuits in Maryland began to pressure the provincial to use his influence to stop Hughes from stirring embers of a fire that had long since died, Hughes had little patience with those who counseled that "it was much ado about a little paltry property." He reminded such advisors that the archbishop and his defenders had brought the most serious

> charges against religious men, that they were "guilty of a breach of a religious trust," that they "purloined," that they were "perjurers," that they should be "unfrocked"—or made bishops—and this spread through Italy, France and England, of a whole Regulars' mission, so that American Jesuits traveling through Europe had to go slinking through, and apologizing, and averring that they had never been cut off from the body of the Society! I am of the same mind—so much ado about a little paltry property. The English Parliament was of the same mind in another case: So much ado about a paltry Stamp Act! But, if the offset to such a paltry thing was an American republic, it is not strange that the offset, after a hundred years, to the wholesale arraignment of a mission of religious men should be a little rectification.[11]

Hughes wasted no opportunity in editing the documents to provide just that. As John Carroll had incorporated the property to preserve it for the Society against all interlopers, including papal congregations, so, Hughes argued, the Maryland Jesuits, foreigners and natives alike, justly resisted Ambrose Maréchal's claims, even when their own general and the pope himself told them to yield. As Hughes reconstructed the long affair, Father General Luigi Fortis was "buying peace at any price"; the pope was getting one-sided information from the archbishop and his agent; Maréchal was arbitrarily using his juridical power to force the Jesuits to meet his demands. Only the Maryland Jesuits appreciated that the very life of the mission was at stake.[12]

For Hughes the meaning of the controversy transcended Maryland and the early nineteenth century, as he intimated to his American assistant at Georgetown University. The extraordinary threat that Maréchal had represented in Maryland in 1820 was a daily fear that the Society lived under in Italy by 1908. "The demand on the Jesuits for the episcopal mensa in Maryland corresponded to what a progressive Government like that of Italy to-day exacts of the episcopal mensa itself for the lay treasury," he noted.[13] Both were species of arbitrary government and tyranny.

11. Hughes to Devitt, Rome, January 25, 1908, GUA, GULSC.

12. Hughes, *History of Society, Documents* (London: Longmans, Green, 1908), 1:571–75.

13. Hughes, *History of Society, Documents*, 1:543n25; Hughes to Devitt; Rome, January 25, 1908,

"Who Can Despise This People?"

The first volume of text covered only the first eleven years of the Maryland Mission; most of the pages (320 of 564) dealt with another controversy, that of the Jesuits with the second Lord Baltimore, Cecil Calvert. By the late nineteenth century, Baltimore was already well noted for having introduced the concept of religious toleration into British America. For Hughes, from the vantage point of two centuries of subsequent history, Calvert's innovation had proven to be a terrible precedent. In his introduction Hughes pointed out that the Maryland experiment of "practical toleration" was the precursor for "every clime in our day" and a microcosm for judging how religious orders could expect to fare with "a dozen European monarchies, empires, or republics, in the matter of general religious politics."[14]

What Hughes found in Cecil Calvert was a Gallican Catholic whose treatment of the Jesuits showed his intentions of subduing religion to the state. Hughes cited with approval the Jesuit General's appraisal of Calvert that

> he has drunk of the muddy waters in the way of Egypt, and is imbued with principles not at all sound; and it is to be feared that not a few others are infected with the same. But I do not see what remedy can be applied, especially in these dubious times, and in a place where every body thinks with impunity what he likes.[15]

That Cecil had not had the advantage of studying at St. Omers, as his younger brothers did, told Hughes much. Baltimore remained a Catholic out of self-interest, but his real convictions were Protestant, and his political principles were Erastian. To Hughes it was no accident that Lord Baltimore's chief associate, John Lewger, was a converted rector of the Church of England.[16]

GUA, GULSC. Occasionally the note of being under siege crept into his correspondence with Devitt. "How politics stand & will turn," he reported in 1909, "is all in the hands of the Lord. There is no Catholic party to save anything. And the Socialists & anticlericals are bent on carrying out the French antecedents here. The ministries [governments] always go from bad to worse"; Hughes to Devitt, Rome, November 24, 1909, GUA, GULSC. When there were rumors in 1912 that the government was about to pass a law confiscating the property of religious orders, Hughes was convinced that the reasons for it were the war debts and a desire to eliminate private education. "All will be State and atheistic," he commented. "New vested interests will be created in the army of hungry brevetted teachers waiting for a place. And then the whole story of France can be rehearsed"; Hughes to Devitt, Rome, November 30, 1912, GUA, GULSC.

14. Hughes, *History of Society, Text*, 1:137.

15. Vincent Carafa, S.J., to Henry Silesdon, S.J., Rome, November 7, 1648, cited in Hughes, *History of Society, Documents*, 1:37.

16. Hughes, *History of Society, Text*, 1:350–53. "I take him to have been an ill-formed Catholic, entirely in the hands of the anti-Jesuit party of Engl.," he commented to Devitt in 1899; Hughes

Calvert's dispute with Thomas Copley over the land the Jesuits had acquired from the Piscataway not only revealed to Hughes Lord Baltimore's contemptuous attitude toward the natives, but more importantly his Erastian ambitions of a Church establishment controlled by the proprietor. Nor was it only the property of Jesuits and Indians that Calvert was bent on confiscating, according to Hughes. Baltimore's feudal designs, which imposed taxes upon property and military service upon the population, clergy included, were to Hughes a seventeenth-century brand of socialism in its absolute claims upon land and persons.[17] Copley, on the other hand, was making but one absolute claim, the principle (as Hughes reminded) "which cannot be denied by a Catholic, that the Church is not under the State."[18]

In this struggle for state control Hughes noted that "the venal proletariate, which had the numbers and votes," were in the pockets of Calvert and Lewger. The quality people in the province were all with the Jesuits.[19] When in 1645 Virginians challenged the proprietor's authority, his "new majority" showed the extent of its loyalty by quickly going over to the invaders.

The change of government was hardly a liberation for the Jesuits. At the end of Hughes' first volume Andrew White and Copley were being shipped back to England in chains; the other Jesuits had fled into Virginia. Of the first twelve Jesuits to serve in Maryland, eight had died on the mission within the first decade. Five were under forty, a testament to the Society's commitment to send some of its most promising young men to the New World, despite the hardships and dangers.

In the second volume of text Hughes followed the precarious fortunes of the Maryland Jesuits and Catholic gentry through the overthrow of the Calverts to the suppression of the Society in 1773. Although the Catholic planters soon lost power and became a tiny minority of the colony, they continued to be a moral and cultural force with the superior education that the English recusant schools at St. Omers and Bruges gave them. From this saving rem-

---

to Devitt, Rome, December 16, 1899, GUA, GULSC. Hughes had suspected Cecil Calvert's orthodoxy long before he began his study of Maryland. "It appears," he wrote in 1878, "that Lord Baltimore was a liberal Catholic, and temporized much and was ready to temporize more, in order to save his property in troublesome times. . . . [T]he history of St. Mary's city is rather that of a city blighted for liberal Catholicism and apostasy"; Hughes to Daniel Considine, cited in *Letters and Notices* 12 (1878–79): 171–75.

17. Hughes, *History of Society, Text*, 1:399–404.

18. Hughes, *History of Society, Text*, 1:405.

19. Hughes, *History of Society, Text*, 1:439.

nant ("the solid and sterling Catholicity of Maryland") came a large number of vocations to the Society, persons of "first-class understanding and judgment" like Robert Brooke, the first native vocation.[20] He and his fellow Jesuits quietly went about the business of their ministry in Maryland in the face of penal laws, attempts to wrest away their property, and the general anti-popery that Hughes saw plaguing the colony through the late Colonial period. To the faithful Maryland Jesuits and Catholic gentry he applied the words of the Assyrians about the Israelites: "Who can despise this people? Is it not right that we should fight against them, and leave not a man alive; or they will circumvent the whole world with their chains!" (Judith 10:19)[21]

A Changing Viewpoint

The second volume of documents, issued in 1910, covered events from the suppression of the Society to the settlement of Archbishop Maréchal's claims in 1838. Again a major focus was the controversy over the property, but the scope was larger and the tone decidedly different. Hughes now suggested that the Maryland Jesuits might have been wiser had they reached an early accommodation with Maréchal. "Whatever they gained in maintaining their rights," he concluded, "they lost in reputation."[22] Actually Hughes was now more sympathetic with the archbishop's arguments. The property was indeed ecclesiastical in nature, he pointed out, no matter what the American Jesuits and U.S. law said about it. It should have been under canonical jurisdiction, as Maréchal was contending and the Maryland Jesuits denying.

Regardless of the canonical rights, Hughes noted that the Jesuits were crippling themselves by so concentrating on the farms and undermining the attempts of enlightened foreign Jesuits like Anthony Kohlmann, who wanted to shift the center of operations from Maryland to New York. Hughes obviously shared Kohlmann's judgment that of the states, Maryland was "the worst and poorest in the Union, from which even seculars retire into the wilderness of Kentucky."[23] The Maryland Jesuits were beginning to pay the price of provincialism, poor management, and the distrust of foreigners, who by 1820 were a strong majority of the mission. Locked into the past, they main-

20. Hughes, *History of Society*, *Text*, (London, 1916), 2:137–38.

21. Hughes, *History of Society*, *Text*, 2:607. Hughes had foreshortened the first sentence of the quote. It reads in full: "Who can despise this people that has such women among them?"

22. Hughes, *History of Society*, *Documents*, 1:1030.

23. Hughes, *History of Society*, *Documents*, 1:945n14.

tained the autonomy of the corporation they had set up to protect the property after the suppression, even though that legal body should have come under the authority of the religious superior after 1805, when the Society was revived in Maryland. Nevertheless, Hughes had to admit that "the blessed Corporation" (one exasperated superior's term for it) was a *felix culpa* insofar as it saved the estates.

"A Kind of Broken Limb"

As Hughes was completing the fourth volume in 1913, he learned that Father General Franz Wernz wanted all the histories to terminate with the suppression. "I was immensely relieved," Hughes later claimed.[24] Five years later he was told to resume the story. Hughes confessed to fellow Jesuit Edward Devitt that he had little idea what particular focus it would take—how it would differ from the provincial history that Devitt was publishing seriatim in *Woodstock Letters* at the time.[25]

The theme he took up was one that he had planted over a decade before in the first volume. There he had observed the importance of studying the period that had led to the American republic. It was vital to study the impact of this milieu upon "the life and destiny of one religious institute," he had argued, seeing how large that order had become in the United States by the early twentieth century and what influence it had across the country. But, he continued, "if this religious Order is fated to decay, its decline and fall do not seem likely to occur through agencies from without.... No; the possibility of decline must be limited to the alteration of internal life or the process of decay from within."[26]

Toward the end of the second part of the Documents Hughes had observed that the Maréchal controversy had saddled upon the Jesuits the reputation of "not being Jesuits at all, but a kind of broken limb barely hanging on to the Society."[27] Hughes himself now seemed determined to substantiate that reputation. If the image of the Maryland Jesuits in the first volumes had been triumphal, one of men who were "superior in learning and ability," zealous, obedient, and heroic, that of their successors in the nineteenth century was one of children dissipating the legacy of their fathers.

24. Hughes, "Reminiscences," 183.
25. Hughes to Devitt, Rome, November 17, 1918, GUA, GULSC.
26. Hughes, *History of Society, Text*, 1:137–38.
27. Hughes, *History of Society, Documents*, 1:1030.

Relying on more extensive material than had appeared in the volumes of documents, Hughes portrayed a post-restoration Society in Maryland that was materialistic and ignorant of its traditions. The Neale brothers, Charles and Francis, who held the vital posts of mission superior and novice master respectively, were basically strangers to the Society's laws and tradition. Charles, Hughes pointed out, had been a mere novice at the time of the suppression. His younger brother had joined the Society only after the Maryland ex-Jesuits were allowed to affiliate themselves with the Society in Russia in 1805. Despite being superior three times Charles knew so little about the laws of the Society that he had possessed private property until his death and willed it to his family.

The Neales, the Fenwicks, and their Maryland confreres were depicted as clerical planters, so preoccupied with their property that they were willing to jeopardize everything else to preserve it, whether it be their standing in the Church during their dispute with Archbishop Maréchal or their very future as a body, by following a policy of closing the novitiate as an economy measure. They opposed the farsighted foreigners among them, especially Anthony Kohlmann, in Hughes' judgment the unmatched "light in his generation" intellectually and spiritually.[28] Men like Kohlmann, Peter Epinette, and John Henry had been trained in Russia and knew the Society from the inside, but they were pushed aside by the native faction. On the other hand, the native Jesuits were all too ready to minimize their differences with Protestants, a tendency, Hughes observed, "which is violently alien to the purposes of the Society of Jesus."[29]

Given these tendencies it was no surprise to Hughes that the foreigners found the younger Jesuits lacking in any spirituality. They were receiving no formation, "had to make bricks without straw, teach without capital and live by their wits."[30] The novices were largely unsupervised when they were not being pulled away to teach at Georgetown or New York. They were admitted virtually without scrutiny and left as freely. Some very promising young Americans had been drawn to the Society, Hughes found, but tiring of their exploitation and "finding nothing of what they expected," most of them soon left.[31]

The foreigners found laissez-faire formation promoting contempt for the

28. Hughes, "History, Text III" (Redaction of 1926), ms. copy in New York Province Archives (hereafter cited as NYPA), 925.

29. Hughes, "History, Text III," 533(2).

30. Hughes, "History, Text III," 393.

31. Hughes, "History, Text III," 748.

traditions of the Society. One of them reported that "One would be ashamed to speak of the rule. Rodriguez would have raised a laugh."[32] The quality of Jesuits produced by such a system that rarely dismissed anyone was predictable. A John McElroy somehow managed to survive it. More typical in Hughes' eyes was a Joseph Carbery, "an ignoramous" who could barely read and had no formal novitiate or training in the Society. What attracted the Marylanders to Carbery was that he was a first-class farmer who would give them another vote on the corporation.[33] Even worse was Adam Marshall, who became for Hughes the reductio ad absurdum of this new generation denied "an honest and genuine formation." An avowed Jacobin who rarely said Mass, went to confession, or exhibited any signs of a religious spirit, Marshall nonetheless became the most powerful figure in the mission as procurator of the corporation. It was appropriate, Hughes wrote, that he had died teaching "as a secular professor" on a U.S. naval ship. "He was fit for a frigate," he concluded, but "had nothing in common with the Order."[34]

An excessive love of liberty and nation were two results of the lack of formation. The Maryland Jesuits' machinations to retain control of their property, despite the commands of general and pope, revealed their true identity as "ecclesiastical democrats" whose ultimate goal was autonomy.[35] Without the proper training to counteract American pressures, Hughes suggested, such behavior was inevitable.

In a State of Secession

As he had done with the previous volumes, Hughes submitted his manuscript to be reviewed by two censors within the Society. One of those appointed was Gilbert Garraghan, who was himself in the process of researching the history of the Society of Jesus in the United States. Garraghan reported anonymously that once again Hughes' work was a model of "thoroughgoing research and scholarly detail." That made it all the more painful, he went on, to return an unfavorable verdict. Not only was Hughes unfair to Carroll, but he was distorting the record in portraying the opposition to Maréchal and

32. Alfonso Rodriguez, S.J., *The Practice of Perfection and Christian Virtues*, 1st ed. (1609), an ascetical work normally read by Jesuit novices; Stephen Dubuisson, S.J., to Luigi Fortis, S.J., cited in Hughes, "History, Text III," 664.

33. Hughes, "History, Text III," 581–83.

34. Hughes, "History, Text III," 662–63, 673.

35. Hughes, "History, Text III," 604.

Rome over the property as strategy peculiar to the Americans. Most of the foreigners, including Kohlmann, had agreed with their stance, he commented.

Garraghan detected a striking shift in tone between *History III* and the documents upon which it purported to be based. "One gets an entirely different view of men or things," Garraghan remarked, "as he uses one or the other source." In this latest volume the "incompetency, the mismanagement, the erroneous views, the sharp practice, the moral delinquencies" so burdened the story that the reader must conclude that "scarcely any one thinks, says or does anything through a spiritual or supernatural motive." Surely, Garraghan observed, even in Maryland things could not have been this bad. The censor noted that Hughes was now applying to the Society itself the polemics that critics of his earlier works had accused him of engaging in against adversaries of the Jesuits. "[I]f any chapter in the history of the Society calls for broad and sympathetic treatment," Garraghan suggested, "it is that which records the efforts of a little group of well-intentioned, but, if you will, misguided men to revive the Society of Jesus in the United States; and broad and sympathetic treatment is precisely what they have not received."[36]

The other censor shared Garraghan's judgment that the manuscript should not be published. Father General Wlodimir Ledochowski told Hughes that he could not publish it in its present form. Hughes agreed that "there are indeed limits" to what should be made public, but he reminded the new general that Father Martín's intention in starting the historical project was the instruction of "our rising generations."[37] Hughes, however, was aiming higher than novices or scholastics in his efforts to instruct. "[O]nly in discovering the historical roots of illnesses can one begin to cure them," he suggested to the general.[38] The Society of Jesus in the United States was not only sick, Hughes contended, but very likely in a state of secession from the Society in Rome.

In an eighty-two-page memorial to the general Hughes attempted to show that his history of the Maryland mission had been no exaggeration, but a revelation of the roots of a crisis in Jesuit America that Father General Martín himself had recognized by the end of the last century. In part it was autobi-

36. Gilbert Garraghan, Censor's report, n.d., Archives of the New York Province (hereafter NYPA).

37. "Thomas Hughes, De Abusibus," an eighty-two page typewritten Latin copy of a memorial to Wlodimir Ledochowski, S.J., dated July 4, 1930, NYPA; GUA, Hughes to Devitt, Rome, April 19, 1913.

38. Hughes, "De Abusibus," 5.

ographical—Hughes' personal discovery of "the Maryland tradition." He recounted the cultural shock of coming from the novitiate in England, with its mature candidates, a third of them converts, to its counterpart in Florissant, where all seven novices were teenagers from Xavier College, the atmosphere stiflingly provincial. Recreation periods were interminable; religious instruction was minimal. The master of novices, Hughes recalled, "communicated no idea either about religion, the Society of Jesus, or any other thing."[39] When the young Hughes complained about the lack of order, the novice master peevishly responded: "They will have to experience everything afterwards; therefore better begin now."[40]

The casual manner in which Americans approached the liturgy and other spiritual exercises scandalized him: provincials saying Mass in less than twenty minutes, priests racing to finish the divine office to win a bet, superiors sending mail during retreat. Hughes claimed that his real awakening to the spiritual deterioration took place at Woodstock, where he was studying theology. A classmate was enthusiastically urging him to read a novel by George Eliot. Finally succumbing to his appeal, Hughes indicated that he would seek permission to read it. "Oh! No!" the other Jesuit exclaimed; and disappeared with the book. "This brought on my first suspicion," Hughes remembered, "of the turbulent waters swirling beneath the surface of the Society of Jesus."[41]

Subsequent trips to America at the turn of the twentieth century only provided additional evidence of the extent of Jesuit declension. The inroads of secularization were even more palpable. Going to theater was now common; the reading of newspapers took the place of meditation and community recreation; confession was becoming a rare exercise; priests were saying Mass once a week. The splendid cuisine and the enormous trunks that carried Jesuit belongings revealed the level of poverty they observed. They were obsessed with money.

In the colleges Hughes alleged an attempt to "modernize" in order to compete with the Harvards and Yales. At Georgetown Hughes found that modernization largely meant baseball. The daily order he encountered there in 1899 included nearly as many hours for baseball as for class. The team spent weeks on the road pursuing the Holy Grail of baseball supremacy in the

39. Hughes, "De Abusibus, 28.

40. Hughes, "De Abusibus.

41. Hughes, "De Abusibus, 22.

moral wildernesses that Hughes considered New Haven and Cambridge to be. The high point of the day, he reported, was the rector's reading of the telegram relating the latest victory to the thunderous applause of the students. The image he best remembered was that of the rector sitting "alone, full of the majesty of Religious Order," watching a hundred boys playing baseball. "Now is baseball queen of studies," Hughes concluded.[42]

The intellectual vacuity of the colleges was for Hughes only a symptom of a larger blindness to the culture that held them captive. He recalled from his diary Father General Martín's words: "They see no dangers in America; more than that, they see nothing. They say we don't understand them in America."[43] Indeed Hughes found very much alive the contempt for Rome that had perplexed former generals like Roothaan and Martín. It had been no accident, Hughes pointed out, that nine of the thirteen superiors of the Maryland mission/province from 1823 to 1901 had been outsiders.

If truth be told, Hughes contended, many Americans had succumbed to Americanism and modernism. The passive virtues associated with prayer, contemplation, and obedience were obsolete in America; the active virtues, "those which best agree with the national genius: to act, make noise, make money, build, be bound hand and feet to the people, whoever they may at length be," were regnant, not only among the populace but, he suggested, even within the Society.[44] That retreat directors were omitting the exercise on hell told much about the decline of faith ("pure and simple modernism").[45] The understanding of the Mass as a mere symbol also had lessons for the discerning. American Jesuits, he concluded, were unconscious modernists. Even the German American Jesuits, renowned for their fidelity to the Society's rules and spirit, were more and more conforming "to the common life of America, not to the common life of the Society of Jesus."[46]

A large part of the trouble was the leadership in the Society in America. The penchant for choosing superiors who had business acumen was the best assurance of perpetuating spiritual and intellectual mediocrity, Hughes contended. Worse still was the appointment of converts like Edward Purbrick and John Whitney, who had been Maryland Provincial and Rector of Georgetown respectively in the 1890s, and abetted the corrosive influence of Prot-

42. Hughes, "De Abusibus, 44, 77.

43. Hughes Diary, February 15, 1896, cited in Hughes, "De Abusibus," 23.

44. "Hughes, De Abusibus," 74.

45. "Hughes, De Abusibus," 25.

46. "Hughes, De Abusibus," 52.

estantism upon the Society there. The worst consequence of this influence, Hughes implied, was the individualism that had marred the Jesuit character in America since the restoration.[47] A "home-rule" spirit was prevailing that could be traced back at least as far as John Carroll, "the most American" of the American Jesuits.[48]

The Revolution as the Key to the Society of Jesus in North America

As early as the second volume of documents (1910) Hughes had noted "some shadows" upon Carroll's character. Carroll, Hughes admitted, was scrupulously correct in trying to restore the property to the Society, but he also manipulated the corporation to advance his own interests. Buried in Hughes' notes was his concern about the archbishop's Gallican tendencies. Carroll's conviction that papal congregations had no just claim upon the temporal possessions of the American Church or indeed any share in the pope's spiritual authority was to Hughes the equivalent of the assertion of episcopal autonomy from papal control.[49] By 1926 Carroll, for Hughes, had become an episcopal boss, fighting the reconstitution of the Society, waging a campaign to keep young men from joining it, starving Georgetown, while he more and more attempted to accommodate the Church to the Protestant milieu.

In a final redaction, which he completed in 1933, Hughes put the nineteenth-century history of the American Jesuits within the context of the Age of Revolution, which he offered as the key to the shape the Society had come to take in the New World. Carroll himself was a child of that age, imbibing the individualism and zest for religious innovation that had marked the first revolution that came to be known as the Enlightenment. By the time he returned to America in 1774 Carroll's secular tendencies were clearly set to embrace the American Revolution, with its illusive promises of religious liberty and separation of church and state.[50] Finally in the year that Carroll was elected bishop by his fellow priests, the third revolution occurred in France, "a world-wide convulsion, a mass of symptoms & eruptions, social, civic and religious, under the effects of which we are laboring a century and half later."[51]

47. "Hughes, De Abusibus," 54.
48. "Hughes, De Abusibus," 5.
49. Hughes, *History, Documents*, 1:619n2.
50. Hughes, "History, Text, III" (Redaction of 1933), 81, 442, NYPA.
51. Hughes, "History, Text, III," 315.

Only in America had the Society "saved" its property. Property, however, was no substitute for the character of the Society, and here was the real loss the Jesuits in America had suffered, Hughes concluded. Kohlmann and Francis Dzierozynski had waged a futile struggle to transplant the ideals of the Society and a knowledge of its fundamental body of laws, the Constitutions, to the Americans. Personal and economic interests had instead triumphed, and the communal character of the Society, the epitome of which was its "devotion to the Church, [and] to its visible head the Papacy," effectively died with the foreigners.[52]

Or rather escaped with them to the West in 1823, when Charles Van Quickenborne led his party of seven novices into Missouri after the corporation closed the Maryland novitiate. But Hughes left the reader doubtful whether these Western Jesuits would long be able to resist the poisons from the East. How pessimistic Hughes had become about the state of the Society in the United States he made clear in his memorial to Ledochowski. There he held out two hopes for the American Society: recruits from the sons of first- and second-generation immigrants and training for them in Rome.[53]

Hughes, Tradition, and Experience

It may seem ironic that Hughes wrote his history in the service of an ultramontane tradition that little valued it.[54] His own vision, however, was on the permanent principles that gave life to the Church and the Society. The "secret" of the Jesuits was "the organization of daily life and work, whether common, exceptional or heroic, on the solid basis of spiritual motives and supernatural aids."[55]

Uniformity was the key, and its source, for the Society as for the Church, was Rome. Had Hughes known better the history of the Society, he would have perhaps better appreciated Carroll's conviction that the Society needed to adapt itself to place and time. Even one of Hughes' heroes, Francis Dzierozynski, came to realize in action the Ignatian principle of adaptation according to circumstances. What worked in Europe, Dzierozynski tried in 1841 to convince another Eurocentric general, Jan Roothaan, would not necessarily

52. Hughes, "History, Text, III," 421, 106.

53. Hughes, "De Abusibus," 78–81.

54. See Stephen J. Tonsor, "Lord Acton on Dlliger's Historical Theology," *Journal of the History of Ideas* 20 (1959): 329–52.

55. Hughes, "History, Text," III (Redaction of 1933), 6.

work in the United States.[56] A later European superior in Maryland who had shared Dzierozynski's insight predicted that "in time the Americans will be equal to the Europeans but give them time."[57]

Such a separate but equal status made no sense to Hughes, either in terms of his understanding of the Society's tradition or his experience of America. He had never been at home there, and it was impossible for him to believe that there could be an authentic American Jesuit tradition, faithful to the spirit and Constitutions of the Society but reflecting its unique environment. What he could see all too clearly was a growing American influence, both in the world and the Society. By 1920 America was a world power, and the American Jesuits accounted for a sixth of the members of the Society of Jesus. The five members in 1805 had grown to nearly 3,000, almost double those in the English assistancy. Hughes was all too aware that their time had come. The combination of his vestigial colonialism and radical ultramontanism made this American advent about as welcome as a new suppression. The ultimate irony was that by the time Thomas Hughes died in 1939, no part of the Society was more oriented toward Rome than the Jesuits in America.

56. Dzierozynski to Roothaan, Frederick, [Md.] June 29, 1841, MD 5-III-6, ARSI.
57. Burchard Villiger to Peter Beckx, Baltimore, September 7, 1860, MD 8-IV-9, ARSI.

Chapter 4

“The Finger of God Is Here”

The Advent of the Miraculous in the Nineteenth-Century American Catholic Community

My discovery of the religio-cultural phenomenon known popularly as “The Prince Hohenlohe Cures” was another consequence of my research in the Maryland Papers of the Roman Archives of the Society of Jesus. There I had come upon a series of reports written by a Jesuit priest, Stephen Dubuisson, labeled “Prodigious Cures in the Visitation Convent of Georgetown and Elsewhere.” Dubuisson’s accounts of the apparent miracles that he had witnessed at the convent from 1831 to 1838 motivated me to explore more deeply into the wave of wondrous happenings that reached back into the early 1820s in the Chesapeake region, beginning with the much publicized cure of Ann Mattingly in Washington City in 1824. Further knowledge of and reflection upon the history of the cures convinced me that they represented an important turning point in the development of religious culture within the American Catholic community.

My initial findings, under the title “The Prince Hohenlohe Cures and the American Catholic Community, 1824–1838,” were presented at a conference on “The Culture of American Catholicism” at the University of Notre Dame in October of 1985. In April 1986 a modified version was given as the annual Catholic Daughters of the Americas Lecture at The Catholic University of America. That paper served as the nucleus of my article entitled “‘The Finger of God is Here’: The Advent of the Miraculous in the Nineteenth-Century American Catholic Community,” which was published in *The Catholic Historical Review* 73 (January 1987): 41–61. Nancy Lusignan Schultz has explored in a larger transatlantic context the Mattingly cure. See her "Prince Hohenlohe's Miraculous Meddlings: Transatlantic Intercessions in Washington, D.C. and Charlestown, Massachusetts," in U.S. *Catholic Historian* 20 (Winter 2002): 1–19.

The Hohenlohe Cures Come to America

[W]e ought to examine every alleged miracle, whether of the first or of the nineteenth century.... [W]e have no power to tell the Almighty that he shall not make a revelation to us at one time, as well as another; and I assert that the proof of the truth of the miracle is to be found in its own nature, and not in the circumstance of the time at which it is wrought. There is nothing in the nature of things, or in the nature of religion to make it impossible for God to do now works similar to those done by him at any former time (John England, October 30, 1826).[1]

Bishop England made these comments in a series of letters addressed to "The Roman Catholics of the United States of North America" between 1826 and 1828 in response to a book published in London that attacked Catholicism. England's defense of miracles was historical and philosophical, with no mention of the United States itself. Yet England himself was in the process of intensely examining an alleged miracle that had created a sensation in this country and beyond, one that had divided the American Catholic community.

Miraculous cures were something new to American Catholic culture. The first generation of Catholic settlers in Maryland had experienced some extraordinary healings among Indian converts, but the phenomenon disappeared with the collapse of the Indian missions in the 1640s. Maryland Catholics, very much within the cultural orbit of English Catholicism, shared the providential world view of their counterparts in the mother country (and most of their Protestant neighbors, for that matter). They believed in a God ready to intervene in the lives of individuals and nations, and could even count stories of occult happenings in their common memory. Nonetheless, their approach to religion was on the whole marked by common sense and practicality.[2] By the late eighteenth century the moderate Enlightenment was

1. Sebastian G. Messmer, ed., *The Works of the Right Reverend John England: First Bishop of Charleston* (Cleveland: A. H. Clark, 1908), 2:292.

2. Stories of divine retribution within the early Catholic community paralleled Puritan providential narratives with distinctive Catholic details. One such Catholic story was that of the Protestant soldier in Saint Mary's City in 1646, who seized the guns of certain colonists who had been firing them in honor of St. Ignatius' feast day. The soldier proceeded to make an obscene

giving a distinct understanding to this tradition under the leadership of the Carrolls and other American Catholics. As Joseph Chinnici has shown, the Enlightenment vision of these American Catholics, grounded in an anthropology of personal experience in a world in which grace and nature were united, promoted among other things "an ecumenical theology, and a definition of spirituality oriented towards service, ministry, public charity and the creation of ecclesial community. In short, this thinking strained for the personal integration of faith and culture."[3]

Between 1824 and 1838 there was a series of miraculous cures and wonders among American Catholics. Of the seventeen that I have found evidence of, all but two occurred in Maryland or the District of Columbia. Most were attributed to the intercession of Prince Alexander Leopold Hohenlohe-Waldenbourg-Schillingfürst, the wonder-working priest around whom a cult had formed in Europe in the 1820s. The cures almost immediately received wide coverage on the Continent and in Great Britain. On this side of the Atlantic there was little or no publicity, but Hohenlohe quickly gained the attention of a number of Jesuits and Sulpicians in the Baltimore-Washington area, all immigrants from the Continent.

As early as June 1822, one of the Sulpicians at St. Mary's Seminary, John Tessier, was writing to Hohenlohe on behalf of a German Jesuit, William Beschter, who was seeking the prayers of the German priest-prince for two of his parishioners.[4] Since Hohenlohe was frequently changing his residence

---

gesture as his "salute" to the founder of the Jesuits. "His buffoonery cost him dear," the superior of the English Province of the Society of Jesus related to the Superior General in Rome in an annual letter much after the event: "for scarce had he gone 200 yards, when he was seized with extraordinary pains in his bowels." Five days later he was dead, "a warning to men of impiety to the Saints"; Annual letter, provincial superior to superior general in Rome, 1670, MPA 4-W-2, GULSC.

Evidence of the occult circulated even among the Catholic gentry. Leonard Neale, the second Archbishop of Baltimore, told of his encounter with an invisible communicant. Once when distributing communion in a parish in southern Maryland, Neale found himself working the communion rail several times to accommodate the many communicants. One spot in the rail, however, was consistently empty when Neale came to it. After Mass a woman asked him why he had not given her communion. She claimed to have been kneeling in the very spot he had found empty; Diary of Joseph Mobberly, S.J., IV, GULSC.

3. Joseph Chinnici, OFM, "Politics and Theology: From Enlightenment Catholicism to the Condemnation of Americanism," *Working Papers Services, Center for the Study of American Catholicism* (Spring 1981): 35.

4. Tessier Letterbook, June 18, 1822, fol. 84, Sulpician Archives, Baltimore (hereafter SAB), AASMSU.

at this time, it was not until January of 1824 that Tessier received a response from the prince, now at Bamberg, Bavaria. By this time two other Jesuits, Anthony Kohlmann and Stephen Dubuisson, were interested in pursuing an appeal for his intercession.

Kohlmann, a native of Alsace, had been in America since 1804. In 1813, as pastor of a church in New York City, he had made legal history by his defense of the seal of confession. Kohlmann, who had been superior of the Maryland Mission of the Society of Jesus and president of three schools (Georgetown, the New York Literary Institution, and the Washington Seminary) was in 1824 novice-master and superior of the Jesuit plantation at White Marsh in Prince Georges County. Dubuisson, born in Sainte-Domingue, had fled with his parents to France during the revolution of 1793. There he had entered government service; during Napoleon's reign he had become comptroller for the Crown. The emperor's first abdication in 1814 gave Dubuisson the opportunity to act on his long-held desire to join the Jesuits. On the advice of a visiting American bishop, he entered the Society in the United States as a member of the Maryland Mission. In 1824 he was assistant pastor at St. Patrick's Church in Washington.

While Kohlmann had been the rector of the Washington Seminary, he had made the acquaintance of Ann Carbery Mattingly. The Carberys were an old Maryland family. One brother, Joseph, was a Jesuit; another was the mayor of Washington. Ann Mattingly, a forty-year-old widow, had been suffering for seven years from a tumor on the breast and other symptoms, including fevers, chills, fits of coughing, and the vomiting of large quantities of blood. Kohlmann asked Dubuisson to write to Hohenlohe on her behalf. Dubuisson, who was collecting everything he could on the European miracles attributed to Hohenlohe, had already written in behalf of other Catholics of the city, but failed to receive a response. Understandably he was apparently reluctant to write again. Months after Kohlmann's request, he finally did so in January 1824.[5]

When Mattingly's condition worsened in February, they decided they could not wait for the prince's particular intention. Beschter informed Dubuisson that Hohenlohe had set aside the tenth of each month to pray for

5. Dubuisson to Hohenlohe, Georgetown, January 2, 1824 (draft), MPA 19-D-I, GULSC. The journal *L'Ami de la Religion* was providing regular and extensive coverage of the Hohenlohe cures. Dubuisson also had a copy of *Cures Miraculeuses obtenues par les priéres du Prince Abbé de Hohenlohe en 1821 & 1822* (Nantes: 1822).

all those outside of Europe who were seeking his aid.[6] In accordance with Hohenlohe's instructions, a novena was made in honor of the Holy Name of Jesus; the afflicted person was to confess and receive communion, as well as have "an unrestricted confidence of being favorably heard."[7]

During the novena, Mattingly, her sight and hearing both failing, seemed at death's door. Her doctor had long since given up on her case and was merely prescribing opium to reduce her pain. On March 10, Dubuisson said Mass for her at St Patrick's at two o'clock in the morning, the time they had calculated that Hohenlohe would be celebrating in Bamberg. After Mass Dubuisson brought communion to Mattingly, who took more than five minutes to swallow the host. Immediately she began to sit up, exclaimed: "Lord Jesus! what have I done to deserve so great a favor," and declared herself completely well. The egg-size tumor, the ulcers on her back, the fevers—all had disappeared.[8] Dubuisson and the five women in the room were in a state somewhere between ecstasy and terror. But they quickly spread the word of her miraculous recovery to friends and neighbors (nearly two hundred persons had been taking part in the novena for her). The news electrified Washington. Thousands visited her daily to see this marvelous woman with their own eyes. By summer the news had spread to Europe through the pages of *L'Ami de la Religion* and other journals.

6. Beschter to Dubuisson, Baltimore, February 6, 1824, MPA 19-D-2, GULSC.

7. *A Collection of Affidavits and Certificates, Relative to the Wonderful Cure of Mrs. Ann Mattingly* (Washington, D.C.: 1824), 37–38. The special prayer that Hohenlohe wrote to obtain cures was not mentioned in this correspondence, nor is there any evidence that it was employed in the Mattingly cure. Later supplicants did employ it. The prayer:

> O God, who directs the hearts of those who believe in thee, vouchsafe at this moment to manifest thyself by act, let thy power and majesty shine on account of thy servant in the same manner as thou actest in the consecration by the words of the Priest, in changing the bread and wine into the true Body and Blood of Jesus Christ, and in the same manner thou doest by thy immediate power, in the words of absolution; so, Oh my God, do I expect now thy immediate operation in the Name of Jesus to whom thou has given all power in heaven and on earth, for his obedience unto His death on the Cross, for thy own Sake O God do I expect this favor, that thy Holy Name be sanctified, that Jesus Christ be blessed and praised, and the true doctrine confirmed, with firm belief and confidence that thou willst act in an immediate manner, I in the Name of Jesus Christ commend by the power given me in holy Baptism,—these infirmities to remove. Confirm my petition, O God the Father, the Son, and Holy Ghost. Amen. [Dubuisson's translation]

8. *Collection of Affidavits*, Depositions of Mattingly, Dubuisson, Dr. William Jones, 2–8, 22–23, 36–40.

Promulgating the Cure

Dubuisson rushed to Baltimore by coach to bring word to the archbishop, Ambrose Maréchal. No doubt Dubuisson and the others involved expected Maréchal to act quickly to authenticate the miraculous nature of the cure. As Thomas Carbery wrote to Maréchal three days after the event, "We shall not make public this affair, till we see or hear from you, which I trust for the honor and glory of the Catholic cause will be soon."[9] Maréchal was in no hurry. In conveying to Dubuisson the instructions that Tessier had received from the prince, the archbishop had made quite clear his lack of enthusiasm for the Hohenlohe cult. "I have certainly no objection to your performing the acts of Devotion prescribed by Prince Hohenlohe. [I] myself on the 10th will join you [in] my prayers, but let no noise be made about it lest impious men should take from thence an occasion of ridiculing or blaspheming our Holy Religion."[10]

The ecstatic reports of the miracle that Maréchal was receiving from Washington did not lessen his wariness. If ever proved, he wrote Father William Matthews, Mattingly's pastor, such an extraordinary event "can not but promote the glory of Alm God in this country." They could also, he added, occasion an enthusiasm that went "beyond the limits traced by enlightened piety & even ordinary prudence." There were to be no public acts of thanksgiving until the miracle was proved "beyond doubt."[11]

Maréchal soon enough saw his worst fears confirmed. Anthony Kohlmann, who had been the most confident of the clerics about the likelihood of a miraculous cure, could not restrain his exuberance. On March 21 the Baltimore *Federal Gazette* published a letter of Kohlmann's to a New York lawyer in which Kohlmann announced the great tidings:

9. Carbery to Maréchal, Washington, D.C., March 13, 1824, AAB 14-B-1, AASMSU.

10. The archbishop was concerned that any Mass to be celebrated in behalf of Mattingly be said in a church, not in her home. He also thought it excessive to be attempting to time the Mass to match the one said by Hohenlohe. "Who can tell where he will be on the 10th of next month?"; Maréchal to Dubuisson, Baltimore, February 13, 1824, AAB 21-O-1, AASMSU.

11. Maréchal to Matthews, Baltimore, March 12, 1824, AAB 21-O-1, AASMSU. Matthews' initial enthusiasm had nearly matched that of his assistant at St. Patrick's. On the tenth he had written the archbishop to inform him "with sentiments of the most profound gratitude to the goodness of our Lord & Saviour Jesus Christ, and unbounded confidence in his Almighty power... [of] the miraculous & instantaneous cure of Mrs. Ann Mattingly"; Matthews to Maréchal, Washington, D.C., March 3, 1824, AAB 19-B-15, AASMSU.

The metropolis of America is moved, as Jerusalem formerly was, at the arrival of three wise men. It is in a transport of admiration and religious awe, and nothing can be thought or spoken of but the astonishing and splendid prodigy, which JESUS CHRIST, the Eternal Son of God, and most amiable Saviour of mankind, had been pleased to work, in the capital of America, and in sight of our national councils.

After recapitulating the details he added that

all those that were there at the moment of her receiving the holy communion, and those that were acquainted with the horrid martyrdom which she suffered during six years, solemnly declare that they consider her miraculous restoration like unto, and equal to, the resuscitation of Lazarus from the grave.[12]

Matthews, under whose jurisdiction the case immediately fell, quickly found himself trying to rein in the enthusiasm of the Jesuits. He was annoyed that Kohlmann was acting like a personal chaplain to Mattingly. He reported to Maréchal that the Jesuits were treating the event as an established miracle: a solemn *Te Deum* had been sung at Georgetown and the college bell rung in celebration.[13] Kohlmann was personally spreading the news in Annapolis, where he had "converted half the town at least in desire."[14] Once Kohlmann's letter was published, Matthews found it necessary to release a short statement giving the essential facts and promising a more complete and authenticated report shortly.[15] People were "indignant" at Kohlmann, Matthews observed, for drawing ridicule on the event. "This miracle has caused a great deal of trouble—happy thing they do not occur often."[16] Matthews was dreading the

12. Kohlmann to Lewis Wilcocks, White Marsh, March 16, 1824, extracted in *An Examination of a Protestant's Objections to the Popish Miracle Lately Wrought in America* (London: 1824), 2–3. Kohlmann's letter to Wilcocks was more restrained than earlier ones he had sent to Jesuits. On the 12th of March he had written a Jesuit: "Laudetur Jesus Christus in aeternum, qui facit mirabilia solus. *Miracle!!!*... The whole city is electrified. In the opinion of the public the miracle is considered... equal to a resuscitation from the grave"; [Kohlmann to unknown], Georgetown, March 12, 1824, MPA, 206-P-23, GULSC.

13. Matthews to Maréchal, Washington, D.C., March 31, 1824, AAB. 19-B-18, AASMSU.

14. Matthews to Maréchal, Washington, D.C., March 19, 1824, AAB, 19-B-16, AASMSU.

15. Matthews to Maréchal, Washington, D.C., March 31, 1824, AAB, 19-B-18, AASMSU; *National Intelligencer*, March 30, 1824, cited in Joseph T. Durkin, S.J., *William Matthews, Priest and Citizen* (New York: Benziger, 1963), 137.

16. Matthews to Maréchal, March 31, 1824. Even before Kohlmann's letter, the zealous behavior of Kohlmann and his colleagues was becoming the occasion of local humor. At the Navy Yard, Matthews wrote, "some wag raised a report that [Dubuisson] broke his leg on his way to Balt[,] that the Abp passed his hand over the fractured leg & said, arise Dubuisson thy leg is cured, & walk home"; Matthews to Maréchal, Washington, D.C., March 19, 1824, AAB, 19-B-16, AASMSU.

arrival of April 10, when Kohlmann and Dubuisson were planning a second effort to cure the other three persons they had been praying for. No doubt this time they would draw a large crowd. If no further cures occurred, Matthews expected that it would prove "a very critical time," since the credibility of the Mattingly cure would suffer, as well. He hoped they would be able to publish the report on the case before Congress adjourned.[17]

For weeks the archbishop hesitated to release the documents that Dubuisson and Matthews had gathered regarding the cure. He was dissatisfied with the length of some statements, including Dubuisson's, and the tone of others. What the report should do, he insisted to Dubuisson, was "make an impression on the spirit of our erring brethren." Anything that could feed the suspicion that the report was the product "of exalted imaginations" would hardly serve that purpose. At the same time Maréchal wanted to respond to the interest that members of the Congress had expressed in the event.[18]

Maréchal's concern for a prudent procedure that would "render the fact respectable" in the larger society (he was particularly intent upon getting the testimony of doctors and non-Catholics) was reinforced by the rector of his cathedral, the English-born James Whitfield. Beschter advised Dubuisson in late March that it was very unlikely that the archbishop would issue a pastoral letter concerning the event. Whitfield was of the opinion that Daniel Murray, the Archbishop of Dublin, had made a serious mistake in issuing a pastoral about a cure in his archdiocese that he had termed "the effect of a supernatural agency."[19] "These Gentlemen," Beschter felt, "are . . . not disposed to suffer any abuse on that account."[20]

17. Washington, D.C., March 27, 1824, AAB, 19-B-17, AASMSU.

18. Maréchal to Dubuisson, Baltimore, March 31, 1824, AAB 19-D-1, AASMSU; Maréchal to Dubuisson, n.d. AAB 19-D-1, AASMSU.

19. "Pastoral Letter of the Most Reverend Dr. Murray, on the Cure of Mary Stuart," in *The Works of the Right Rev. John England, First Bishop of Charleston*, ed. Ignatius Aloysius Reynolds (Baltimore: 1840), 3:461–63.

20. Beschter to [Dubuisson], Baltimore, March 24, 1824, MPA 19-D-1, GULSC. Tessier added that "if some of us here have thought that some of you there have acted with too much exuberance and fervor," it was good to remember how impossible it was to contain zeal in encountering a miracle "so evident"; for those who had been involved not at all, like "our Gentlemen of Baltimore," it was easy to keep cool; Tessier to Dubuisson, Baltimore, May 4, 1824, MPA 19-D-1, GULSC).

Maréchal was in the midst of his long controversy with the Maryland Jesuits over the legal status of the latter's extensive property in southern Maryland (see chapter 1). Kohlmann had been superior in 1818 when Maréchal first raised his claim to the property. There is no evidence, however, that the archbishop's actions in the Mattingly case were being consciously influenced by the land dispute.

When Maréchal finally allowed the pamphlet to be published in early May 1824, he attached a very reserved note, attesting to "the considerable attention" that he had given to the following certificates and affidavits, evidence that he assured his readers was "certainly entitled to the greatest respect and credibility, about facts which were obvious to the senses." There was no mention of miracle.[21] The archbishop was keeping a discreet distance from the event, to let it rise or fall on its own merits.[22]

The Cure as Litmus Test

If the archbishop expected such discretion to end the polemics over the miracle, he was badly mistaken. An anonymous pamphlet published in Georgetown in July seized upon this reticence of Maréchal to attack the whole affair. In the heated climate of March and April, the author pointed out, to have spoken merely of "a *wonderful* cure . . . was to incur the charge of criminal unbelief." After all the anticipation of the publication and all the delay, now only one layman could be found to call it a miracle in print. "[S]o much like the birth of a mouse from the parturient labours of a mountain." Sensible Catholics, he concluded, must be mortified.[23]

21. *Collection of Affidavits and Certificates*, 3–4.

22. Dubuisson was particularly exasperated that Maréchal would not even allow him to publish the letter in which he had permitted the original novena to be held for Mattingly. "It certainly behooves your grace," he wrote, "to show great circumspection in pronouncing the cure to be a miracle, but it is my part to state the facts"; Dubuisson to Maréchal, Washington, D.C., April 27, 1824, MPA 19-D-1, GULSC.

23. The forty-one-page pamphlet claimed that Mattingly had been suffering, not from an internal cancer, but from an abscess that conveniently broke shortly before Dubuisson brought communion to her; *The Washington Miracle Refuted: Or, a Review of the Rev. Mr. Matthew's Pamphlet* (Georgetown: 1824). The author signed himself "A Friend of Truth." The July date of publication is inferred from a letter of Beschter to Dubuisson in which the former related that Maréchal "appears very much humbled, to find himself treated in a quite different manner [than] he expected; Baltimore, July 10, 1824, MPA 19-D-1, GULSC.

Dubuisson intended to issue a second pamphlet refuting the charge that the tumor was an abscess. One of the doctors Dubuisson contacted for expert testimony was the archbishop's own physician, Pierre Chatard. Chatard responded:

> That case is indeed, an extraordinary one, one that has puzzled your humble servant who has never been very ready to believe marvelous things; however, he is not to be ranked among those who would not acknowledge the resurrection of a dead body, were they to witness it. I confess that the illness of Mrs. M. . . . an obscure one for me, it was certainly not an internal Cancer. I rather incline to believe that it was a *vomica* or Sac, emptying itself, from time to time, and increasing the distress of the patient, at each time. I have met with such cases in my practice more than once; and one that terminated in death after having lasted eight

In notes that Dubuisson prepared to rebut the wide-ranging charges of the pamphlet, he wrote that among the worst failings of the author was his attacking Matthews, who had been his friend and protector. Dubuisson was sure that he knew his identity. Although he nowhere records the name of his suspect, it is almost certain that he meant a fellow Jesuit, Thomas C. Levins.

Levins was a native of Ireland who had studied at Clongowes and Stonyhurst before joining the Society of Jesus in England. He had been at Georgetown for three years, teaching natural philosophy and mathematics. A young man of wide learning and interests, Levins made little attempt to disguise his disdain for the enthusiastic piety of Kohlmann and Dubuisson. That Levins would openly ridicule such a staple of Jesuit formation as Alphonso Rodriguez' *Practice of Perfection and Christian Virtues* and restrict his Mass-saying to Sundays (and then reportedly at a "gallop" of "15 or 16 minutes") shocked the rule-conscious Dubuisson, as did Levins' taste for Byron and other "licentious poetry."[24] The Irishman's rapid entrance into the political society of Washington was also a source of uneasiness with the continental Jesuits, who were highly critical of American culture in general and tended to isolate themselves from it as much as possible.[25]

---

years. Doctor Jones mentions a Skirrhous tumor in one of the mammae; I suppose there was one: but I am sorry that the doctor did not give us more details on its size and progress; and what was very essential, that he did not assure us the skirrhous tumor existed when he saw Mrs. M. at his last visit, on the 5th of March. . . . the lady says positively, and so the witnesses do, that at the very moment the marvelous cure was obtained, there was a hard much inflammed and painful lump. If that lump that disappeared in the twinkling of an eye was a skirrhe ready to open and form an ulcerated cancer, surely the sudden disappearance of such a tumor would, by itself, constitute a miracle; because such a thing can not happen either by a crisis or by medicines. I think the doctor could relieve our anxiety by adding to his certificate, and giving us his opinion about it in a more positive manner. However, the duration of the lady's illness; her sufferings; the emaciation and reduction of her system together with the sad symptoms existing at the moment of her instantaneous and perfect cure, is indeed a wonderful thing, and I would betray my conscience were I to say that I do not see the finger of God in it"; Chatard to Dubuisson, November 1, 1824, MPA, 19-D-1, GULSC.

Whether Dubuisson ever obtained this additional information from Jones is unknown. In May of 1824 Archbishop Maréchal had a long conversation with the doctor, after which he requested that Jones give a supplementary affidavit. Jones promised to do so, but months later there was still no indication that he had complied with the request; Dubuisson, Notes on the Refutation Pamphlet, MPA 19-D-1, GULSC.

24. Dubuisson to Luigi Fortis, Georgetown, January 26, 1825, MD 3-IV-3, ARSI.

25. Dubuisson himself, perhaps because of his Sainte-Domingue and French experiences, was always extremely sensitive about the connection between church and state. Later as pastor of St. Mary's in Alexandria, he agonized over what liturgical acknowledgment he should make of

Levins' closest Jesuit associate was Roger Baxter. A native of England whose views had evidently been shaped by the Enlightenment theology of Joseph Berington and others, Baxter had preceded Levins by some five years to Georgetown, where he had greatly strengthened the faculty in the areas of language and polite literature. Baxter had also published an apologetic work in 1820 that featured a remarkably ecumenical ecclesiology and minimal devotionalism.[26]

Charles Plowden, who had been Baxter's novice-master in England, gave him a letter of introduction upon his leaving for the United States, in which he had described him as a person of "abilities and knowledge, and an easy style in writing, which may be of great use. He is besides a youth of good temper, and does not want principles of virtue which I trust he will exert, if your Reverence only take care to keep him well employed at home and sequestered, as much as may be, from the company of externs, according to the rule."[27] Baxter quickly confirmed Plowden's judgment about his intelligence and eloquence in the classroom, pulpit, and press. His virtue and general orthodoxy were another matter. He shared Levins' scorn for the monastic religiosity of those like Dubuisson, as well as his fidelity to the English Catholic tradition of limited power for the papacy. Because of their nonconformist views and scandalous behavior, the regional superior, Francis Dzierozynski, like Kohlmann, from the Russian Province, was by the beginning of 1824 ready to send Levins and Baxter back to Ireland and England, respectively.[28]

Two months later Dzierozynski was reporting that Levins was responsible for the "greatest scandal" the mission had ever seen.[29] Someone under the nom de plume "Deocritus" had written a letter in the *National Intelligencer* about the Mattingly miracle. "Democritus" claimed to be a Catholic "in the strictest sense ... but no enthusiast." The letter proceeded to skewer Kohl-

---

President Harrison's death in 1841. For Dubuisson even a sermon and a prayer for a dead president smacked of politics.

26. As Joseph Chinnici has pointed out, Baxter's reckoning as anonymous Catholics those who maintained "the essentials of Christianity" without formal membership in the Church was very much in the English Catholic tradition; Roger Baxter, *The Most Important Tenets of the Roman Catholic Church Fairly Explained* (Washington, D.C.: 1820), 11; Chinnici, "American Catholics and Religious Pluralism, 1775–1820," *Journal of Ecumenical Studies* 16 (Fall 1979): 742–43.

27. Plowden to Grassi, January 10, 1817, cited in Thomas Hughes, "The History of the Society of Jesus in North America," Text III, 761 (second redaction of 1926), GULSC.

28. Dzierozynski to Fortis, Georgetown, February 10, 1824; Latin extract of Polish letter, MD 3-I-4, ARSI.

29. Dzierozynski to Fortis, Georgetown, April 5, 1824; Latin excerpts of Polish letter, MD 3-I-7, ARSI.

mann for his overwrought description of the miracle. It denied that Kohlmann had anything to do with Georgetown College, but suggested that too many of Kohlmann's pietistic friends had replaced "men of varied and solid learning" there (one of the latter, no doubt, being Baxter, who by then had been isolated in a mission in the remotest part of southern Maryland).[30]

The letter caused an immediate uproar in Catholic Washington and its environs. Sermons and letters denounced "the apostate priest" whom many persons, including Dzierozynski and Dubuisson, identified as Levins. All the internal and external evidence indicates that their conclusion was correct, but when Dzierozynski commanded under the vow of obedience that Levins and the rector of the college, Benedict Fenwick, say whether or not either was the author of the letter, both refused to respond. Personal privacy rights outweighed in their minds any claims of religious order. All Levins would tell Dzierozynski was that in his judgment the letter had caused no injury to either Kohlmann or the Society.[31]

If Levins was skeptical about the miracle, he was more upset about the manner in which Kohlmann and the Continental Jesuits were promoting it. As he confided to Baxter, "the fanatical gang . . . have nearly worked its ruin by their folly."[32] That they were attempting to routinize the event on a monthly basis disgusted him.[33] All the tensions between the native Jesuits and their British colleagues on the one hand and the Continental Jesuits on the other were finding expression in the Mattingly cure. Differences over religious observance, ecclesiology, and American values were predisposing Jesuits toward their position on the miracle.[34] Levins was convinced that "The Friars," as he

30. *National Intelligencer*, April 1, 1824.

31. Dzierozynski, who had been sent to the United States in 1821, in part to provide leadership to counteract the independence that the Jesuit authorities in Rome saw plaguing the Society in America, could only conclude about this incident: "So you see, Father General, what America is and what kind of Jesuits we have here"; Dzierozynski to Fortis, Georgetown, April 5, 1824, MD 3-I-7, ARSI. Although Levins wrote Baxter that the Democritus letter had spared him the trouble of "forging one," the style and substance of the letter point clearly to Levins, as those of *The Washington Miracle Refuted* do not, despite Dubuisson's conclusion; Levins to Baxter, Georgetown, April 7, 1824, MPA 206-N-2, GULSC).

32. Levins to Baxter, April 7, 1824, MPA 206-N-2, GULSC.

33. "No miracle in G[eorge]t[o]wn or Washington," he noted in his diary a month after the Mattingly cure, "though [John] De Theux [a Continental Jesuit at the college] &c had been working"; Levins Diary (John Gilmary Shea transcript), April 10, 1824, GULSC.

34. Even property was a factor here. The civil owner of the Jesuit lands was the Corporation of Roman Catholic Clergymen, the members of which had to be American citizens, which disqualified many of the Continental Jesuits, including Dzierozynski. The latter at this very time

dubbed the Continental Jesuits, were a menace to the cause of Catholicism in the United States. Kohlmann, for his part, was sure that he was reenacting sacred history. "Miracles," he felt, would "always have the same fate with those of Christ: simple people admired them and glorified God, the scribes and Pharisees were enraged at them." It was consolation enough for him to know that the Lord still worked them.[35]

When Levins, despite Dzierozynski's refusal to grant permission, accepted an invitation from the Secretary of War to serve as one of the examiners of the cadets at West Point in the late spring of 1824, his days were numbered. The following fall a series of articles about the fallout of the miracle appeared in the *National Journal* under the nom de plume "Ebezebron the Pilgrim." In decrying the pressures that had been brought upon the archbishop to lend his authority to the miracle, Ebezebron attacked the

> ignorant and shallow men, petulant & snarling old women [who] raise their voices to denounce the facts, because heaven does not send its ministering angels to wait on their high commands! Is this the result of your novenas, your ecstasies, visions and affidavits?[36]

Once again Dzierozynski confronted Levins, with no better results. The superior removed his priestly faculties and intensified his efforts to deport both Levins and Baxter. Baxter departed in late November for England. Levins left Georgetown upon receiving his dismissal papers from the superior general in February 1825. He was quickly taken into the Diocese of New York, where he became heavily involved in the clerical and sectarian politics of the city, to the consternation of another French émigré, Bishop John Dubois.[37]

With the removal of Baxter and Levins the controversy over the miracle ceased. Meanwhile the Continental Jesuits were intent upon gaining recogni-

---

was attempting to force the trustees to surrender effective control of the property into his hands. Levins warned Joseph Carbery, the brother of Mattingly stationed at St. Inigoes with Baxter. "Let [Dzierozynski] become possessed of the property, and then watch the tricks of the developed animal"; Levins to Carbery, Georgetown, April 15, 1824, MPA 206-N-5, GULSC.

35. Dubuisson Diary, September 2, 1825, GULSC.

36. Mobberly Diary IV, November 5, 1824, quoting *National Journal*, October 25, 1824, GULSC.

37. Dzierozynski to Fortis, Georgetown, November 24, 1824, *MD* 3-I-16, *ARSI*; Dzierozynski to Fortis, January 29, 1825, *MD* 3-I-19, *ARSI*; Levins Diary, November 22, 1824, GULSC. Baxter, once in England, pressed to return to America, specifically to New York. Dismissed from the Society, he eventually found his way back to the United States, only to die in Philadelphia in 1827; Excerpts from the English Provincial, August 21, 1825, *MD* 3-I-27, *ARSI*. For Levins' New York career, see Richard Shaw, *John DuBois: The Founding Father* (Yonkers, N.Y.: United States Catholic Historical Society, 1983).

tion for it at the highest level of the Church. In May 1824, Anthony Kohlmann was recalled to Europe to teach dogma at the Roman College. An audience was arranged with Pope Leo XII, during which Kohlmann related the details of the Mattingly cure. The pope was so impressed that he ordered the Matthews pamphlet to be translated into Italian and published by his own printer. Kohlmann was elated. In late December he wrote his friends in America that Leo was speaking with great reverence about the event. Just as encouraging was the pontiff's request that Kohlmann write out for him his thoughts about what was most needed for the progress of religion in America.[38] With a miracle of its own, so Kohlmann and Dubuisson hoped, America could command new respect in Rome, and those who had nurtured this marvelous intervention would be in a favored position to help set the course for the Church in the United States.

"This Is Indeed the House of God"

In the dozen years following the Mattingly cure there were at least seventeen claims of additional miracles or cures affecting fifteen individuals. With one exception they happened to women, mostly members of religious orders (ten of thirteen).[39] Six of the cures occurred in the Convent of the Visitation in Georgetown, three at St. Joseph's, Emmitsburg, two among the Sisters of Charity of Nazareth in Kentucky, and one in the Carmelite monastery at Portobacco, Maryland. With the exception of the Carmelite community, all the convents or monasteries involved had connections with French Jesuits or Sulpicians. At Portobacco an older sister of Ann Mattingly was a professed nun.

The pattern of the cures followed the Mattingly precedent: a long illness (in most cases of at least two years' duration); symptoms of headaches, pains in chest, hemorrhaging, inability to retain food;[40] the failure of physicians

38. William McSherry to Richard McSherry, Rome, January 1, 1825, Alumni File, GUA, GULSC; Beschter to Dzierozynski, Baltimore, [1825], MPA 207-R-14, GULSC; Dubuisson Diary, March 21 and September 2, 1825, GULSC.

39. The sex of one of the persons cured is unknown. Of the thirteen women involved, the ages of nine are known. At the time of their cures, they ranged from 49 to 20 years old, the median being 37 and the average 34.5. In his study of *Miracles and Prophecies in Nineteenth-Century France* (New Brunswick, N.J.: Rutgers University Press, 1982), 54, Thomas A. Kselman found that the highest percentage of *miraculés* were widowed or single adult women.

40. A few of the alleged cures were far less significant than the others. The one male who claimed to have been cured, a mathematics professor at the Sulpicians' college in Baltimore, proved to have been suffering from what he described as attacks of "a canine appetite." Even Tessier could not take his "recovery" very seriously. "If God intends to work another miracle, as is

to cure the patient, despite drastic measures of bleeding, the application of leeches, and purging; a novena during which the afflicted person often got worse; the indifference to being cured; the instantaneous cure on the last day of the novena at the moment of the reception of the Eucharist; new strength and vigor that surpassed that which the person had possessed before.

At the Georgetown Visitation convent so many cures occurred (one nun wrote to her family in 1838, "this is indeed the house of God & the Gate of Heaven")[41] that they developed a morphology of their own, with the subjects increasingly self-conscious of the roles they were expected to play. Ann Maria Digges, Sister Mary Appollonia, had been suffering from pulmonary ailments even before she entered the convent in 1816. (Tuberculosis ran in the family; a mother and brother had already died from it.) In 1825 she had been one of four nuns at visitation for whom a novena in league with Hohenlohe had been made (she was already considered "dangerously consumptive"), but she refused to pray for her own cure, since God seemed to will her death.[42] When Digges's condition became desperate in 1831, out of obedience she began another novena in union with Hohnlohe. Even though her symptoms grew worse during the novena, she was confident that she would be cured this time, since she was acting from obedience. She remembered thinking that

> were it left to my choice, I should prefer to die, but... all my desire was *that the glory of God might be promoted, and that I might perform his adorable* will.... Fr. D[ubuisso] n came, and the awful moment *arrived* [with communion]... the awe [she had felt

very probable," Tessier wrote Dubuisson in May 1824, he thought he would do something more impressive than what the faculty member was claiming had happened to him through divine intervention; Baltimore, May 5, 1824, MPA 19-D-1, GULSC; Louis Deluol to Dubuisson, Baltimore, April 25, 1824, MPA 19-D-1, GULSC. There was a second cure involving Mattingly, this one in 1831 at the Visitation convent where she was staying. The "cure" was her recovery from a bad ankle sprain. It was probably inevitable, given the close scrutiny of Mattingly's health after 1824, that any rapid healing would be cause for the discovery of new evidence of the miraculous.

Twelve of the cases, however, were certainly of a serious nature. Six involved tumors, of either the breast or the liver. Four manifested symptoms of advanced tuberculosis; there was one case of symptoms suggesting cirrhosis of the liver; and one involving both an impaired liver and spinal meningitis.

41. Sister Mary Bernardine [Ward], Georgetown, February 17, 1838, Georgetown Visitation Archives (hereafter GVA).

42. The chaplain of the nuns, Joseph P. de Clorivière, said nothing about Digges's resistance in his report to the archbishop. The first mention of it is found in the pamphlet that Dubuisson wrote six years later when she was finally cured; Clorivière to Samuel Eccleston, Georgetown, February 10, 1825, AAB, 14-L-61; *Narrative of Two Wonderful Cures Wrought in the Monastery of the Visitation at Georgetown in the District of Columbia in the Month of January 1831* (Baltimore: 1831), 14.

during the whole novena] *penetrated* my whole frame, in a manner *more easily conceived than expressed.* As our Lord entered the door, I said to him, O My Saviour, Jesus! I offer & resign myself into your hands as a victim. Grant me life or death, as it will please you, for I have *no other will than* yours. I then received, and, in an instant, . . . in the very *act of swallowing* [the host] I felt a sensation from my head & through my whole frame, *even* to the extremities, *which exceeded all that I can express.* It *appeared* to me that I was *raised* in my bed *from the awful impression* of the powerful hand of God, & . . . lost in the awful power of God.[43]

Physical prowess became an important test of the supernatural character of the cures at Visitation. Lifting heavy objects was the favored means of proving the new power of the cured person. Dubuisson had Digges lifting chairs and weights the morning of her cure; the next day he insisted that she lift a fifty-two-pound clock weight with one hand. For the next eight days he had her repeat the exercise of lifting a twenty-eight-power weight with the little finger of her left hand.[44] As Dubuisson concluded about a later cure at Visitation:

when it is observed, that the person has not only been brought back to integrity of health, but is now found to possess physical, bodily forces which she never had before,—forces far surpassing what is ordinarily possessed by individuals of the same sex and complexion,—forces that endure, that bear any test,—then indeed, the mind, overwhelmed, cannot resist the inference, *Digitus Dei est hic.*[45]

Another mark of the cured that was cited as evidence of God's special touch was the enduring state of the extraordinary health that they enjoyed. A few weeks after the cure of the Visitandine Sister Mary Eugenia (Millard), another nun at Visitation duly noted that "her complexion, before so ghastly and disfigured, is now that of a person in perfect health; and she is now entirely free from all disease . . . [and teaching again] with all possible alacrity and zeal."[46] Dubuisson could not resist observing that "what is the *commencing* wonderful state of Sister Eugenia, has been the *established permanent*, wonderful state of Sister Apollonia, of the same Convent, these seven years, and of Mrs. Ann Mattingly, of Washington, these fourteen!"[47]

No one tracked the charts of the cured as persistently as did Dubuisson.

43. Apollonia Digges's account of her cure, January 25, 1831, MPA 210, GULSC.

44. *Narrative of Two Wonderful Cures*, 19–22.

45. Dubuisson, *et al.*, *A Narrative of the Wonderful Cure of Sister Mary Eugene Millard, a Nun in the Convent of the Visitation, in Georgetown (District of Columbia) on the 10th February 1838*, 26, GVA.

46. Mary Bernardine, February 24, 1838, GVA.

47. Dubuisson, Narrative, 26–27, GVA.

He secured accounts of the miracles from the cured persons themselves, wherever possible. As late as 1862 he was writing from Rome to inquire about the health of Eugenia Millard, the last person to be cured. He was particularly interested, not only whether the rumor of her death was true, but whether she had died of the same ailment she had been so wonderfully freed from in 1838. "If so," he remarked, the "prodigy would lose something of its first supposed character."[48] In 1828 he happily noted that Mrs. Mattingly's health was "better perhaps than that which any other person in Washington would boast of."[49] Twenty years later she was still thriving. Apollonia Digges lived an active life as a Visitandine until her death in 1889. The later lives of some of the others were not so blessed. Sister Beatrix Myers of Georgetown Visitation, whose tuberculosis had been remitted through a Hohenlohe novena in 1825, suffered a relapse eight years later. She was then cured for a second time, but died eight years later at the age of 45. The Carmelite Elizabeth Johnson (Sister Magdalen) died two years after her cure; she was 51 at the time of her death.[50] Wilhelmina Jones, Sister Mary Stanislaus of Georgetown Visitation, who was cured of cancer in 1838, lived on until 1879, but suffered greatly from various heart and kidney ailments. Eugenia Millard had not died when Dubuisson made his inquiry in 1862. But she had evidently slowly sunk back into the spinal paralysis that had first plagued her. As the Annals of the Visitation Convent noted on her death in 1863, "the cross [was] given back to her, to be borne twenty long years."[51]

A New Devotional Contender

Although the intercession of Prince Hohenlohe was central to all the early cures (1824–1831), the new devotion to Mary's immaculate conception began to supplant Hohenlohe as the focus of the novenas in the 1830s. The cult of the Miraculous Medal that grew out of the apparitions of Mary to Catherine Labouré in 1830 quickly spread to the American Catholic community. At both St. Joseph's in Emmitsburg and Georgetown Visitation, novenas were begun in 1835 in honor of the Immaculate Conception, and Miraculous Medals were put on the afflicted persons. Ironically the sister at Georgetown was Beatrix

48. Dubuisson to [Angela Harrison], May17, 1862, GVA.

49. [Dubuisson notes on Mattingly cure, 1828], MPA, 19-D-1, GULSC.

50. Profession and Death Books, Carmelite Monastery Archives, Baltimore.

51. Annals, II, GVA.

Myers. Both novenas produced the same effects as the successful ones made in union with the prince-priest.[52]

Dubuisson had been stationed in Philadelphia in 1835. Three years later he was again a regular visitor to the Georgetown convent from his new station in Alexandria. When Eugenia's crisis occurred, Dubuisson apparently arranged for Hohenlohe's intercession. Alarmed by Eugenia's rapid deterioration in January of 1838, the sisters decided they could not wait until the tenth of the following month, and instead began a novena to the Immaculate Conception. It is interesting to note that when the friends of Ann Mattingly found themselves in a similar crisis in 1824 (knowing that Hohenlohe was going to offer his Mass for their specific intention at a date they could not afford to wait for), they had still made the novena in general union with him. Now in 1838 the Immaculate Conception novena failed in securing their intention; two weeks later the Hohenlohe one occasioned the cure. Afterward Dubuisson could not resist a comparison of the results:

> This, surely, can be considered as a marked, fresh sanction from heaven of the devotions performed in union with Prince Hohenlohe. And why would it not be a peculiar trait of heavenly regard for that Prince?... Did he not say to his Disciples: *He that believeth in me, the works that I do, he shall do also, and greater than these shall he do?* (John 14:12)[53]

The implication of Dubuisson, conscious or not, was that Hohenlohe, as priest, was in the apostolic succession in a way that eluded Mary herself.

The Hohenlohe cult had already been on the wane in Europe when it made its way across the Atlantic. Shortly after it published the news of the Mattingly miracle, *L'Ami de la Religion* ceased carrying accounts of Hohenlohe cures because of the repetitious details and growing skepticism about them.[54] The persistence of the clerical support in the United States for the cult suggests a particular attraction that a priest like Dubuisson had for a fellow priest as the central mediator in the miraculous process.

52. Annals I, GVA; Marie Augustine [Barber] to Kohlmann, Georgetown, May 24, 1835, MD, 7-XI-2, ARSI; Dubuisson [Notes on the cure of Sister Mary Romana, Catherine Martina Hemmall], January 23, 1838, MPA 19-D-1, GULSC.

53. Dubuisson, Millard Narrative, 14–15, GVA.

54. The Hohenlohe cult continued to decline until Hohenlohe's death in 1849, but never completely disappeared. His help was still being sought in Europe as late as 1844; Kselman, *Miracles and Prophecies*, 23. But interestingly, the Millard cure seems to be the last one attributed to him.

The Cures as Confirmation of Catholicism's Superior Claims

Thomas Kselman has noted the efforts of the Church in France in the nineteenth century to institutionalize cures within the framework of orthodox rituals and symbols supervised by the clergy.[55] The Eucharist was the centerpiece of this ecclesiastical canopy. Ann Taves has traced the emergence of a eucharocentric devotional culture in the United States in the mid-nineteenth century, a culture that was increasingly oriented to Rome and the papacy.[56] The Eucharist, as we have seen, was at the heart of the Hohenlohe cures, both in Europe and the United States. There was a difference, however, in the role the Eucharist played in the cures on the respective continents. In Europe the cures most often came at the elevation of the Host during the consecration.[57] In the United States the vital moment was the actual swallowing of the Host, as though Jesus had to be physically encountered for the cure to be effected. Time and again the instantaneous cure was traced to that act of swallowing. In Jesus' sacramental burial in the "tomb" of the communicant, the latter experienced an instant resurrection from her living death. One of the distinguishing qualities of the restored person was the enduring sweetness of breadth, comparable to the newborn. So too the extraordinary strength of the cured was a sharing in Jesus' own power.[58]

"[H]ow express the love of my Jesus in holy Communion[?]" Ann Mattingly later wrote. "Oh unworthy that I am[,] yet to receive, such marks of tenderness & love, it appears to me when I approach the Holy Table, that I shrink up to nothing, fear & dread of the majesty of God, ... yet I feel a longing desire to be united to him."[59] The novenas themselves were an occasion for the more frequent reception of communion by the community than was customary. The subsequent devotion to the Eucharist of one of the cured nuns led to the extraordinary permission to receive it daily.

Three of the cures in the mid-thirties were unrelated to the reception

55. Kselman, *Miracles and Prophecies*, 36.

56. Ann Taves, "Context and Meaning: Roman Catholic Devotion to the Blessed Sacrament in Mid-Nineteenth-Century America," *Church History* 54 (December 1985): 482–95.

57. Hohenlohe's prayer itself made an explicit comparison between the radical change in transubstantiation achieved during the consecration of the Mass and that sought in the cure.

58. A laywoman found Millard's new strength a proof from the scripture passage: "and virtue went out from him and healed all" (Luke 6:19); Ann T. Nicholes, n.d., MPA 19-B-1, GULSC.

59. Mattingly to Dubuisson, Washington, D.C., May 22, 1828, MPA, 19-D-2, GULSC.

of the Eucharist. Marie Donatienne Maisonneuve of the Nazareth Sisters of Charity was cured at the elevation during Mass. Catherine Martina Hemmall, Sister Mary Romana, of St. Joseph's, Emmitsburg, who used the Miraculous Medal, experienced her transformation outside of Mass entirely when she was in her workroom. Sister Stanislaus Jones of Georgetown Visitation had the most non-institutional cure. Indeed Jones apparently had not even prayed to be cured. Her "large and ugly tumor" had simply disappeared during the night. Dubuisson read in this a return to the "Simplicity" of "apostolic times." Still he considered the cure appropriate for "private edification only.[60]

The miracles for public consumption were those that would clearly show the power of the Eucharist, especially to non-Catholics. As one Jesuit observed immediately after the Mattingly miracle, "the power & mercy of our amiable Saviour could not be more sensibly expressed before infidels, as well as dishonorable members of the Catholic Church... [since] they see the Value of the great Sacrafice [*sic*] of Mass, they behold the surprising effects of the holy Eucharist."[61] Another saw in the cure of Beatrix Myers that "God continues to work wonders to show to an unbelieving world that the flesh & blood of his divine Son are present in the adorable Sacrament of the Altar."[62] The writer of the pamphlet *The Washington Miracle Refuted* could insist that there was no need for miracles in the modern age in order for Christianity to establish its claims, but the Catholic boosters of these miracles could answer that they were confirming the superior claim of Catholicism to the mantle of Christianity through their revelation of the wonder-working effects of the Real Presence.[63]

Even the one miracle that did not involve a cure served to promote the same aim. Cecilia Reeves, a widow, had been received into the Church a few months before her death of consumption in March 1825. Dubuisson had given her the last sacraments shortly before she died. The next morning her relatives discovered the letters "IHS" impressed on her wrist, just above the hand in which she had been holding a crucifix. The relatives, all non-Catholic, were startled, but had no idea what the letters meant. When they found out,

60. Ward, Georgetown, February 17, 1838, GVA; Narrative of Millard Cure, 2–3, GVA; Dubuisson to Hohenlohe, Georgetown [1838] (draft), MPA 19-D-2, GULSC.

61. Francis Neale to [Dubuisson], St. Thomas Manor, March 23, 1824, MPA, GULSC.

62. Mobberly Diary, IV, February 1825, GULSC.

63. *The Washington Miracle Refuted: Or, a Review of the Rev. Mr. Matthew's Pamphlet* (Georgetown, 1824), 34–35. As the Sisters of Georgetown Visitation expressed their conviction, "all the lovers of religion will rejoice with us... in seeing Jesus glorified, his real presence and action manifested in his adorable sacrament in so beneficial a manner"; Georgetown *Metropolitan*, March 1, 1825.

they asked to take instructions in the Church. Dubuisson saw in the event "something soothing and highly encouraging to lovers of the Lord Jesus, in the bare fact, that a person, who expired with his image before her eyes, and his name on her lips, had the day after her decease, the emblem of that sacred name, IHS impressed . . . just above that hand which held his image."[64] And those letters were also the ones traditionally inscribed on the Host.

In this campaign to impress Protestants and gain converts the *Orthodox Journal* of London saw a special reason for the Mattingly miracle in the United States:

> Hitherto it has been alleged that these miracles have been wrought in corners, and on the person of some nun or individual of no rank in society.—Here, however, the case is different. To confound the incredulous, God has manifested his power in the midst of a shrewd and sensible people, who are not shackled with restrictions, nor harassed with penalties for exercising the right of conscience, and time will show us the result.[65]

From the beginning Dubuisson and his colleagues realized the stakes in the Mattingly case. In identifying her in his letter to Hohenlohe, Dubuisson underscored that "nothing would make a greater impression than a miracle by your prayers."[66] When she was cured, Tessier had no doubt about God's intention "in working this miracle in the capital, and during the session of Congress; on a person so well known, being the sister of the Mayor of the city, and whose affliction has been so long and so extraordinary."[67] The many conversions that followed in the District of Columbia and Maryland were attributed at least in part to the miracle. By the middle 1820s a Catholic could report with excitement to his cousin in Paris that "there is in Maryland, & everyone remarks it, a general fermentation as to Catholicism."[68]

Bishop John England, in his quest to show the compatibility between Catholicism and American culture, was also attracted to the Mattingly cure precisely because of the open character of the event, its evidence so available to public scrutiny. England studied the cure for nearly six years, interviewing Mattingly and other principals in the event, as well as doctors. In a long

64. There were no initials or letters on the crucifix itself; Dubuisson, Account of Cecilia Reeves' miracle, AAB 21-A.B-1, AASMSU.

65. Cited in *Examination of a Protestant's Objections*, 7.

66. Dubuisson to Hohenlohe, February 10, 1824, MPA 19-D-1, GULSC.

67. Tessier to [Maréchal], [Baltimore], April 2, 1824, AAB 20-U-21, AASMSU.

68. W[illiam Joseph] Williams to Samuel Eccleston, Baltimore, September 12, 1826, AAB, AASMSU.

open letter to Maréchal's successor, James Whitfield, in April 1830, England concluded that it "was an immediate and miraculous interference of the Creator himself." That being the case, the bishop rhetorically asked, "what must be the consequence when we unite this fact with the declaration of the Saviour? . . . they shall lay their hands upon the sick, and they shall recover."[69]

The Significance of the Cures

Such a reasonable miracle may have been the perfect oxymoron, in England's eyes, to convince Americans that Catholicism had claims that could not simply be dismissed out of ignorance or prejudice. Unfortunately, the public disposition to listen declined sharply in the 1830s in the wake of Irish immigration and the Second Great Awakening. England himself was a transitional figure in American Catholic society. The enlightened republican tradition he represented was rapidly fading.

The virtual monopolization of the cures by women tempts one to reflect upon a certain feminization of American Catholic culture, to play upon Ann Douglass' phrase. Here, instead of liberal Protestant clergymen and women, we have conservative Catholic priests and sisters. Such gender domination in the culture of nineteenth-century miracles was, of course, not peculiar to America. But the high percentage of nuns among the cured does seem to have been an American Catholic phenomenon. Males were certainly prayed for (as were other women, both religious and lay), but apparently in vain.[70] This pattern did not escape the notice of the nuns. As Apollonia Digges remarked to Dubuisson in 1831, "according to the general saying, we will have to double and treble our prayers, as there is question of obtaining the miraculous cure of *men*."[71] If the cures increased the sentimentalization of devotional life, they also were a source of superiority for women, whether religious or lay, giving them a special access to the divine. If obedience and self-denial were keys to obtaining divine favor, the cured and their feminine colleagues were by no means the suggestible subjects of male authority figures. While, for example, it took Dubuisson and his Sulpician associates months to get Archbishop Maréchal to allow them to publish their pamphlet, the Visitandines had one

69. Messmer, *Works of the Right Reverend John England*, 6:156.

70. Among the women who failed to be cured were the two superiors noted as seeking Hohenlohe's help, one at Georgetown Visitation, the other at Carmel Portobacco. Both died shortly afterward.

71. Digges to Dubuisson, Georgetown, May 5, 1831, MPA 210 extra, GULSC.

out barely a month after the Apollonia Digges cure in 1831, even though the new prelate was James Whitfield, who had been the chief voice of caution in Maréchal's council in 1824.[72] The abandonment of the Hohenlohe ritual for that of the Immaculate Conception could also be read as a sign of feminine assertion against a male-controlled process.[73] The miracles provide further testimony of the relatively liberated status of the American nun in the nineteenth century that Mary Ewens and others have documented.[74]

A half-century after the last cure, the historian John Gilmary Shea wrote that the Mattingly cure "seemed to revive the dormant faith of Catholics, and was followed by an increase of piety and devotion."[75] What Shea failed to note was that the piety and devotion were of a kind that John Carroll would have found foreign. Although the Hohenlohe miracles were a passing phenomenon, they revealed and affected some important changes that were occurring in the intellectual and devotional life of the Church. The French émigrés and their Continental associates were hardly the wave of the future, but their isolation from their new culture and their rigid ecclesiology foreshadowed the Catholic America to come. The ultramontanism they embraced continued to grow within that community long after the Hohenlohe miracles were a faint memory. Marian and Eucharistic devotions became more and more popular, especially in the new Irish and German communities. Other miraculous cults arose in time. In the miracles of the 1820s and 1830s one gets an insight into the origins of that ethos Jay Dolan has described as "devotional Catholicism," with its peculiar stress on authority, sin, ritual, and the miraculous, that came to characterize American Catholicism by the late nineteenth century.[76]

72. Peter Kenney, the Irish Jesuit superior of the Maryland Mission in 1831, professed to be "frightened" at the way the Georgetown visitation nuns had been pressuring the archbishop about the miracle. "Some of them," he wrote, "are I hear more like Furies, than Christians!"; Kenney to Dubuisson, April 5, 1831, MPA 210-W-1, GULSC.

73. Before the Georgetown Visitation superior gave Sister Beatrix the miraculous medal to wear in 1835, she allowed each of the nuns "to approach and kiss" "this new found treasure"; Foundation Book, GVA.

74. Mary Ewens, O.P., "Removing the Veil: The Liberated American Nun in the Nineteenth Century," *Working Papers Series* (Spring 1978).

75. John Gilmary Shea, *History of the Catholic Church in the United States* (New York: John G. Shea, 1890), 3:87.

76. Jay P. Dolan, *The American Catholic Experience: A History from Colonial Times to the Present* (New York: Doubleday, 1985), 221–40.

Chapter 5

Rome, the American Church, and Slavery

THIS PIECE, like the one in chapter 3, originated as part of a *festschrift* (Joseph C. Linck, C.O., and Raymond Krupke, eds., *Building the Church in America: Studies in Honor of Monsignor Robert F. Trisco on the Occasion of his Seventieth Birthday* [Washington, D.C.: The Catholic University of America Press, 1999], 30–49). It was the outgrowth of the paper I had given nearly twenty years earlier about Jesuit slaveholding in Maryland. Eugene Genovesi, who was the commentator at the session, in his response remarked about how little we know of the Catholic slaveholding community, although it was a significant one in certain parts of the American South, particularly in Maryland, Louisiana, and Kentucky. Genovesi went on to wonder what difference, if any, their religion meant to Catholics as slaveholders. Catholics were an American religious community that uniquely recognized an earthly source of authority beyond the shores of the United States—i.e., the Holy See. What impact, if any, did Rome have, or try to have, on the American Catholic community regarding slavery? And what effect, if any, did the American experience with slavery have on the development of papal teaching on the subject? This essay represented an initial exploration of the questions.

In Supremo Apostolatus

In 1839 Pope Gregory XVI published an apostolic letter, *In Supremo Apostolatus*, in which he explicitly condemned the slave trade and seemed to condemn by implication the institution of slavery itself. "We consider it our pastoral duty," Gregory stated, to make every effort to turn the faithful away from the inhuman traffic in negroes, or any other class of men.... [W]e... do vehemently admonish and abjure in the Lord all believers in Christ, of whatsoever condition, that no one hereafter may dare unjustly to molest Indians, negroes, or other men of this sort; or to spoil them of their goods; or to reduce them to slavery; or to extend help or favor to others who perpetrate such things against them.

The pontiff forbade any Catholic to defend such practices "under any pretext or... excuse."[1]

The letter initially received little attention in the United States, either within or outside the Catholic community. The following year, however, it briefly became an issue in the presidential campaign. In an issueless election in which the Whigs were out-Jacksoning the Jacksonians in their exploitation of political symbolism ("Tippecanoe and Tyler, Too"), a prominent Democrat, Martin Van Buren's Secretary of State John Forsyth, desperate to secure votes for Van Buren and not above using anti-Catholicism to smear William Henry Harrison, the Whig candidate, claimed the pope's letter as evidence that the Catholic Church was a promoter of abolition. Forsyth, speaking before a Georgian audience, was arguing that Harrison had been forced upon Southern Whigs by a combination of sinister forces that included anti-Masons, abolitionists, the British government and the pope, whom he implied had written his letter on slavery under the pressure of British influence.

Forsyth's published remarks occasioned a series of public letters from Bishop John England of Charleston to Forsyth in which he treated the history of the Church's position on slavery.[2] England argued that the present pontiff, Gregory XVI, had clearly distinguished between slave traffic and domestic slavery as it existed in the United States. The latter, the bishop insisted, had not been condemned by Rome. England pointed out that at their triennial meeting in 1840, the American bishops, a majority of whom were from slave states, had formally accepted the pope's letter. If even one of them had found in it anything that he could not accept in conscience concerning the teaching of the Church regarding slavery, he would have been under obliga-

1. Apostolic Letter, December 3, 1939, reproduced in *Letters of the late Bishop England to the Hon John Forsyth, on the Subject of Domestic Slavery*, ed. E. George Read (Baltimore: John Murphy, 1844), ix–xi.

2. There were eighteen letters in all over a two-year period, all devoted to a historical exposition of the Church's teaching on slavery. England's death in 1842 prevented him from taking up the other two topics he intended to treat: the question of slavery in the New World and the condition of blacks in the United States.

tion to raise a protest to the pontiff. But none did. If they had found in the letter anything contrary to the institution of slavery as it existed in the United States, they would have made it their duty to do all they could to eradicate the evils that the pope had identified. But none felt so obligated. Indeed the pope himself, England reported, in a private audience with the Charleston bishop, had shown his awareness that the American South was heir to a system that had been saddled upon the region long before. American Southerners were not engaged in the kind of slave trafficking condemned in the apostolic letter. No American, he concluded, should think that any Catholic, including the pope, was an abolitionist. "Slavery," he informed Forsyth, "is regarded by that church of which the Pope is the presiding officer, not to be incompatible with the natural law, to be the result of sin by Divine dispensation, to have been established by human legislation, and, when the dominion of the slave is justly acquired by the master, to be lawful, not only in the sight of the human tribunal, but also in the eye of Heaven."[3]

Despite Forsyth's scare tactics, Harrison won the election (he even carried Georgia). Three years later *In Supremo Apostolatus* momentarily surfaced again when Daniel O'Connell, the Great Liberator of Irish politics, used it in a futile attempt to woo Irish Americans to the abolitionist standard.[4] Abolitionists periodically brought up the letter during the remainder of the antebellum period as proof that the Church opposed slavery, a claim American Catholic leaders were quick to dispute.[5] But *In Supremo* had no lasting impact on American Catholic society itself. It was after all a letter that had been occasioned by European efforts to eliminate the international slave trade. Pope Gregory, who was deeply interested in the evangelization of Africa, was naturally attracted to such a goal. Moreover, the papal magisterium was still in the process of becoming the reality we take for granted. In the early nineteenth century the pope spoke rarely as a moral teacher. As it was, the American bishops continued to keep their peace about the issue that gradually polarized the country to the point of civil war. If the gag rule did not ultimately prevail in the United States Congress, within the American Catholic community there

3. Read, ed., *Letters*, 19–21, 24.

4. Gilbert Osofsky, "Abolitionists, Irish Immigrants, and the Dilemmas of Romantic Nationalism," *American Historical Review* 80 (October 1975): 889–912.

5. See John E. Quinn, "'Three Cheers for the Abolitionist Pope!' American Reaction to Gregory XVI's Condemnation of the Slave Trade, 1840–1860," *Catholic Historical Review* 90 (January 2004): 67–93.

seemed to be a self-imposed gag rule that was extremely effective. Catholics, like most other Americans, proved loyal to their respective sections, but the American Catholic Church, unlike other churches, did not split over the issue. Still, in the American Church's failure to face this dominant social question, there was a Roman factor—of which Gregory XVI's letter was the most dramatic manifestation—in which the Holy See proved a progressive force in the American Church's confrontation with the slavery issue.

American Catholics and Slavery

The American Catholic Church and slavery had to a large extent grown up together in this country. During the Colonial and early national periods, Catholics were even more confined to the South than slavery was. Only in the early nineteenth century, at the very time slavery was being abolished in the Northern states, did mass immigration shift the center of the Catholic Church in America from Southern plantations and farms to Northern cities. But until the 1820s the largest concentrations of Catholics were in Maryland, Kentucky, and Louisiana. The two greatest churchmen of antebellum Catholicism, John Carroll and John England, were Southern bishops. In 1840, the year of the Council of Baltimore that formally received (without making comment) Gregory's letter on slavery, the majority of Catholic episcopal sees were still located in the South. American Catholicism until that time was largely a Southern phenomenon, and the "peculiar institution" was an integral part of it.

Catholics easily accommodated themselves to slavery. The traditional moral theology of the Church held that slavery was not in itself evil, so long as the mutual rights and duties of slaveholder and slave were respected. Even before the discovery of America, however, Pope Pius II denounced the enslavement of African natives. His successor, Leo X, in the early sixteenth century condemned the attempts of the Spanish and Portuguese to enslave the Indians as something "not only the Christian religion, but Nature herself cried out against."[6] By the seventeenth century the papal strictures were in no common memory of French or English Catholics settling in Louisiana and Maryland. When slavery gradually became the dominant source of labor in

6. Ludwig Pastor, *History of the Popes from the Close of the Middle Ages*, vol. 8 (St. Louis: 1908), 447; cited in Madeleine Hooke Rice, *American Catholic Opinion in the Slavery Controversy* (New York: Columbia University Press, 1944), 16.

the staple agricultural economies of the Southern colonies, Catholic planters became slaveholders.

Nor was the practice confined to the laity. Priests, religious, even bishops held slaves. The Maryland Province of the Society of Jesus in the 1820s was one of the largest slaveholders, certainly in Maryland, if not in the South itself, with its workforce of nearly four hundred slaves on its six estates. Originating in the need to support their ministries, the plantations acquired by the Jesuits had seldom returned enough profit to fulfill their initial purpose. As the tobacco economy of the Chesapeake region became increasingly stagnant in the first decades of the nineteenth century, the condition of the Jesuit properties continued to decline. In 1820 one Jesuit visitor from Ireland found them the epitome of "splendid poverty... so much apparent wealth & real poverty."[7] Such appearances occasioned several controversies about the Maryland Jesuit plantations and their slaves that reached to Rome itself.

As seen in chapter 2, as early as 1788 Jesuit slaveholding in Maryland had brought a protest to Rome from an Irish missionary priest, Patrick Smyth, who attributed the languishing condition of the Church in the Chesapeake area squarely to the scandalous image Jesuits projected as slave masters and the neglect of the religious needs of their people that a preoccupation with plantations brought.[8] John Carroll thought the charges serious enough, and likely to be believed in Rome, where they were circulating, that he issued his own pamphlet to rebut Smyth.

Twenty-five years later two other Irish priests raised the same question, not as publicly, but in higher circles.[9] In 1814 the protestors were two Dominicans, William Vincent Harold and John Ryan, who had recently returned to Ireland from Philadelphia, where they had provided valuable service to Catholics in that city. John Carroll, prizing Harold's renown as a devoted missionary and outstanding preacher, had lamented his departure from the United States in 1813. A year later Carroll was doing everything to block Harold's appointment to the vacant see of Philadelphia. What turned him against

7. "Temporalities," 1820, MPA, X-T-1, GULSC.

8. Patrick Smyth, *The Present State of the Catholic Mission, Conducted by the Ex-Jesuits in North America* (Dublin : P. Byrne,1788), 17–18.

9. The prominence of the Irish on both sides of the question of slavery and Catholicism has to be noted. The Irish, of course, were involved in their own fight for freedom. Of those Irish who stayed in America, like John England, the Purcells, and the Kenricks, where they fell out on the matter depended very much on where they made their homes, whether in Charleston, for instance, or Cincinnati.

the Dominican was an account he received in the fall of 1813 from a London friend about the reports Harold and Ryan were circulating in England and Ireland concerning clerical slaveholding in Maryland. The two were savaging the American Jesuits for holding great estates, trafficking in slaves, and being a scandal to slave and nonslave alike. Carroll himself they accused of being a great holder of slaves.[10]

Carroll, in his response to Archbishop John Troy of Cork (where the two were at the time), admitted that slaveholding was widespread among the clergy in America. He noted with some contempt that there was not yet in the United States "that enthusiasm for [the slaves'] emancipation" that had become so fashionable in England, the very country responsible for the introduction of slavery into its former colony. But he denied that the clergy ever engaged in slave traffic. Harold and Ryan should have known, Carroll added, that the clergy they had attacked, the Jesuits in Maryland, were actually working out a program to emancipate their slaves gradually. As for himself, he pointed out that he had freed the slaves he had inherited and possessed none at all.[11]

Carroll was very sensitive about the slavery question. Like his cousin Charles Carroll of Carrollton and fellow Maryland Catholic Roger Taney, he regarded slavery as a social and economic affliction.[12] Taney and the Carrolls favored gradual emancipation as a solution. The two laymen were officers of the Colonization Society. What the three could not tolerate were the abolitionists, whom they tended to associate with the radical freethinkers of the French Revolution, in particular Rousseau and Raynal, both of whom had condemned slavery on moral grounds. In 1801 John Carroll had removed a priest, John Thayer, from Kentucky, who had among other things stirred up the people because of his opposition to slavery. Thayer was suspected of being a disciple of Raynal.[13]

10. Dale B. Light, *Rome and the New Republic: Conflict and Community in Philadelphia Catholicism between the Revolution and the Civil War* (Notre Dame and London: University of Notre Dame Press, 1996), 75.

11. Carroll to John Troy, Baltimore [1813], in *The John Carroll Papers*, ed. Thomas O'Brien Hanley, S.J. (Notre Dame: University of Notre Dame Press, 1976), 3:312–13. Hanley dates this letter in 1815, but the extract in the archives of Propaganda Fide gives the date of 28 December 28, 1813; *Congregationi Particulari*, 1814, vol.146, folios 533r–536v, APF.

12. Taney, the future Chief Justice of the Supreme Court, regarded slavery in 1818 as "a blot on our national character"; cited in John T. Noonan, Jr., "The Catholic Justices of the United States Supreme Court," *Catholic Historical Review* 67 (July 1981): 369–85.

13. Annabelle M. Melville, *John Carroll of Baltimore, Founder of the American Catholic Hierarchy*

Harold and Ryan immediately answered Carroll. Ryan, writing for his fellow Dominican, perhaps because of Harold's episcopal ambitions, expressed surprise to Archbishop Troy that Carroll had not only defended slavery on abstract principles but condemned the opponents of the system as hypocrites. Pace Carroll, the Dominican informed the prefect, not all priests were slaveholders; indeed, from Boston to Maryland there was not one. The problem was the Maryland Jesuits with their hundreds of slaves. The scandal was aggravated by the contiguity of Maryland to Pennsylvania, where slavery had been abolished by the efforts of the Quakers and others precisely on the grounds of its incompatibility with Christian social morality. Unlike New York and Pennsylvania, where the Irish had settled heavily in the past generation, the Church was declining in Maryland because of its association with slavery. The Jesuit mission at Bohemia was a stark metaphor of the condition of the Maryland Church. Once a flourishing parish (according to Ryan), the chapel was now collapsing, the birds of the air circulating through the holes in the roof and leaving their droppings on its altar. The once large congregation now consisted of fifty adult slaves and their children.

Ryan also insisted that the Maryland Jesuits trafficked in slaves, if that term meant the buying and selling of individuals for various reasons, some of which, he admitted, were commendable, given their commitment to the system itself, such as the selling of a slave to keep families together. The real question, Ryan maintained, was not the theoretical justification of slavery according to traditional moral theology, but rather the actual scandal that de facto slaveholding by priests was giving in the United States to Catholics and non-Catholics alike. "Even tho the reverend gentlemen," he argued,

> could ever so triumphantly prove on abstract principles that their system is not a defrauding the labourer of his hire, a sin which is somewhere said to call to heaven for vengeance, yet if having the appearance of evil it render the Incorporated clergymen so many stumbling blocks in the way of their Quaker brethren and of thousands besides among their fellow citizens: if metaphysical distinctions, and finedrawn casuistry be too subtle for the mental vision of these blunt, honest folks:—and that labouring under the incapacity of comprehending Doctor Carroll's reasoning on this subject they identify the principles of the Catholic Religion with a practice on the

(New York: Charles Scribner's and Sons, 1955), 188–89. Carroll had, to an earlier complaint from Thayer about the evils of slavery, assured him that he shared his uneasiness about "the treatment & manners of the Negroes. I do the best I can to correct the evils I see; & then recur to those principles which . . . influenced the many eminent & holy missionaries in S. America & Asia, where slavery equally exists"; Carroll to Thayer, Baltimore, July 15, 1794, in Hanley, *Carroll Papers*, 2:122–23.

part of its ministers, so apparently uncharitable, they become so prejudiced . . . as never to inquire fairly as to the truth of that religion.

Ryan claimed never to have heard anything about a plan of gradual emancipation. If the Jesuits had a plan, he suggested, it was *in petto*, a secret one for some indefinite future that could not justify the losses to the Church that their scandalous involvement with slavery was causing.[14]

Ryan in 1814 took their case to the Congregation for the Propagation of the Faith, the body responsible for the governance of the Church in America. He had heard that another Irish Dominican, John Connelly, had been appointed Bishop of New York, and he thought the time a propitious one to urge Rome to use the new prelate to investigate the Church's slaveholding in Maryland. He urged the cardinal prefect to bring the matter to the attention of the pope himself.[15]

There is no evidence that Propaganda ever did anything about the complaint of the Dominicans about the Jesuit slaveholding. Shortly after he returned to the United States in 1820, Harold tried to put the best face on their criticism of Carroll in a letter to the cardinal prefect: that the Archbishop of Baltimore was caught up in a system of which he did not approve, as was demonstrated by his emancipation of the patrimonial slaves he had received.[16] It was as though Harold were trying to protect his own fading episcopal possibilities. Whatever, Harold was appointed to no see, and Jesuit slaveholding on a grand scale continued for another two decades.

Although Ryan and Harold were not privy to it, the Maryland Jesuits, through their legal body, the Corporation of Roman Catholic Clergymen, had in fact adopted a policy of gradual emancipation long before 1815. Some slaves had gained their freedom in that way. What seems noteworthy, however, is a resolution passed by the trustees of the corporation, of which Carroll was one, in June of 1814, six months after Carroll had learned of the Dominicans' attack. The trustees resolved to hire out most of the slaves on their plantations for a set number of years, after which they would be free.[17] But

14. Ryan to John Troy, College of St. Thomas, Bloomfield, March 20, 1814, *Congregazioni Particolari* (hereafter CP), 1814, vol. 146, fols. 533v–36v, APF.

15. Ryan to Rt. Rev. Dr. Milner, November 14, 1814, CP; 1814, vol. 146, folios 656(1)rv–657(1) v, APF.

16. Harold to Cardinal ?, January 5, 1821, *Scritture Riferite nei Congressi America Centrale*, 1821–1822, vol. 7, folios 155–156v, APF.

17. Corporation Minutes, June 14, 1814, MPA, GULSC.

the resolution was never carried out, to Carroll's "surprise and mortification." A month before he died in 1815, the archbishop protested the sale of several individuals on the White Marsh plantation.[18] There is record of only one slave being freed as a result of the resolution. It seems obvious that Carroll was the force behind the resolution, and with his death, the impetus for the policy died, as well. In 1820 the corporation repealed the resolution with the explanation that "mature reflection" had convinced them that such a plan was "prejudicial."[19]

The reflection, no doubt, had two sources: the Superior General in Rome had told the Maryland Jesuits to delay any action involving the plantations. In addition the Archbishop of Baltimore, Ambrose Maréchal, was contesting the Jesuits' claim to ownership of the property, including the slaves. That dispute was finally settled in 1828 with the Jesuits retaining their lands. By the 1830s a new generation of leaders in the new Maryland Province was determined to sell the slaves and lease the property to tenant farmers. By that time deferred emancipation had effectively become a social impossibility in Maryland, so the Jesuits looked toward a mass sale. In October 1836 Father General Jan Roothaan approved the proposal, with the stipulations that they not separate families and that they make provision for the continuing spiritual care of the slaves.

More than 270 slaves of the Maryland Jesuits were sold to two planters in Louisiana in 1838. The scale and nature of the sale sent shockwaves beyond the Catholic community. The specter of Jesuits selling their slaves to the Deep South, even to a heavily Catholic state like Louisiana, was one that scandalized many Jesuits and non-Jesuits alike. The European Jesuits in Maryland, who tended to romanticize the master-slave relationship as a superior form of feudalism, were most vocal in their opposition. Native Jesuits, who were superiors of the plantations, also strenuously objected to the sale, and at least a few apparently managed to warn their slaves that the provincial and the sheriff were coming to collect them. Some of the blacks escaped to the woods to return later to the estates. Most were shipped south, and some families were evidently separated. The resulting scandal, news of which reached Roothaan from outraged Jesuits and laity alike, forced the resignation of the Maryland provincial, Thomas Mulledy, and his exile to Europe.

All this, of course, happened before *In Supremo Apostolatus*, and there is no

18. Carroll to Francis Neale, Baltimore, October 3, 1815, in Hanley, *Carroll Papers*, 3:361.
19. Minutes of Corporation, St. Thomas, August 22, 1820, MPA, GULSC.

evidence that it had any influence on the shaping of that document. Benedict Fenwick, the Bishop of Boston and a Jesuit from Maryland, thought that his Maryland brethren might have sold their slaves as quickly as they did because they knew of the impending papal letter, but nothing survives to support Fenwick's suspicion.[20] It is, however, quite possible that Jan Roothaan knew of such a letter by the early part of 1839, and that it played a part in his sharp reaction to the sale.

With the sale of the Jesuit slaves the most visible example of Catholic slaveholding had largely disappeared, but Southern Catholics were by and large more committed to the institution in 1840 than they had been in 1820. It was virtually impossible to find a Southern Catholic like William Gaston, a justice of the supreme court of North Carolina, who as late as 1832 termed slavery "the worst evil that afflicts the Southern part of our confederacy."[21] By that time Gaston, who even supported voting rights for free blacks, was dangerously out of step in the South. John England, who privately shared Gaston's abhorrence for slavery, nonetheless, as we have seen, defended it publicly. Catholics north and south opposed the growing abolition movement on several grounds. They identified it with nativism, perfectionism, and Great Britain. As John England put it, "I witnessed [in Ireland] the yearly display by the anti-slavery society of the preparation and presentation to parliament of two petitions; one for abolishing the slavery of the negroes in the West Indies, the other for riveting the chains of the white slaves in Ireland, by continuing to enforce the penal laws against the Roman Catholics."[22] But the American Catholic opposition to abolitionism went beyond its association with anti-Catholicism. The immediate abolition of slavery, Catholic spokesmen like Orestes Brownson argued, would be an injustice to the slaveholder and a disaster for the freedman. Then, too, they feared that the assertion of federal power that abolition involved would be a dangerous precedent for the federal government's interference in other areas, including the religious.

The nativism of the 1830s through the 1850s made the American Church all too conscious of its status as an alien minority in America. By 1850 Catholics were still less than nine percent of the population, but, having become the largest denomination in the country, were under stronger attacks than ever. Self-preservation became a priority. The bishops as a group concen-

20. Benedict Fenwick to Samuel Eccleston, Boston, March 11, 1840, AAB, AASMSU.

21. Rice, *American Catholic Opinion*, 134–15, citing *American Catholic Historical Researches*, 8:71.

22. Read, ed., *Letters*, 14–15.

trated on private behavior rather than social ethics. Except for the area of public education, the bishops foreswore any activity that could be deemed political. When the prelates held their first plenary council in Baltimore in 1852, they limited their remarks about slavery to the need to provide for the spiritual needs of the individual slaves. The Irish-born Francis Kenrick, successively Bishop of Philadelphia and Archbishop of Baltimore, lamented that the condition of slaves (he could have enlarged this to blacks in general) had deteriorated since the rise of the anti-slavery movement, but could only conclude that "such is the state of things, nothing should be attempted against the laws."[23]

Rome and Slavery

And what of Rome? Only when the Church began missionary efforts in Africa in the early nineteenth century and confronted directly the slave trade did the papacy address African slavery. In 1815 Pope Pius VII, in response to appeals from European statesmen, agreed to support the efforts to abolish the international slave trade. A quarter century later Pope Gregory XVI, who as a former head of the Church's department of missions had a deep interest in the African missions and knew intimately the evils of the slave trade, issued his encyclical, *In Supremo Apostolatus*, which, reflecting the Swiss theologican Johann Sailer (who taught that slavery was to be condemned precisely because it converted persons into "mere things" and robbed them of their individuality), condemned "that inhuman trade by which Negroes, as if they were not men, but mere animals, . . . are . . . contrary to the laws of justice and humanity, bought, sold, and doomed."

Except for that apostolic letter of 1839, there was little said about slavery. Partly that was the result of the way in which Propaganda functioned. It tended to be reactive, responding to complaints brought or questions raised. And there were few of either regarding slavery. Those that did arise tended to come from foreigners, like Harold and Ryan. Thus in 1816 Charles Nerinckx, a Belgian priest working in Kentucky, raised several matters about which he was in doubt concerning Kentucky society. One was slavery. He seemed at sea about it. "What judgment must one make," he asked, "about the selling of slaves. . . ? What if they are sold to heretics, or at a public auction?" Propaganda for-

23. Francis Kenrick, *Theologia Moralis* I, tract V, cap. V, translated in U.S. *Catholic Miscellany*, December 9, 1843, quoted in Rice, *American Catholic Opinion*, 71.

warded it to the Holy Office, whose response was "non licere" ("This is not allowed)."[24] Yet the selling continued, even, as we have seen, by religious themselves. In 1828 an immigrant bishop, Guiseppi Rosati of St. Louis, sought guidance about the validity of clandestine marriages of slaves (in some states slave marriage was not allowed). The question once again was forwarded to the Holy Office, which assured the bishop that the ceremonies were indeed valid.[25]

American slavery in fact was no higher a priority for Propaganda than it was for the American Church. When in January 1861 the Sacred Congregation was preparing a set of issues that it thought the American bishops should take up at their next plenary council, slavery or the evangelization of the blacks was not among them (the evangelization of Indians was).[26]

Rome and the Civil War

Rome, although aware of the slavery controversy in the United States that had brought that nation to the brink of war, was at the time preoccupied with its own insurrection in the Papal States. Initially it had a common interest with the United States government in affirming the right of self-defense against rebellion. Finding itself increasingly isolated as a temporal power in the European sphere, certain papal officials, such as Giacomo Antonelli, the Cardinal Secretary of State, were looking to the United States as a rising power to foil Great Britain's supposed encouragement of *risorgimento* in the Italian peninsula (the United States and the Papal States had diplomatic relations at the time).[27] By the fall of 1862, however, this tilt toward the North began to shift. Ironically, the Lincoln administration's reluctant decision to make the abolition of slavery an implicit war goal in the form of the Emancipation Proclamation proved crucial in reversing the Holy See's previously favorable attitude toward the North's prosecution of the war. As the casualties in America mounted to horrifying numbers, the Roman perception grew that the

24. *Dubbi propositi dal Sig. Nerinckx*, April 1, 1816, 13r, 24v, *Atti*, 1816, vol. 179, APF.

25. Prop. Fide to Rosati, October 25, 1828, *Lettere e Decreti*, 1828, vol. 309, fol. 758, APF.

26. *Ponente L'Eminentissimo e Reverendissimo Sig Cardinale Costantino Patrizi Ristrello con Somnario e Note Di Archivio Sul Metodo attualmente vigente nelle elezioni dei Vescovi per gli Stati Uniti d' America e sopra diversi inconveniente che occorono in quelle Diocesi*, January 21, 1861. Printed. *Atti*, 1861, vol. 225, January 1861, APF.

27. David J. Alvarez, "The Papacy in the Diplomacy of the American Civil War," *Catholic Historical Review* 69 (April 1983): 233–34.

Lincoln administration seemed intent, not on using the measured force appropriate to a just war to restore the union, but on the complete submission of the South; the adoption of an unconditional surrender policy by the federal government only reinforced this attitude. The news of the Emancipation Proclamation was seen as a desperate measure to encourage slave rebellion in the South. The very government that had justified its call for volunteers on the grounds of putting down an insurrection now appeared to be consorting in servile insurrection. And that conjured up visions of slaves murdering defenseless women and children in the Deep South. The Emancipation Proclamation in fact rekindled the prejudices and fears about the United States as a radical republic that the Holy See, like other European powers, had long harbored.

The North's commitment to abolish slavery seemed then, from Rome, to be cynically self-serving and hypocritical. As *L'Osservatore Romano* remarked in October 1862: "We are certain that [emancipation] will not come about from the benevolent initiative of the North." Instead the editors professed themselves ready to believe that the Confederates, once they gained independence, would work out a peaceful solution to the issue. "Will not the example of France and England," they concluded, "be imitated by a race which is intelligent and chivalrous, as the Confederates of the South have always shown themselves to be?"[28] Obviously the Confederacy was winning the propaganda war in Rome.

In part the Southern influence upon the Holy See came from an American Catholic, Martin Spalding, the Bishop of Louisville. In the spring of 1863 Spalding wrote to Cardinal Alessandro Barnabò to protest the abolitionist position that three Catholic clergymen of Cincinnati, the diocese immediately north of Louisville, had taken: Archbishop John Baptist Purcell, his priest brother, Edward, editor of *The Catholic Telegraph*, and Purcell's auxiliary, Sylvester Rosecrans, the brother of the Union general. In a twenty-three page letter Spalding defended the constitutional right of secession (Kentucky had attempted to remain neutral when war had broken out between the Northern and Southern states, but many Kentuckians, including Spalding, sympathized with the Confederacy's quest for independence; others openly supported it, including joining Confederate armies). He reviewed the chief causes of the

28. *L'Osservatore*, November 8, 1862, quoted in "Roman Views on the American Civil War," by Anthony B. Lalli, S.X., and Thomas H. O'Connor, *Catholic Historical Review* 57 (April 1971): 34.

war, which he identified as the tariff and slavery. The bishop admitted—as he claimed all good and moderate men did—that slavery was a great inherited social evil. The important question was how to free the slaves without ruining the country and the blacks themselves. Spalding pointed out the dismaying plight of free blacks, especially in the segregated North, as well as the hypocrisy of the North, particularly in the refusal of several Northern states to allow emancipated blacks to settle there. "Our philanthropists of the North," Spalding commented, "wish certainly to see the slaves freed, but they wish by no means to have them among themselves."[29] He castigated the Punic War aims of the Lincoln administration: confiscation of property, including blacks, and the arming of the freed blacks. He underscored the connection of abolitionism with anti-Catholicism among Northern religious and political leaders: "Down with slavery and popery."[30] As Spalding surveyed the American landscape after two years of bloody conflict, he saw an escalation of violence and bloodshed that promised nothing short of genocide in the South:

> our miserable war, first begun to restore the broken Union, has now become a war of confiscation of property, of violent emancipation of the Negroes, of threatened and encouraged slave insurrection, of destruction and desolation of the vast and fair territory of the South, and finally of extermination of all the whites, and perhaps at the same time also of the Negroes themselves, if the revolt can not by any other means be suppressed. Such is at least the present spirit of our government.[31]

What should the Church do amidst such carnage and treachery? To Spalding it should simply stay out of the way. The passions that were killing hundreds of thousands of soldiers and maiming many more, and the destroying and plundering of property, were surely not going to cease with the end of the slaughter. To identify in any partisan way with the struggle was to invite persecution of the Church after the war.[32]

Spalding's apocalyptic account must have seemed prophetic when news came shortly afterward of the draft riots in New York, at the heart of which were Irish Catholics. Significantly, Spalding's essay was published anonymously in serial form in *L'Osservatore* (in October 1863). Six months later he was appointed Archbishop of Baltimore.

29. David [Thomas M.] Spalding, C.F.X., ed., "Martin John Spalding's 'Dissertation on the American Civil War,'" *Catholic Historical Review* 52 (April 1966): 78.

30. Spalding, "Dissertation," 79.

31. Spalding, "Dissertation," 81.

32. Spalding, "Dissertation," 83–85.

Rome Speaks

While Spalding was attempting to get Propaganda to silence those prelates who were speaking out in favor of abolition, the Papal States' consul in New York City, Louis B. Binsse, was suggesting that the Sacred Congregation apply pressure in the opposite direction. In September 1863 Binsse addressed the tradition of silence about slavery within the American Catholic Church. In the face of civil laws that denied natural rights to slaves, such as those connected with marriage and family, and the telling evidence that religion made little progress where slavery prevailed, Binsse wondered how much longer Roman authorities could be silent. He cited with approval the moral stand taken in Cincinnati against slavery. "I regret to say," he added, "that among the Catholic clergy, there are a good number, especially among those teaching in the colleges of the south, who favor the cause of separation and who are hostile to the cause of the government."[33] Binsse's source of concern about the need for the Church to take a stand about slavery was apparently Isaac Hecker. In January 1864 the consul was conveying to the Cardinal Prefect Hecker's conviction about the urgency of the question and the need for the Church to declare itself. "The question of the future solution of slavery is the question of the day for the United States," he informed Barnabò. Binsse confessed that he could not comprehend the thinking of those who opposed abolition, who were persisting in protecting the institution and ignoring its role "as the sole cause of our terrible civil war."[34]

The Holy See, as noted, not about to be party to the Lincoln policy on emancipation—indeed, had begun to send signals that it favored the Confederacy. When Pius IX sent a letter addressing President Jefferson Davis as the head of the Confederate States, the Confederacy claimed this as evidence of the Holy See's recognition of its independence. This occasioned a protest from the new American minister to the Papal States, Rufus King, that the government of the Holy See should be the last one to sympathize with "the enemies of Human Liberty."[35] Pope Pius IX assured King that he could never sanction a system of slavery. His Secretary of State, Cardinal Giacomo Antonelli, subsequently admitted that upon further study of the U.S. Constitu-

33. Binsse to Barnabò, New York, Sept. 18, 1863, *Scritture*, 1864–1865, vol. 20, folios 213r–214rv, APF.

34. Binsse to Barnabò, New York, January 5. 1864, *Scritture*, 1864–1865, vol. 20, folios 503rv–506rv, APF.

35. Alvarez, The Papacy," 245.

tion, the South's war for independence seemed an illegitimate one. But real sympathies remained with the Confederacy. There was no attempt to communicate the Holy See's stated position on the war to the American hierarchy.

Late in the war Propaganda did finally examine the issue of slavery in connection with the American conflict. The occasion was the pastoral that the Bishop of Natchitoches, Augustus Martin, had issued in August 1861. In his address to the people of northern Louisiana he defended as divinely ordained not only the de facto institution of slavery in the South, but the very enslavement of Africans. For Martin "the will of God" was manifest in the exchange of the Africans' labor for the necessities of life, both material and spiritual, that they received in slavery, no matter what "extravagant humanitarian utopians...[,] sentimental...English philanthropists[,] and northern Puritans thought."[36]

More than three years later, in the fall of 1864, the consultor of Propaganda who was charged to examine the pastoral, a Dominican, Vincent M. Gatti, found Martin's position on slavery completely opposed to the teaching of *In Supremo Apostolatus* and predicated on some fallacious biblical assumptions, such as the blacks being the descendants of Canaan and subject to Noah's curse. Even if they had been, Gatti noted, all such ethnic distinctions were obliterated by Christ. Martin, he suggested, was really the sentimental one in imagining that slavers were somehow applying Adam Smith's invisible hand to the peculiar institution—that in pursuing their selfish ends through such violence, the greater good of the blacks was really being promoted. Even the blessing of Christianity was no "justification for the iniquity which such traffic" entailed.

Slavery, Gatti continued, was wrong because it was a violation of the natural right of liberty. He admitted that the Church had not condemned every form of slavery in the past, but was certainly opposed to the kind that originated in the unjust deprivation of individual liberty, to the kind that was defended on the grounds of some intrinsic difference between whites and blacks. Original sin was something shared by all, and was no excuse for perpetuating injustice. Education was the key to eliminating differences in human capacity. In serving as an apologist for the "peculiar institution," Martin, Gatti concluded, was contradicting the popes who had "condemned not

36. *Lettre Pastorale de Mgr. L'Eveque De Natchitoches A l'occasion de la guerre du Sud pour son Indépendance* (August 1861), *Scritture*, 1864–1865, vol. 20, fols. 1207r–1213v, APF.

only the enslavement of individuals, but the continued keeping of them as slaves."[37]

Gatti was making the distinction between the chattel slavery of the United States and the milder forms of slavery that the Church had traditionally legitimized. In effect Gatti's report explicitly condemned chattel slavery as well as slave trading, and Pope Pius IX accepted its recommendation to condemn the pastoral and place it on the Index of Forbidden Books, should Martin not retract it. The Holy Office officially promulgated the distinction in 1866. As Maria Caravaglios has observed in her *The American Catholic Church and the Negro Problem in the XVIII–XIX Centuries*, in this byzantine way a small revolution in papal teaching was effected. Pius IX's successor, Leo XIII, became the first pontiff to publicly condemn not only slave trading, but the institution itself in his 1890 encyclical *Catholicae Ecclesiae.* By that time, of course, the Civil War was long over, and the Thirteenth Amendment had abolished slavery not only in the areas in rebellion against the Federal Government, but throughout the land.

Conclusion

During his controversy with Secretary of State Forsyth, John England confessed that many persons had asked him about his personal view about slavery: "whether I am friendly to the existence or continuation of slavery? I am not—but I also see the impossibility of now abolishing it here. When it can and ought to be abolished is a question for the legislature and not for me."[38] Slavery might be an evil, but it was out of the Church's domain to decide the practical means by which it was to be ended. The Church could enunciate the general principles, but had to leave applications to those competent. So too Francis Kenrick: the slavery discussion pertained "to politics." Indeed

37. Gatti, Minerva, November 25, 1864, *Scritture*, 1864–1865, vol. 20, fols. 1199r–1205 v., APF. Gatti seems to have been influenced by the German moral theologian Johann Sailer, Bishop of Ratisbon, whose *Handbuch der Christichlen Moral* (vol. 2, 1830–1841), developed the Pauline doctrine of equality in Christ in regard to slavery. "The state of slavery," Bishop Sailer wrote, "and any treatment of human beings as slaves, turns people who are persons into mere things, turns people who are ends in themselves into mere means, and does not allow the responsibility of people for what they do, or do not do, to develop properly, and in this way cripples them in their very humanity; hence it is contrary to the basic principle of all morality"; cited in John Francis Maxwell, *Slavery and the Catholic Church: The History of Catholic Teaching Concerning the Moral Legitimacy of the Institution of Slavery* (Chichester and London: Barry Rose Publishers, 1975), 102–3.

38. Rice, *American Catholic Opinion*, 69.

Kenrick was all too typical of the prelates who felt that the whole controversy over slavery was simply polarizing the country to the detriment of the slaves themselves.[39] In effect, on the question of slavery the American bishops were making a rigid separation between the private and public orders, making any public criticism of slavery unthinkable.[40] Such a separation, John Noonan has suggested, makes more understandable why a Catholic, Roger Taney, could have freed his own slaves and treated blacks as equals within the Church, yet still issued the Dred Scott decision in 1857. As a result the prelates kept their peace about even the worst evils of the system. Pace John England, they did not speak out against the evils, which were all too visible. To the extent that they defended the system, they created a fantasy that had little to do with the reality of slavery in the United States, and certainly had nothing to do with their own experience of the institution. Not until January 1861 did a bishop speak out publicly on the evils of slavery: a Southern bishop, Augustin Verot of St. Augustine. Verot defended the institution of slavery, but called for significant reform if the new Confederacy was to endure.[41] Verot also was responsible for the topic of the freedman getting onto the agenda of the Second Plenary Council in 1866, but with no better results than came from his efforts to reform slavery.

The slavery controversy was occurring at the very time the Church in this country was under attack as an anti-American institution. The tendency to identify the abolitionist and nativist movements only reinforced the conviction that silence was the best policy for American Church leaders. Ecclesiastical self-preservation and unity proved to take priority over even such a fundamental question of social ethics as slavery.

One historian has observed: "there was an element of unreality in any claim of North American Catholics to be loyal followers of the common

39. See Kenrick to Barnabo, Baltimore, May 11, 1863, *Congress. Amer. Cent.*, Section XX, fols. 213v and 214 rv, APF.

40. In *A Vindication of the Catholic Church*, Kenrick had written in 1855: "As regards political institutions, she is wholly independent of any, and suited to all. It is not her province to model or fashion them; but being indifferent to each particular form of social organization, she studies only to infuse the spirit and maxims of Christ, and thus to modify and mitigate whatever may be exorbitant and unjust"; Kenrick, *Vindication* (Baltimore: John Murphy, 1855), 332. By its persistent silence on the realities of American slavery by the 1850s, however, the Church in America was failing Kenrick's own moral standard.

41. See Michael Gannon, *Rebel Bishop: The Life and Era of Augustine Verot* (Milwaukee: Bruce Publishing, 1964), 31–56.

Catholic teaching. For they must have been well aware that the form of slavery which existed under the inhuman slavery legislation in the slave-holding States was an extreme form of chattel-slavery."[42] The fact of the matter seems to have been that they were not. They were very much children of their culture, and to that extent captives of it. Until the war itself the persons who did look to Rome for guidance were all foreigners.

For its part Rome seemed reluctant to intervene. Although it would respond occasionally to *ad hoc* requests for solutions to dilemmas regarding slavery, there was no effort made to enunciate any overall teaching regarding slavery in the United States. It is significant that the letter from the Holy See that had the greatest impact in this country was written not for the United States, but Africa. Rome itself had more pressing concerns. The Church itself was still a much more decentralized institution than it would be by the end of the century. Only with Pius IX did the papal encyclical become a prominent means of exercising the magisterium. Catholics throughout the world, including America, did not tend to look to Rome as the center of authority the way they would after the First Vatican Council. Hence the role that the Holy See might have played in forcing American Catholics to transcend the chains of culture went largely unfulfilled. On the matter of the "peculiar institution," Rome respected the wisdom of the local Church that survival dictated silence and conformity. That strategy worked, but one can today wonder at the price that was paid.

42. Maxwell, *Slavery and the Catholic Church*, 112.

Chapter 6

The First American Jesuit Province and the Shifting Center of Catholicism

On the occasion of the nation's bicentennial, the Maryland Provincial of the Society of Jesus asked Joseph Durkin, Gerald Fogarty, and myself to write a history of the Maryland Mission's own bicentenary: from its origins in 1633 to its elevation to provincial status in 1833. *The Maryland Jesuits, 1634–1833* (Baltimore: Corporation of the Roman Catholic Clergymen) subsequently was published in 1976. Some years later a new provincial approached us about doing a sequel to bring the history up to the present: to celebrate the 350th anniversary of the founding of Maryland in 1984 and of the presence of the Society of Jesus in British America/the United States. As with the initial volume, we divided the work among ourselves, but reversed the order of who would be responsible for what period. For the 1976 book I had covered the last period: from the partial restoration of the Society in the United States in 1805 to the creation of the Maryland Province in 1833. This time I was responsible for the initial period: from the creation of the province to its merger with the New York Mission in 1879. For several reasons that project never reached print. My manuscript remained in a drawer (this was just before the advent of the personal computer that so dramatically changed the ways of scholarship).

Time's passage made me much more aware of how those forty-five years constituted the entire life of the Maryland Province; after 1879 it became something very much different. It also sharpened my appreciation of how much the shifting forces of the Society of Jesus in the eastern United States was a microcosm of those remaking American Catholicism in the Chesapeake and New York regions. The modifications I have made in the original essay have been largely done to reflect that more recent understanding.

The Maryland Mission

For nearly two centuries the Maryland Mission was the body that represented the major presence of the Society of Jesus within the portion of British America that became the United States. With Maryland as its center, Jesuits during the Colonial and early national periods had expanded their ministry into Pennsylvania, New York, and New England. Throughout the Colonial era the mission was dependent on the English province for its personnel and financial support. With the suppression of the Society by papal decree in 1773, the mission ceased to exist. When several American ex-Jesuits were allowed in 1805 to rejoin the remnant of the Society of Jesus that had survived in Polish Russia, the mission revived as a dependent of the Society as a whole. During the first three decades of the mission's second period, foreign Jesuits, mostly from Ireland, Belgium, Germany, and France, constituted a majority of the Society's members in the mission. Their work was largely confined to the country parishes attached to the farms in Maryland and Pennsylvania. The mission had a brief presence in New York City in the first decade of the century, when the immigrant Anthony Kohlmann established the New York Literary Institution. Despite the school's quick growth, Jesuit superiors, concerned about overstretching their limited resources, ordered Kohlmann to close the school in 1813 and recalled the Jesuits there to Maryland. Kohlmann's protests that they were abandoning what was rapidly becoming the largest (nearly 100,000 inhabitants) and most important city in the country, the biggest beneficiary of the market revolution that was transforming the economy, "the Emporium of America," to be entombed in Maryland, "the poorest and most beggarly of the whole union," went unheeded.[1] Not for three decades would the Jesuits return to New York, and then it would be members of the Society from the Canadian province, not Maryland. The Mission had also had a toehold in New England in the person of a convert, Virgil Barber, whom the Maryland Mission superior had sent to New Hampshire in 1822 to minister to his father's Episcopal congregation, which, along with its priest, had recently made a group conversion to Roman Catholicism. There

1. Kohlmann to Giovanni Grassi, New York, October 25, 1813, MPA 204-T-18, GULSC; Kohlmann to Grassi, White Marsh, April 24, 1815, MPA 204-H-3, GULSC.

Virgil, with his father Daniel, had begun an academy that eventually suffered the same fate as the New York Literary Institution: forced to close because the Maryland Mission could not provide the necessary support in funds and personnel. After a short stay in Maine working with the Penobscot tribe, he was recalled to Maryland to join the faculty in the newly opened St. John's Literary Institute at Frederick.

In 1832, through the initiative of Peter Kenney, the Irish Jesuit who was an official Visitor to the Mission for the second time (his earlier visit had been in 1820), Rome granted the two colleges of the mission—Georgetown and St. John's—a dispensation from the Society's rule prohibiting the acceptance of stipends in order to charge tuition, a move that freed them from their dependence on the plantations, which had proven to be poor providers of financial support for either the colleges or the Jesuits' pastoral ministries.[2] It was becoming increasingly clear that the Jesuits' future in the United States was as urban educators, not as planter-preachers. At the same time, the number of native Jesuits within the mission was growing. In the early 1820s, the best among the indigenous scholastics (seminarians) had been sent to Rome for their training. By the early 1830s a critical core of Roman-trained American Jesuits had returned to the mission to assume leadership. These changes in ministries and demographics were two factors that led Kenney and the new leaders of the Maryland Mission in 1832 to petition the Society to raise Maryland from the status of mission to that of province. The following year the Maryland Province became the first province to be established by the Society in the United States. There were ninety members of the new province: thirty-eight priests, twenty scholastics, and thirty-two brothers. Roman-trained Americans held all the key positions within the new province: William McSherry was named provincial; his assistant was Aloysius Young. Thomas Mulledy was rector/president of Georgetown; James Ryder was vice-rector.

A Conflict of Visions

In July 1835 the Maryland Province held its first congregation. Out of its week-long deliberations came recommendations (*postulata*) to the superior general of the Society that the province sell its slaves, along with some of

2. "Instructions Given by Rev. Fr. Kenney, Superior of the United States Mission, to Rev. Fr. McSherry, Procurator of the Same Mission," September 4 1832, MPA X-M-2, cited in Thomas Morrissey, S.J., "*As One Sent*": *Peter Kenney, S.J., 1779–1841* (Washington, D.C.: The Catholic University of America Press, 1996), 301.

the land they worked, that the money from the sale be invested, and the remaining lands leased to tenant farmers. The delegates urged reduction in the number of missions in rural Maryland and Pennsylvania in order to concentrate their energies on the cities, especially in erecting colleges in Baltimore, Philadelphia, Richmond, and elsewhere, where bishops were inviting them to do so.[3]

The farms or plantations had long been a source of concern both in Rome and America. Generals worried that the planter-pastor lifestyle in Maryland and Pennsylvania did not really promote the Institute of the Society. The Maréchal controversy had deepened the suspicions of Superior General Luigi Fortis that the Maryland Jesuits loved their land more than the Society or the Church. Priests like Anthony Kohlmann regarded the farms more as obstacles to the pursuits of the traditional apostolates of the Society, especially education, rather than the supports the farms were intended to be. Procurators grew more and more pessimistic about the possibility of a slave-based economy providing support for anything, whether it was churches, colleges, or houses of formation.

In 1830 Fortis's successor as superior general, Jan Roothaan, had dispatched Kenney to America for a second time to reexamine the state of affairs in the Maryland Mission. Among Kenney's charges was to determine whether the lands and/or slaves should be sold. Kenney's earlier visit had already convinced him that the Maryland Jesuits' slaveholding was "an immense burden" that was severely limiting their mission and gravely damaging the reputation of the Society in the country.[4] Before Kenney could present any recommendations about the question to Roothaan, the latter decided that one last attempt should be made to improve the farms. That apparently satisfied the majority of the Maryland Jesuits, who continued to regard the ancient places as the backbone of the province's work and an integral part of the Society's American heritage. Two Jesuits who did not share this view were William McSherry and Thomas Mulledy, who were convinced that the problems that plagued the Society in Maryland—pressing debts, lack of funds, struggling colleges, corrupt slaves—all stemmed from the attempt of the Maryland Jesuits to be both priests and planters (see chapter 2). Until the province was able to liberate itself from the farms and the mission churches that had grown from

3. *Acta Primae Congregationis, Provinciae Marylandiae Societatis Jesu*, 1835, MPA, GULSC.
4. "Temporalities," 1820, MPA XT-1, GULSC.

them, it would never be able to develop colleges and shift its resources to the cities where the future obviously lay.

The province congregation provided Mulledy, McSherry, and their Roman-trained colleagues, who constituted half the delegates, an opportunity to effect their grand plan. Since none of the older Maryland Jesuits had received the theological training to qualify for profession or the fourth vow, they were not eligible to be delegates. The younger, Roman-educated Americans subsequently dominated the congregation, to the consternation of some of the older Jesuits, both native and foreign-born, who resented the ambition and arrogance of a Mulledy who was clearly the force behind the radical proposals that were sent to Rome. "These new men," Fidèle de Grivel wrote to Roothaan's assistant, "wish to sell the farms, [and] to erect colleges in the cities, especially in Virginia, where Fr. Mulledy is from. But the money from the sales, if they occur, will quickly be dissipated to little effect."[5] As it was, conditions on the plantations of the Society in Maryland were steadily improving under the careful management of new Jesuit managers. This economic and moral improvement was an argument that Stephen Dubuisson tried desperately to make with the general in urging that he reject the request to sell the slaves and lands. Dubuisson, one of four delegates who had opposed the changes at the congregation, solicited testimonials from Joseph Carbery, Peter Havermans, and the other local superiors of the farms about the thriving state of Catholicism in Southern Maryland. The picture he relayed to Roothaan was one of faithful blacks, churchgoing white Catholics, and a well-disposed non-Catholic population that promised harvests for the future.[6]

Despite these protests, in the fall of 1836 the superior general approved

5. De Grivel to Luigi Fortis, Baltimore, October 24, 1835, MD 5-II-1, ARSI.

6. Havermans at Newtown reported even larger numbers of parishioners making their Easter duty: "12 at St. John's, 800 at Medley Neck, 500 at Sacred Heart, 300 at Newtown itself. I remember once," the Belgian Jesuit wrote, "that I went to church about sunrise..., and finding at that time...already a good collection [of people], it happened that day, that at mass, at 10 o'clock, I heard [confessions of] about half [the congregation], after mass I continued again till 3 o'clock, gave communion again, thinking that in that case, after people had been waiting from morning till most night, to receive the bread of life, it would not be wrong to give holy Communion, in an extraordinary case at that hour; after all was over and the sun about to set, leaving the church I happened to speak to one of them,...I told him... I am sorry you had to wait so long. I am not better than you he answered. I asked him, when [had] he arrived at church, and how far he came. He told me it was nearly ten miles, and got at church at sunrise"; Havermans to Dubuisson, St. Thomas, June 2, 1838, MPA, GULSC; Carbery to Dubuisson, St. Inigoes, April 22, 1838, MPA, GULSC.

the sale with the stipulation that the religious needs of the slaves be provided for, families not be separated, and the money invested for the support of Jesuits in formation. When William McSherry's rapidly spreading cancer forced him to resign as provincial superior in 1837, Thomas Mulledy succeeded him and rapidly found buyers for nearly 275 slaves in Louisiana. By November 1838 the last of them had been transported by ship to New Orleans.

Mulledy claimed that all the Catholics in the vicinity of the Jesuit farms approved of the sales. Dubuisson and Havermans reported that Protestants and Catholics alike had been scandalized. The event does seem to have sent shock waves through the Catholic community. Some Maryland Catholics were apparently disturbed enough by what had happened that they went to Archbishop Eccleston with their complaints, and the archbishop took the matter to the superior general.

Exile, Death, and Attempts toward Change

Thomas Mulledy, both his friends and enemies admitted, was a man of considerable talent and energy. Under his leadership Georgetown College had flourished, but he had left a debt of over $47,000 from the two buildings he erected during the middle 1830s. Impulsive and tendentious, Mulledy alienated many Americans by his imperious manner, while his fondness for the manorial lifestyle of Chesapeake society, especially its drinking habits, seemed in the eyes of the Europeans to be unbecoming a religious. They found him too lax as a superior, allowing his subjects to break silence during the appointed hours, overindulge in alcohol, go out without a companion and visit lay persons at night, and receive guests of both sexes in their rooms. As one European concluded: "This is the worst of all the provinces."[7] In March of 1838 Roothaan ordered Mulledy to prohibit any use of alcohol.[8] In June of the following year he forbade "in virtue of holy obedience" any nocturnal trips outside the houses of the Society except for pastoral reasons, any

7. Stephen Dubuisson thought this judgment by an Italian Jesuit at Georgetown an exaggeration, "but was himself highly critical of the general state of the province"; Dubuisson to Roothaan, Alexandria, August 10, 1838, *MD* 7V-6, *ARSI*. Philip Sacchi, another Italian Jesuit at Georgetown told Roothaan: "We have fallen so far from the spirit of Mother Society." In Sacchi's estimation Mulledy was acting more like a businessman than a provincial, "too absorbed in temporal things," and unconcerned about providing the necessary supports for the fostering of the spiritual life of the members of the province; Sacchi to Roothaan, Georgetown, July 22, 1838, *MD* 7-III-1, *ARSI*.

8. Roothaan to Mulledy, Rome, March 30, 1838, MPA, GULSC.

unaccompanied daytime social visits to the houses of lay persons, and any reception of females in the private rooms of Jesuit houses.[9]

Mulledy had also used the $25,000 he had received as a down payment for the slaves to meet some of the debts on the new buildings at Georgetown, despite the explicit instructions of the general. In March of 1839 Roothaan informed him that if it were true that he had used part of the money for some other purpose than the support of the scholastics, he had incurred an ecclesiastical censure.[10] By that time the general was in correspondence with McSherry about the scandal Mulledy had created in the mass sale of the slaves. By August Roothaan was convinced that greater scandal would be given if nothing was done. He ordered McSherry to inform Mulledy to resign as provincial. By the time Roothaan's letter reached Georgetown, Eccleston and McSherry had already persuaded Mulledy in late June to take his case to Rome. That same day he resigned and made McSherry acting provincial. When he finally saw the general, the latter had little to say beyond the observation that "all was now settled." He assigned Mulledy to Nice to teach English to young boys. The general's advice that he take along his secular clothes led the former provincial to hope that his stay in France would not be a long one.[11]

As Roothaan had instructed, McSherry called together the eight professed members of the province to solicit their opinion about who the next provincial should be. Six of the eight voted for McSherry, and he was duly appointed by the general. McSherry, however, was in no condition to exercise leadership. In November he had to confess that his health was so bad that he was scarcely able to attend to half his duties "and my inability may be of some long continuance."[12] In fact McSherry had courageously been battling stomach cancer for at least five years. In the midst of great suffering in 1835 he sought medical treatment and obtained relief, although the doctors were unable to do anything about the growths. By the fall of 1839 one had reached the size of an orange, giving him constant pain. So little could he concentrate that he was forced to write his letters to Roothaan in English rather than the customary Latin. By the end of November he was in bed, unable to retain any solid food.[13] He died on December 21, 1839. He was forty years old.

9. Roothaan to Mulledy, June 6, 1839, MPA, GULSC.

10. Roothaan to Mulledy, March 4, 1839, MPA, GULSC.

11. Mulledy to McSherry, Nice, October 13, 1839, GUA 185-4, GULSC.

12. McSherry to Roothaan, Georgetown, November 21, 1839, MD 7-I-19, ARSI.

13. Georgetown, November 29, 1839, MD 7-I-21, ARSI.

The professed in the province, in accordance with the wishes of McSherry, chose Francis Dzierozynski to be vice-provincial and rector of Georgetown until the general could make permanent appointments. Dzierozynski, as a former superior and the oldest of the professed, was a caretaker choice. Francis Vespre, the provincial's assistant, stressed to Roothaan the province's need for "a superior who has the prudence and the firmness to make us respect his authority."[14] Dzierozynski, however, remained as the vice-provincial for the next three years, despite his initial plea that Roothaan appoint someone from outside the province. "Your Province can heal itself," the general told him. "Certainly, St. Ignatius, who has taken under his mantle his companions in Maryland for more than two centuries will not desert them now in the crisis in which they find themselves."[15] That Dzierozynski was not made provincial was an apparent reminder that Roothaan considered the province to be on probation.

Stephen Dubuisson had thought that the former superior was the best choice in the province: not only did he know the Institute of the Society, but he favored Europeans, something neither McSherry nor Mulledy could have been accused of. If Dubuisson and his fellow émigrés expected Dzierozynski to put the province into the order they thought proper, they were quickly disappointed. Complaints resumed about the lax state of religious discipline and zeal in Maryland, about Dzierozynski's inaccessibility, his indulgence of others' failings, his general inactivity. As one put it, "he is a saintly man but that is not enough."[16]

When he was made vice-provincial Dzierozynski had been the master of novices in Frederick. He continued to live there until Roothaan forced him to move to Georgetown in the fall of 1841 following complaints that Dzierozynski rarely ventured beyond the novitiate grounds. He was over sixty. He had reluctantly become superior again. But, unlike some of the Europeans, he had learned much about America since coming here in 1821. He had come to appreciate the Ignatian principle of adaptation according to circumstances. What worked in Europe, what could ideally govern behavior there, was not *a priori* to be expected to work in the United States, to be set down as a code to be rigidly observed. It might be the ideal to have no visitors at a college,

14. Vespre to Roothaan, Georgetown, December 21, 1839, MD 7-I-22, ARSI.

15. Roothaan to Dzierozynski, Rome, March 10, 1840, MPA 500.88b, GULSC.

16. De Grivel to Assistant to Superior General, Georgetown, September 8, 1841, MD 7-I-38, ARSI.

Dzierozynski admitted, but "considering the circumstances of this society, namely a new world and a new population, and many of them Protestants" (including a good portion of the students at Georgetown and St. Johns), an absolute prohibition was out of the question. On the contrary, allowing visitors in the library, museum, and chapel made a good impression upon them, especially the non-Catholics.[17]

Europeans continued to protest that the Americans were still too much the children of their culture, too imbued with the national spirit of liberty and materialism. One of them was appalled that the Maryland Jesuits enthusiastically took part in the "national feasts" of Washington's birthday and the Fourth of July, staging grand banquets at which the students inevitably became inebriated. "By thus praising the founding fathers," he observed, "they think they will win popular respect which they love too much and are too much influenced by."[18]

Dzierozynski vehemently denied that the Americans suffered from a spirit of nationalism. Such complaints, as well as those concerning the degenerate state of the province, were to Dzierozynski the products of overvivid imaginations with no foundation in reality. Roothaan was not persuaded. He told Dzierozynski: "Ours see them, externs [lay people] see them with grave damage to the reputation of the Society—and the Superior alone does not see them!!" Dzierozynski was not cowed:

> I often am also amazed, most beloved Father.... I rejoiced about the state of the whole Province but especially about that of the College at Georgetown, because it was greatly noted and praised by all of Ours and by the externs... and because... I have always found it in excellent condition, as also I have found the whole Province, which lately I have visited in its entirety, everything is being done, thank God, with the greatest edification and to the good of souls.... And now I am told that I neither see nor wish to see the evils that are open to the eyes of all.[19]

17. Dzierozynski to Roothaan, Frederick, January 1, 1841, MD 7 I 35, ARSI. As James Ryder remarked about one immigrant Jesuit, he seemed incapable of distinguishing between the essential and the trivial; Ryder to Roothaan, Georgetown, August 14, 1841, MD 7-II-10, ARSI. Even worse, this person, even after seven years in the country, was still refusing to speak English.

A college like Georgetown, which was both a boarding school and a training center for Jesuit scholastics (seminarians), was something unknown on the Continent. One European marveled that it was neither urban nor rural, neither a religious house nor a secular boarding school, but some strange combination of them all; Sacchi to Roothaan, January 23, 1839, MD 7-III-4, ARSI.

18. Philip Sacchi to Roothaan, Georgetown, July 22, 1838, MD 7-III-1, ARSI.

19. Dzierozynski to Roothaan, Frederick, June 29, 1841, MD 7-I-35, ARSI.

Roothaan's displeasure with Dzierozynski only increased thereafter. In August 1843, when the superior general established a commission composed of John McElroy, James Ryder, and Francis Vespre to find the best way to disengage the province from the farms and missions in rural Maryland and Pennsylvania, he did not even inform the vice provincial. Roothaan knew all too well Dzierozynski's feelings about the farms.

Under the skillful administration of Peter Havermans, the supervisor of the new tenant system on the former plantations, the farms were finally beginning to provide some support for the province. The superior general, nonetheless, was determined to remove the province not only from the farms, but from the country churches as well, once and for all. Parishes, except those connected with schools, were more properly the work of secular priests. Eliminating them from the responsibility of the Maryland Province was one way the general intended to bring the Maryland Jesuits more into conformity with the Constitutions of the Society. With the slaves gone, few beyond Dzierozynski were resisting the logic of the cities. Even Augustine Bally, who was so successful during his long pastorate at a village in southeastern Pennsylvania that the place was renamed for him, had to admit that the opportunities and needs for the Society were much greater in the cities than in the country places as Catholic immigrants began to flood Boston, Philadelphia, Baltimore, and other East Coast cities.[20]

McElroy's commission proposed that the best way to quit the farms was by a series of piecemeal sales, done quietly so as not to alarm Archbishop Samuel Eccleston (the Maréchal controversy still shadowed them); in the meantime they could appeal to Eccleston to take over now one, now another church. "Much as we desire and admit the necessity of withdrawing Ours [Jesuits] from the duties of parish Priests, they concluded, "there would be at *this time*, an insuperable objection on the part of the Arch-bishop." It would not be easy to do, "at least in a short time, still with the exertions of the Provincial, zealously enlisted in the business, we have no doubt it may be accomplished." But so little confidence did they have in the provincial's willingness to confront the matter that they were keeping him in the dark until they received further instructions from Roothaan.[21]

Anthony Rey, an immigrant Jesuit, confided to the general his observations about the province of which he had been a member for less than two

20. Bally to Roothaan, Goshenhoppen, January 31, 1842, MD 7-VII-3, ARSI.
21. McElroy, et al., to Giovanni Grassi, Frederick, June 17, 1843, MD 7-II-14, ARSI.

years. There was an "urgent need" for a provincial who would combine talent, prudence, knowledge of the Institute [the core of the Constitutions of the Society of Jesus], "and the desire to have it observed to the letter, as the circumstances and your instructions permit." They especially needed "an interior man, who will give his special attention to the morale of our Province, and motivate us to that interior and truly religious spirit, which we now more or less are lacking." They needed new blood, and, to Rey's thinking, it should be European, not American. Rey pointed out that of forty-one priests listed in the catalogue, hardly half that number were active (three were dead, one—Havermans—had left, three were useless, others old or infirm); nor was the list of scholastics any more promising.

> If you abandon us to ourselves, the same I believe will be well said of us, as of the Fathers of Mexico: the Maryland Province is dispersed. . . . But if you can give us together with a provincial who has your whole confidence six priests who are formed, but still young enough to learn English well, solidly virtuous and capable of occupying after two or three years here the places of consultors [advisors to the provincial], of minister, of rector, and indeed of the Provincial, if you can send us from time to time some novices from Europe, as our Fathers have gotten in Missouri; I believe that our Province will be very capable of contributing to the greater glory of God.[22]

Some of the Europeans thought they already had one such religious in Rey. "If we had 5 or 6 like him," Grivel judged, "there would be cause for great hope."[23] Even the normally serene Dzierozynski had to admit that "We are desperate" and urged that the general send back Mulledy from his European exile as the province congregation of 1841 had requested.[24]

A year later Roothaan sent Francis Dzierozynski back to Frederick, where he gave great edification as spiritual father at the college for several more years. The superior general appointed James Ryder provincial, but Ryder held the office for scarcely a year. Roothaan, apparently having at last decided that the province could not cure itself, replaced him with an outsider. It marked the beginning of a pattern of non-Maryland Jesuits being appointed by Rome to govern the province that would prevail for its lifetime. The new provincial, whom the general also designated an official visitor, was the Belgian Peter Verhaegen of the independent Missouri Vice-Province. As his socius Verhaegen chose Anthony Rey.

22. Rey to Roothaan, Georgetown, July 22, 1842, MD 7-I-51, ARSI.

23. De Grivel to Assistant, Georgetown, September 8, 1841, MD 7-I-38, ARSI.

24. Dzierozynski to Roothaan, Georgetown, July 22, 1842, MD 7-I-50, AARSI.

Catholic Revivalism

In 1842 there were 107 Jesuits in the province: thirty-five priests, thirty-one scholastics, and forty-one coadjutors (brothers). Slightly more than half, fifty-seven, were engaged in the colleges at Georgetown and Frederick, including all of the fourteen scholastics in theology and philosophy at the former college. There were twenty-four missions or parishes, only three of which were urban (in Alexandria, Georgetown, and Philadelphia). Thus a large portion of the Maryland Jesuits was still engaged in rural ministry, despite the efforts of Roman and provincial superiors to shift the province's focus from the country to the city. True, there were nearly thirty more Jesuits than there had been ten years before, but the number of priests was virtually the same, while the general Catholic population was exploding. In that same period the Catholic population in the United States had doubled (from an estimated 600,000 to approximately 1,300,000), most of that growth having come on the Eastern seaboard.

One of the reasons Father General Roothaan wanted the Maryland Jesuits to give up the rural missions and farms was to free some of them for "bands of missionaries" who would be ready to give retreats to clergy or laity throughout the eastern part of the United States. Significantly, John McElroy, arguably the most outstanding Jesuit in antebellum America, was already heavily engaged in this work. McElroy had emigrated to the United States from Ireland in 1803 and, three years later, entered the newly restored Society of Jesus at Georgetown as a lay brother candidate. As an instructor of students at the college, the largely self-educated McElroy so impressed his religious superiors that they made him a candidate for the priesthood. Ordained in 1817, the indefatigable giant (he was well over six feet) over the next sixty years left a very large imprint on the American religious landscape, founding churches and colleges for the immigrant poor, serving, during the Mexican-American War, as one of the first Catholic priests to be appointed a chaplain to U.S. forces, and committing himself with extraordinary zeal to the preaching of retreats and missions. In 1839 alone McElroy gave retreats in Frederick (where he had built a church and established a college), Emmitsburg (for the Sisters of Charity, their boarding students, and the students at Mt. St. Mary's), and Georgetown (for the students at the college and for the boarders at the Visitation Convent). He also gave retreats in Cincinnati to both the clergy and laity of the diocese. The one for the clergy lasted ten days, that for the laity a week. "From my little experience in . . . retreats," he wrote in 1840,

I am convinced, it is the *most profitable part* of our ministry, and to *form a band exclusively for such*, say 3 or 4, would deserve almost any sacrifice, this *be means under God, of laying solidly, the foundations of our holy religion in this new world* of renovating the Clergy, and through them the Laity—. . . I w[oul]d willingly offer myself as the last & the least, to labor with them in this glorious enterprise—by such a band it is not only a single city or village, that would profit by our labors; but *the whole United States!*[25]

Not even the United States could contain the ubiquitous McElroy, whose lack of formal education was more than offset by a native shrewdness, indefatigability, and zeal that enabled him through some four decades to give missions and retreats to clergy, religious, and laity from Canada to Mexico. As late as 1863, when he was 81, he traveled over 2,000 miles by steamer, rail, and carriage in less than four months to give retreats in Baltimore, New York, St. John's, and Halifax. McElroy and his compatriot, James Ryder, were the two most active members of the province in this work. Many of the Americans seem to have been initially cool to it, at best. This attitude perhaps stemmed from the lack of a tradition of missions within the English/American Catholic community, whereas missions had strong roots within the Ireland that McElroy and Ryder had left. This heritage gave them an advantage in America, where the engine of revivalism was sweeping and resweeping through the land, leaving "burned-over districts" and a transformed culture. Missions were in effect the Catholic counterpart of revivalism, in regenerating the faith of natives and immigrants through the week-long exercises that included Mass, instructions, meditations, litanies, the rosary, benediction, and the sacrament of penance.

What McElroy and Ryder gave appears to have been something between the Spiritual Exercises of Ignatius Loyola and the missions that Jesuits, Redemptorists, Paulists, and others made such an institution of American Catholicism later in the century. McElroy wrote about one such "retreat" to laity in the cathedral in New York in November, 1840:

The usual confessors for the Cathedral are three . . . but during the week, the Bishop invited others to assist, . . . so that eight daily, the last day ten Confessors, were employed and could not suffice for the number who presented themselves at the tribunal—The Zeal & piety of these good people, consoled us very much—On yesterday morning (Sunday) it is said 1,000 persons approached the Holy Table in the Cathedral, the greatest number ever known to approach on one occasion in this City. This

25. McElroy to Roothaan, Frederick, June 4, 1840, *MD* 7-V-6, *ARSI*.

is additional proof of the great good of Retreats, given throughout this Country—your paternity [Roothaan] was kind enough to approve of my suggestion to have two or three fathers associated as Missionaries, as I have been informed by Father Provincial, but Alas! he has no one to spare for that purpose.[26]

The new provincial, Verhaegen, was very committed to the work. Within his first months in office he gave the exercises at Holy Trinity in Georgetown and at a church in Baltimore (with McElroy). Ignatius Brocard, his successor (1847–1852), was even more persuaded of the need for a "band of two or three peripatetic priests like the Protestants have," not only to rekindle Catholic faith, but to gain converts, as well. By 1851 newly ordained priests in the province, as part of their final year of formation, were giving missions in Maryland and Pennsylvania to blacks and whites, slaves and masters, with thousands of communicants and scores of converts. "Many [of the blacks] were not satisfied," they wrote, "to hear the saving truth once in their own churches, but followed the fathers to a second or third mission twelve or twenty miles away, and when the end had come they were sad that they were forced to say goodbye to us too soon."[27]

Giving missions became a regular feature of tertianship (the final year of formation) in the 1850s. In 1854 the Tertians were not merely working the towns and villages of Maryland and Pennsylvania, but Savannah and Augusta, as well. But the lack of manpower prevented the establishment of a permanent mission band as colleges increasingly absorbed the available priests, brothers, and scholastics.

Nativism, Refugees, and Expansion

"Here we have had a mighty contest for the office of President of the U.S.," Peter Kenney had written to one of his fellow Jesuits in Dublin in January 1833.

26. McElroy to Roothaan, New York, November 23, 1840, *MD* 7-V-7, *ARSI*. One Maryland Jesuit pleaded that the superior general make available to them an English translation of the Spiritual Exercises of Saint Ignatius. Without that, he explained, "the Literal Meditations & Contemplations [of the Exercises] are scarcely used"; James Lucas to Roothaan, Baltimore (1843), *MD* 7-I-56, *ARSI*.

27. At one of the parishes in southern Maryland, the official report of the missions given in 1851 observed: "Many persons because of the cold" stayed home. "The exception was the negroes who from the first day flocked to the exercises and the sacraments. You might say that the masters were reserving the earth for themselves, while their slaves were being allotted heaven"; Missions of Third Year Fathers for 1851, *MD* 9-XI-64, *ARSI*.

General Jackson is known to be reelected by a more powerful majority than that which first placed him in the chair of the first magistrate of this great country. It would highly amuse you to witness the effusions in speeches & prejudices of the electors. The Irish are mostly all favorable to Jackson. . . . To gain them they were made to believe that all the friends to the National Bank to which Jackson is opposed, were Orangemen & that Genl Jackson was a great favourite with Bishop Conwell [The Irish-born Bishop of Philadelphia] & Pius the 8th.[28]

Such tactics may have amused Kenney, but they added substance to charges that the Roman Catholic Church had replaced deism or "infidelity" as the greatest threat to America's becoming a Protestant empire. The sharp influx of Catholic immigrants, the conversion of prominent Protestants, the attempts of Catholic prelates to secure public funds for their parochial schools—all combined to alarm many evangelical Protestants. Lyman Beecher, the foremost Protestant preacher in the East, was so concerned about the spread of the Church into the West, where he saw the future lay, that he moved his family to Cincinnati to be better able to meet the threat on the front lines. Nor was it only evangelical churchmen who were worried. Horace Bushnell, the leading American Protestant theologian of the day, concluded that: "Our first danger is barbarism [read immigration], Romanism next." And, of course, most immigrants were, at least nominally, Roman Catholics. Anti-Catholic and anti-Jesuit tracts became something of a cottage industry in the three decades before the Civil War. One of the most virulent was penned by the inventor-artist Samuel B. Morse, who saw Jesuits lurking everywhere from the Mississippi to the halls of Congress. In an 1835 tract entitled *Imminent Dangers to the Free Institutions of the United States Through Foreign Immigrations*, Morse sounded his shrillest alarm:

[The Jesuits] have already sent their chains and oh! to our shame be it spoken, you are fastening them upon a *sleeping victim*. Americans you are marked for their prey, not by foreign bayonets, but by *weapons surer of effecting the conquest of liberty*, than all the munitions of physical combat in the military or naval storehouses of Europe. Will you not awake to the apprehension of the reality and extent of your danger? . . . Up! Up! I beseech you, Awake! To your posts! Let the tocsin sound from Maine to Louisiana. Fly to protect the vulnerable places of your Constitution and Laws.[29]

One of the major objects of nativist attacks was the European mission societies that were aiding the Church in America. Morse and others saw the

28. Kenney to Robert Haley, Georgetown, January 18, 1833, MPA X-Z-6, GULSC.

29. Samuel B. Morse, *Imminent Dangers to the Free Institutions of the United States Through Foreign Immigrations* (New York: 1835).

societies as devious attempts to sabotage republican institutions in this country. The Maryland Province was a major beneficiary of the French Society for the Propagation of the Faith. In a report to them in 1841, Stephen Dubuisson remarked:

> One knows that the spirit of opposition to Catholicism among the sectaries, sometimes results in hostile acts. . . . The principles and the law of the country are with [the Catholics]; it is probable that they will finally prevail; . . . In our Province we are pleased to have made the majority among our separated brethren have a more favorable spirit.[30]

Indeed in 1842 Maryland Catholics felt secure enough to celebrate the 208th anniversary of the landing of the *Ark* and *Dove* on St. Clement's Island. Or perhaps they felt that the time had come to remind nativists how long Catholics had been in this country. Approximately seven hundred persons, including the mayor of Washington and several members of Congress, went by boats from Washington and Baltimore to St. Inigoes, where Mass was celebrated by Archbishop Eccleston, and Bishop Benedict Fenwick of Boston preached. They then sailed up the river to St. Mary's City, where a crowd of four thousand joined them for a procession to the ruins of the old capital. There the rector of Georgetown, James Ryder, and George Reed, a Baltimore convert, eulogized the first planters of Catholicism in the original colonies, "and all without giving the least offence to the Protestants who were present."[31]

Most of the attacks in the nativist crusade were rhetorical, but there was occasional violence. In 1834 a crowd, stirred by the preaching of Beecher and others, burned the Ursuline Convent at Charlestown, outside Boston. The ecumenical relations that the Maryland Jesuit Benedict Fenwick had assiduously cultivated as Bishop of Boston were one of the first victims of the assault. The bishop became increasingly embittered by the failure of the civic authorities to provide protection, the acquittal of the principle arsonists, and the inability of the nuns to get any real indemnity (two months after the fire the Charlestown collector levied the annual assessment on the property!).

The bishop had been considering the erection of a college in the city, and had even purchased property to do so.[32] The Charlestown burning and

30. Dubuisson, Commentary on the Maryland Province, MD 7-IX, ARSI.

31. Extract of a letter of Anthony Rey, May 21, 1842, MD 7-I-49, ARSI.

32. Anthony J. Kuzniewski, S.J., *Thy Honored Name: A History of the College of the Holy Cross, 1843–1994* (Washington, D.C.: The Catholic University of America Press, 1999), 20.

aftermath may well have been a factor in his looking elsewhere to build his school. In the same year as the Charlestown burning, Fenwick acquired a tract of 11,000 acres in Maine, where he planned to build a college for Irish immigrants. By 1842 he had built a two-story school in the settlement (named Benedicta) and offered this, first to Canadian Jesuits, then, upon their rejection of the offer, to the Maryland Jesuits.[33] Dzierozynski and his consultors much preferred an urban college to one in the wilderness. They also favored a day school rather than a boarding college. The former would enable them to attract poorer youths, as John McElroy had done in Frederick at St. John's. Within a few months a compromise was struck in which the bishop acquired the property of a school in Worcester that a local priest had been conducting for several years. The Maryland Jesuits agreed to open a boarding college there, with Fenwick's promise that in the near future they would have the opportunity to begin a day school in Boston.[34] Five Jesuits were assigned to the school, including Thomas Mulledy, who was named rector. Fenwick had insisted that Mulledy head the new institution, and accordingly Roothaan had finally allowed him to return to America.[35] In the fall of 1843 the province opened a boarding college there; in accordance with Bishop Fenwick's stipulation, it was to be for Catholics only.[36] The significance of the opening did not escape Dzierozynski: "Prodigies indeed! A Catholic College of the Holy Cross and of the Society of Jesus and among *Yankees*! Who would ever have thought it possible!"[37] In the heartland of New England, the font of higher education in the United States, Catholics finally had a college.

New England had no monopoly on violent nativism. In Baltimore in 1839 a mob tried to repeat the Charlestown success, this time at the expense of the Carmelites. As in Boston, the confrontation was occasioned by a "runaway"

33. Kuzniewski, *Thy Honored Name*, 20–21.

34. Kuzniewski, *Thy Honored Name*, 26.

35. Walter J. Meagher, S.J., and William J. Grattan, *The Spires of Fenwick: A History of the College of Holy Cross, 1843–1963* (New York: Vantage Press, 1966), 36–42; Dzierozynski to Roothaan, Georgetown, September 6, 1842, MD 7-VIII-1, ARSI; Dzierozynski to Roothaan, March 14, 1843, MD 7-VIII-2; Dzierozynski to Roothaan, Georgetown, April 30, 1843, MD 7-I-55, ARSI.

36. The bishop's determination to limit his school to Catholics was the result of several things: the violent nativism he had experienced in Boston, his conviction that an all-Catholic environment would promote religious vitality and vocations, and his sense of the appeal that an exclusively Catholic institution would have upon Catholic parents, all other Catholic schools being of a mixed character; Kuzniewski, *Thy Honored Name*, 21–22.

37. Dzierozynski to Roothaan, Georgetown, August 22, 1843, MD 7-VIII-3, ARSI.

nun, in this case a mentally disturbed one. A mob quickly formed in the streets and proceeded to head for the convent, with the intention of putting it to the torch. The mayor of the city attempted to calm the crowd. At the invitation of the nuns he and another public official inspected the convent and questioned each of the women individually to ascertain whether any of them was being forcefully detained. All confessed that they were there by their free choice. Still the mob was unsatisfied, and the militia was called out to guard the monastery. A curfew was put into effect. Stones were hurled by the mob against the troops, but there was no bloodshed, although the mob vented its anger outside the convent for the next two days. The militia remained for three weeks.[38]

The worst violence came in the spring and summer of 1844 in Philadelphia. Job-related conflicts first broke out in May, when an attack of Catholic Irish upon a meeting of their Ulster countrymen precipitated a massive Protestant retaliation, during which they burned two churches, two schools, and thirty homes in the Catholic community. In July there was greater violence that raged for four days before 5,000 state militia restored order. The July rioting left fifteen dead and several dozen seriously injured.[39] "We are here," Francis Vespre commented from Frederick on the turbulence in Philadelphia, some sixty-five miles distant, "as we are everywhere else, in the hands of divine Providence, but if this example spreads, we could be among the first towns affected. Things are in such a state that it will not take a conflagration, a spark will be enough."[40]

Within two years the United States was at war with a Catholic country, Mexico. The federal government, sensitive about the loyalty of its Catholic citizens, especially those among the expeditionary force (nearly half), quickly made efforts to secure Catholic chaplains. Through bishops John Hughes and Patrick Kenrick it approached Verhaegen for two priests to join the army in Texas. After an elaborate consultation involving, among others, the bishops of Boston, New York, Philadelphia, and Mobile, Catholic officials decided that the government's request "was a proper one." McElroy and Rey were chosen as the chaplains. Hughes and Kenrick personally accompanied Verhaegen to

38. Joseph G. Mannard, "The 1839 Baltimore Nunnery Riot: An Episode in Jacksonian Nativism and Social Violence," *The Maryland Historian* 11 (Spring 1980): 13–27.

39. David R. Contosta, *Saint Joseph's: Philadelphia's Jesuit University—150 Years* (Philadelphia: St. Joseph's University Press, 2000), 23.

40. Vespre to Roothaan, Frederick, June 5, 1844, *MD* 7-V-13, *ARSI*.

the State Department to make the arrangements. The provincial was optimistic about the development. "It will serve to destroy those calumnies of the adversaries of our Religion," he wrote Roothaan, "who for so long have been reporting that Catholics and especially the Catholic clergy of the United States, are opposed to our form of government, that they are not faithful subjects, that they always take the part of the enemy."[41] He was pleased that President Polk had wanted to see them before they left for the front. For the next year McElroy ministered to the Catholic soldiers in General Zachary Taylor's army at their base at Matamoras, Mexico. Rey, who accompanied the expeditionary force across northern Mexico, won recognition for his heroic ministry during the battle of Monterrey. In January he disappeared en route to visit McElroy. The latter, after many attempts, finally learned that a party of Mexicans had killed both Rey and a companion. Verhaegen recalled McElroy in May, 1847, thinking that the war was over. It dragged on for more than a year. "What a great calamity for each Republic!" Verhaegen wrote Roothaan.[42] The war had long since transcended any occasion for proving Catholic loyalty. For the Maryland Jesuits it had cost them one of their most valuable members.

Jesuit Immigrants and College Building

By the time peace was concluded with Mexico Verhaegen had returned to Missouri. He too had disappointed the general. He pleaded that Roothaan allow him to return to the West and work with Indians. He regretted that he had failed to carry out the general's wishes in Maryland, but it was not for lack of trying. The problem lay with the four men whom Verhaegen saw giving "its form to this Province": Ryder, George Fenwick, and the two Mulledy brothers, Samuel and Thomas. They had all been Roman-trained, Verhaegen pointed out, and thus set the tone for the rest, especially the scholastics. So long as they remained, Verhaegen saw no hope of reforming the province. He had tried to deal with the situation by rotating them between Holy Cross and Georgetown, but the change of skies had not improved their character, so far as he could determine. He was obviously pleased to be relieved of his office in January 1848.[43]

41. Verhaegen to Roothaan, Worcester, June 5, 1846, MD 8-I-17, ARSI.

42. Verhaegen to Roothaan, Georgetown, October 28, 1847, MD 8-I-28, ARSI; John McElroy, S.J., "Chaplain for the Mexican War," *Woodstock Letters* 16 (1887): 226; hereafter WL.

43. Verhaegen to Roothaan, Georgetown, July 10, 1847, MD 8-I-25, ARSI; Verhaegen to Roothaan, August 14, 1847, MD 8-I-27, ARSI.

The new provincial was Ignatius Brocard from Switzerland. He too could not escape *miramurs* from Rome. (One gets the impression that the superior general began to think that everyone he sent to reform the Maryland Province quickly succumbed to the sirens of the Potomac.) But Brocard was a wise choice. He knew the Society, and he quickly came to know America. He early realized that which has confounded so many idealists: how differently "things work out in America from what is planned; even" he was not above pointing out to Roothaan, "when your Paternity has intervened."[44] He was compassionate, but decisive. He was determined to give the scholastics a proper education for their future work. He also was intent upon seizing the opportunities for expanding the work of the province, particularly in education. Fortunately for Brocard, the moment was right for his vision and commitment.

While one war was ending on the North American continent, a series of uprisings was convulsing Europe. The revolutions of 1848 generated thousands of refugees, many of them members of religious orders. In the Society entire provinces were dispersed. The Upper German Province sought sanctuary in America, as did many members of provinces in Italy. It was an extraordinary migration that included the astronomers/physicists Benedict Sestini and Angelo Secchi, as well as Johan Bapst, Michael Tomei, John Baptist Pianciani, Bernard Wiget, and Burchard Villiger.

Even before the uprisings, the province had been actively seeking help from Europe. In 1845 Ryder had gone to Italy to recruit priests and scholastics. He had returned with eight. Once the news of the massive displacements caused by the uprisings of 1848 reached America, Brocard wasted no time in extending an offer of asylum to as many as the province could accommodate. In August 1848 forty-one Germans arrived. All twenty-one of the scholastics plus four priests remained in Maryland. In November twenty-one Italians arrived. Bernard Maguire, a scholastic, greeted them on behalf of the Georgetown community and the province. He admitted that they would not find in America the civilization they had known in Europe. What he could offer them was

> a land of freedom to be evangelized, a people generous, hospitable, kind, wandering in the paths of error, yet anxious to embrace the truth. We offer you thousands of poor degraded beings who scarcely know that there is a God who made them

44. Brocard to Roothaan, Georgetown, August 12, 1850, MD 8-II-27, ARSI.

and who constantly cry out for the bread of life and . . . there is no one to bring it to them. . . . We offer you, in fine, twenty millions of souls redeemed by the blood of Calvary to be saved by our labors. And will not this gift compensate for all your losses?[45]

By 1851 there were 213 Jesuits working in the Maryland Province. Nearly a third, 69, were from European provinces.[46] The additional manpower allowed Brocard to pursue his plans to strengthen the existing colleges and to open new ones in the South and East. He saw the opportunity to provide for the first time an excellent theological and philosophical faculty for the scholastics and a chance to strengthen the curriculum at Georgetown, especially mathematics and astronomy (an observatory had been built in 1841). "Perhaps also with their arrival," Brocard suggested to the superior general, "new houses can be formed in Pennsylvania, Virginia and other states where we have been unable to fulfil our hopes of having schools."[47]

Over the past two decades Catholics had been prominent players in the higher education boom that had added hundreds of colleges across the country. Between 1829 and 1849 no fewer than thirty-one Catholic colleges or literary institutes were founded. The Maryland Province's involvement had been minimal: St. John's and Holy Cross. For years provincials, lacking the manpower, had been declining the requests of bishops to establish schools in their dioceses. Within months of taking office Brocard, suddenly possessing human resources that his predecessors had not known, was seriously considering starting colleges in Charleston, Erie, and Richmond. Bishop Ignatius Reynolds of Charleston had been offering his school to the province for over two years. Verhaegen had even visited Charleston to inspect it, but came away convinced that the town was a poor prospect due to its few Catholics, native hostility, and the heat of the place. Brocard was much more optimistic. Not only was he prepared to staff the college once the bishop raised the money for a new building, but he was negotiating with the Provincial of Turin for a priest and two brothers to develop some land in Georgia, which the bishop had also given the province. Unfortunately neither project went any further.

As we have seen in the founding of Holy Cross, the preference now was for day schools. The latter required a smaller investment of money and man-

45. [1848] MD 9-XIV-4, ARSI.

46. *Catalogus Provinciae Marylandiae Societatis Jesu Ineunte Anno MDCCLI* (Georgetown: 1851).

47. Brocard to Roothaan, Georgetown, April 16, 1848, MD 8-II-5, ARSI.

power; some even argued, pace Benedict Fenwick, that they also promoted more vocations than boarding schools did. Brocard quickly adopted this strategy. While he was attempting to secure a college in Charleston, he accepted back from Father William Matthews the Washington Seminary that had been sold to Matthews in the 1820s. As Brocard explained to Roothaan, there was no other Catholic school in the nation's capital (Georgetown was still a separate municipality), and many Catholics were attending "the Protestant 'Columbian'" (George Washington University today).[48] In October 1848 the Washington College opened its doors. The first Jesuit community included John Blox (the superior), Francis Vespre, two scholastics, and two brothers. Both Catholics and Protestants were delighted with the new institution, according to Brocard. "Many of them," he reported, "especially the leading citizens and those in government, are sending their sons there." He expected that the enrollment would reach 200. By 1851 it was nearing 350 students.[49] Seven years later it was incorporated by Congress as Gonzaga College.

Although Philadelphia was the largest city in the province and counted between 150,000 and 170,000 Catholics, about a third of the total population, the Maryland Jesuits had given it rather little attention. True, they had had a church there for over two hundred years. But there had never been an effort to establish a college. Mulledy was one of the first to see the potential there. "Philadelphia is an immense field for our society," he wrote in 1839. "[T]he citizens are heart and soul for us—Within two years we can have the beginnings of a College."[50] At St. Joseph's, Felix Barbelin was experiencing great success in conducting a Sunday school for over four hundred students of both sexes, including many blacks. The number of converts he was attracting was extraordinary. As a later provincial observed of Barbelin, "he works day and night in sacred ministries . . . an extraordinary worker, piety and innocence itself."[51] Peter Havermans had also at that time approached Father General Roothaan about starting a college there, and the latter had encouraged him

48. Brocard to Roothaan, Georgetown, April 16, 1848, MD 8-II-5, ARSI.

49. Brocard to Roothaan, August 28, 1848, MD 8-II-8, ARSI; Brocard to Roothaan, November 8, 1848, MD 8-II-9, ARSI; Brocard to Roothaan, March 16, 1851, MD 8-II-36, ARSI.

50. Mulledy, while provincial, had tried to start a school in Washington, but Roothaan had denied permission. "Allow me here to observe," Mulledy wrote the superior general, "if we do not accept the occasions offered for colleges—perhaps—when we wish to open them—further occasions will not occur because others will be in possession; Mulledy to Roothaan, Georgetown, April 17, 1839, MD 7-I-12, ARSI.

51. Ashwanden to Roothaan, Georgetown, June 2, 1852, MD 8-II-52, ARSI.

to consult the provincial. Havermans found both McSherry and Dzierozynski somewhat lukewarm toward the idea, and within two years he left the Society. The province decided it could not yet open a college there, despite the urging of Barbelin and McElroy. As Vespre explained to the general,

> Who is the priest or rather the two priests who have the diverse qualifications necessary to begin . . . a college . . . in a city like Philadelphia where the sciences and the arts are the most cultivated. . . . These are the unfortunate facts . . . and all the aspirations, the desires and the speculations can neither wipe out nor change them.[52]

The riots of 1844 aggravated their efforts to secure contributions to build, since much Catholic money went to rebuild the ruined churches.

Within weeks of taking office Brocard authorized Barbelin to buy property adjacent to St. Joseph's Church for a college.[53] On September 15, 1851, approximately ninety boys formally started elementary classes in the still unfinished building on Willings Alley. "This can be considered the beginning of the college so long expected and promised to Philadelphia," Brocard wrote Roothaan.[54] Although all the students who enrolled during the first year were Catholic, there was no intention, as at Holy Cross, of excluding others, hence the school had no difficulty securing its charter in the following year. That same year James Ryder, now stationed in Philadelphia, embarked on the first transcontinental fundraising trip with Brocard's permission, but to Roothaan's displeasure. Ryder, who had many friends in California, unfortunately failed to find much gold for St. Joseph's among them. By the middle 1850s enrollment had outstripped the very limited facilities at Willings's Alley, and in January of 1856 the school moved west across town to St. John's, where James Ryder became president.[55]

Baltimore was another city that the province had long eyed as the seat of a college. For over a decade Archbishop Eccleston talked about his desire to have the Maryland Jesuits establish a house there, but nothing came of it. The

52. Vespre to Roothaan, Georgetown, January 21, 1842, MD 7-I-43, ARSI.

53. That same year a man offered to build a school for the Society in Philadelphia, two miles from St. Joseph's Church, on the condition that it be open to Catholic and non-Catholic alike (he wanted an alternative to Gerard College, which was closed to Catholics, among others), and that they pay back two-thirds of the cost ($30,000) in ten years; Brocard to Roothaan, Georgetown, October 3, 1851, MD 8-II-9, ARSI.

54. Brocard to Roothaan, Georgetown, October 3, 1851, MD 8-II-40, ARSI; Francis X. Talbot, S.J., *Jesuit Education in Philadelphia: St. Joseph's College: Philadelphia, 1851–1926* (Philadelphia: St. Joseph's College, 1927), 37–50.

55. Contosta, *Saint Joseph's*, 32–33.

main obstacle was the Sulpicians' college, St. Mary's. Until Brocard there was little interest among the Jesuits of starting or taking over a parish in Baltimore, so long as a Catholic college was already in existence. Brocard, however, decided that having a house in the town was a critical investment for the future. "To have a piece of ground in Baltimore," he explained to the general, "will be extremely promising . . . ; that town being the crossroads of routes from the South, the West and the North and being at the same time a seaport." If they failed to seize the day, he noted, it "will perhaps be a long time before we have another such chance."[56]

Two years later Brocard's investment paid off when the Sulpicians decided to close their college. A year to the day after St. Joseph's opened its doors in Philadelphia, Loyola College began classes in a building on Holiday Street in the business district of Baltimore. By August 1854, within the shadow of the Washington monument, the brick structure was rising on Calvert Street that would house the school for the next seventy-five years. A year earlier the Maryland legislature had granted the new college a charter. As the successor to St. Mary's College, Loyola continued the former's tradition of providing a liberal arts education for the middle class of Baltimore. As the only college for men in the city, Loyola, like St. Mary's before it, attracted a substantial minority of students who were not Catholic. Unlike the other colleges the province established during the 1840s–1850s, Loyola continued to reflect the ethnic and religious pluralism of an earlier, less segmented America. Moreover, unlike the other urban colleges the Maryland Jesuits opened during the decade, few of the sons of the immigrant poor were among Loyola's students in its first half century.[57]

The third major city within the province that lacked a Jesuit college was Boston, whose Catholic population, thanks to waves of famine-fleeing Irish, was approaching the 100,000 mark by mid-century. John McElroy had been assigned to Boston upon his return from Mexico in 1847 to take over St. Mary's of the Sacred Heart in the North End, whose care Bishop John Fitzpatrick had entrusted to the Maryland Jesuits. McElroy, as he had done in Frederick, quickly began an elementary school for boys, taught by laymen, and one for girls under the Sisters of Notre Dame de Namur. In 1854 the bishop invited the Maryland Jesuits to open a college. One of the reasons for agreeing to accept

56. Brocard to Roothaan, Georgetown, April 4, 1849, MD, 8-II-13, ARSI.

57. See Nicholas Varga, *Baltimore's Loyola, Loyola's Baltimore, 1851–1986* (Baltimore: Maryland Historical Society, 1990), 13–37.

Holy Cross had been the hope that in the near future they could begin a second New England college in Boston. When a fire destroyed the main building at Holy Cross in 1852, there was deep division within the province about reopening the school. Some wanted to shift the Jesuits in Worcester to Baltimore. The provincial superior, now Charles Stonestreet, was himself committed to rebuilding, since he feared the consequences the reputation of the Society would suffer, particularly in New England, should it abandon Worcester. Rome supported Stonestreet, and the provincial quickly had cause to believe his judgment further confirmed when the Bishop of Boston began raising money for the construction of a Jesuit college in that city.

Stonestreet believed, like McElroy, that a Jesuit college in Boston had a great role to play in educating poor Catholic immigrants. Like McElroy he appreciated the generosity of the Irish in building churches and schools, despite their pressing poverty. In America the Society could no longer restrict itself to educating the sons of the gentry.[58] Other Jesuits in Maryland shared this concern: "If the Society wishes ever to do anything truly great," one member stationed in Baltimore wrote in the late 1850s, "it must begin to have special care of the lower classes, for it is only by retaining our own there, and by making conversions amongst them, that the Catholic Church can ever hope to have a strong hold on the American people."[59] Resurgent nativism, in the form of Know-Nothings, obstructed the project, but the Church of the Immaculate Conception on Harrison Avenue in the South End finally opened in the late winter of 1861. Next to the church stood the completed brick college building that McElroy, for lack of a Jesuit faculty, was unable to open. Boston College finally obtained a charter in 1863, two years before its older sister institution in Worcester, and began classes in 1864 with a faculty of three and forty-eight students.[60] Tuition was a modest $30 per semester.[61] It became the first Maryland Jesuit college to attract large numbers of the sons of immigrants.

58. McElroy had some seven thousand members in his congregation, only three of whom owned their homes. McElroy had pointed out to Stonestreet one tenement in which twenty-seven families lived. When a riot broke out in the area on the Fourth of July, Stonestreet, from an old Catholic family in Southern Maryland, could not resist telling McElroy: "See, my dear father, the pious congregation of St. Mary's!"; Stonestreet to Beckx, Georgetown, August 9, 1854, MD 8-III-7, ARSI.

59. Unsigned memorandum[1858–60?], MD 9-X-1, ARSI. The author was particularly decrying the practice of pew rents, which effectively denied the poor any seats in church.

60. David R. Dunigan, S.J., *A History of Boston College* (Milwaukee: Bruce Publishing, 1947), 72–78.

61. Thomas H. O'Connor, *The Boston Irish: A Political History* (Boston: Back Bay Books, 1995), 92.

At Georgetown the college had been floundering when Brocard arrived. There were fewer than eighty students. Ignatius Combs blamed the lagging enrollments, at a time when "other Catholic colleges in the United States are well filled," on the failure of the foreign Jesuits to accommodate their teaching philosophy and discipline to American students. He saw cause for hope in Brocard, whom he found favorable toward American mores and ideals. The first thing Brocard did was to recall James Ryder as president in order to rebuild the reputation of the school. Ryder greatly improved the morale of professors, prefects, and students, which had been at ebbtide under Thomas Mulledy (again, rector from 1845 to 1848). Ryder's heart, however, was more in preaching and missions than college administration. He was frequently away, which would have been more tolerable had his subordinates been better united than they were.

The addition of the distinguished faculty from Italy and Germany also accelerated the revival of the college. But the refugee professors, especially the Germans, found the discipline in the college to be sadly lacking, an old theme that two generations of foreigners had raised about American educational governance or the lack of it. In early January 1850 they found an occasion to strike a blow for discipline. When some of the students went on a rampage of trashing their rooms, breaking windows, and creating the kind of havoc that Southern juveniles prided themselves upon, two of the culprits were expelled. Many of the other students involved pleaded the case of their colleagues with the vice-rector, Father James Ward (Ryder had been away for several weeks on a preaching tour). Ward told them that if they were guilty, they could consider themselves expelled, as well. The word spread rapidly that the entire student body had been dismissed. Some sixty students decamped to a hotel in Washington. Their defiance was soon filling the papers of Washington and Georgetown. At this point the provincial superior got involved, pleading with Ward that he go to the students and work out some compromise. Ward replied: "If you want things done that way, name another Vice-President."[62] Brocard did just that, making Angelo Paresce the acting vice-rector. Through the negotiations of Paresce and Bernard Maguire, most of the students eventually made their submission and returned.[63]

62. Brocard to Roothaan, Georgetown, December 21, 1850, MD 8-II-33, ARSI.

63. Brocard to Roothaan, Georgetown, January 23, 1850, MD 8-II-22, ARSI; Brocard to Roothaan, April 12, 1850, MD 8-II-24, ARSI; see Joseph Durkin, S.J., *Georgetown University: The Middle Years* (Washington, D.C.: Georgetown University Press, 1963), 30–31; also Robert Emmett Curran,

The provincial discovered that Ward had been under the influence of a particularly rigorous German, Joseph Duverney, the spiritual father of the community. Duverney and Francis Xavier Knackstedt, virtually from their arrival in America, had isolated themselves from the other priests, but had considerable influence with the German scholastics and a few of the young Americans, like Ward. "They have done more to embarrass me," Brocard wrote Roothaan, "than all the rest of the Province."[64] The next year Duverney was in Philadelphia and Knackstedt at St. Inigoes, on the tip of Southern Maryland. Charles Stonestreet also replaced Ryder in 1851, and the college began a decade of growth that saw enrollments move well beyond three hundred students.

In the eyes of the American Jesuits, Duverney and Knackstedt were but the worst examples of the rigidity they found characteristic of the immigrants. They no doubt blamed them also for inspiring an article in the *Freeman's Journal* in 1849 that charged that the Jesuits were monarchophiles. Ryder responded by claiming that, not only were the Jesuits not partial to monarchy, but the structure of the Society itself was republican.[65] Another issue that aggravated ethnic relations in Jesuit communities was the use of alcohol. Ironically, by the end of the 1840s it was the foreigners, especially the Italians, who were complaining about the elimination of wine at table. Americans like Ryder were advocating this measure in order to refute the reputation the Society had acquired in this country, and Brocard thought it was a price the Europeans could pay to avoid any possible occasion for scandal.

Despite the ethnic tensions, the provincial realized what a disaster it would be to have refugees recalled to Europe. As it was, Brocard reluctantly had deferred any further expansion until more Jesuits were available. He pleaded with the general not to withdraw the Europeans and thus deny the province the chance to become finally "what you have wanted for a long time and which you so strongly recommended to me in sending me here."[66] He pointed out the number of ne'er-do-wells he had purged from the province ranks. More importantly, the province had lost through premature death an extraordinary number of experienced or promising men such as McSherry,

The Bicentennial History of Georgetown, vol. 1, *From Academy to University, 1789–1889* (Washington, D.C.: Georgetown University Press, 1993), 184–86.

64. Brocard to Roothaan, Georgetown, January 23, 1850, MD 8-II-22, ARSI.

65. Brocard to Roothaan, Georgetown, October 6, 1849, MD 8-II-17, ARSI.

66. Brocard to Roothaan, Georgetown, April 12, 1850, MD 8-II-24, ARSI.

Rey, Gabaria, and others. Still others who had given promise had had to be dismissed. Then too, he reminded the general, the province had welcomed the exiles as sons and spent much money on them. Did not they owe the province something now in return? "I fear that if the work begun is lost, the next state [of this province] will be worse than the former one."[67] Vocations were still too rare in this country. Europe had a surplus. And reflecting on the ominous events that had created so many clerical refugees, he added: "If one fine day... Italy and Europe should become a foreign mission, it will be good for us to prepare missionaries."[68]

In March 1852 Brocard cut his finger while exercising. He soon experienced dizziness and a severe fever. The doctors diagnosed erysipelas, but it proved to be typhoid fever. He was dead within a week, perhaps the worst loss the province had suffered in its brief history.

Apostolic Challenges and a Revival of Nativism

When Archbishop Kenrick had approached Ignatius Brocard in 1851 about the possibility of a Missouri Jesuit becoming Bishop of Philadelphia, the provincial suggested that the day of Jesuit bishops was past, now that there were many secular priests available.[69] In truth only one Jesuit from the Maryland Province, Benedict Joseph Fenwick, had become a bishop. Several others, including Mulledy and Ryder, were at one time or other rumored to be candidates for a particular see, but nothing came of the speculation. Relations between the Maryland Jesuits and the archbishops of Baltimore since the accession of Ambrose Maréchal had varied from stormy to mixed. But the virtual absence of Jesuit bishops was but one consequence of a continuing shortage of personnel that continued to plague provincials throughout the 1850s as it had their predecessors.

Pleas continued to be made to the superior general for help, although the provincials were becoming more discriminating in their requests. Burchard Villiger in 1860 cautioned that the general not send discards, but "those with virtue and knowledge."[70] Compounding the shortage of priests was an attitude that increasingly manifested itself as the province expanded northward.

67. Brocard to Roothaan, Georgetown, October 31, 1851, MD 8-II-41, ARSI; Brocard to Roothaan, December 23, 1851, MD 8-II-43, ARSI.

68. Brocard to Roothaan, Georgetown, November 25, 1850, MD 8-II-41, ARSI.

69. Brocard to Roothaan, Georgetown, October 31, 1851, MD 8-II-41, ARSI.

70. Villiger to Peter Beckx, Baltimore, September 7, 1860, MD 8-IV-21, ARSI.

If some immigrant Jesuits, especially the Germans, suffered from ethnocentrism in America, some natives of the Maryland Province manifested a certain lococentrism. The farther they were sent beyond the reaches of the Chesapeake and its estuaries, the more out of sorts they became. As one provincial in the 1850s, Charles Stonestreet, reported to the new superior general, Father Peter Beckx, when Stonestreet assigned some of his fellow Marylanders to Boston or Worcester or Maine they feared they were being exiled. "One recently said to me (who had been very unhappy in Worcester)," Stonestreet wrote, "the whole time I was living there I was trembling that I would not see Maryland again."[71]

Offers to staff colleges and parishes or to give the Exercises continued to be turned down or deferred for lack of Jesuits. One sign of hope for a different future was the increase in novices in the decade. By 1857 there were twenty-two candidates, of whom sixteen were accepted. Most were from the province's colleges.[72] Another encouraging sign in the 1850s was the quality of the provincials. Charles Stonestreet and Burchard Villiger were outstanding leaders during a particularly crucial decade for the province and the nation. Stonestreet, a native of Charles County in Southern Maryland, was the first Marylander to be appointed provincial who was not Roman-trained. (He was professed on the day he received his appointment.) Villiger, like Brocard a Swiss, had come to this country in 1848. He was keenly aware of being an outsider but, unlike many of his compatriots, rapidly acculturated himself to his new country. As he pointed out to Superior General Peter Beckx (who like Roothaan had difficulty understanding Americans):

> If I may suggest, Americans can not be forced to sanctity, can not be forced to perfection, can not be forced to religious discipline, but nonetheless they can more quickly and securely be brought [to this state] with gentleness and exhortation than with rigor...
>
> In time the Americans will be equal to the Europeans but give them time.[73]

Both men brought uncommon intelligence, a deep spirituality, and much courage to the office. Both continued the work that Brocard had begun.

Throughout the fifties the number of students increased in the schools in Georgetown, Baltimore, Philadelphia, and Washington. Stonestreet even

71. Stonestreet to Beckx, Georgetown, August 9, 1854, MD 8-III-7, ARSI.

72. In 1856, for instance, six novices were from Holy Cross, two from Georgetown, one from St. Joseph's, and one from Loyola; Stonestreet to Beckx, Georgetown, July 12, 1856, MD 8-III-19, ARSI; Stonestreet to Beckx, July 30, 1857, MD 8-III-25, ARSI.

73. Villiger to Beckx, Georgetown, June 23, 1859, MD 8-IV-9, ARSI.

wanted to establish schools at all the missions in Southern Maryland and elsewhere, to be taught by laymen or brothers; one parochial school had begun at St. Thomas Manor in 1854. But many of the colleges were still weak, with teachers ill-prepared and enrollments swollen through a lack of requirements. Some rectors, Villiger felt, were more concerned about finances and numbers than they were about quality education.[74] There was also pressure to replace the classical curriculum with a business-oriented one that would attract more students. Holy Cross, from its beginning in 1843, had offered a commercial course that paralleled the classical one. Loyola and St. Joseph's both began commercial tracks in response to parental complaints about their sons being compelled to study the classics. But the chief problem facing the colleges continued to be the lack of Jesuits.

Nativism raised its ugly head once more in the 1850s. Persistent immigration (2,598,214 in the decade alone), attempts to secure public funds for parochial schools, and restiveness over the growing sectional crisis all nurtured a xenophobia that found convenient targets in Catholics, especially Jesuits. In 1853 a papal diplomat, Archbishop Gaetano Bedini, sent to the United States to establish full diplomatic relations with Washington, was forced to abandon his mission after crowds threatened him in Pittsburgh, Wheeling, and Cincinnati. A year later in Ellsworth, Maine, a crowd attacked John Bapst, a Swiss Jesuit refugee who had been sent north to work with Indians and Irish immigrants. Bapst's work in the town of Ellsworth quickly led to Protestant conversions. He also became the most outspoken critic of the local public school policy of forcing Catholic children to read the King James version of the Bible. Tensions grew through the early months of 1854. In the summer, churches in Manchester and Bath were destroyed. The bishop removed Bapst to Bangor for his own protection. When he returned to Ellsworth in October, a crowd dragged him from the home of a parishioner, tarred and feathered his bare body, and paraded him about the town for hours on a plank. Bapst assured the general that he was hurt "neither in body nor mind." Indeed he felt that the intended shaming had instead won him sympathy from many non-Catholics in the state. Nonetheless, he saw himself as but the temporary center of "a rising storm."[75]

74. Villiger to Beckx, Georgetown, June 4, 1860, *MD* 8-IV-17, *ARSI*. St. John's College in Frederick was on its last legs. It had never recovered from a riot there in 1851, when Thomas Mulledy was rector; Thomas R. Bevan, 220 *Years . . . A History of the Catholic Community of the Frederick Valley* (Frederick: 1977), 32.

75. Bapst to Beckx, Bangor, January 10, 1854, *MD*, 9-XXII-3, *ARSI*. Bapst's experience affected

Nowhere was the American Party, the political organ of the nativists, stronger than in Maryland. In 1854 it elected its candidate mayor of Baltimore. The following year it captured the state legislature. In 1856 Maryland became the only state to cast its presidential vote for the American or Know-Nothing Party candidate, Millard Fillmore. By 1850 twenty percent of the city's population was foreign-born. During the ensuing decade, German and Irish immigrants, many of them Catholics, streamed into the city from the docks in increasing numbers. In 1852 a Catholic delegate in the legislature introduced a bill to secure funds for sectarian schools. That same year the Maryland Province finally opened Loyola College, and the First Plenary Council of the Church hierarchy convened in Baltimore. Scores of robed prelates and priests marching in solemn procession to the cathedral in downtown Baltimore created a scene of pomp, a New York journalist noted, "such as Republicans are not wont to look upon."[76] To many Marylanders the growing power of the Church seemed all too evident. In a community disrupted by demographic and socio-economic changes that included the decline of slavery, immigrants and Catholics "served, like lightning rods, to attract the apprehensive attentions of citizens whose old ways of life were disappearing."[77]

In the District of Columbia, Charles Stonestreet felt the shockwaves from Maryland. "[We] are in a crisis," he wrote Beckx in 1856. Stonestreet worried that nativism might poison the presidential election that year. "In such a situation prudence seems very much in order for us, so that we . . . project an image of calm regarding the outside world."[78] Calmness, though, did not mean absolute silence. In February 1855 the provincial wrote a letter to *The Metropolitan*, a Baltimore magazine, to respond to the hoary charge that Jesuits took an oath to overthrow non-Catholic rulers. "I am humiliated as a Marylander," he wrote,

---

him more deeply than he realized at the time. He ended his life in an asylum haunted by nightmares of attackers storming his room; *WL* 16 (1887), 324–25, cited in James Hennesey, S.J., *American Catholics: A History of the Roman Catholic Community in the United States* (New York and Oxford: Oxford University Press, 1981), 125.

76. The New York *Observer*, cited in *The Premier See: A History of the Archdiocese of Baltimore, 1789–1989*, by Thomas W. Spalding (Baltimore and London: The Johns Hopkins University Press, 1989), 155.

77. Jean H. Baker, *Ambivalent Americans: The Know-Nothing Party in Maryland* (Baltimore and London: The Johns Hopkins University Press, 1977), 23.

78. Stonestreet to Beckx, Boston, March 11, 1856, MD 8-III-17, ARSI. Two years earlier Stonestreet had already begun to consider opening houses in the Deep South, where he thought there was less opposition to Catholics and danger of persecution; Stonestreet to Beckx, Georgetown, November 4, 1854, MD 8-III-8, ARSI.

> to . . . repel the charge of more than latent treason! The Western shore of Maryland, the home of my childhood, has ever been a classic place, cherished in my heart with patriotic pride. There are the remains of my grandfather, a revolutionary soldier, and there, in an adjoining county, is the landing place of "The Pilgrims of St. Mary's," whose brightest scenes and best memories are imperishably connected with the Jesuits' name. . . .
>
> I can not help seeing in this, an effort to render me and my brethren in religion, aliens at home and strangers by our own fireplace.[79]

Of course many of the Jesuits in Maryland *were* aliens. The persistence of Germans and Italians in clinging to their native languages and openly decrying American ways was providing welcome ammunition for the nativist attacks. As one Marylander warned, the general, ethnic differences that had previously "unsettled only our houses and colleges" now had much larger repercussions.[80] No one was more sensitive to the delicate position of foreign Jesuits than Villiger. "Would that we had an American Provincial in this region!" he wrote the general in 1859.[81] Villiger thought that Father General Beckx was making his position even worse by attempting to impose certain regulations regarding nocturnal visits and the like. Villiger delicately pointed out the major fault of the regulations: their failure to take circumstances into account. Enforcing them, he warned, would take more of his time than all the rest of his governance of the province. "But if your Paternity thinks it necessary to make the rules public," he concluded, "then it will be necessary to elect an American Provincial, because I can not succeed in this barring a miracle."[82]

A few months later the general informed him that he was sending still another official visitor, the third in less than twenty years. The latest was no stranger to Maryland. Father Felix Sopranis had originally come to the province as a refugee in 1848. As Visitor he quickly put into effect the regulations that Villiger had balked at. In addition he ordered that the province give up parishes in Baltimore, Philadelphia, and Richmond, and urged it to divest itself of as many places in southern Maryland as possible. He also directed that the province examine the feasibility of having laymen teach business courses in their schools. But the ordination that produced the greatest con-

79. *WL* 31 (1902), 221–22.

80. James Ward to Beckx, Baltimore, November 17, 1854, *MD* 8-III-9, *ARSI*.

81. Villiger to Beckx, Worcester, May 21, 1859, *MD* 8-IV-8, *ARSI*.

82. Villiger to Beckx, Georgetown, June 25, 1859, *MD* 8-IV-9, *ARSI*.

sternation among Maryland Jesuits, especially those attached to Georgetown, was the designation of Conewago, the Jesuit farm just above the Maryland-Pennsylvania border, as the future site of a common scholasticate. Scholastics, Sopranis observed, needed to be free to concentrate on their studies. They could not be both students and teachers/prefects as they were at Georgetown. Until appropriate quarters could be built at Conewago, all scholastics in the Maryland and Missouri provinces, as well as the New York, California, and Louisiana missions, would use the vacant college building in Boston.[83]

For nearly a decade Maryland provincials had debated the need for a common scholasticate that would be separate from a college. Brocard thought its advantages far outweighed its disadvantages. Stonestreet felt that removing the scholastics and their faculty would be fatal to Georgetown. Villiger disliked the exploitation of scholastics and began sending them abroad for their theology. He too was attracted to Conewago. For the present he thought Boston was the best alternative.

As the scholasticate was being transferred in 1859, the decision was also being made to relocate the provincial's headquarters in Baltimore. Such a move was necessary, Villiger explained, for several reasons: Baltimore was more nearly at the center of the province by both rail and steamboat; all the business concerning the farms and missions was handled in Baltimore; and with a decline in the number of Jesuit houses in Maryland, there was a need to ensure that there would be a minimum number of Jesuits residing in Maryland to serve as members of the corporation, the legal body of the province.

War and Reconstruction

Villiger moved to Baltimore in the late summer of 1860. By December Abraham Lincoln had been elected president and South Carolina had seceded. "Political affairs here are in the greatest turmoil," Villiger reported. "The dissolution of the states seems inevitable; the economy is nearly destroyed."[84] Villiger thought that contingency plans should be prepared to divide the Society into two provinces along sectional lines. The northern province would include Philadelphia, New York, Boston, and Worcester; the southern one Maryland and the other Southern states.[85] By the time Villiger received the

83. Ordinations of Felix Sopranis, 1860, MD 8-VI, ARSI.

84. Villiger to Beckx, Baltimore, December 13, 1860, MD 8-IV-24, ARSI.

85. Villiger to Beckx, Baltimore, February 27, 1861, MD 8-IV-26, ARSI.

news that Angelo Paresce had been named to succeed him as provincial, Fort Sumter had fallen. "Our schools will probably be closed soon for a time," he wrote the superior general, four days after the first cannon had fired in Charleston harbor.[86]

On April 19 Paresce was read in as provincial. Less than a mile away fighting was erupting in the streets of Baltimore between civilians and Massachusetts troops on their way south. Within a month Federal troops had occupied both Baltimore and Washington. The latter city, by the late spring of 1861, was becoming a constellation of camps as the government prepared to begin the march on Richmond. Father John Early, the rector of Georgetown, warned his community to avoid all conversations with soldiers. Since a majority of his community almost surely had Confederate sympathies, that was prudent advice. But Early had deeper fears in mind. He informed the general: "There seems to be no imminent danger for religion, but because things are not as favorable for Catholics as they should be through the constitutions of the United States, God knows where finally this civil upheaval will lead."[87]

As soon as he took office Angelo Paresce urged that all his subjects abstain "from every spirit of party."[88] Such noninvolvement in politics was part of the Maryland Jesuit tradition. John Carroll himself, realizing that priests and politics rarely mix well, had warily consented to being part of the mission to persuade the Canadians to join the Revolution in 1776. But Carroll had not only gone, but became a staunch supporter of the Patriot cause. Maryland Jesuits had prided themselves on their patriotism. As recently as the Mexican War the province had taken advantage of the opportunity to demonstrate its allegiance. 1861 was not 1846, of course. This was civil war. Washington's enemy was not Mexicans, but fellow countrymen, relatives, former students. Southern Maryland was full of Confederate sympathizers, as was Washington itself. Where was one's country in 1861?

If the English ex-Jesuits in America had found themselves confused in the face of divided loyalties in the American Revolution, there was something new in the policy of caution and silence that superiors in Maryland imposed at the outbreak of the Civil War. To understand it one must appreciate not only the damage that nativism had done to the Jesuit psyche over the past generation, but more importantly the defensive attitude that refugee Jesuits

86. Villiger to Beckx, Baltimore, April 16, 1861, MD 8-IV-27, ARSI.

87. Early to Beckx, Georgetown, May 12, 1861, MD 9-XIV-21, ARSI.

88. Paresce to Beckx, Frederick, April 22, 1861, MD 8-V-1, ARSI.

brought with them. Being uprooted in a revolution could make one very sensitive to giving the least pretext for offense. Thus Stephen Dubuisson, himself a refugee as a young child from revolution in Sainte Domingue, agonized over what liturgical acknowledgment he should make of President Harrison's death in 1841 when Dubuisson was pastor of St. Mary's Church in Alexandria. For Dubuisson even a sermon and prayer for a dead president smacked of politics. That the Society in Italy was itself in the midst of a revolution that was threatening Rome by 1860 conditioned the fears that some American Jesuits harbored about the American situation. Father General Beckx kept instructing Paresce that he do everything possible to ensure that no cause be given for offending one side or the other.

"We are between Scylla and Charybdis," Angelo Paresce responded in November 1861. Still the provincial superior was happy that no one in the province had taken a public stand on the war, "although there is not lacking among us," he admitted, "those who hold tenaciously to their private opinions."[89] A month later, when war between the United States and England seemed imminent over the seizure of the *Trent*, Father General Beckx instructed Felix Sopranis that as Visitor he was to act as the general's alter ego, should communications be cut off between Rome and America.[90]

The admonishment of superiors for their members to maintain a strict neutrality in public seems to have been generally effective throughout the Maryland Province, even at Georgetown, where a majority of the faculty were Confederate sympathizers. Controlling the speech of students was another matter. At Georgetown, for instance, where a vast majority of the students were from below the Mason-Dixon line, many from the Deep South, students gathered in February 1861 for a public burning of the effigy of President-elect Lincoln. Three months later, when two U.S. Cavalry officers were dispatched to the campus to reconnoiter the countryside from its elevated position above the Potomac, students lined up along the road to the main gate and serenaded the officers with "Three Cheers for Jeff Davis and the Southern Confederacy!"[91]

Many students left Georgetown and the other colleges of the province to join the armed services of their respective regions. Enrollments in all the col-

89. "I have rigidly enjoined all superiors," he added, "that they diligently read all letters of Ours; and mail none in which even the least allusion is made to political affairs"; Paresce to Beckx, Baltimore, November 26, 1861, MD 8-V-8, ARSI.

90. Beckx to Sopranis, Rome, December 21, 1861, MD 9-X-3, ARSI.

91. "A Remembrance of the War," Georgetown *College Journal* 7 (December 1878): 20–21.

leges fell during the course of the war, particularly at Georgetown, so dependent upon the South for its students. By the middle of the war the student population was less than half what it had been in 1860. Both Georgetown and Holy Cross, which had, before the war, been national schools in the make-up of their student bodies, now became much more narrowly regional institutions. Loss in revenue from shrinking enrollments and wartime inflation also greatly taxed the finances of the colleges. Georgetown and Holy Cross were both forced to have significant increases in tuition to meet the economic challenge. These conditions forced St. Joseph's to close in 1863; a year and a half later it managed to reopen for the 1864–65 academic year.

Maryland Jesuits quickly began to serve as chaplains to the soldiers. Bernard Wiget, the rector of Gonzaga, was among the first to respond. Wiget eventually secured a commission as chaplain in the U.S. Cavalry and became a familiar sight astride his horse, Jackson, visiting the troops in their camps in and around the city. Robert Brady ministered to wounded soldiers in the various hospitals that sprang up around the city as war casualties mounted to numbers no one had imagined possible. Paresce also assigned Francis McAtee and Joseph O'Hagan to the Army of the Potomac. Tertians went out from Frederick to minister to federal troops at Harpers Ferry, Point of Rocks, and other strategic sites along the Baltimore and Ohio tracks. The huge prison camp that opened in the fall of 1863 for Confederate soldiers at Point Lookout in southern Maryland became a mission for Basil Pacciarini, the superior at St. Inigoes.

When a draft was introduced to raise troops in late 1862, novices, scholastics, and coadjutor brothers were not initially exempted, but after some friendly government officials intervened, the exemptions were extended to cover all Jesuits. Buildings, however, were not exempt. Georgetown College became the headquarters for the New York 69th and 79th regiments during the late spring of 1861. The villa outside Washington was occupied in 1862. Federal troops were stationed at St. Thomas Manor through much of the war. After the second battle of Bull Run federal forces took over Holy Trinity Church in Georgetown, as well as parts of Georgetown College and the novitiate at Frederick to serve as hospitals for the wounded and dying. Hundreds of them converted, including virtually all of the 120 who died.

Joseph O'Hagan served as chaplain of the New York 73rd for much of the war. The heavily Catholic regiment O'Hagan initially found to be "the scum of New York society, reeking with vice and spreading a moral malaria around them." Some indeed had been recruited from prisons. Military discipline and removal from their old corrupting environment gradually transformed most of them. O'Hagan eventually served as the pastor of a military parish consisting of Catholics serving in ten Union regiments. The masses he celebrated in the field regularly attracted more than 1,500 soldiers. O'Hagan was in the thick of the action during the Peninsula Campaign in the spring of 1862. He was at Fredericksburg late the following fall when General Ambrose Burnside was preparing to mount a massive attack upon the impregnable Confederate defenses on the hills behind the town that the Union commander hoped would open the way to Richmond and the end of the war. "[I]f he attempts it here," O'Hagan wrote Bernard Wiget at the end of November, "it will be at a terrible sacrifice of life."[92] O'Hagan proved to be all too accurate a predictor. In the desperate charges against Marye's Heights and elsewhere two weeks later the Army of the Potomac suffered more than 13,000 casualties in killed and wounded, many of them Irish Catholics. "I never imagined," O'Hagan wrote Wiget five days after the battle:

> that so many dead could be left on one field. They were actually in heaps. . . . I do not know what the next programme will be, nor do I care much, provided our poor men are not led to another butchery. It is horrible, and I am only surprised that the entire nation does not rise up against it unanimously.[93]

"There is yet no hope of peace," Paresce reported in June 1863 as Lee was threatening both Baltimore and Washington; "the Civil War gets more fierce by the day."[94] The war had become a seemingly endless repetition of murderous battles, each leaving more casualties than the last. "So many thousands of men wounded! It scarcely can be believed," was all that Wiget could comment in 1864 after tending the victims for more than three years. He added: "The hospitals again and again have been vacated only to be filled once more and our work in them is unending."[95]

A few Jesuits saw heaven's hand in the declining fortunes of the Confederacy. After the battle of Gettysburg, John Barrister, a German who had changed his name from Bauermeister, wrote from Alexandria:

92. O'Hagan to Bernard Wiget, near Falmouth, November 30, 1862, in *WL* 15 (1886): 111–12.
93. O'Hagan to Bernard Wiget, Falmouth, December 18, 1862, in *WL* 15 (1886): 112–13.
94. Paresce to Beckx, Baltimore, June 23, 1863, *MD* 8-V-16, *ARSI*.
95. Wiget to Beckx, Washington, D.C., July 22, 1864, *MD* 10-XXIII-1, *ARSI*.

How the Almighty punishes American pride by the very thing which once made these people so boastful and haughty, I mean their "*Glorious Union and heavenborn Constitution.*" *O tempora! O mores!* There was a time when the haughty Virginian looked down upon the poor Irishmen or the humble mechanic from his . . . window with an air of contempt. Now an Irish soldier or a Massachusetts cobler [sic] sits on his lofty porch of Corinthian columns, smoking his pipe, or chewing tobacco.[96]

Had Angelo Paresche been able to foresee in 1861 how the war would end, he might well have feared for the safety of the Maryland Province and American Catholics in general. The day after Abraham Lincoln was assassinated, soldiers arrested a Georgetown Jesuit, John Guida, because of his striking resemblance to the suspected presidential killer, John Wilkes Booth. Guida was quickly released, but others with Jesuit connections were among those convicted of plotting or abetting the assassination: three Georgetown alumni—David Herold, Samuel Arnold, and Dr. Samuel Mudd—and Mary Surratt, whose confessor was Bernard Wiget. Herold and Surratt were hanged, Arnold and Mudd imprisoned for life. But despite the hysteria and fury that swept the city and nation in the wake of the assassination, no one struck the chord of a Catholic or Jesuit plot to bring down the republic. The Catholic record in the war had effectively discredited the nativist shibboleths of the previous decades.[97]

What the Church's response should be to the people liberated by the armies of the North during the war was one of the issues taken up at the Second Plenary Council of Baltimore in 1866. Among their recommendations was the call for religious communities to open churches and schools for blacks. A few Maryland Jesuits had been pioneers of this work in the cities. Felix Barbelin in Philadelphia and Thomas Lilly in Georgetown and Frederick had begun schools for blacks. With the encouragement of Archbishop Martin Spalding of Baltimore, one of the more vigorous promoters of the work

96. Barrister to [John Cattani], Alexandria, July 17, 1863, GUA, GULSC.

97. Thomas Reed Turner, in his study of the popular reaction to the assassination, points out how many Protestant clergy in Washington and elsewhere stoked the fires of revenge, but they confined their targets to Confederate leaders and their sympathizers; neither Catholics nor Jesuits were singled out; Turner, *Beware the People Weeping: Public Opinion and the Assassination of Abraham Lincoln* (Baton Rouge: Louisiana State University Press, 1982), 25–52; 77–89.

Although Wiget was a character witness at Mrs. Surratt's trial and accompanied her to the gallows, no one ever apparently raised a suspicion about the priest's involvement. Some, however, who recalled the name of Wiget's horse, may have wondered what particular Jackson he had been named for.

of evangelizing the freedmen, the province began a church in Baltimore, St. Francis Xavier, for a black congregation. When blacks in Washington urged the archbishop to erect a church and school for them, Spalding asked Paresce to have Wiget take on this important work. The provincial hesitated, reluctant to increase the debt of the province at a time when expenses were still exceeding income and the commitment had been made to build the scholasticate. "I do not know what to say," Wiget wrote to the general; "it is certainly true that the negroes are greatly in need of spiritual help." He realized that if effective action was not taken, the Church would lose many black Catholics who had come into the city from southern Maryland. "I am indeed very ready to help," he offered; "perhaps some means can be found for carrying out this work."[98]

Nor was money the only shortage. The province still lacked the men to do all it was committed to doing, much less to staff new missions. Patrick Lynch, Bishop of Charleston, appealed to Beckx to come to the province's aid by sending some men who could work among the blacks on Port Royal Island, one of the earliest areas liberated during the war and a government showcase for a reconstruction of the South in which blacks would prosper under the stimulus of free enterprise. There were 50,000 blacks there, the bishop pointed out, "perhaps not 50 Catholics. . . . I think that all things considered," he concluded, "this is an excellent place to commence a mission among the Negroes, . . . I will do everything to cooperate, that a poor Bishop like myself can do, for I wish to see the work started. . . . Every month that passes is so much time lost."[99]

Like the American Church in general, the province's response to such opportunities in the unsettled situation following the war was mixed at best. In southern Maryland Jesuits continued to minister to black and white alike in mixed congregations in which little appeared to have changed since 1863. Francis McAtee came back from the army to be pastor at St. Thomas Manor. Half of his 3,000 parishioners were black. Life hardly was more comfortable there than it had been in the army camps. A fire had destroyed the church and residence in December 1866. Poverty was everywhere. "Those who before the civil war wore purple, now lack food and clothing," he reported to the general

98. Wiget to Beckx, Washington, D.C., October 3, 1866, MD 10-XXIII-5, ARSI. The debt in the province in 1867 was $42,303. Income for the year had been $81,910. Expenses were $85,517; Financial Account, January 1, 1866 to January 1, 1867, MD 10-I-19, ARSI.

99. Lynch to Armellini, Baltimore, October 26, 1866, MD 10-X-2, ARSI.

in 1871. But he found the faith of the people "outstanding." He apologized for having written less often than the rules required because he found himself occupied in his work "day and night, there is scarcely time for reciting the Breviary."[100]

As blacks flocked into Baltimore and Washington, however, Jesuit superiors began to look elsewhere for a religious community that was prepared to specialize in this ministry. In 1869 they thought they had found such a group in France, and were deliberating whether they should turn over their Baltimore parish to them as a base. "[F]or this work seems so great," wrote the provincial, "and of such moment that it must be committed to such a congregation which does this one thing."[101] Two years later the Mill Hill Fathers, organized by Bishop Herbert Vaughan for the black apostolate, came from England to America and took over St. Francis Xavier in Baltimore.

The Maryland–New York Province

Since William McSherry and his companions had sailed for Rome in 1820, ocean travel had improved considerably. The growing body of government regulations, both in the United States and Europe, had slowly bettered conditions aboard ship. The mortality rates plummeted. But the trip under sail across the Atlantic was still a long one (steamships would not begin to dominate the traffic until the 1870s) and at times very dangerous. In January 1869 three Jesuits were making the crossing. Two were returning from the Procurators' meeting that had been held in Rome the previous fall. Joseph O'Callaghan had represented Maryland and Joseph Keller Missouri. The third Jesuit, Brother Salvatore Berari, was on his way to join the Maryland Province. In the middle of its passage the ship encountered a severe storm that raged for several days. O'Callaghan risked his life at one point to go to the aid of a seaman who had fallen from a mast during the storm. The next morning, as they were attempting to read their breviaries below deck, a portion of the roof caved in, killing O'Callaghan and mortally wounding Berardi.[102]

O'Callaghan's death was but the latest of a series of losses of key personnel that the province had suffered over the past three decades. It had been widely expected that O'Callaghan would be the next provincial. Many

100. McAtee to Beckx, St. Thomas Manor, January 25, 1871, MD 10-XXII-1, ARSI.

101. Joseph Keller to Beckx, Baltimore, September 15, 1869, MD 10-II-3, ARSI.

102. *Navigatio funestra Patrum Procuratorum qui ex America Roman venerant, anno 1869*, MD 10-I, ARSI.

considered him the outstanding Jesuit in the province. Seven months after O'Callaghan was buried at sea, Keller was named to succeed Angelo Paresce. The Bavarian native Keller was shaken by the news: "I am truly punished," he wrote Beckx, "for having lost my companion at sea: if at least, he had left me his mantle and his spirit, it would be more easy to occupy his place."[103]

A month later Woodstock College opened. In the winter after Appomattox Paresce had acquired 139 acres of land fifteen miles west of Baltimore for $4,500 as a site for the first rural scholasticate in the Society.[104] Pressures had been building, as we have seen, to move the scholastics from a college setting. The economic costs of a rural scholasticate would be far smaller than those that had been increasingly taxing the province when the scholastics had been housed at Georgetown or at Boston.[105] There was also growing concern, at least in Rome, about the temptations of the city. On the general's instructions Father Paresce warned the scholastics in Boston in 1861 about visiting certain sections of the city, wearing secular clothes, and riding trains.[106]

What is unclear is why they purchased new land when there was abundant land available at Conewago. Paresce himself favored Conewago, but had been the only one to support that site during the Provincial Congregation in 1862. All the other delegates had supported Georgetown. "I scarcely suspected the extent of the opposition to Conewago," Paresce admitted.[107] Woodstock, half the distance that Conewago was from Georgetown, seems to have been a compromise.

The cost of the building was a prodigious $232,000, forcing the province to make an annual appeal in all its churches for money to retire the debt. But Missouri, now also a province, and the New York Mission (of the Canadian Province) had committed themselves to sending their scholastics to Woodstock for a common training. From Georgetown came the nucleus of a library

103. Keller to Beckx, St. Louis, August 7, 1869, *MD* 10-II-1, *ARSI*.

104. Patrick J. Dooley, "Woodstock and Its Makers," *WL* 56 (1927): 5.

105. The expenses for the scholasticate in Boston for the year 1861 were $17,440.02. That same year the farms produced only $14,961; Paresce to Beckx (1862), *MD* 8-V-9, *ARSI*. By 1862 the Boston operation represented over half the expenses of the province; Paresce to Beckx, Baltimore, February 16, 1863, *MD* 8-V-14, *ARSI*.

106. Baltimore, November 26, 1861, *MD* 8-V-13, *ARSI*.

107. Paresce to Beckx, Baltimore, October 13, 1862, *MD* 8-V-13, *ARSI*. At the time Paresce had been communicating with the Duchess of Leeds, a Carroll descendant, who was interested in donating to the Society land she held in Pennsylvania. Paresce thought that this would help support the scholasticate there. In 1863 she turned over the property to the province, but it added no weight, as it turned out, to Conewago as an option for the theologate.

and a faculty. Paresce moved out from Baltimore to become the first rector. Keller sent fourteen scholastics there the first year, despite the needs of the colleges for their services. By 1871 there were seventy-five scholastics there from Maryland, Missouri, and New York. That same year they published the first issue of *Woodstock Letters*, a journal encompassing historical articles and news reports on Jesuit activities in the country and the world.

The withdrawal of the scholastics had forced the colleges to turn to lay professors to fill the vacuum. Georgetown and Loyola each brought in four lay faculty; Gonzaga, Holy Cross, and Boston College each added three to their faculties. With the exception of Georgetown, the change was a substantial one, representing from one third to one half of the faculty. It was also a painful one, at least in Baltimore. James Ward, the prefect of studies at Loyola, thought that the "bringing in of laymen to teach our classes was a blow to the school that almost destroyed its character. The parents were displeased and withdrew their children of all grades."[108] The Loyola students themselves evidently did not share the feelings of these parents. They seem to have responded well to the lay faculty, on one occasion even giving them all gold canes.[109]

Father Provincial Keller was concerned about the need for curriculum change, as well. He favored the creation of separate business schools rather than the introduction of business classes into the existing colleges. None of the colleges attempted to heed the provincial superior's preference. Loyola College did reinstitute the commercial course, which had lapsed during the war. Holy Cross and Georgetown continued to offer the classical course only. Keller also advocated making the natural sciences and mathematics more prominent in the curriculum of the colleges. In America, he felt, it was more necessary to stress these disciplines than the Jesuits traditionally had done. The curricular changes taking place at Georgetown and elsewhere since the war gave him encouragement. "We are somewhat like France and England in that regard," he informed Beckx; "not yet on the same plane with those countries but we are approaching it and these studies form a great part of the course in all the colleges; in order to give influence to our men, it is one very useful means to make them very adept in the sciences."[110]

Loyola, by the 1870s, was including chemistry and physics in the course

108. Ward to Armellini, Baltimore, May 6, 1878, *MD* 10-XI-3, *ARSI*.

109. Varga, *Baltimore's Loyola*, 83.

110. Keller to Beckx, Baltimore, September 21, 1869, *MD* 10-II-4, *ARSI*.

of studies for its upper three classes. At Georgetown Patrick Healy, the prefect of studies, very much shared Keller's appreciation for the sciences and had made them an integral part of the curriculum. As early as 1869 Keller wanted Healy to become rector of Georgetown. Healy's genesis as the son of a Georgia planter and his common-law slave wife kept Rome from making the appointment. Finally in 1873, events in the form of the sudden death of the rector of Georgetown conspired to make Healy acting president of the institution, and a year later rector. Healy almost immediately began to pursue very ambitious plans for making Georgetown a university. The most visible symbol of that commitment was the magnificent Flemish Renaissance structure that Healy built on the east lawn of the campus. The project broke his health and nearly bankrupted the college, but the results spoke for themselves. "At Georgetown they are building at last," James Ward reported to Rome in May 1878. "The new building promises to be a very grand one & will present to the cityside an imposing appearance. Washington has changed so much for the better & extended its limits so far that you would not know it."[111] The city had incorporated the town of Georgetown in 1871. Healy was saying through his building that Georgetown was aspiring to be nothing less than a great university in a national city, such as Louvain, which had been the inspiration of both his architectural and educational vision.[112]

When Rome fell to the armies of *Risorgimento* in 1870, provincial superior Keller sent monies to the superior general Beckx for his support and an open offer to any Jesuits seeking sanctuary. "America is open to you," he wrote, "perhaps the only home left us in this world. We are looking for a large increase in our numbers."[113] A few additional Italians joined the province, but a larger consequence of the fall of the pope's last vestige of temporal power may have been attitudinal. "The afflictions of the Holy Father have made ultramontanes of all of us here who have any good within," Keller reported to Beckx in December 1870.[114] Earlier the provincial reported the attention that the topic of personal infallibility was getting in the journals:

111. Ward to Armellini, Baltimore, May 6, 1878, MD 10-XI-3, ARSI.

112. Keller at the same time was pursuing a plan to establish a Catholic university in Philadelphia through the auspices of the archbishop of that city. If successful, he wrote to the prelate, it "would make Philadelphia the educational headquarters of the whole country." The archbishop and his clergy, however, decided against the project; Francis X. Talbot, *Jesuit Education in Philadelphia*, 81–84.

113. Keller to Beckx, Baltimore, 21, May 1871, MD 10-II-17, ARSI.

114. Keller to Beckx, Baltimore, December 23, 1870, MD 10-II-14, ARSI.

We think that that article can be proclaimed by acclamation. Let it happen! For whoever knows well the idea of the Church as the body of Jesus Christ can not doubt for a moment the infallibility of its head. It is the head that directs, it is the head who speaks for all the members, and if the Church is infallible, she is so by her head . . . in a word in the Pope, as the visible head of the body.

Pardon that speech—I presume on your goodness and your sympathies: above all I ardently desire that a *coup de grace* will be dealt to those nonCatholicly catholic systems which exist in the Church as spies in the camp, as enemies disguised as friends.[115]

Keller's "speech" would have puzzled, if not embarrassed, John Carroll and his confreres of the Colonial and early national periods. For them infallibility was a character of the Church, not a personal charism of the pope. As late as 1849 charges were raised in the *Freeman's Journal* and elsewhere that Jesuits were not sufficiently obedient toward the pope, that the philosophy they taught gave too much autonomy to reason and led to infidelity. The European refugees, of whom Keller was one, undoubtedly set the intellectual life of the province in a much more conservative direction. Woodstock by the 1890s would be the intellectual center of the ultramontanist forces in the American Church.

In the course of the 1870s the number of Maryland Jesuits increased from 253 to 298. In 1879 that number nearly doubled when the New York Mission was joined to Maryland. For a long time Marylanders had complained about the fragmentation of the province, with New York wedged between New England and the rest. During the Civil War the Visitor, Felix Sopranis, proposed a fusion of the province and the mission, but the superior general, getting conflicting opinions from America, deferred any action. By 1871 there was a new factor, or rather an old one in a new place. Keller reported to Beckx that he had been startled by the depth of ethnic opposition he found at Woodstock between the Canadians and the Americans of the New York Mission. The provincial suggested that the Canadian houses be set up as a separate mission and the rest joined to Maryland. He also favored making the New York superior the head of the province. "The termination of that mission

115. Keller to Beckx, Baltimore, January 6, 1870, MD 10-II-7, ARSI. It is revealing to compare Keller's attitude to that of Brocard and his fellows in 1850 when the papal declaration of the doctrine of the Immaculate Conception was being considered. The American Jesuits urged that no such declaration be made for several reasons; Brocard to Roothaan, Georgetown, January 6, 1850, MD 8-II-21, ARSI.

would be less displeasing to them," he explained, and, citing a reason that Anthony Kohlmann would have applauded, "the seat of the Provincial ought shortly become the city of New York." As Keller envisioned the union, New York would strengthen "the spirit of religious discipline" (Keller had a lingering concern about the Maryland tradition) and Maryland would provide more English-speaking teachers for the New York colleges.[116] He might have added that New York had long since fulfilled Anthony Kohlmann's prediction and become, not only the largest and wealthiest city in the country, but the most important area of Catholic America, as well. The Society's future in the eastern United States lay primarily in New England and the Middle Atlantic region, of which New York was the center.

When the merger finally took place, the Maryland Provincial, Robert Brady, remained as superior. His curia, however, moved from Loyola College in Baltimore to the College of St. Francis Xavier on 15th Street in New York City. The name of the province was also changed to "New York." That was too much for the Marylanders. The next year the catalogue read: "Maryland–New York Province," a small victory for tradition, but no change in the reality that the center of gravity for the province, along with the power and influence, had shifted to New York from Maryland. The Maryland Province, as such, had run its course, completing a history that fell short of even a half century.

116. Keller to Beckx, Baltimore, May 21, 1871, *MD* 10-II-17, *ARSI*. By this time superiors were beginning to think in terms of organizing the Society more along ethnic lines. An ethnic enclave had already been established in 1869 with the formation of the Buffalo Mission, which was given territory with a heavy German presence, such as Buffalo, for its area of ministry.

Part 2

New York

Chapter 7

Prelude to "Americanism"

The New York Accadèmia and Clerical Radicalism in the Late Nineteenth Century

WHEN I WAS SEARCHING for a dissertation topic in the spring of 1970 my director at Yale, Sydney Ahlstrom, urged me to do a study of Michael Augustine Corrigan, Archbishop of New York from 1884 to 1902. There was a real need for such a study, Ahlstrom argued, since Corrrigan was the sole figure among the leading American Catholic prelates in the late nineteenth century who had not yet been the subject of a historical examination. I resisted my director's proposal, knowing all too well the frustrating experience of Gerald Fogarty, who four years earlier, as a student of Ahlstrom's, had been similarly encouraged to do his dissertation on Corrigan, only to discover that there was little or nothing in the archives of the Archdiocese of New York upon which to base any work on the archbishop. After Ahlstrom found one reason or other to deflect several alternate dissertation topics that I came up with, I reluctantly agreed to his original suggestion, swayed by his reasoning that, even if my research was restricted to what was available in the public record, a Corrigan study was worth taking up. Just to confirm that the New York Archives were indeed as essentially barren of relevant material as Fogarty had found them to be, I traveled the sixty miles from New Haven to Dunwoodie Seminary in Yonkers, where the archives were then located. As it happened, the librarian at Dunwoodie was temporarily doubling as archivist. He unlocked the door to the archives and informed me that I was free to work with whatever I found. Upon entering the room I was struck by a large pile of boxes in no particular order in one corner. Eventually I found my way to examining them. They proved to be a trove of material from the papers of several previous prelates of the archdiocese. Material from the Corrigan papers clearly dominated the pile. I later learned that the week before my visit, a faculty member at Dunwoodie had literally dumped the material there. He had, a good many years before, been asked to do a history of the archdiocese and had, during all that time, had these materials squirreled away in his room. He had very recently been reassigned from the seminary and had apparently abandoned any hope of completing an archdiocesan history. I, unlike Fogarty, had had the good fortune of showing up at just the right time to reap the suddenly accessible harvest of resources.

Among the pile of materials was the multi-volume diary that a New York priest, Richard Burtsell, had kept, off and on, from the 1860s through the 1890s. Perusing the early pages of that diary I learned of the informal ecclesiastical think tank that Burtsell and a group of fellow priests in the archdiocese had formed immediately following the Civil War to discuss religious and political issues. The "Accadèmia," as it came to be known in the upper circle of administration within the archdiocese, provided a window into the liberal mindset that Burtsell and his peers manifested in their pursuit of reform within the Church and nation. An earlier version of this essay appeared in *Church History* 47 (March 1978): 48–65.

The Republican Tradition Moves North

With John England's death in 1842 the republican tradition in Catholic America had essentially passed, as well. Twenty-five years later there were new stirrings of republicanism, not in the South where Carroll and England had advanced their vision of a republican Church, but in the North. Those stirrings proved to be short-lived, but they marked the emergence of an American Catholic liberalism in the postbellum period that culminated in the Americanist crisis in the last decade of the nineteenth century, precipitated by a group of liberal prelates and their associates to adapt Roman Catholicism to republican institutions and values in the face of conservative opposition. The history of a remarkable association of New York priests provides insight into the background of the Americanist controversy that better enables us to appreciate the peculiar lines that the episcopal struggle assumed. It makes clear that as early as the 1860s certain American priests were adumbrating the key issues that would constitute Americanism, and that these clerics had an important influence upon the conflict that tore apart the hierarchy in the 1890s.

By 1860 the American priest found himself a prime victim of the power struggle that the episcopacy had waged with the laity during the peak of trusteeism. Autocratic episcopal government might have been an effective means for preventing the schism of various ethnic groups and for consolidating the rapid expansion of the Church, but for the American priest it meant chiefly an erosion of his own authority and independence.[1] Groups of priests across the country began pressing for their full rights under canon law. One such group in the Cleveland diocese began to gather for monthly meetings in 1862 to discuss issues related to dogma, scripture, and moral theology, in addition to those regarding canon law. On the eve of the Vatican council its leader, Eugene O'Callaghan, wrote a series of articles under the *nom de plume* "Jus" for the New York *Freeman's Journal and Catholic Register* that called for an ecclesiastical process based upon canon law to replace the existing arbitrary system, in which bishops had the right to transfer or even dismiss priests at will. A thousand clerics responded to the *Journal* in support of "Jus."[2]

Elsewhere canonists such as Sebastian Smith of Newark took the bishops to task for failing to observe not only the provisions of canon law, but the hierarchy's own conciliar directives, as well.[3] Smith's *Notes on the Second Plenary Council*, published in 1874 (New York: P. O'Shea), became a rallying point for reformers, as had the "Jus" letters five years earlier. Smith was part of a loosely associated Newark clerical clique that pressured both James Roo-

1. For an analysis of this development, see Jay P. Dolan, *The Immigrant Church: New York's Irish and German Catholics, 1815–1865* (Baltimore: The Johns Hopkins University Press, 1975), 163–66. Dolan considers nineteenth-century Catholic theology, with its model of monarchial authority, to have provided the rationale for the new style of episcopal government and urbanization to have fostered its implementation in America.

2. For a short account, see Nelson Callaghan, *A Case for Due Process in the Church: Father Eugene O'Callaghan, American Pioneer of Dissent* (Staten Island, N.Y.: Alba Press, 1971).

3. Both priests and bishops used the law when it suited their interests and ignored it when it did not. That, at least, was the conclusion of George Conroy, the Irish bishop who was sent on a fact-finding mission to the United States in 1878 after Vatican officials decided they needed some better information to settle the numerous appeals they were getting from American priests against their ordinaries. Conroy found that few wished to abide by the body of laws set down by the old canon law or the Councils of Baltimore. For an excellent survey of this whole question of the relationship between episcopal and clerical rights, cf. Robert Trisco, "Bishops and Their Priests in the United States," in *The Catholic Priests in the United States: Historical Investigations*, ed. John Tracy Ellis (Collegeville, Minn.: St. John's University Press, 1971), 111–292.

sevelt Bayley and his successor, Michael Augustine Corrigan, to change their arbitrary administrative practices as ordinaries of that diocese.

The Accadèmia

The most notorious of these groups of clerical dissidents was one based in New York City and known, at least in chancery circles, as the Accadèmia. The focal point of conservative suspicions for over twenty years, the Accadèmia came to be regarded as the epitome of the unrest fomenting against the established order of American Catholicism, a cabal of liberalism in which the question of priests' rights was only the tip of an ideological iceberg that threatened the faith and polity of the Church. Although there was little or no contact among the Accadèmia and other groups of priests, conservative leaders like Corrigan and Bishop Bernard McQuaid became convinced that these groups were deviously promoting what amounted to a national conspiracy against episcopal authority.

The Accadèmia began in 1865 as an approved theological society of the Archdiocese of New York after the model of a society begun in London by Cardinal Manning. Under the initiative of Jeremiah Cummings, the first American graduate of the Urban College of the Sacred Congregation for the Propagation of the Faith (Propaganda Fide), and of Henry Brann, who had studied at the same college, the society was originally intended as a forum for the continuing theological education of the former Roman students in the area. From the outset, however, the society's meetings for the reading and discussion of original papers were open to all members of the clergy. After less than a year's existence, the society voted to disband, because many New York priests, according to one member, Richard Burtsell, found it dominated by abolitionists and those trained in Rome. At their last meeting the members appointed a committee to obtain Archbishop John McCloskey's approval for a new society, one presumably more representative and less dominated by Propagandists—those who had studied at the Urban College.[4]

4. Burtsell Diary (hereafter Diary), vol. 2, April 17, 1866, Archives of the Archdiocese of New York (hereafter AANY). Propagandists had two special privileges that tended to set them apart from their fellow clergy. First, they had the right of appeal to the pope upon being removed or disciplined by their ordinary. Second, their letters to Propaganda would not be returned to their ordinaries, as was the standard procedure. In fact they had the obligation of making annual reports to the Sacred Congregation, a tradition that many American bishops considered an undermining of their own authority.

A different version of the official Accadèmia's demise is given in an unsigned typed manu-

By the fall of 1866 Archbishop McCloskey had not yet taken any initiative toward setting up a new society, and Thomas Farrell, the pastor of St. Joseph's Church on Sixth Avenue, was privately threatening to set up his own theological group if the archbishop did not establish a similar body for his clergy when the prelate returned from the Second Plenary Council being held in Baltimore that fall.[5] Shortly thereafter Farrell began hosting almost weekly meetings at his rectory. The regular attendants were Farrell, Patrick McSweeny, Sylvester Malone, James Nilan, Thomas McLoughlin, Richard Burtsell, and Edward McGlynn, who would eventually become its most famous member with his controversial support of the economic reformer Henry George in 1886. On the periphery of the group were several Paulists, including the noted converts Isaac Hecker and Augustine L. Hewit, as well as John Moore, a Propagandist who was doing pastoral work in Florida and would later become bishop of St. Augustine. Most of them were young (Burtsell, McSweeny, Nilan, McGlynn, and Moore were in their twenties) and most had been trained in Rome.

We know all too little of their ideology during these years. Outside of Hecker, who was not a regular member, they published virtually nothing. A major source of our knowledge of their thought is the diary that Burtsell kept at the time.[6] We do know that the regular members prided themselves on their radical views. They supported Radical Reconstruction in the South and Fenianism in the North. They defended the public school as a legitimate educational environment for Catholic children. They were opposed to the temporal power of the pope and had open minds about the inspiration and inerrancy of the Scriptures, infallibility, celibacy, and many other topics that were considered beyond discussion in higher circles of the archdiocese.

Monsignor Thomas Preston, Burtsell's pastor during these years, later claimed that the aim of Farrell's Accadèmia was to "establish an American school of theology with liberal ideas" by minimizing the authority of the Holy See and adapting Catholicism to democratic forms and institutions.[7] Burtsell himself confessed to James Nilan in January 1867, about the time Farrell's

script housed in the Archdiocesan Archives of New York and entitled "Private Record of the Case of Rev. Edward J. McGlynn." According to this 1901 account McGlynn himself led the move to dissolve the society. Thereafter—in the "Private Record's" version—the Accadèmia, now limited to the McGlynn circle, drifted into heterodoxy (AANY 50–53, 517–25).

5. Diary, vol. 2, September 17, 1866, AANY.

6. Burtsell's diary for the years 1865–1868 has been published; see Nelson J. Callahan. ed., *The Diary of Richard L. Burtsell, Priest of New York: The Early Years, 1865–1868* (New York: Arno, 1978).

7. McGlynn, "Private Record," 521, AANY 50–53.

group was forming, that "a revision of the fundamental principles of theology" was badly needed and that he considered his theological studies to be commencing "*ab ovo*."[8] The genesis of Burtsell's radical approach to theology, as well as that of the other young priests in the group, apparently did not go back to any Roman education. Although they chafed under the authoritarianism of the Urban College and the aristocratic prejudice of the Roman clergy, especially the Jesuits, both Burtsell and McGlynn, by Burtsell's admission, had been staunchly conservative seminarians with very orthodox ideas.[9] The trauma of the Civil War was evidently the catalyst that radically committed them to American democracy and all its implications for the form that Catholicism should take in America.

As Michael Gannon has suggested, the Civil War was "a watershed in the maturation of the American Church," forcing bishops and priests to enter "national politics on an issue not directly affecting Catholicism as such."[10] This seems especially true of clerics like Burtsell, Malone, and McGlynn. When Henry Brann in 1865 excoriated the Protestant ministers, North and South, for having brought on the war, and praised Catholics for having "kept aloof altogether" from the sectional controversy that had dominated the 1850s, Burtsell's comment was that Catholics had done so "through cowardice, because we ought to have spoken in favor of the Union and the abolition of slavery."[11] Burtsell had returned to America in the bitterest year of the war—1862—and apparently was disconcerted by the Church's continuing failure to support emancipation as a war goal.

Sylvester Malone was a staunch and outspoken unionist in his Brooklyn parish, which was sharply divided about the war. After Appomattox a tour of the South committed Malone all the more to securing full justice for the freedman. Edward McGlynn had returned on the eve of the war in 1860. Before it was over he had charge of a floating parish in Central Park made up largely of Irish squatters and a hospital for Federal soldiers. He was there in July 1863 when the New York Irish began rioting and hanging blacks in protest of the draft laws. It was the perfect setting for some inescapable reflections on the meaning of the war.

8. Diary, vol. 3, January 25, 1867, AANY.

9. Diary, vol. 2, September 10, 1866, AANY.

10. Michael Gannon, "Before and After Modernism: the Intellectual Isolation of the American Priest," in Ellis, *Catholic Priest*, 311–12.

11. Diary, vol. 1, May 31, 1865, AANY.

Their war experiences evidently made them aware that their fellow Irish were still below the middle-class status that the families of the Accadèmia had attained. Moreover, these priests seemed to sense that the "new freedom" that Northern intellectuals saw coming to birth on the fields of Antietam, Gettysburg, and Cold Harbor raised new hopes for Irish nationalism, as well. Supporting the cause of the Fenians in abolishing English oppression was a natural commitment for one embracing the Radical Republican ideology.

When Brann expressed shock at Burtsell's mercurial change from the Roman conservatism to the radicalism he was exhibiting by the late 1860s, Burtsell told him: "I once thought rulers ought to take care of the people: in America I have learned that the people knows how to take care of itself."[12] Burtsell and his fellow reformers learned from the war experience of democracy in action, and drew conclusions for American Catholicism. The country had survived because of the basic wisdom and courage of the people themselves, and the structure and principles of the Church in America should be determined with the participation of its members. As with another generation of American Catholics a century later, political radicalism fostered religious radicalism.

The inspiration of Scripture and the infallibility of the pope were two doctrinal questions the members of the Accadèmia most frequently discussed. Regarding the former there was a range of opinions. For James Nilan, to call the Scriptures inspired meant no more than calling Dante's Divine Comedy "inspired."[13] Burtsell, on the other hand, thought that the Old and New Testaments were uniquely inspired and free of error insofar as they dealt with matters of faith and morals defined by the Church. All its members doubted the authenticity of the Genesis account of the fall of the first parents; indeed they held that there were probably more than one set of such parents, although they did not venture to consider evolution as a hypothesis.[14]

With Pius IX's definition of the dogma of the Immaculate Conception

12. Diary, vol. 3, January 25, 1867, AANY.

13. Diary, vol. 3, January 25, 1867, AANY.

14. "We doubted the inspiration of the history of our first parents' fall," Burtsell recorded, "and thought that many Adams may have been created, as long as the whole human race fell from original justice. The reasoning [of] Rom[ans]. 5 about sin entering by one man, is not of faith. . . . St. Paul's reasoning there is very illogical"; Diary, vol. 3, February 27, 1867, AANY. Strangely there is no mention of the theory of evolution although Hecker's *Catholic World* was taking up the issue during these years. This of course was before the publication of *The Descent of Man*, in which Darwin explicitly included man within his theory.

hardly more than a decade old, infallibility was a live topic. The Accadèmians found that neither dogma was sufficient to prove the other. Conversely they interpreted history to prove that the Church had earlier held that the pope could err in matters of faith. With their democratic convictions they preferred to profess a more traditional understanding of infallibility: that of the Church as opposed to that of the pope. They were uneasy with the definition of the Immaculate Conception precisely because it seemed to rest on the pope's unique infallibility. The latter claim was particularly unacceptable to Burtsell, because he interpreted it to include the pope's indirect power to depose sovereigns.[15]

Many of the practices of the Church they found exceedingly legalistic. Convinced that the material integrity of confession (the exact recitation of one's sins) had not been a prime concern for the Apostolic Church, they felt that their large congregations warranted the use of general absolution. It was absurd, Burtsell and McGlynn concluded, for a priest to waste five hours listening to "the tomfooleries of servant girls!"[16] Other practices such as the wearing of vestments and Latin masses they dismissed as medieval vestiges that had come to be considered peculiarly sacred. They were promoting the adoption of English in the popular devotions as the first step toward making the vernacular the normal language for the liturgy.

Most of the Accadèmians opposed mandatory celibacy, since it retarded emotional growth and tended to produce too many selfish and lonely priests. Eliminating this requirement, they reasoned, would attract more talented and attractive men to the priesthood. In the present dispensation the influence of the celibate clergy stemmed from "a superstitious reverence" on the part of the laity for a clerical mystique created by the priest's separation from the laity.[17] Religious orders they likewise found outmoded, stifled by their tra-

15. Diary, vol. 3, May 19, 1867, AANY. The theory of the pope's indirect temporal power asserted that while church and state are independent societies, the pope has the right to intervene in temporal affairs, even to the point of deposing heretical rulers, when the faith and morals of the people are endangered.

16. "If anyone wishes special advice," Burtsell suggested, "let him confess that special sin privately"; Diary, vol. 3, January 23, 1867, AANY.

17. Nilan, McSweeny, and Burtsell agreed that "celibacy never allows priests to become men, marriage sobers men at once: Celibacy brings lonesome hours to the priest: marriage would give him a perpetual object to be loved: Celibacy makes priests selfish: marriage would make him more social.... So few choose celibacy, that few smart and good men become priests. The Protestant clergy has more social influence than the Catholic"; Diary, vol. 2, July 21, 1866, AANY.

ditions and dominated by small-minded men whose vision was fixated on the past. Burtsell remarked in 1866 that he had once looked to the Jesuits as the leaders of the age; in the light of his subsequent experience he now saw them trying to "fossilize" Americans "with the habits of the Middle Ages." Hecker especially condemned the Jesuits' insistence on making all the decisions in their direction of others, thus stripping people of their responsibility in making moral judgments.[18]

The Accadèmians expected authority in the Church to be exercised in a manner suiting human maturity. "A diocese or the Universal Church is not to be governed as a large friary or college," Burtsell observed in a discussion with Patrick McSweeny in 1865.[19] Burtsell himself had nearly left the Urban College because of its authoritarian regimen. In democratic America the "boss rule" of a John Hughes appalled Burtsell and his colleagues all the more.[20] What especially irritated them were the growing efforts of the episcopacy to make laws governing the whole lifestyle of the clergy, from the prohibition of beards to the wearing of the Roman collar. This they saw as a further removal of the priest from the general life of the people, to be confined to a more cloistered range of activities closely monitored by his bishop. The contemporary style of authority, they were convinced, induced priests to look on bishops as demigods; the laity, in turn, had the same attitude toward priests. It was an enervating situation that impelled the Accadèmians to seek root changes that would revitalize the Church.

In brief, the Accadèmians believed that in America the Church had to be radically different from what it had been in the Old World. It had to be open to the uniqueness of its new milieu and reflect that milieu. If only the American Church could break out of its feudal patterns, there was no limit to its possible effect upon the country.[21] American Catholicism had to abandon its tradition of prudent silence on social questions and begin taking the lead in the reform movement. It had to cease its isolation from Protestants and its

18. Diary, vol. 3, December 31, 1866, AANY.

19. Diary, vol. 1, June 20, 1865, AANY.

20. When some New York priests approached Hughes about their rights under canon law, the prelate told them "that he would teach them [County] Monaghan canon law; he would send them back to the bogs whence they came"; Diary, vol. 1, July 26, 1865, AANY.

21. "We agreed," Burtsell wrote of a conversation he had with McGlynn in 1865, "that a different spirit is to be brought into the church's legislation. We have the country whence a new activity may spread throughout the whole Christian world. A little more democracy would be of use"; Diary, vol. 1, March 30, 1865, AANY.

condemnations of American groups like the Masons, simply on the basis of the reputations of their European counterparts.

By 1867 McGlynn was already preaching this "American Idea" from the secular pulpits that would make him a national figure over the next thirty years. Speaking in Cooper Union McGlynn alluded to the destiny God had given America by creating this continent on such a vast scale, preparing it for a "gigantic race of men not in physical but moral stature of enterprise, intelligence and virtue." To fulfill its destiny America had to become Catholic, McGlynn asserted, because Catholicism, unlike Protestantism, denied the total depravity of human nature, a doctrine that would ever impede human progress.[22] As Orestes Brownson wrote in the *Catholic World* that same year (and likely a chief source for McGlynn's remarks):

> there is no ground [in Protestantism] on which to assert the natural rights of man, for the fall has deprived man of all his natural rights; and for republican equality the reformation [sic] founds at best the aristocracy of grace, of the elect, as was . . . attempted to be realized . . . by the Puritans in New England, who confined the elective franchise and eligibility to the saints, which is repugnant to both civil and religious liberty for all men.[23]

The vision of McGlynn was that only under Catholicism could the country achieve its potential and realize true unity. To make this possible, the Church had to Americanize. "It will be [American] in spite of us," McGlynn warned.[24]

"A Class of Young Priests . . . Pretend[ing] to Know More Than the Church"

With these convictions it was inevitable that conflicts should have early arisen between members of the Accadèmia and the chancery. Burtsell and McGlynn became archdiocesan gadflies to spur the archbishop to more vigorous measures to serve the pressing spiritual needs of a growing immigrant population, among which were many Irish Catholics with little or no contact with the Church. The two priests continually pointed out the lack of churches and accused the chancery of underestimating the number of Catholics in the metropolitan area in order to justify the archdiocese's stand-pat policies.[25] In

22. Diary, vol. 3, April 28, 1867, AANY.

23. [Orestes Brownson], "The Church and Monarchy," *Catholic World* 4, no. 23 (February 1867): 638.

24. Diary, vol. 3, April 28, 1867, AANY.

25. Burtsell and McGlynn were arguing that the Catholic population of New York was at least

the archbishop's presence they charged him with being too remote from his people and allowing his clergy to live too luxuriously while spiritual necessities were going unheeded. They attacked the helter-skelter administration of the archdiocesan charitable institutions and the practice of charging fees for dispensations from the laws of the Church. If such fees had to be charged, they insisted that the revenue at least go toward building new churches and training additional priests. Sharing the misgivings of other New York Catholics about the prodigious growth of the parochial school system, Burtsell and McGlynn argued that the Church in New York was consuming too much money and energy in building and running schools at the expense of neglecting the religious ignorance of the vast numbers of poor immigrant Catholics in the city. Secular education, they contended, was the proper realm of the state, not the Church.[26]

Burtsell, McGlynn, and Nilan clashed with McCloskey over the latter's policy of denying the sacraments to the Fenian Brotherhood, the Irish-American organization dedicated to securing independence for Ireland. Not only did the three priests challenge the hierarchy's right to dictate politics to the Irish, but Burtsell and Nilan wrote a pamphlet setting forth the philosophical and theological justification for the Fenians' position.[27] Furthermore, the Accadèmians defended the Masons in the United States as a legitimate organization that should not fall under the Church's ban, inasmuch as it did not seek the overthrow of religion or the civil government, the reason for the Church's condemnation of the Masons in Europe. McGlynn and his colleagues also deepened the suspicions of conservatives by taking part in ecumenical affairs with Protestant clergymen, such as the Christian United Association. Cooperating with non-

---

500,000, whereas the archbishop contended it was not above 300,000; Diary, vol. 1, May 25, 1865, AANY. Donna Merwick, in her study of the Boston Archdiocese during this period, finds a similar pattern of polarization between a rising group of Irish-American clerics and a native-born archbishop (John Williams) hesitant to endanger the Church's standing with the Yankee community by responding in a dynamic fashion to the challenges that a rapidly growing immigrant population was raising for the structures of the Church and the larger society; Merwick, *Boston Priests, 1848–1910: A Study of Social and Intellectual Change* (Cambridge, Mass.: Harvard University Press, 1973), 61–93.

26. Diary, vol. 1, May 25, 1865, AANY. In that year seventy-five percent of the New York parishes had schools, with a total student population of 16,000. This was an estimated one-third of the Catholic children; Dolan, *Immigrant Church*, 105–08.

27. When Burtsell and Nilan visited Fenian headquarters in Union Square, the officers there were surprised to encounter two sympathetic priests; Diary, vol. 1, November 29, 1865, AANY. Rome subsequently condemned the Fenians as a secret society in January 1870.

Catholics in charitable work was a measure that even as intransigent a convert as Thomas Preston could and did conscientiously support. Joining with Protestants, often in liturgical settings, in pursuit of common traditions and values, was something quite different.[28]

With the pope's dominions in central Italy reduced to the environs of Rome, the temporal power of the pontiff was an especially sensitive issue. When Thomas Farrell publicly questioned certain papal prerogatives, including the temporal power, a special diocesan committee appointed to consider possible disciplinary action against Farrell voted unanimously for his removal from St. Joseph's, but the recommendation was stayed by McCloskey's perennial desire for peace.[29] Burtsell published a series of letters in the *Catholic Standard* of Philadelphia under the pseudonym "*Excelsius*" in which he attacked the attempt of the Papal States to preserve the temporal power of the pope by raising a loan in the United States. When McCloskey learned that Burtsell was *Excelsius*, he summoned him to express his objections to Burtsell's apparent direction and warned him against any future repetitions.[30]

By May of 1867 the members of the Accadèmia learned that the archbishop was decrying "a class of young priests" who "pretended to know more than the Church" knows.[31] Five months later he told the pastors of the archdiocese that the prevailing talk outside of New York held that some of his clergy were holding opinions condemned by the Holy See.[32] That same fall the Accadèmians considered abolishing their society, since imprudent members were leaking reports of their freewheeling discussions, and the group was widely regarded as systematically opposed to ecclesiastical authority.[33]

It is unclear how long Farrell's theological society lasted. In the wake of the ultramontane victory at Vatican I the intellectual and social ferment of the late 1860s ebbed, and the ebullient radicalism of most of the Accadèmians cooled with advancing age and vested interests within the archdiocesan bureaucracy. Burtsell, for instance, whom even McGlynn in 1866 had accused of being too imprudent in the expression of his radical ideas, had learned the

28. Burtsell was appalled when Archbishop McCloskey refused to take part in an ecumenical service for the assassinated president in April 1865 on the grounds that "it would not look well for him to be praying where Prot[estant] clergymen were present! Oh bright theology!" Burtsell commented, "Oh, cowardice! Does the Catholic Church forbid us to bless our countrymen!"; Diary, vol. 1, April 15, 1865, AANY.

29. McGlynn, "Private Record," 522–23, AANY 50–53.

30. Diary, vol. 3, February 18, 1867, AANY.

31. Diary, vol. 3, May 15, 1867, AANY.

32. Diary, vol. 3, October 8, 1867, AANY.

33. Diary, vol. 3, September 10, 1867, AANY.

lesson of discretion from his *Excelsius* experience, and thereafter was very cautious not to lose his influence within the archdiocese by provocative remarks. In time Archbishop McCloskey's suspicions were overcome, and promotions for the Accadèmia members began to follow. McGlynn was even chosen for the prestigious role of archpriest at the Mass in New York celebrating McCloskey's elevation to the cardinalate in 1875.

Nevertheless, stories of the unreconstructed views of Farrell's circle continued. In 1874 Cardinal Alessandro Barnabò, the prefect of Propaganda, instructed McCloskey to warn Burtsell and McGlynn about "the ultra liberal ideas they were indulging in."[34] James Nilan, who had begun a controversial school plan at his parish in Poughkeepsie under which the town government exercised certain controls over the school in return for certain subsidies, heard in 1883 that diocesan authorities were disturbed about bimonthly meetings that Nilan was sponsoring for his fellow priests in the area. Nilan felt constrained to explain that these meetings were not intended to rival the diocesan clergy conferences that had finally been reinstituted, but were merely designed to afford entertainment and stimulation of the mind.[35] Such assurances did little to assuage chancery suspicions that Nilan was reviving the Accadèmia in an upstate branch.

Edward McGlynn

By 1883 Edward McGlynn had publicly cast his lot with the radical Irish nationalists who had discovered Henry George as the messiah who would return the land to the people through his single-tax panacea. McGlynn played a key role in persuading Irish Americans that George's land doctrine was "good gospel, not only for Ireland, but for England, Scotland, and for America, too."[36] Whether through Michael Corrigan, who had in 1880 become

34. Cited in a letter from Archbishop Corrigan to Cardinal Giovanni Simeoni, October 12, 1888, draft, AANY, unclassified.

35. Nilan to Corrigan, Poughkeepsie, September 20, 1883, AANY, C-10.

36. Stephen Bell, *Rebel, Priest and Prophet: A Biography of Dr. Edward McGlynn* (New York: Devin-Adair, 1937), 26–27. By a fortuitous coincidence, Henry George's *Progress and Poverty* was published in the very year that the Land League was formed. The Land League was the result of the movement known as the "New Departure" that brought together the Home Rule forces of Charles Steward Parnell, the Irish proponents of social reform led by Michael Davitt, and the American Fenians under John Devoy. George's indictment of the land monopoly as the primary source of economic inequity had an enormous impact upon Irish-American reformers both here and in Ireland; cf. Thomas N. Brown, *Irish-American Nationalism, 1870–1890* (Philadelphia and New York: J. B. Lippincott, 1966).

McCloskey's heir in waiting, or Ella Edes, the American journalist in Rome who had close ties with both the Vatican Congregation for the Propagation of the Faith (Propaganda) and the New York chancery, Giovanni Simeoni, the cardinal prefect of Propaganda, received clippings of McGlynn's speech. The Vatican was then in the delicate process of trying to reestablish diplomatic relations with England. Having priests involved in the Irish question would certainly impede any rapprochement. Simeoni informed Corrigan that certain statements attributed to McGlynn regarding the ownership of land contained propositions opposed to the Church's teaching and advised that the clergy abstain from political disputes.[37] Shortly afterward a second epistle arrived from Propaganda communicating the pope's order to suspend McGlynn from his ministry unless McCloskey judged otherwise. Other prelates, such as Silas Chatard of Vincennes, Indiana, and William Henry Elder of Cincinnati, were urging McCloskey to take action against McGlynn. McCloskey did drop McGlynn without explanation from a key diocesan committee, but declined to impose any further sanctions upon him after McGlynn promised to abstain from future political gatherings.[38]

When McCloskey died in 1885, Corrigan as his successor came to be very much under the influence of those who were continuing to smell heterodoxy in the actions and motivations of McGlynn and his clerical associates. Corrigan's vicars general, Thomas Preston and Arthur Donnelly, and the former president of the first Accadèmia, Henry Brann, were three hardliners who most shaped Corrigan's response to McGlynn's support of Henry George during the mayoralty campaign of 1886 and the sequence of events that extended the controversy for the next eight years. The memories of the radicalism associated with the Accadèmia continued to color the interpretations that the archbishop and his advisors put upon the position of the clerical dissidents during the controversy. Corrigan, for instance, informed Cardinal Simeoni in November 1886 that McGlynn was persisting in preaching doctrines that were against Catholic teaching. He accused him of denigrating the pope and expounding the heresy that ministry "is not from the bishop but

37. Simeoni to Corrigan, Rome, August 9, 1882, AANY, 1–41. Propaganda was sending similar directives regarding clerical political abstinence to the Irish hierarchy during this summer.

38. McGlynn later claimed that he had voluntarily promised to refrain from making Land League speeches, "not because I acknowledge the right of any one to forbid me, but because I knew too well the power of my ecclesiastical superiors to impair and almost destroy my usefulness in the ministry of Christ's Church"; New York *Daily Tribune*, February 4, 1887.

derives its power from the laity," an impudent attempt, Corrigan thought, to democratize "sacred cult in the church" and to substitute George for Leo XIII as the "pontiff of a democratic church without dominion or tiara."[39] In another letter to Simeoni he claimed that McGlynn was denying the principle of *ex opere operato* in contending that the sacraments were valueless without the presence of love.[40]

When McGlynn issued a public statement denouncing the right of "Bishop, Propaganda, or Pope" to prevent him from exercising his civil rights as an American citizen, Corrigan concluded that "the poison of anti-Catholic opinions," which McGlynn had long cultivated in private, was now being spread openly.[41] In McGlynn's refusal to respond to the pope's summons to come to Rome in the spring of 1887 Corrigan found the heresy of denying the primacy of the pope in matters that pertain, not only to faith and morals, but also to the discipline and government of the Church throughout the world. Significantly, the archbishop on his visitations throughout the archdiocese that spring instructed congregations on the article of faith regarding papal primacy that Vatican I had declared.[42]

The excommunication of McGlynn in July 1887 for his failure to heed the pope's order only seemed to increase the threat of schism and made it all the more imperative to discipline the clerical friends of McGlynn who were main-

39. [Corrigan] to [Simeoni], New York, November 24, 1886, draft, AANY, unclassified.

40. Corrigan to Simeoni, March 18, 1887, draft, AANY, unclassified. The basis of Corrigan's charge was a letter that McGlynn had written to a Protestant minister at the time of the death of Henry Ward Beecher, one of the best-known Protestant clergymen. In his letter McGlynn had stated: "I am glad . . . that the theology of the old church agrees with his [Beecher's] in this, that the essence of religion is in communion with God through the love of Him for His own sake, and in loving all men for God's sake with the best love with which we love ourselves; and while sacrifice and sacrament, creed and ritual prayer and sermon and song, may be and are powerful helps and necessary manipulations of this religion, which is love; without it, they are a mockery, a sacrilege and a blasphemy"; New York *Daily Tribune*, March 14, 1887.

41. Corrigan to Preston, Nassau, February 11, 1887, AANY, unclassified.

42. The definition of the Vatican Council that the archbishop was citing against McGlynn read in part: "If anyone therefore says that the Roman Pontiff has only the office of inspection or direction, but not the full and supreme power of jurisdiction over the whole Church, not only in matters that pertain to faith and morals, but also in matters that pertain to the discipline and government of the Church throughout the whole world . . . or if anyone says that this power is not ordinary and immediate either over each and every church or over each and every shepherd and faithful member, let him be anathema"; *Constitutio de Ecclesia Christi*, *sessio* 4, *Conc. Vaticanum* 1869–170, in *Enchiridion Symbolorum Definitionum et Declarationum: De Rebus Fidei et Morum*, by Henricus Denziger, ed. Karl Rahner (Freiburg: Herder, 1955), 505.

taining contact with him and absolving Catholics who attended the weekly meetings of his Anti-Poverty society to listen to McGlynn's diatribes against "the ecclesiastical machine." In early 1888 Corrigan obtained instructions from Propaganda to impose silence upon McGlynn's clerical colleagues, forbidding them to advocate or discuss the theories of George or take part in the Anti-Poverty meetings. None of the other former members of the Accadèmia were promoting Georgian theories, but they persisted in asserting that McGlynn had been condemned without the due process guaranteed by canon law for economic doctrines on which the Church had made no pronouncement.

The chancery pressured the clerical friends of McGlynn in various ways, one of which was to threaten to examine the finances of their parishes. As early as October 1887 Corrigan had instructed his fiscal procurator to call Burtsell and Nilan to his court, presumably to examine their account books, "unless they can explain away their objectionable utterances on the Land Theory."[43] Another tactic was to eliminate them from key diocesan positions. Thus in November 1889 Burtsell was dropped as a synodal examiner. Nilan was removed from the school board, and McSweeney was discontinued as a diocesan consultor. Transferral of priests to upstate parishes ("The brains of the diocese are up the Hudson" became a common saying during the period), as well as a refusal to promote any priests who were sympathetic to McGlynn, were other sanctions that the chancery exercised.[44]

43. Corrigan to Bernard McQuaid, New York, October 4, 1888, Archives of the Diocese of Rochester (hereafter ADR). For some reason this instruction was not carried out, but another McGlynn supporter, Thomas Ducey, the pastor of St. Leo's on Twenty-Eighth Street, was subsequently ordered to turn over his books for examination. When the examination revealed a deficit of some forty thousand dollars a year, the diocesan consultors began to consider several options, including the removal of Ducey from St. Leo's and/or the closing of the parish. That the concern was not merely financial, however, is clearly evident in the minutes of the diocesan consultors for November 5, 1890, when they decided to defer action until they could study Ducey's next sermon; Corrigan to Ducey, New York, January 31, 1888, AANY, C-18; Corrigan to Ducey, New York, April 5, 1889, copy, AANY, C-18; Minutes of Meeting of Diocesan Consultors, Wednesday, November 5, 1890, AANY, unclassified.

The financial condition of St. Stephen's was also one of the reasons given by Corrigan to Propaganda for removing McGlynn as pastor in January 1887. In 1886 St. Stephen's showed an indebtedness of $154,464.54. Even McGlynn's friends admitted he was a poor administrator, but pointed out that he had reduced his church's debt by more than $142,000 during his last four years as pastor; Financial Report of St. Stephen's Church, 1886, AANY.

44. From the available evidence it is clear that at least six assistants were moved for their support of McGlynn. Chancery officials obviously regarded three parishes as strategic centers of McGlynnites among the clergy: St. Stephen's, Epiphany (Burtsell's church), and St. Leo's. Thus

Burtsell as "The Backbone of the Rebellion"

Since none of these measures successfully stifled the McGlynn controversy, Richard Burtsell drew increasing attention from archdiocesan officials as the major cause of the continuing dissent among the clergy. Burtsell was no McGlynn. He did not support the land theories of George or the Anti-Poverty Society. He was not going to take to the hustings to harangue "the ecclesiastical machine," nor was he about to lead a schism. The lesson of the *Excelsius* experience was now second nature to him. But he was deeply respected at home and in Rome for his understanding of Church law and, in a way, this made him a special menace to episcopal authority. Burtsell was continually a goad as a canonist, much in demand across the country to defend priests in their contests with ordinaries. His advocacy of priests' rights was making him a threat to episcopal authority far beyond New York. His book on *The Canonical Status of Priests* published in December 1887 had enhanced his influence.[45] Two months later he was a key witness in a suit brought against the trustees of St. Patrick's for refusing burial in the archdiocesan cemetery to a man who had died suddenly at an Anti-Poverty meeting, and contended that, since the archbishop had issued no regulation forbidding Catholics from attending the meetings, he could hardly deny Christian burial to someone who in good faith had gone to hear McGlynn. The church recognized, Burtsell maintained under questioning, that people could disobey out of good conscience.[46]

Chancery officials were sure that to allow Burtsell and his fellows to continue to preach about the rights of conscience of Anti-Poverty people would destroy ecclesiastical government in New York. When the archbishop subsequently made attendance at the meetings a case that priests had to refer to the

---

James Curran, John Barry, Thomas McLoughlin, and P. F. Maughan were transferred from St. Stephen's, John Power from the Epiphany, and Daniel Burke from St. Leo's.

45. "The whole tendency of the book is . . . calculated to do harm," Corrigan wrote his secretary, Charles McDonnell. What especially bothered the archbishop was a note inside the cover requesting recipients to send one dollar to a New York address for the creation of a fund that would be employed "for the defense of priests unjustly deprived of their ecclesiastical positions." The archbishop ordered Burtsell to withdraw it from publication, since he had not gotten his approval, but Burtsell claimed that he had not suspected that Corrigan would impose the normal regulations on a pamphlet that had already appeared in a Catholic newspaper (as a series of articles in the New York *Tablet* in the spring of 1887), had been privately printed, and was not for public sale; Corrigan to McDonnell, New York, December 15, 1887, copy, AANY, C-18; Corrigan to Burtsell, New York, December 14, 1887, copy, AANY, C-18; Diary, vol. 6, December 16, 1887, AANY.

46. Court Record, Philip McGuire vs. Trustees of St. Patrick's Cathedral, November 15, 1888, copy, AANY, unclassified.

chancery, Burtsell was finally forced to take a stand in the matter. In October 1889 he buried with full honors of the Church a woman parishioner who had been a regular attendant at the Anti-Poverty meetings.

Corrigan, convinced by now that Burtsell was "the backbone of the rebellion," transferred him to a parish in upstate New York; Burtsell thereupon appealed to Propaganda, as was his right as an alumnus.[47] Corrigan defended the necessity for removing Burtsell in an extrajudicial manner rather than going through the normal channels of censuring him for his disobedience. The experience of the McGlynn case was evidence enough for the archbishop that any outright attempt to suspend Burtsell would have renewed the turmoil and mass protest that McGlynn's suspension and removal had first ignited.[48]

Thomas Preston was confident that Rome would sustain Corrigan once more, but he was taking no chances. In early January 1890 he laid out to a Vatican official what was at stake in the Burtsell case. It was a question, he said

> of a few priests who are really disloyal to the Holy See. They minimize all the declarations of His Holiness. They were opposed to the Infallibility until its definition, and now are disposed to make it as little as possible consistent with a profession of faith. They are opposed to parochial schools. . . . They have spoken in favor of saying Mass in the English language, of doing away with the vestments and ceremonies prescribed by the church, of getting rid of what they call medieval customs and obsolete practices, and of Americanizing the Catholic Church here, and adapting it to our liberal and republican institutions.[49]

47. Corrigan to Ella Edes, New York, October 29, 1889, copy, AANY, C-18. In his *Canonical Status of Priests in the United States* Burtsell admitted that ordinary rectors like himself were removable at the will of the bishop, but "natural equity and the Plenary Councils and the Propaganda," he argued, "have interpreted that this 'will' must be determined by serious motives and be guided by anxious care to save the good name of any one affected by the removal." Since his removal as rector of the Epiphany would be interpreted as a punishment for some "serious wrongdoing," Burtsell contended that he had the right to a trial to preserve his reputation. Corrigan took shelter in the March 1887declaration of Propaganda that American bishops were not bound to follow the canonical procedure, so long as there was "serious reason for such action, and full account taken of the past merits"; *Canonical Status*, 46, 101; Burtsell to Corrigan, New York, December 16, 1889, AANY, C-18; Simeoni to Gibbons, Rome, May 20, 1887, Latin, printed copy, ADR; AANY, C-18, Corrigan to Burtsell, New York, December 17, 1889; AANY, C-18; Corrigan to Burtsell, New York, December 21, 1889, copy, AANY, C-18.

48. *Relatio Translationis Statutae Quidem, sed Nundum Peractae, Doctoris Richardi L. Burtsell, Rectoris Amovibilis Ad Nutum Ab Ecclesia Epiphaniae Ad Ecclesiam Sanctae Mariae, Et Ejusdem Doctoris Recursus ad Superiorem* (1890), AANY, unclassified.

49. Preston to Archbishop Domenico Jacobini, New York, January 2, 1890, copy, AANY, S-1.

Burtsell was unable to prevent his own transfer, but Francisco Satolli, the apostolic delegate sent to America by Leo XIII in the fall of 1892, revived the hopes of the old radicals for the Americanization of the Church, especially when clerical dissidents, including McGlynn, found Satolli an effective court of appeal against their ordinaries. When the delegate lifted the excommunication against McGlynn shortly before Christmas of 1892, the New York *Tribune* found that it meant that American Catholicism was finally "adjusting to the free institutions of the country." Hereafter, it predicted, "the priests of the Church will enjoy a freedom of utterance and action that in many cases has heretofore been denied them, and the whole church will grow into closer touch with American life and institutions. The ultra-montane type of Churchmanship in this country has received a serious blow from which it may never recover."[50]

It was poor prophecy, for the McGlynn restoration was to be the high-water mark for the dissidents in New York and elsewhere. Archbishop Corrigan's exploitation of divisions within the Roman curia was to be instrumental in ending the alliance between the American liberals and the apostolic delegate.[51] Richard Burtsell experienced at firsthand the changing climate in Rome toward the American liberals in the fall and winter of 1893–1894. After being kept waiting for nearly eight months while trying to obtain a hearing for himself and a parish for McGlynn, he came away with nothing more than some advice from a Vatican official that Americans like himself were wasting their time in trying to "bring Republicanism into the Church."[52]

The Accadèmia and the Americanists

By the 1890s Burtsell, McGlynn, and Hecker had come to be largely pawns of a new movement toward liberalism that derived its leadership from the hierarchy itself, notably Archbishop John Ireland of St. Paul and Bishop John Keane of the Catholic University of America. Ireland and Keane's attempt to intervene with Vatican officials regarding the McGlynn case in 1886 had been one of the first skirmishes in the ideological struggle that was dividing the American hierarchy into liberal and conservative camps in the last decade of the century. Already in 1890 Corrigan was warning Rome of the "ultra-Americanism" of the

50. *New York Tribune*, December 25, 1892.

51. For an analysis of this strategy, see Robert Emmett Curran, *Michael Augustine Corrigan and the Shaping of Conservative Catholicism in America*, 1878–1902 (New York: Arno Press, 1978), 422–27.

52. Diary, vol. 9, May 5, 1894, AANY.

liberal party that he saw Ireland and other prelates forming. To Corrigan, Preston, and their conservative allies, the Americanist movement of Ireland and the liberal prelates was the natural outgrowth of the clerical radicalism that had first manifested itself in the sixties.

The relationship of the Accadèmians to the Americanists is an intriguing one. Sylvester Malone was a close friend of John Ireland, although how much the latter knew of the Accadèmia is uncertain. Beginning in 1887 Richard Burtsell had regular contact with the Americanist prelates. The two groups took basically similar stands regarding secret societies, the rapid Americanization of immigrants, and parochial schools. It is significant that John Ireland adopted James Nilan's Poughkeepsie Plan as the model for his own controversial school arrangements in Minnesota in 1891. Both groups tended to play down the relevance of religious orders in a democratic society. They both were pressing for some form of democratization in the Church to enable it to internalize the values of individual initiative and freedom that they saw as the hallmarks of American life. While the Americanists restricted their reform aims largely to Church polity, the Accadèmians were raising some basic doctrinal questions that foreshadowed the Modernist crisis in Europe a few years after the Americanist controversy. Changes in the discipline and liturgical life of the Church were also questions that went beyond the concerns of most Americanists, although Denis O'Connell's proposal of substituting the common law as a much more appropriate basis than Roman law for the law of the Church had implications for the reform of ecclesiastical discipline that would have been much more radical than the demand of the Accademians for the full institution of canon law in this country.[53]

Both groups favored the Republican Party, but by the 1890s the GOP had shed any radical idealism that had attracted the Accadèmians. It now stood unequivocally for the new capitalism that Ireland thought to be the foundation for the success of American democracy.

Both the Accadèmians and the Americanists accepted the separation of church and state as the ideal environment in which the Church could grow in America. An inference of the liberal program as developed by Ireland was that the American Church under liberal leadership would obtain a favored position because of the liberals' ties with the Republicans, and Americanists

53. Cf. Gerald F. Fogarty, S.J., *The Vatican and the Americanist Crisis: Denis J. O'Connell, American Agent in Rome, 1885–1903* (Rome: Università Gregoriana Editrice, 1973), 263–65.

successfully used this argument in certain Vatican circles in the early 1890s to win papal support for their claims to serve as brokers between Washington and Rome. Such posturing was alien to the concept of church and state that the Accadèmians had developed in the 1860s. The Americanists, moreover, went much further than the Accadèmians in touting the American experience as a paradigm for the rest of the world, including the Church universal. Just as the American triumph over Spain in 1898 signaled to Americanists like O'Connell that the axis of civilization was providentially passing from Europe to America, so too were they confident that the American Church was to be the fulcrum for the Roman Catholicism of the twentieth century. The Americanists unmistakably manifest a cultural imperialism that makes *Testem Benevolentiae*, Leo XIII's encyclical condemning Americanism in 1899, seem a mixed blessing.

No doubt the euphoria of the Spanish-American War accounts for some of the jingoism of O'Connell and Keane in the late nineties, but they seem never to have realized how much ethnocentrism colored both their geopolitical and georeligious thinking. They would have done well to heed the warning that Orestes Brownson raised in *Catholic World* in 1867 about such culturally bound ideology:

> The mistake is that people are too ready to make a religion of their politics, and to seek to make the system of government they happen to be enamored of... a universal system, and to look upon all nations that do not accept it, or are not blessed with it, as deprived of the advantages of civil society. They make their system the standard by which all institutions, all men and nations are to be tried.... Our government is best for us, but that does not prove that in political matters we are wiser or better than other civilized nations, or that we have the right to set ourselves up as the model nation of the world.[54]

With *Testem Benevolentiae* the liberal prelates got the same message that Burtsell had received in Rome in 1894, and they quietly abandoned their movement. Despite this setback, the first years of the new century saw an intellectual fermentation in the Catholic University and several seminaries that promised to renew the spirit of theological openness and investigation that had marked the Accadèmia. The outstanding forum for this renewal was appropriately enough the *New York Review*, which began in 1905 at St. Joseph's Seminary in Yonkers under the spirited sponsorship of Archbishop John Far-

54. [Brownson], "The Church and Monarchy," 639.

ley, Corrigan's successor. The first scientific Catholic theological journal in America, the *Review*, its editor promised, would "interpret with becoming care and reverence the old truths in the light of the new science."[55] Major contributors to the *Review* were three of St. Joseph's faculty: the editor, James F. Driscoll, professor of Semitic languages; Joseph Bruneau, professor of dogmatic theology; and Francis E. Gigot, the leading Catholic Scripture scholar in America.

The *Review* lasted but three years, a victim of the repression that quickly set in after another papal condemnation of an intellectual movement, the renunciation of Modernism by Pope Pius X in his 1907 encyclical *Pascendi Dominici Gregis*. The double condemnation of Americanism and Modernism had a devastating impact upon the intellectual awakening among American Catholics. As the historian Michael Gannon judged:

> Free intellectual inquiry in ecclesiastical circles came to a virtual standstill. The nascent intellectual movement went underground or died. Contacts with Protestant and secular thinkers were broken off. It was as though someone had pulled a switch and the lights had failed all across the American Catholic landscape.[56]

To extend the metaphor, when the lights, after a blackout of half a century, finally began to come back on in the 1960s, one could recognize shafts of intellectual inquiry that the Accadèmia had explored a century before.

55. James F. Driscoll, S.S., quoted in Gannon, "Before and After Modernism," 334.
56. Gannon, "Before and After Modernism," 341.

Chapter 8

The McGlynn Affair and the Shaping of the New Conservatism in American Catholicism, 1886–1899

EDWARD MCGLYNN, the New York priest who was excommunicated in the 1880s as a result of his support of the economic reformer Henry George, arguably represented the pinnacle of dissent within the American Catholic community in the nineteenth century. Certainly the protest movement that formed around McGlynn had the most consequential effects upon recasting the ideological leanings of the American hierarchy by the last decade of that century. The following chapter attempts to examine "The McGlynn Affair" within its larger ecclesiastical context and to point to the impact it had upon the formation of the episcopal bloc that epitomized the conservative ascendancy within Catholic America. This essay originally appeared in *The Catholic Historical Review* in its April 1980 issue. It has been slightly modified.

"All the Furies Let Loose"

On a Saturday night in June 1887, an estimated 75,000 people marched in the streets of New York in protest of Edward McGlynn's suspension from his priestly ministry for his support of Henry George. A week later George was telling the thousands who packed the Academy of Music that the mass demonstrations taking place in New York, Chicago, and elsewhere were a resounding message to Michael A. Corrigan, Archbishop of New York, and his backers that they could not isolate McGlynn by the threat of excommunication.[1] Another McGlynn partisan noted: "I think they will have to excommunicate some millions of American Catholics."[2] Recalling those days of protest, Maurice Francis Egan, who had been editor of the New York *Freedman's Journal and Catholic Register* in 1887, described the atmosphere of the city as one of a society reduced to near anarchy with "all the furies let loose."[3]

The controversy between Edward McGlynn and Archbishop Corrigan constitutes one of the most significant cases of dissent within the American Catholic community of the late nineteenth century. Its full significance, however, lies within an appreciation of the tapestry of issues that increasingly polarized the Church after the Third Plenary Council of Baltimore in 1884. For the struggle between the Corriganites and the McGlynnites far transcended the economic theory of Henry George or socialism or the civil rights of American Catholic priests. What made the McGlynn affair so extraordinary, and gave it such staying power as a controversy, was the number of key issues that made up the sum of its parts. It touched upon, among other things, social reform, Irish nationalism, parochial schools, the relationship between church and state, and the polity and identity of American Catholicism. Among the

1. New York *Herald*, June 27, 1887.

2. New York *Herald*, July 4, 1887.

3. Maurice Francis Egan, *Recollections of a Happy Life* (New York: George H. Doran, 1924), 133. A substantial body of literature exists on the McGlynn affair. Stephen Bell's *Rebel, Priest and Prophet: A Biography of Dr. Edward McGlynn* (New York: Devin-Adair, 1937), is useful, but the author's limited sources (mainly newspaper accounts and interviews) enable him to tell little of the internal history of the case. James Roohan makes an illuminating study of McGlynn's relation to the development of Catholic attitudes on social reform in his 1952 Yale dissertation, later published as *American Catholics and the Social Question, 1865–1900* (New York: Arno Press, 1976), 322–83. James Jeremiah Green's "The Impact of Henry George's theories on American Catholics" (Ph.D. diss., University of Notre Dame, 1956) is a related treatment of McGlynn's connection with George. Two extensive accounts of the affair are in John Tracy Ellis, *The Life of James Cardinal Gibbons, 1834–1921* (Milwaukee: Bruce Publishing, 1952), 1:549–628, and Frederick J. Zwierlein, *The Life and Letters of Bishop McQuaid, prefaced with The History of Catholic Rochester Before His Episcopate* (Rochester: Art Print Shop, 1927), 3:1–83. For the campaign of 1886 see particularly Charles Barker, *Henry George* (New York: Oxford University Press, 1955). For McGlynn's relationship with the radical Irish nationalists, see Thomas N. Brown, *Irish-American Nationalism, 1870–1890* (Philadelphia and New York: J. B. Lippincott, 1966), 133–51. A rich source for the Roman involvement in the case is Alfred Isaccsson, O.Carm. *The Determined Doctor: The Story of Edward McGlynn* (Tarrytown, N.Y.: nd). With the exception of the last-mentioned, none of the above pursues the developments beyond 1892. A wealth of relevant source-material is contained in an unsigned, typed document under the title "The Private Record of the Case of Rev. Edward J. McGlynn," a 1901 manuscript in the archives of the Archdiocese of New York. This article utilizes much of the latter material as does also Robert Emmett Curran, *Michael Augustine Corrigan and the Shaping of Conservative Catholicism in America, 1878–1902* (New York: Arno Press, 1978).

factors that began to divide liberal and conservative Catholics in the late 1880s, none was as important as the McGlynn affair in setting in motion the synergistic effects that recast American Catholicism by the end of the century.

Edward McGlynn in 1886 was pastor of St. Stephen's Church on East 28th Street between Lexington and Third Avenues, the largest and one of the most prestigious parishes in the city. As an activist who for twenty years had been working for social reform, McGlynn was extremely popular among New Yorkers, both Catholic and non-Catholic. His parish operations, the largest of which was the St. Stephen's Home for over 500 children, were a forerunner of the methods of the institutional churches that would be the major instrument of the Social Gospel movement among American Protestants later in the century. Intelligent as well as indefatigable, McGlynn's forte was on the speaking platform in the best tradition of revivalism before it parted ways with social reform. He was one of the most charismatic speakers of his day.

In 1882 McGlynn had begun preaching the gospel of Henry George for the radical Irish nationalists in New York. George's indictment of the land monopoly as the primary source of economic inequity had an enormous impact upon Irish reformers, both in America and in Ireland in the 1880s. The Holy See, at the same time, was in the delicate process of trying to reestablish diplomatic relations with England. Even though Rome was unwilling, as a *quid pro quo* for renewed relations, to condemn the Land League's efforts to secure land reform in Ireland, at the very least it did not want priests promoting the movement, especially those whose politics were as socialistic as McGlynn's seemed.[4] Cardinal Giovanni Simeoni, Prefect of the Congregation for the Propagation of the Faith (Propaganda), accordingly instructed Archbishop Corrigan, at that time coadjutor to Cardinal John McCloskey, that certain statements attributed to McGlynn "contained propositions openly opposed to the teachings of the Catholic Church." Simeoni directed that McGlynn abandon his political activities.[5] McCloskey reluctantly rebuked the priest for

4. Bishop Herbert Vaughan to Corrigan, Salford, December 17, 1881, AANY, C-3; Vaughan to Corrigan, Salford, February 2, 1882, AANY, C-3; see Emmet Larkin, *The Roman Catholic Church and the Creation of the Modern Irish State: 1878–1886* (Philadelphia: American Philosophical Society, 1975).

5. Simeoni to Corrigan, Rome, August 9, 1882, AANY, I-41. Propaganda was sending similar directives concerning political abstinence for the clergy to the Irish hierarchy during this summer.

Bernard Smith, an Irish Benedictine in Rome and an agent for Archbishop Corrigan, was also the contact for Irish Catholic Whigs who were attempting to secure papal condemnation of the Land League in exchange for diplomatic relations with England. It is likely that Smith was using his influence with Simeoni; see Larkin, *Roman Catholic Church*, 59–60.

his "socialistic" addresses, and McGlynn promised to abstain from all future political gatherings.[6]

Within a short time McGlynn drifted back to the political circuit, but the plenary council of 1884 was absorbing too much of the energy of his ecclesiastical superiors for them to pay close attention to him. By the summer of 1886 McGlynn was fully involved in Henry George's campaign for mayor of New York.

The political atmosphere was especially tense, 1886 marking the height of the second of three social earthquakes that shook the country to its core in the last quarter of the century. As in 1877, railroad strikes had swept across the country, often leaving a wake of violence and fears of class warfare. By 1886 the meteoric rise of the Knights of Labor, through a series of successful strikes, gave substance to the fears. The mayoralty campaign of George was bringing together in an explosive mix the various elements of Irish nationalism, the labor movement, and socialism. Patrick Ford gave George the support of the *Irish World* and toured the tenement districts with him. Terrence V. Powderly, the Knights' Grand Master Workman, came into the city to make speeches on George's behalf. Daniel DeLeon, the radical socialist at Columbia University, as well as Walter Rauschenbusch and Heber Newton, the liberal Protestant reformers, were in his camp. But none was more key to his success than McGlynn.

The New York Church and the Democratic Party

When one considers the tenuous balance of power that prevailed between the two national parties in the middle 1880s and the vital position that New York City occupied in that equilibrium, it becomes clear what a threat the George campaign represented to Tammany Hall and the Democratic Party. The source of Democratic power in New York was the vote of the Irish Americans. In 1886 they most likely already constituted a majority of the population.[7] Reformers and Irish nationalists had for years been trying in vain to wean the Irish from their loyalty to Tammany and the Democrats. McGlynn

6. Corrigan to Archbishop William Henry Elder, New York, September 18, 1882, Archives of the Archdiocese of Cincinnati.

7. The census of 1890 lists 190,000 Irish-born New York inhabitants out of a total population of 1,489,000. Another 409,000 were second-generation Irish. Beyond these were a considerable number of third- and fourth-generation Irish not identified in the report; William V. Shannon, *The American Irish* (New York: Macmillan, 1966), 760.

was an ideal nurse for the weaning. A longtime Republican, his credentials of concern for the poor and the Irish were impeccable, his standing in those communities unequaled by that of any other Catholic spokesman in New York. His effectiveness in promoting George in the fall of 1886 brought a letter from a Tammany leader to Corrigan's vicar-general, Monsignor Thomas Preston, seeking confirmation that the Catholic Church in New York was not endorsing George's candidacy. Preston obliged by declaring that "the great majority of the Catholic clergy in this city are opposed to the candidacy of Mr. George."[8]

Understandably Tammany made full use of Preston's condemnation of George in trying to offset McGlynn's inroads upon their traditional constituency. Who benefitted the most from this ploy is a moot point, since some Catholics apparently voted for George in reaction to the chancery's heavy-handed attack upon McGlynn. The Tammany candidate prevailed in the election, but George's remarkably strong showing convinced many that McGlynn's influence had been a major factor.[9] Reports later circulated that several Catholic laymen with connections to Tammany were responsible for Corrigan's suspension of McGlynn during the campaign. Bourke Cockran, a prominent Tammany politician, boasted that he had convinced the archbishop of the danger of George's candidacy.[10]

Although the archbishop rightly resented the charge that he was in Tammany's keep, he did have close ties with several Tammany figures and was well aware of the local Democrats' longtime support of state aid for Catholic charitable institutions. Corrigan's own background and status predisposed him to have little understanding of the labor movement and of reformers. William Shannon, in his study of the American Irish, observed that the Catholic hierarchy in New York tended to be extremely conservative, primarily because of the accidents of personality. But he suggested that another important cause was the fact that the Irish first captured political power in New York and built up a substantial group of upper-middle-class property owners. Corrigan's world was really limited to this class. His own father, an immi-

8. Thomas Preston to J. O'Donoghue, New York, October 26, 1886, cited in Zwierlein, *Life and Letters of Bishop McQuaid*, 3:6–7, quoting the Rochester *Union and Advertiser*, October 29, 1886.

9. George polled at least 68,000 votes against the regular Democrat, Abraham Hewitt. (The Republican candidate, Theodore Roosevelt, finished third.) Many had serious doubts about the honesty of the votes.

10. Bell, *Rebel, Priest, and Prophet*, 35.

grant who through his grocery business and real estate interests became one of the richest men in Newark, was a perfect illustration for Russell Conwell's thesis that the resourceful could mine "acres of diamonds" in their backyards. Thanks to his father, the archbishop himself was now a man of considerable wealth. He could appreciate the concerns of men of substance about the need to conserve the fabric of society from the attacks of socialists and liberals. He was particularly sensitive to their concerns as contributors to the many churches, schools, and other institutions that the Church was racing to put up in New York to keep pace with a Catholic population that was swelling each year from immigration and a high birth rate. In a year of labor uprisings and fears of impending class warfare, he shared the alarm of many conservatives over McGlynn's support of apparently socialistic reform methods.

Suspension and Excommunication

Corrigan needed no prodding from the Democratic machine to take action against McGlynn. He had begun to pressure the priest to desist from his support of George even before the latter's formal nomination on September 23. On August 21, in a letter to McGlynn, the archbishop expressed his uneasiness about the newspapers' reports of the priest's relations with George and urged him to "leave aside anything that . . . would *seem* even to coincide with socialism."[11] When he learned that McGlynn was to address a mass rally in the city on October 1, he forbade him to take part in future political meetings without permission from Propaganda.[12] McGlynn promised to sit out any further political campaigning, but he felt obliged to fulfill his commitment at Chickering Hall.[13] There McGlynn proceeded to anoint George as "the most unselfish man of this country, formed by providence to preach the new gospel."[14] The next day Corrigan privately suspended McGlynn from his priestly duties for two weeks for "so flagrant an act of disobedience," noting that the censure had "nothing whatever to do with this or that political party,

11. Corrigan to McGlynn, New York, August 21, 1886, printed in the New York *Daily Tribune*, February 4, 1887.

12. Corrigan to McGlynn, New York, September 29, 1886, copy, AANY, unclassified. Ironically the archbishop had not hesitated to use McGlynn's political influence six months previously, when he asked him to intercede with President Cleveland on behalf of General John Newton, who was seeking a promotion; McGlynn to Corrigan, New York, March 11, 1886, AANY, C-10.

13. McGlynn to Corrigan, New York, October 1, 1886, AANY, C-10.

14. Burtsell Diary, vol. 6, October 1, 1886.

but is founded on the instructions of the Holy See, and the nature of Episcopal authority and sacerdotal obedience."[15]

The archbishop had already written to Rome about McGlynn's latest political activities. When in late November Corrigan once again suspended McGlynn for a newspaper interview in which the priest urged people to read *Progress and Poverty*, the archbishop informed Cardinal Simeoni that McGlynn was persisting in preaching doctrines that were both against Catholic teaching and unacceptable to the vast majority of the American people. Furthermore Corrigan accused McGlynn of denigrating the pope and expounding the heresy that "ministry is not from the bishop but derives all its power from the laity."[16] The increasing attention the press gave to McGlynn led Corrigan to cable Rome at the beginning of December for some prompt action.[17] On December 4 the cardinal prefect of Propaganda cabled Corrigan to have McGlynn proceed immediately to Rome. In January the pope himself issued the same order and took personal charge of the case.[18]

McGlynn maintained that he was unable to go to Rome for three reasons: his poor health, his slender financial resources, and family obligations. In addition, he adamantly insisted to the archbishop that he would continue to teach "as long as I live, that . . . private ownership of land is against natural justice, no matter by what civil or ecclesiastical laws it may be sanctioned," and that he would, if given the chance, confiscate all private property in land "without one penny of compensation to the mis-called owners."[19] He denied the right of anyone, "Bishop, Propaganda or Pope," to punish him for opinions in political economy that had not been condemned by the Church.[20]

In May 1887, Leo approved Archbishop Corrigan's attempt to "crush the vicious seeds of doctrines, scattered under the pretext of helping the masses," and ordered McGlynn to repair to Rome within forty days under pain of excommunication.[21] McGlynn pleaded conscience over obedience and was excommunicated in July.

15. Corrigan to McGlynn, New York, October 2, 1886, AANY, unclassified. The suspension itself did not become a public issue until after the election.

16. [Corrigan] to [Simeoni], New York, November 24, 1886, AANY, unclassified.

17. Corrigan to Simeoni, New York, December 24, 1886, abstract, AANY, unclassified.

18. "Private Record," 21, AANY, L-3.

19. McGlynn to Corrigan, New York, December 20, 1886, AANY, C-10.

20. New York *Daily Tribune*, February 4, 1887.

21. Leo XIII to Corrigan, May 4, 1887, duplicate, AANY H-5; Simeoni to McGlynn, Rome, May 4, 1887, copy, AANY, H-5.

The Stakes in the McGlynn Affair

To grasp the full impact of the McGlynn affair, one must appreciate the extent to which it developed out of a background of growing fear among a sizable portion of American bishops and priests of the mounting liberalism within the American Church. Since the late 1870s a conservative bloc had been forming in reaction to Roman legislation advancing priests' rights and abetting the incipient liberalism among the clergy that was threatening to undermine episcopal authority.[22] Prelates like Bernard McQuaid of Rochester and Richard Gilmour of Cleveland began to press for concerted action within the hierarchy that would utilize Rome to bring about uniformity under a strong episcopacy within the Church in America, while maintaining a certain independence from Rome. The question of priests' rights, they were convinced, was merely a symptom of more deeply rooted dissent. For the past twenty-five years they had experienced groups of priests fomenting unrest against the established order and allegedly questioning everything from celibacy to the inspiration of Scriptures.

Edward McGlynn had long been one of the most celebrated dissidents. As the previous chapter noted, he was the outstanding member of a group of New York priests who had become notorious for their radical ideas regarding politics, theology, and the Americanization of the Church. As early as 1867 McGlynn was publicly proclaiming that the Church in America had to be radically different from what it had been in the Old World. In 1870 he created his first sensation by attacking all public aid to religious institutions as a violation of the separation of church and state and by insisting that the Church was misdirecting its energies in trying to build and maintain schools.[23] Four years later the Cardinal Prefect of Propaganda, Alessandro Barnabò, warned him about "the ultra liberal ideas" he was espousing.[24]

In 1882 McGlynn had defied the warning of chancery officials in Cleveland not to speak to an Irish American group there, the Parnell Branch of the Land League, whose women members had incurred Bishop Gilmour's excommunication for promoting revolutionary politics. When Cardinal Mc-

22. For an excellent treatment of the impact of this legislation, see Robert Trisco, "Bishops and Their Priests in the United States," in *The Catholic Priest in the United States: Historical Investigations*, ed. John Tracy Ellis (Collegeville, Minn.: St John's University Press, 1971), 194–292.

23. Report of Thomas F. Lynch (n.d.), AANY, unclassified.

24. Cited in a letter from Corrigan to Cardinal Giovanni Simeoni, October 12, 1888, draft, AANY, unclassified.

Closkey was unwilling to order McGlynn to refrain from going to Cleveland, several bishops had seen signs of an impending authority crisis. As William Elder of Cincinnati wrote Corrigan, "if this act of Dr. McGlynn's should pass without adequate reparation, it would be the most disastrous blow to discipline, and to faith itself." He urged Corrigan to persuade the cardinal to take appropriate action before McGlynn's "poison" had sunk further into the "minds and hearts of the people, perplexing and perverting their ideas of justice, property, of deference for the Church."[25] Cardinal McCloskey, as noted above, eventually reprimanded McGlynn for his "various Communistic addresses," but took no further action after McGlynn promised to discontinue his political activity.

With the crisis of 1886 McGlynn was raising those fundamental questions that Elder feared regarding the rights of individual conscience and the limits of ecclesiastical authority over American Catholics, whether clerical or lay. Significantly, much of McGlynn's persistent support in his Anti-Poverty Society came not from the working class, but from middle-class Catholics, including a disproportionate number of women.[26]

When Archbishop Corrigan sought the advice of his consultors in December 1886 about transferring McGlynn from St. Stephen's because of his persistent insubordination, the archbishop contended that he was the heir of a problem that Cardinal McCloskey should have dealt with long before. Monsignor Preston added that the land issue was hardly the only charge against McGlynn. He had refused to build a parish school, despite the decree of the last plenary council. He was considered too lax in allowing people to receive communion too frequently and without previous confession. Another consultor maintained that McGlynn claimed that as a Propagandist (one who had studied at the Urban College of Propaganda in Rome), he did not owe obedience to the archbishop. "Dr. McGlynn must be put down," he concluded, "or the Archbishop of New York might as well not be the archbishop of New York."[27] In McGlynn's refusal to respond to the pope's order to come to Rome

25. Elder to Corrigan, Cincinnati, August 20, 1882, AANY, C-2; Elder to Corrigan, Cincinnati, August 28, 1882, AANY, C-2.

26. One layman who attended several of McGlynn's lectures in the spring of 1892 found his audience small, but largely middle-class and heavily female; E. F. Dunne to Corrigan, New York, April 3, April 10, April 17, April 25, May 1, May 8, 1892, AANY, unclassified. Even when McGlynn was attracting thousands to his addresses, the proportion of middle-class supporters, especially women, seems from the newspaper accounts and other informal reports to have been high.

27. This account of the meeting was written by Patrick McSweeny and is found in the

to explain his position, Corrigan and his advisors found a natural manifestation of McGlynn's heterodoxy, a virtual denial of the primacy of the pope.

Praise quickly poured in to Corrigan when he issued a pastoral letter in which he denounced George's land theory. Patrick Ludden, soon to be named Bishop of Syracuse, congratulated him on taking the offensive against liberalism. Silas Chatard, Bishop of Vincennes (later Indianapolis), who had issued a similar pastoral at about the same time with much less reaction, thought Corrigan's letter would "do more for the Church in America, than the liberal Priests can do harm." ("The more we strengthen each other's hand," Corrigan owned in complimenting Chatard on his own stand for the rights of property, "the better for discipline, and better for the faithful.") Ignatius Horstmann, chancellor of the Archdiocese of Philadelphia, hoped that now that Corrigan had set the example, "all our Bishops will come out in condemnation of the George heresy."[28]

Playing the Roman Card

McGlynn's excommunication in July 1887, for his refusal to heed the pope's summons, only intensified the controversy. The mass demonstrations declined, but the attempts of both sides to obtain a favorable solution from Rome persisted for the next eight years, with some important consequences for the American Church. The New York hierarchy resorted to various means, including loyalty oaths, the transfer of priests, and the making of attendance at Anti-Poverty Society meetings a reserved sin, to break the backbone of McGlynn's support among clergy and laity. The McGlynn case became a litmus test for judging orthodoxy and establishing one's credentials as conservative or liberal. The pledge of loyalty that New York priests were pressured to sign in the spring of 1887 became for years the norm for promotions and appointments. The laity's involvement in the affair became a similar criterion. Thus in 1889, when delegates to the Catholic Congress in Baltimore were being

---

archives of Mount Saint Mary's College, Emmitsburg, Maryland, where McSweeny's brother, Edward, was a professor. A passage in Richard Burtsell's diary indicates that it was not composed until 1889; Diary, vol. 7, February 14, 1889. Propagandists had the right of appeal to the pope upon being removed or disciplined by this ordinary. This as well as other privileges tended to make American prelates suspicious of them as subjects.

28. Ludden to Corrigan, Troy, November 19, 1886, AANY, C-16; Chatard to Corrigan, Indianapolis, November 23, 1886, AANY, C-15; Corrigan to Chatard, New York, December 28, 1886, Archives of the University of Notre Dame (hereafter AUND); Horstmann to Corrigan, Philadelphia, November 27, 1886, AANY, C-15.

chosen, Archbishop Corrigan was allowed to nominate the candidates, all of whom he made sure were "loyal and conservative."[29]

By 1890 McGlynn was becoming a pawn in the ideological struggle that developed between the liberal and conservative camps within the hierarchy. In the new alignment of the prelates a significant addition to the old conservative bloc was the German American bishops. Prelates like Corrigan and McQuaid were finding that they shared much more in common with Frederick X. Katzer, Archbishop of Milwaukee, than they did with Archbishop John Ireland or Bishop John J. Keane or the other liberal prelates of Irish extraction concerning parochial education, The Catholic University of America, or secret societies. The Germans were also drawing McGlynn's fire for their anti-Americanization attitudes. In fact, Corrigan's warming toward the Germans was very likely due in large measure to the strong support he had received from German priests and prelates during the McGlynn crisis. It was the German priests of the archdiocese who had presented him with the first testimony of loyalty. Nor was any German prelate trying to intervene in the McGlynn case, as some of the liberal prelates were.

Corrigan's continuing concern was that his action against McGlynn would be overturned by Rome on the grounds that McGlynn's removal from St. Stephen's had been uncanonical, since he had never had the chance of a hearing.[30] The appeals to Rome on McGlynn's behalf by dissident priests like Richard Burtsell or Sylvester Malone were disturbing enough, but even more

29. Preston to Orestes Brownson, Jr., New York, April 8, 1889, Brownson Papers, AUND.

30. Some canonical authorities, such as Richard Burtsell, were arguing that no bishop could transfer or depose even a movable rector for any crime of violation of discipline without the offer of a trial. Propaganda had left this point deliberately vague when the question came up in April of 1887.

Burtsell and others were contending that McGlynn's superiors had denied him equity at every stage of the case. Cardinal Simeoni had ordered him to retract his economic teaching in 1882 without even giving him the chance for an explanation. Four years later the archbishop had dredged up this condemnation to prohibit McGlynn from publicly supporting George's campaign and had suspended the priest for making a scheduled appearance for George, even though McGlynn promised to abstain from all further activity in George's behalf. Subsequently, Corrigan had renewed the suspension on the basis of a newspaper report, again without allowing McGlynn any chance to defend himself. Then he had been ordered to Rome without being told what the charges against him were. Corrigan had stated in the press that there were other charges lodged against him in Rome besides his land theories, but none had even formally communicated to McGlynn. Nonetheless, McGlynn had authorized Burtsell to write Cardinal James Gibbons of Baltimore that he would come to Rome, provided he were first reinstated, and he had even wired Gibbons to that effect. Gibbons had never even acknowledged the letter.

disconcerting to ecclesiastical authorities in New York were the attempts of other bishops such as Ireland and John Moore of St. Augustine. In September 1887, Moore attempted to have the American archbishops agree to propose reopening the case in Rome. By November, McQuaid was convinced that the bishops needed to take some joint action to uphold Corrigan. William Elder of Cincinnati agreed to write to Rome warning of the disastrous consequences that would follow any concessions to McGlynn, and asked several of his suffragans to do the same. The vast majority of prelates, in fact, even though they might have felt that Corrigan had not acted with prudence, were all too aware of clerical threats to their authority to support a dissident priest in any diocese. As McQuaid wrote Corrigan: "If you are to rule your diocese, you must have all necessary power to inflict discipline on recalcitrant priests. If you can effectively crush this open and defiant rebellion on the part of the McGlynn faction, and you can if Rome sustains you, . . . you will have won a great battle not only for yourself, but for the whole country."[31]

The New York archdiocesan officials were also trying to discredit McGlynn in Rome on the grounds of immorality. During the winter of 1887–1888, Corrigan's secretary, Charles McDonnell, presented to Roman officials extensive testimony from several women charging McGlynn with promiscuous behavior and heretical teaching concerning the sixth commandment. That Corrigan and his advisors were predisposed to believe that McGlynn's slippery slope had inevitably led to debauchery is understandable. Convincing Rome that such allegations were true and deserving of censure was another matter entirely, as Cardinal Henry Edward Manning of Westminster was discovering about the same time.[32] Nonetheless, the Holy Office was persuaded by the evidence that Corrigan forwarded to condemn McGlynn for solicitation and "perverse doctrines in sexual matters."[33]

Having McGlynn condemned in secret, however, would never destroy his influence. Some supporters of Corrigan were sure that nothing short of

31. McQuaid to Corrigan, Rochester, April 5, 1887, AANY, C-16.

32. Manning had been attempting for years to have the Holy Office uphold his suspension of Monsignor Thomas Capel, the rector of Manning's ill-fated University College of Kensington, for immoral behavior. Ironically Corrigan furnished the proof that finally convinced Rome. Capel, who had been wandering about America while under suspension, caused a scandal in a New York hotel in 1885, which Corrigan documented for Manning; Corrigan memorandum, February 9, 1885, AANY, unclassified.

33. Corrigan to [Cardinal Lucido Parrocchi], New York, October 12, 1888, copy, AANY, unclassified.

a condemnation of the source of McGlynn's ideas would effectively undermine his influence. Urged by his Roman friends to make a direct appeal to Leo XIII for an official denunciation of George's writings, Corrigan, in October 1887, formally petitioned the pope that the Congregation of the Index examine *Progress and Poverty*. Cardinal James Gibbons, with the close support of the rector of the North American College in Rome, Denis J. O'Connell, coordinated extensive appeals from the American hierarchy against any such condemnation on the prudent grounds that George's ideas should be allowed to die the natural death that speculative schemes found in the United States. Even conservatives like Gilmour and Elder thought it better to have Rome condemn the proposition about the injustice of holding private property in land and avoid the whole matter of George's book. A year and a half later the Holy Office compromised by condemning George's writings, but it refused to allow any promulgation of the condemnation. "How *peculiar* to condemn a book," Monsignor Preston understated his exasperation to Corrigan, "& then to keep the condemnation secret! I hope some of the Bishops will leak."[34] None did.

Preston and Corrigan continued to seek a public Vatican condemnation of George as the key to isolating McGlynn. In May 1890, Corrigan renewed to Cardinal Camillo Mazzella his plea for "some explicit declaration regarding the right of private property" to combat the socialistic theories that the archbishop saw spreading in the United States through such popular tracts as Edward Bellamy's *Looking Backward*.[35] Even some of the hierarchy, Corrigan informed a representative in Rome, thought that the promotion of liberal doctrines would be "the high road to American favor, and a passport for the claims of the Catholic Church."[36] When *Rerum Novarum* followed in May 1891, Ella Edes, the veteran American journalist in Rome with close ties to the New York chancery, reported that the pope's aim was to condemn George's theory without condemning his books.[37] Whether it was his aim or not, the encyclical gave the conservatives the magisterial sanction they had been seeking. Declaring that private property was in "perfect harmony with the natural law," Leo condemned "certain obsolete opinions" that denied any individual own-

34. Preston to Corrigan, New York, April 26, 1889, AANY, C-24.

35. Corrigan to Mazzella, May 16, 1890, in "Private Record," 254–55.

36. Corrigan to Smith, New York, April 2, 1891, Smith Papers, Archives of the Abbey of St. Paul Outside the Walls (hereafter AASPOW).

37. Edes to Corrigan, Rome, May 28, 1891, in "Private Record," 265–67.

ership of land. Corrigan's partisans began hailing the encyclical as the great authoritative vindication of the archbishop's long struggle against McGlynn and George. Corrigan himself stressed the obligation that Catholics had in obeying even such *non ex cathedra* statements as *Rerum Novarum.*

In the summer of McGlynn's excommunication Corrigan had mentioned to Gibbons that the crisis had had one good result—it had strongly increased his attachment to the Holy See. "I realize more and more clearly, day by day, he told the cardinal, "the profound truth of the axiom, 'Ubi Petrus, ibi Ecclesia!'"[38] One very concrete way of manifesting loyalty was the yearly Peter's Pence collection. New York as the richest diocese in the United States annually sent the largest amount, between fifteen and twenty thousand dollars in the 1880s. Baltimore, by contrast, was sending between five and ten thousand. At a time when the Holy See had lost its traditional support from the Papal States, such voluntary contributions assumed increasingly large importance. Nor did the New York officials simply let the money speak for itself. When Charles McDonnell went to Rome to lay out the evidence about McGlynn's alleged immorality, his official mission was to present the proceeds of a special collection taken up in honor of Leo's jubilee. But McDonnell was keenly aware of how interrelated his two missions were. "This evidence [of McGlynn's alleged immorality]" he confided to Corrigan, "and the . . . Jubilee collection, will be a powerful offset to the machinations of Smith's [McGlynn's] friends and followers." "I want to bring out the fact that New York's offering is larger now than ever before, a proof of the loyalty of the people in the face of the desperate efforts made to cut down the Peter Pence."[39]

Another effect of the loss of the Papal States in 1870 had been the Holy See's need to secure and invest its funds abroad. As an investment center New York was also unique within the American Church. The year Michael Corrigan became McCloskey's coadjutor, 1880, Rome had begun to entrust funds to his custody and management. The following year Propaganda had asked him to invest almost $45,000 in securities.[40] In 1889 the Propaganda

38. Corrigan to Gibbons, New York, August 5, 1887, AAB, AASMSU.

39. McDonnell to Corrigan, Rome, December 6, 1887, AANY, C-16; McDonnell to Corrigan, Rome, January 22, 1888, AANY, C-16. One of the archbishop's fears during the McGlynn crisis was that the size of the collection would greatly decrease. There was some decline in the Pence in the late 1880s, but whether this was owing to the poor economy of the period or the boycott of McGlynn partisans is difficult to judge.

40. Corrigan to Cardinal Cajetan Aloisi Masella, New York, October 18, 1889, copy, AANY, unclassified.

official in charge of finances, Cardinal Aloisi Masella, decided to withdraw the funds under the belief that the growth rate was too slow. Archbishop Corrigan's realization of the importance of being the custodian of these funds is reflected in his efforts to convince Propaganda officials that the interest rates were much higher than they appeared to be.[41] Fortunately for the archbishop, Masella was transferred from the Sacred Congregation before the securities could be sold, and New York continued to be an investor for the Vatican.[42] By 1898 the value of the funds was nearly $172,000.[43]

In the fall of 1889 the announcement of the Peter's Pence collection gave the archbishop an opportunity to issue a pastoral letter on the temporal power of the pope. While it was within God's providence, Corrigan admitted, to devise many ways of ensuring the perfect liberty that the pope needed to exercise his spiritual jurisdiction, "still, as far as human prudence can determine, and as things actually exist, temporal sovereignty is the most natural means, and indeed . . . a necessary means for securing the good government of the Church."[44] This would become an increasingly recurrent theme for the archbishop.

A decade before, Corrigan, along with many of his fellow prelates, had been concerned about maintaining a balance between their loyalty to Rome and their collegial independence as American bishops. Corrigan had played a key role in preserving this balance in the Roman deliberations that prepared the Third Plenary Council. But events were now sweeping him along in a way that was forcing him to assume a position that would have a profound effect upon the equilibrium between loyalty and independence that the American hierarchy had long been seeking to attain.

Francisco Satolli and the Restoration of McGlynn

Part of the high priority the American hierarchy had put on unity in the 1880s was the fear that disunity would provide an inevitable occasion for the lessening of their independence by the establishment of a Roman delegation

41. Corrigan to Simeoni, New York, October 25, 1889, copy, AANY, unclassified.

42. Rome also proposed that Corrigan receive the Peter's Pence collection from all dioceses in the country and directly invest it. The archbishop rightly felt that this would offend some of his fellow prelates, and suggested a more indirect procedure, whereby the funds would still be sent to Rome, while their ultimate investment would take place in New York; Preston to Corrigan, June 6, 1889, AANY, unclassified; Corrigan to Masella, June 6, 1889, copy, AANY, unclassified.

43. [Cardinal Vincent] Vannutelli to Corrigan, Rome, July 28, 1899, AANY, I-41.

44. Pastoral Letter of Michael Augustine Corrigan, Feast of the Holy Rosary, October 1889, AANY, H-3.

in the United States. When Leo appointed Francisco Satolli in August 1892 as an apostolic ablegate or official visitor, the announced purpose of his visit was to represent the pope at the World's Columbian Exposition in Chicago. Among his unannounced purposes, however, was to bring about a reconciliation of McGlynn with the Holy See. As Satolli secretly told Corrigan's vicar-general, John Farley, many in Rome felt that Corrigan had acted too hastily in his handling of the case.[45] Cardinal Mariano Rampolla, who as the Vatican's Secretary of State was taking a much more active role in American affairs, had been especially dismayed over Corrigan's actions and his alleged involvement with Tammany Hall. With the proponents of "*ralliement*" holding the balance of power within the Vatican, Corrigan as the leader of the anti-liberal party in America was finding more doors closed to him in Rome.

O'Connell and Ireland, having decided that helping the Vatican to establish the American delegation would aid their own liberal program, had been responsible for the invitation to the Chicago Exposition.[46] By August O'Connell could assure Ireland that Satolli was entirely in their hands.[47] Attempts at restoring McGlynn were very much a part of the liberal-conservative struggle that was peaking in 1891–92. It was a propitious time for such a reconciliation. McGlynn was out of the headlines. Even Burtsell admitted in February 1892 that the Anti-Poverty Society, now in its fifth year, was "dwindling away." The Academy of Music was a growing cavern of empty seats for McGlynn's Sunday addresses. This was the background for Satolli's having the McGlynn case as one of his chief priorities when he sailed for America in September. By the middle of December McGlynn was told to prepare a statement of his economic theories. Four professors of The Catholic University of America found nothing in it contrary to Catholic doctrine, and Satolli, two days before Christmas of 1892, restored McGlynn to good standing with the Church without even consulting Corrigan.[48]

The conservatives were dumbfounded. McGlynn's dubious restoration seemed to them to sanction not only the "socialistic" theories he had made

45. Farley Diary, September 24, 1892, AANY.

46. See Gerald P. Fogarty, S.J., *The Vatican and the Americanist Crisis: Denis J. O'Connell, American Agent in Rome, 1885–1903* (Rome: Università Gregoriana Editrice, 1973), chap. 8.

47. O'Connell to Ireland, Rome, August 3, 1892, quoted in Fogarty, *The Vatican and the Americanist Crisis*, 231.

48. The four professors were Thomas Bouquillon, Thomas O'Gorman, Charles P. Grannan, and Edward A. Pace; Burtsell Diary, vol. 9, December 20–22, 1892; Burtsell Letterbook, December 21, 1892, AANY.

his hallmark, but also the defiance of episcopal authority that McGlynn had come to incarnate. "Our people are terribly worked up, particularly the better classes," Corrigan lamented to McQuaid. "Many say they will go to Church no more."[49] Corrigan refused to receive McGlynn back into the archdiocese until the priest made public reparation for the scandal he had caused.[50] Roman friends were advising the archbishop to hold firm. By January newspapers were carrying headline accusations against Corrigan as the chief force behind the outpouring of letters and articles against Satolli and Ireland, which had begun appearing in newspapers across the country in November when Satolli announced his liberally tilted guidelines on the education of Catholic children, and which had sharply increased in number and passion with McGlynn's restoration. Rumors began to spread that Corrigan would be forced to resign or accept a coadjutor.

Paradoxically the sensational accusations against Corrigan consolidated conservative support for the New York prelate. John Lancaster Spalding of Peoria was but one of many bishops who encouraged Corrigan to stand his ground. To allow McGlynn to be taken back without apology or penance, Spalding wrote, would be "a fatal blow at ecclesiastical authority—a bribe held out to every priest to become disobedient and rebellious."[51] "You are fighting a great fight," Archbishop William Gross of Portland, Oregon, assured Corrigan. "You are the leader and champion of genuine Catholicity against . . . false liberalism."[52] On no account, Gross urged, should he resign or accept a coadjutor. With Satolli playing into the hands of the liberals by downgrading parochial schools and restoring dissident priests over the protests of their ordinaries, many conservatives were ready for the confrontation with the delegate that Corrigan was providing by refusing to give McGlynn a parish or even to allow him to say a public Mass.

Favorable Vatican Winds for the Conservatives

When McGlynn left secretly for Rome in the spring of 1893, Corrigan sent his Italian secretary, Father Gherardo Ferrante, to represent him at the Vati-

49. Corrigan to McQuaid, New York, December 28, 1892, ADR.

50. He was also justifying his stand on the ground that the Holy Office's condemnation of McGlynn for solicitation was unaffected by Satolli's decision about his economic teaching; Corrigan to Cardinal Monaco, New York, December 27, 1892; Italian copy, AANY.

51. Spalding to Corrigan, Peoria, January 1, 1893, AANY, G-4.

52. Gross to Corrigan, Portland, January 18, 1893, AANY, G-4.

can. Ferrante quickly proved beneficial to Corrigan as he began to win the favor of key officials, including the Prefect of Propaganda, Cardinal Mieceslaus Ledochowski. A larger issue was working in Corrigan's favor. The establishment of Satolli's mission had been the work of the pope, his Secretary of State, and Denis O'Connell. Ledochowski had never even been consulted about Satolli's appointment. O'Connell and Ireland had hoped that the institution of the delegation would free the Church in America from the jurisdiction of Propaganda and increase its independence. But Satolli, as well as the American Church, still fell under the direction of the Sacred Congregation, and Satolli's tendency to deal directly with Leo or Rampolla only increased the hostility toward him in Propaganda. The latter resented Rampolla's assumption of certain traditional prerogatives of the congregation, including being consulted about apostolic delegates to missionary countries such as the United States.[53] This tension was but part of the larger opposition between Leo and Rampolla, on the one hand, and Propaganda, on the other, about the restoration of the papal lands and relations with European powers.[54]

Given this Byzantine situation, Corrigan's opposition to Satolli became an asset for him at Propaganda. In supporting Corrigan, Propaganda could help check the designs of Rampolla and the pope.[55] Rampolla warned Satolli in June 1893 that Corrigan could cause much trouble for them, presumably a reference to the New York prelate's new strength at Propaganda.[56] Two months later Leo had Rampolla suggest to Satolli that he give Corrigan some public sign of esteem.[57] On August 15 the delegate made his public peace with the archbishop during a pontifical Mass in St. Patrick's Cathedral. Realistically both knew a public reconciliation had become mutually necessary, even though suspicion and distrust continued on both sides.

There followed a series of events in which Satolli's stance toward the conservatives changed radically as he began to support prelates against the appeals of dissident priests, to praise parochial schools, and to put pressure upon the

53. Ferrante to Corrigan, Rome, June 24, 1893, AANY, unclassified.

54. Leo ironically was pursuing his *ralliement* policy partly to gain support against the Triple Alliance, specifically Italy, for a restoration of the temporal power. The American liberals mistakenly interpreted Leo's strategy as a commitment toward democracy.

55. Denis O'Connell had come to realize this strategy of Propaganda by the fall of 1893; see Burtsell Diary, vol. 9, October 28, 1893.

56. Rampolla to Satolli, June 14, 1893, 5:54; Eduardo Soderini, "Leo XIII and the U.S. of America," unpublished manuscript, AUND.

57. Rampolla to Corrigan, Rome, August 4, 1893, in "Private Record," 377–78, AANY, L-3.

liberal Catholic press. The conservatives' confidence in Satolli grew as he came more and more under the direction of Propaganda. Patrick J. Ryan, Archbishop of Philadelphia, even suggested that Propaganda submit ecclesiastical cases to the apostolic delegate that had previously been reserved to Rome.[58]

December 1894 found McGlynn in Brooklyn, still waiting for Corrigan to receive him back. The archbishop had learned that the pope had finally acknowledged that Satolli had acted too quickly in restoring McGlynn and would soon order him to retract certain propositions. But no order came. By this time the McGlynn case had become such an impenetrable web of issues, facts, and allegations that Rome was bewildered, as one Vatican official admitted.[59] Leo's apparent tendency to lend encouragement to anyone who had his ear at the moment seems to have made a final resolution even more difficult. Moreover, O'Connell was telling Leo that in ordering any retraction by McGlynn he would effectively be rebuking Satolli and The Catholic University of America for attesting that no such retraction was necessary.[60] Given the opposition between Leo and Propaganda, the pope was not about to give such a gratuitous censure to Satolli or the university.

A Pyrrhic Victory

The delegate finally persuaded Archbishop Corrigan to name McGlynn pastor of St. Mary's in Newburgh, a small town in upstate New York. The archbishop was sure enough of his position now to take McGlynn back without it seeming to be a sign of his declining authority. What had become the symbolic goal of the McGlynnites—to have McGlynn restored to a parish in New York—now could be read as an indication of the archbishop's growing power. For by 1895 the signs were increasingly clear that the aims of the American liberals were slowly collapsing. From Newburgh McGlynn continued to vent his unreconstructed views on the single tax, parochial schools, and the plight of American labor. He still believed that the establishment of the Apostolic Delegation in Washington had overturned the "benevolent paternal despotism" of the bishops and created "a new order" that would finally enable the Church in America to be fully American.[61] Neither he nor the lib-

58. McDonnell to Corrigan, Brooklyn, April 21, 1895, AANY, G-16.

59. Burtsell Diary, vol. 9, November 7, 1893.

60. Henry Gabriels to Corrigan, Rome, December 21, 1893, AANY, G-4.

61. Edward McGlynn, "The Results of Cardinal Satolli's Mission," *The Forum* 22 (February 1897): 695–705.

eral prelates were very astute readers of the signals from Rome. Less than a year before McGlynn died in 1900, Leo XIII condemned Americanism.

The interplay of events and issues that climaxed in January 1899 with *Testem Benevolentiae* was a highly complex one. The McGlynn affair was but one of the larger strands of the Americanist tapestry. Given the centralizing trend that both Pius IX and Leo XIII vigorously pursued during their reigns and the growth during this same period of a conservative episcopal bloc seeking to strengthen its authority over clergy and laity, the conservative triumph was probably inevitable. But the importance of the McGlynn affair in relation to this long-term development is that it was one of the most effective shapers of the particular divisions that grew up among the American hierarchy during these last fifteen crucial years of the century and forced a stance toward Rome, on the part of the conservatives, that had extremely serious consequences. The affair dominated Archbishop Corrigan's concerns during those eight years from 1886 to 1894 and critically affected his trust of key liberal prelates like Gibbons, Ireland, and Keane. For many other conservative prelates the McGlynn case confirmed their worst fears of the liberal cancer they saw maturing in the Church.

When they perceived that cancer spreading from clerics like McGlynn and Burtsell to prelates like Ireland and Keane, the conservatives reluctantly resorted to Rome more and more to find a cure. The official one that *Testem* provided for them had a higher price than they undoubtedly had anticipated. For by the first years of the twentieth century the American Church was less independent of Rome than it had been in the 1870s. The old balance between loyalty to Rome and collegial independence was largely lost, as the veto power of the apostolic delegate over episcopal appointments clearly symbolized. Michael Corrigan's tendency to maximize the primacy and infallibility of the pope set the pattern for the ultramontanism that would characterize the Church in America in the first half of the twentieth century. Whereas an older conservative like McQuaid had found infallibility an inopportune dogma, Corrigan had ended up flaunting it. In turning so completely to Rome to save themselves from the designs of the liberals, the conservatives lost some of their own heritage as well.

Chapter 9

"Listen to Our Voice . . . Walk in the Ancient Paths"

The Episcopacy and the Road to Universal Parochial Education

THE *New York Times*, in January 2009, reported that the Catholic school system in the United States, which forty years ago was educating half of the children within its faith community, now found itself facing the threat of extinction, with its schools, which once numbered more than 12,000, increasingly shrinking (2,000 closed over the past two decades, most of them since 2000), and now accounting for only fifteen percent of the American Catholic student population. In the 1960s more than five million children were in parochial schools; today there are fewer than half that number, with one fifth not Catholic. The precipitous decline of parochial education has been the consequence of a number of factors, including rising costs, particularly those of a lay faculty virtually replacing the religious sisters and brothers who traditionally staffed the schools; of fewer parents willing or able to commit their children to parochial education; of inadequate management; of changing demographics. A major study by the White House Domestic Policy Council concluded that the dwindling presence of parochial schools constituted a crisis, not just for American Catholics, but for American society in general.[1] That conclusion was a reflection of just how integral to American primary education Catholic parochial schools had become in the twentieth century, when it emerged as the largest private educational network in the world, a

1. Paul Vitello and Winnie Hu, "Catholic Schools, Under the Threat of Extinction, Are Being Reinvented," *New York Times*, January 18, 2009.

remarkable accomplishment when one considers the relative poverty of the American Catholic community, especially in the formative years of the nineteenth century, when the parochial system was put in place.

This chapter originated as a paper given at a conference on "The Evolution of a Vision: 100 Years of Catholic Education in America," held at Ursuline College in Cleveland in June of 1984 to celebrate the centennial of the Third Plenary Council of Baltimore, whose actions culminated the movement to make education an essential part of the Catholic experience in America. The provincial and plenary councils in the nineteenth century played a key role in the development of the Catholic empire in primary education in the United States. Not only did they gradually define the place of education within the American Catholic community, but they provided the rationale, if not the mandate, for the unique phenomenon that American Catholic parochial education became by the twentieth century: the largest private school system, not only in the United States, but in the world. To appreciate the work that the councils did regarding education is to appreciate the changing landscape within which Catholics developed their schools at all levels, from the eighteenth century on.

John Carroll and the Beginnings of Catholic Education

To say that Catholic education in America begins with John Carroll is not to deny that there were Catholic schools before him. Indeed, Carroll himself went to one, on a Jesuit plantation in the northeast corner of Maryland's Eastern Shore. Missionaries in New Spain, New France, and British America founded schools for natives and colonists, but with one exception they were short-lived, as was Carroll's school at Bohemia. The exception was the Ursuline School in New Orleans, founded in 1727 by a group of ten Ursulines from Rouen, France, with Mère Marie de St. Augustine Trancepain as superior. Of note was the comprehensive nature of the Ursuline school: there were actually two schools, one a "free" school for poor students, including blacks and Indians, and a boarding school for children of the wealthier settlers. The Catholic school in the nineteenth century would increasingly be such a comprehensive school.

That there were but few Catholic schools—and those very short-lasting—is not surprising. Catholics in British America lived under civil disabilities in most colonies, including Maryland, where most of them were. Among the penal laws that governed Catholics in Maryland was one that ordained that

"Papists" keeping school would be transported out of the colony. To send a child abroad to be educated in a Catholic school on the Continent, as many Maryland Catholic gentry did in the eighteenth century, was to risk a fine of £100 and, more importantly, the loss of the child's inheritance.

That was the situation until the American Revolution, when John Carroll fortuitously arrived on the scene in Maryland—fortuitously because, in any normal course of events, Carroll would never have returned to America, which he had left in 1748. He had become a Jesuit after his school days at St. Omer's, been ordained, then assigned to teach at the Jesuit schools at Bruges and Liége. For a man of Carroll's talent and scholarship, it was highly unlikely that the Society would have sent him back to the mission in America. But the suppression of the Jesuits by Pope Clement XIV in 1773 left Carroll with no reason to remain in Europe. Hardly had he returned to America than the Colonies revolted against Great Britain. With independence came religious freedom and the emancipation of Catholics. It was now possible for Catholics to consider doing what had been scarcely possible before: found schools.

No one saw the possibilities and the needs regarding education more clearly than Carroll. The success of a republic that professed the sovereignty of the people depended on an educated citizenry. Carroll himself came to realize that Catholics had an important stake in providing their own institutional means to achieve this enlightened goal. In the wake of the Treaty of Paris, Carroll, newly appointed superior of the American clergy, began to raise funds to begin an academy for Catholic males, but received little encouragement. His fellow ex-Jesuits opposed his efforts to sell some of the former Society's property in order to endow a school. Lay Catholics were also very slow to come forward to provide any financial support. For a time Carroll thought very seriously of using his influence to secure places for Catholic faculty in the existing nonsectarian colleges in Maryland and Pennsylvania. He was already a trustee of both St. John's College in Annapolis and Washington College in Chestertown. In 1784 he wrote to a friend that, since Catholics were now enjoying the same toleration as everyone else, was it right to think of "separating ourselves from the Community?" If they did, he wondered, would they not bring on a hostility that would have some very "disagreeable" consequences?[2] The following year he was ready to acquire residences for

2. Carroll to Ferdinand Farmer, December 1784, in *The John Carroll Papers*, ed. Thomas O'Brien Hanley (Notre Dame: University of Notre Dame Press, 1976), 1:158, cited in Philip Gleason,

Catholics attending the new public colleges, with Catholic faculty serving as housemasters.

Had Carroll held to this plan, Catholic education in this country may very well have had a very different history, most certainly a shorter one. But within a year he was once more pursuing what he repeatedly referred to as "the object nearest my heart"—a Catholic academy for the education of youth. To this day it is not clear what caused Carroll to change his mind. There was, indeed, a brief flare-up of anti-Catholic feeling in the region, occasioned by the publication of a pamphlet written by a former Jesuit and cousin of Carroll who had converted to the Protestant Episcopal Church. Concerned that the pamphlet would lead to a full-scale revival of the discrimination that had dogged Catholics during most of the Colonial period, Carroll published a lengthy rebuttal of Wharton's attack on the Church. The anti-Catholic feeling proved very fleeting. That should have renewed Carroll's confidence in the suitability of Catholics finding their education within the public square. In the end it did not. We can only speculate about what led him to renew his plan to begin his own academy. One thing we need to bear in mind is Carroll's primary concern in planning his own institution in the first place. It was to provide an education for future priests. There is evidence that the more he pondered the need for priests to serve the rapidly growing Catholic population, the more he concluded that a Catholic school was the only way to provide for them. Carroll, by 1786, had come to believe firmly that establishing their own school was the best investment Catholics could make in protecting their own future. That conclusion, reached by many different paths, would be one that Catholic prelates would consistently echo over the course of the next century.

In 1786 the Select Body of the Clergy, the representative group that Carroll had organized to administer the property and goods held by the Church, finally approved the project and provided the funds to purchase a site for the school in the town of Georgetown. Four years later the first student enrolled. By 1792 there were sixty-six students.

In the pastoral letter that followed the first synod that Carroll held as bishop in 1791, he explained that he had founded Georgetown because the education of youth is such a central concern of the Church. "I know & lament," he wrote, "that the expense will be too great for many families, and

"'The Main Sheet Anchor': John Carroll and Catholic Higher Education," *The Review of Politics* 38 (October 1976): 592. Father Ferdinand Farmer, a German ex-Jesuit, had himself become a trustee of the University of Pennsylvania in 1779.

that their children must be deprived of the immediate benefit of this institution."[3] Carroll hoped that some Georgetown graduates, from a student enrollment that was indeed national in its scope, would in turn begin schools in their own home areas so that the effect would proliferate. But the burden of his letter was on the responsibility that parents had for the spiritual nurturing of their children. The family was still seen as the primary arena for education.

Carroll continued to promote educational institutions that would meet the needs of the growing Catholic population. The French Revolution produced an exodus of extraordinary priests who profoundly affected Catholic education, including Benedict Flaget, William DuBourg, John Dubois, and Gabriel Richard. In 1790 the Sulpicians established a seminary in Baltimore (part of Carroll's vision for a national Church in which the clergy would be trained in America, not Europe); in 1800 they expanded their operations in Baltimore by opening a lay college. Eight years later, in the hamlet of Emmitsburg, amid the Blue Ridge Mountains of Western Maryland, Dubois began Mount St. Mary's College. DuBourg, while Bishop of Louisiana, was instrumental in establishing in France, in 1822, the Society for the Propagation of the Faith, the first of three major European missionary societies that would support various apostolates in the American Church during the nineteenth century, including that of education.

Nor did Carroll neglect the education of women. When the first group of religious women, the Carmelites, came to the United States in 1790, Carroll secured for them a dispensation from Rome in order that they might open a school for girls. The mother superior, the daughter of an old Maryland family, politely but firmly informed the bishop that they had come to this country not to teach, but to pray. A decade later the Poor Clares did begin a school in Georgetown that eventually became the Georgetown Visitation School. In the first decade of the nineteenth century, Elizabeth Ann Seton began a school in Baltimore. When she later organized her religious community that became the Sisters of Charity, she made education a primary ministry of her new community. St. Joseph's Academy in Emmitsburg was the first institution of many across the country that were the result of that commitment.

A striking note of most of these schools founded during this period be-

3. Carroll, "Pastoral Letter of 1792," in *Catholic Education in America: A Documentary History*, ed. Neil G. McCloskey, S.J. (New York: Teachers College, Columbia University, 1965), 48.

fore 1830 was their ecumenical character. They were open to Protestants as well as Catholics. Such was the case with Georgetown, as well as St. Joseph's College in Bardstown, Kentucky, founded in 1820, the New York Literary Institution (1809), and the Ursuline Academy in Charlestown, Massachusetts (1822). In a society in which formal education was still a private concern, Catholics had at least one advantage: the religious orders that provided what came to be called "the living endowment" for schools. Often enough the Catholic school was the best, if not the only one available in a town or area, and enjoyed broad public support.

The Provincial Councils and the Rise of the Common School

As Americans moved west in the nineteenth century, Catholics were very much among them in Kentucky, Ohio, Indiana, Michigan, and elsewhere. In the Michigan territory, no Catholic was more prominent than Gabriel Richard. Father Richard, like Carroll, was deeply committed to education. It was Richard, indeed, who initiated the establishment of the University of Michigan in 1817, some twenty years before the territory became a state. The project was an interdenominational one, with the single Protestant clergyman, John Monteith, as fully involved as Richard. On Richard's recommendation Monteith was named first president of the institution. Richard served as a member of the board of trustees.

Such cooperation between Catholics and Protestants became increasingly rare by the 1830s. By that decade two events had occurred that were changing the face of American society: mass immigration and the second great outburst of revivalism. The 1820s began the century-long influx of European peasants into America. Many, if not most of them, were Catholics. In the late eighteenth century John Adams could be glad that Catholics were as rare as earthquakes in America. Those days were long past. In the 1820s, 54,000 Catholics entered the country, over half of them Irish, the poorest immigrants America had ever known. By 1830 the Catholic population had climbed over the 300,000 mark. In the ten-year period between 1845 and 1855 more than a million Irish, fleeing the famine that would claim even more of their countrymen in their native land, emigrated to this country. By mid-century the Catholic Church in America had become the nation's largest denomination.

At the same time, the country was in the midst of an evangelical "awakening" that was deeply affecting the culture both in the towns and on the frontier. A "Benevolent Empire" of itinerant preachers, tract and Bible societies, Sunday schools, religious journalists, and reform societies labored to make this a truly Christian (read Protestant) republic. By the 1830s Roman Catholicism had replaced deism or infidelity as the greatest threat to America's becoming a Protestant country. The sharp influx of Catholic immigrants, the conversion of prominent Protestants to Catholicism, the attempts of Catholic prelates to secure public funds for their schools—all combined to alarm many evangelical Protestants, as was pointed out in chapter 6. Anti-Catholic tracts became something of a cottage industry in the three decades before the Civil War. Violence against Catholics was sporadic but real enough, such as in Charlestown, Massachusetts, in 1834, when a crowd, stirred by evangelical preaching about the threat to American society that Catholics represented, burned the Ursuline convent; or in Philadelphia, where nativist mobs twice in the spring and summer of 1844 went on destructive rampages through the Catholic community. The Charlestown event proved to be a factor in Bishop Benedict Joseph Fenwick's decision to restrict the enrollment to Catholics only in the school he founded in 1843 in Worcester, Massachusetts. Holy Cross became a precursor of the single-religion schools that came to dominate the Catholic educational landscape by the Civil War.

While Catholic education was increasingly becoming one for Catholics only, the "public" or "common" school was coming into being. Benedict Fenwick was not the only resident of Boston deeply disturbed by the convent burning at Charlestown. Horace Mann was morally outraged at the event. A subsequent riot in Boston between Catholics and Protestants deepened his concern over the survival of such a fragmenting society. In his brooding over the hatred and bigotry that led to such outbreaks, he began to look to education as the key to building a common culture that could overcome ethnic, religious, and economic divisions. Mann became the great advocate for the common school and was instrumental in developing the first state system of public education.

As Neil McCloskey has pointed out, the very concept of a common school was a contradictory one in nineteenth-century America. How could one provide a common education when religion was considered so integral to education, but religion itself in America was so pluralistic? Mann himself opposed sectarian education, but felt that the public school could inculcate a nonsectarian Christianity. Sidney Meade once observed that the reason public education was so easily accepted in America in the second quarter of the nineteenth century was the growing conviction among Christian denominations that what they shared was the essence of Christianity; what divided them—matters of theology, or polity, or liturgy—was in the final analysis incidental. To many who felt this way, like Mann, the common school was perfectly capable of imparting the essence of Christian wisdom and morality, especially through the reading of the Scriptures.

What to Mann was the common inheritance of Christians was pure and simple Protestantism to Catholic leaders. That the Bible typically used was the King James or Authorized Version only underscored the Protestant bias of the next half century. As the common school spread throughout the states north of the Potomac, Catholics would seek—with rare success—relief in the courts from such obligatory Bible reading in public schools.

Anti-Catholic bias in textbooks was another persistent problem. Even in the McGuffey readers there was a residue of Protestant Christianity amid the middle-class culture that the books promoted in their young readers. In other texts the anti-Catholic slant was blatant. Laurina Kaiser studied the texts used in teaching geography, history, and literature to children during this period. The anti-Romanist tone was pervasive. An 1818 history book dealing with the colonization of South America asked its readers: "Was the papal religion planted there?" And the printed answer: "Yes; with all its ignorance, and superstition; and it continues there to this day, with all its degrading effects on that southern world." And it continued: "What is the comparative difference of character, between North and South America?" "Greater than language can express." "To what may this be imputed?" "Entirely to the difference of character between the Papal and Protestant religions."[4] Two decades later another history text declared: "The Spaniards are zealous Catholics. In no country is there more pomp and superstitious ceremony as regards religion; and perhaps in none is there less true Christianity."[5] A compendium of geography anticipated by three decades the spirit of manifest destiny regarding Mexico that would rage during the 1840s: "The Roman Catholic religion is established [there] in its most bigoted form. It is hoped, however, that this rich and extensive country will assume self-government; and invite

4. Frederick Butler, *A Catechetical Compendium of General History* (Hartford: 1818), 110, 115; quoted in *The Development of the Concept and Function of the Catholic Elementary School in the American Parish*, by M. Laurina Kaiser, O.S.B. (Washington, D.C.: The Catholic University of America Press, 1955), 82.

5. S. G. Goodrich, *The Child's Second Book of History* (Boston: 1836), 107, quoted in Kaiser, *Development of the Concept*, 84.

the industrious of all nations and religions to her friendly shores."[6] Another geography text published in 1835 asserted: "The diffusion of knowledge in civilized countries will be found proportioned to the freedom of the people. It is greatest where the government is most free, and where the Protestant religion prevails.[7]

Anti-popery still very much lived on in the texts. "What has been... [the popes'] general moral character?" one history book asked in 1818. "Corrupt in the extreme; practicing, and tolerating all the vices, and the blackest crimes." "Have they generally died suddenly?" "Yes; and very often by violence."[8]

When the first provincial council of Baltimore met in 1829, these developments were still largely in the future. There was concern about the lack of educational opportunities for poor Catholics. The prelates discussed the need for establishing a religious society of men who would devote themselves to the education of boys as Catholic religious women were doing for girls. The prejudicial textbooks were another concern. The prelates recognized the need for publishing Catholic textbooks as an antidote. They declared that a Catholic school was the "best mode" for educating Catholic children, even if it could not provide the best "worldly training," for nothing was more important for a child than his spiritual cultivation. They concluded that it was "absolutely necessary that schools should be established in which the young may be taught the principles of faith and morality, while being instructed in letters."[9]

That education was such a prominent issue for the bishops during their first council was in large measure due to John England, the Irish immigrant bishop of Charleston who had been most responsible for bringing the prelates together and was given the task of writing the pastoral letter that was issued at the end of their meeting. For England, as for Carroll, education was the key to self-governance, a *sine qua non* in a republic. So he had established the first Catholic newspaper in the United States, set up schools, and begun a

6. John McCulloch, *Epitome of Workman's Geography* (Philadelphia: 1816), 122, quoted in Kaiser, *Development of the Concept*, 86.

7. William C. Woodbridge, *A System of Universal Geography* (Hartford: 1835), 194–203, quoted in Kaiser, *Development of the Concept*, 88.

8. Butler, *Catechetical Compendium*, 118, quoted in Kaiser, *Development of the Concept*, 93.

9. Decree 35, *Concilia Provincialia, Baltimorei Habita Ab Anno 1829 usque ad annum 1849*, Editio *Altera* (Baltimore: Murphy, 1851), 84.

seminary to train an indigenous clergy. He was not looking for state support. Like Carroll, he believed in a free Church in a free society. If providing a proper education for its members was a necessity for the Church in America, it had to be done in the tradition of voluntarism that England brought with him from Ireland. He thought it healthy for the hierarchy to be dependent upon the laity, not the state, for supporting its works. He was optimistic that if the laity's rights were respected, their financial support would follow. Through England's initiative the diocese of Charleston became the sole local church in the history of American Catholicism to adopt a constitution that established the framework of a basic body of law under which bishop, priests, and laity shared responsibility for the governance and well-being of the diocese.

England, in fact, wrote the pastoral letters following each of the first four provincial councils. In the first one following the council of 1829, England enjoined parents to "attend to the education of your children; teaching him first to seek the kingdom of God and his justice." The pastoral urged parents to "seek those teachers who will cultivate the seed which you have sown." Education was now clearly seen as something that transcended the home. The ideal was to maintain the continuity of a Catholic environment, whether at home or in school, in the formation of Catholic children.

Four years later, in 1833, the prelates met again in Baltimore. The bishops reaffirmed the need to provide appropriate textbooks for children in Catholic schools, not to mention those in non-Catholic institutions. The England-penned pastoral letter urged parents to support Catholic colleges and schools. In turn the prelates promised to ensure the high quality of the faculty. The same plea was made after the Third Provincial Council in 1837.

Despite the recurring episcopal pleas, as the major historian of Catholic parochial education has noted, the response from the Catholic masses was largely lethargy and apathy. Several causes may have been at work here: a Catholic population that was becoming increasingly immigrant and poor, the hope (shared by many, if not most, of the bishops) of attaining public funds for schools, the lack of strong episcopal leadership on the issue (aside from England), and uncertainty about the acceptability of a common school system.

When the bishops gathered in Baltimore in 1840 for the Fourth Provincial Council, there was still optimism about obtaining public funds. John Hughes, the bishop of New York, had the support of Governor William Seward in seeking state aid for the Catholic schools in his diocese. In Kentucky the new superintendent of public instruction for the state, the Protestant Episcopal bishop Benjamin Smith, was adumbrating a plan for a school system organized along denominational lines. The Archbishop of Baltimore, Samuel Eccleston, was telling the Society for the Propagation of the Faith that "in my opinion the public mind will never be more favorably disposed toward the Catholic Religion than at present."[10]

Bernard Meiring, in his study of the educational legislation of the councils of Baltimore, contends that the bishops at this council of 1840 were still willing to settle for a truly nonsectarian public school. He notes, for instance, that the Bishop of Bardstown (Kentucky), Benedict Flaget, a strong advocate of education, made no protest about the type of public school that Bishop Smith was proposing to establish in his state. One should note, however, that this was a "public school" that would be Catholic in all its aspects—control, staffing, curriculum—save for the source of its financing. In one decree of the council, it is true, the bishops swore to be vigilant in attempting to weed out the noxious textbooks that were used in all too many public schools. But their greater concern was the tendency of Catholic parents—for financial reasons—to send their children to public schools at all. The pastoral letter warned parents who made this choice that the loss of their children's faith was the likely price they would pay for any financial savings they realized. If they thought they were building an endowment for their children by skimping on their education, they were dealing in fool's gold. For those parents whose children were exposed to Bible reading in public schools, the bishops recommended that they counter it with Bible reading in their own homes from an approved version of the sacred text. The ultimate solution for this proselytizing, the bishops added, was for Catholics to establish their own comprehensive network of schools "fitted according to our own principles." By painful experience, they concluded, they had found that the common school movement involved the dominance of Protestant beliefs and ideology at the expense of Catholic ones. The Council of 1840 could be seen as the Church's first public declaration of universal Catholic education as the ideal in the American situation.

10. *Annals of the Propagation of the Faith*, September 1838, quoting a letter from Samuel Eccleston, January 31, 1838, cited in *Educational Aspects of the Legislation of the Councils of Baltimore, 1829–1884*, by Bernard Julius Meiring (New York: Arno Press, 1978), 87–88.

Nativism and Baltimore Plenary Councils I and II

John Hughes' attempt to secure public funds has been told in many places. The catalyst for his quest was the Public School Society, which controlled public monies for education in New York City. The society was itself the result of an eighteenth-century law that originally had provided funds to several religious denominations, including the Catholic Church, that were conducting schools. The Public School Society was set up to provide for those children not being served by the various denominational schools. By the 1840s the society had come to possess a monopoly over the public funds. Hughes, by making this monopoly a public issue in the municipal elections of 1840, succeeded in breaking the power of the Public School Society, but failed to obtain any public monies for his own schools. He remained optimistic that Catholic pressure would eventually result in Catholics getting their fair share of the funds. In the meantime, he began to develop a separate parochial school system.

Some historians have suggested that a less aggressive prelate than John Hughes might well have fared better in the attempt to secure justice for Catholics in New York City. The Catholic record elsewhere in such attempts does not favor this interpretation. John England's newspaper, the *U.S. Catholic Miscellany*, read the signs of the times quite accurately in commenting on the outcome in New York in 1841. "We do not think it likely," it stated, "that a public body can be found in the United States which does not, without its own consciousness or suspicion, think and act under the influence of great prejudice against Catholics, their claims, their rights, their principles, their religion, and their politics."[11] By 1859 Hughes himself was admitting that "the time has almost come when we shall have to build the school-house first and the church afterward."[12] A resurgence of violent nativism during the 1840s, most notably in Philadelphia, where two churches and thirty homes were burned and fourteen persons died, no doubt had a large role in leading Hughes and many other Catholic leaders to the conclusion that Catholics had no choice but to build their own school system.

Nativism raised its menacing head once more in the 1850s. Persistent immigration (two and a half million immigrants, largely Catholic, in that decade alone), persistent attempts to secure public funds for parochial schools,

11. *U.S. Catholic Miscellany* 22, no. 34 (1841), quoted in Meiring, *Educational Aspects*, 109–10.

12. Hughes, Pastoral of 1850, quoted in Meiring, *Educational Aspects*, 110–11.

and restiveness over the growing sectional crisis nurtured a xenophobia that found convenient targets in Catholics. In 1853 a papal diplomat, sent to the United States to establish full diplomatic relations with Washington, was forced to abandon his mission after crowds threatened him in Pittsburgh, Wheeling, and Cincinnati. A year later in Ellsworth, Maine, a crowd attacked an immigrant Jesuit priest who had become a very outspoken critic of the local public school policy of forcing Catholic children to read the King James or Authorized Version of the Bible. The mob stripped John Bapst of his clothes, tarred and feathered him, and paraded him about town for hours on a plank. Bapst thought the harrowing incident won him sympathy from many non-Catholics in the state. Nonetheless, that very year the Supreme Court of Maine upheld the compulsive Bible reading practice. In Massachusetts, a stronghold of nativism, a Catholic couple in Boston brought suit against a public school teacher for beating their son after he refused to recite the Protestant version of the Ten Commandments. The court acquitted the teacher.

Nowhere did nativism as a political movement prove to be stronger than in Maryland, the original center of Catholicism in the United States and itself the terminus of much Catholic immigration during the antebellum era. By the middle 1850s the American Party had gained control of the mayor's office in Baltimore and the state legislature. The periodic gathering of the Catholic prelates in Baltimore offered stark evidence of the growing presence and power of the Church in the United States. When the bishops convened in Baltimore in 1852, the Church had grown beyond the provincial level. Catholics, previously all organized under the Province of Baltimore, now made up six provinces across the country—thus the First Plenary Council of Baltimore. When the council opened in May of 1852 there was a lull in nativism. But the prelates were under no illusion that conditions had improved nearly enough for Catholics to seek their education in any common school system. Indeed, they had identified a new enemy, besides the traditional Protestant-bias of many common schools—secularism.

Francis Kenrick, the Archbishop of Baltimore who presided at the council, set the keynote for the discussion on education in a paper he had prepared for the occasion. "[T]he effort to educate youth without giving any religious tinge to the mind, tends to indifferentism and infidelity," he wrote. Kenrick admitted that the common system of education might be acceptable to religious groups who shared certain tenets and were careful to guard against any "irreligious influence." For Catholics, however, such a system would always be "objectionable and dangerous," for any educational system, if it were to inculcate moral values, could do so only through religion, and here Catholics would always be at odds with Protestants.[13]

The theologians on the Committee on Education continued the assault against public education. They found "the radical disease" in the theory of common education that excluded religion from any place in the classroom. This was the consequence, they observed, of the state's arrogating to itself the right to educate. As bad as the system was in theory, they found it even worse in practice. In the working system, religion in the form of a sanitized Protestantism actually got into many public classrooms. Indeed, they contended that in most parts of the country public education was "directly or indirectly under the control of Protestant ministers." For those parents who willfully refused to send children to "good" Catholic schools, the theologians recommended that the bishops deny these Catholics the sacraments.

The prelates ignored the last recommendation, but did enact a decree that would set in motion the movement that would make the parochial school the standard for Catholic elementary education. The decree called for the establishment of schools in connection with parish churches and to support them from parish revenues, as far as circumstances permitted. The pastoral letter was the eloquent work of Peter Richard Kenrick, the Archbishop of St. Louis and brother of the presiding prelate. "Listen to our voice," Kenrick wrote, "which tells you to walk in the ancient paths; to bring up you children as you yourselves were brought up by your pious parents." But of course it was no longer possible to walk in the ancient paths. They were embarking on a radically new path that would involve a massive commitment of personnel and money in setting up an autonomous Catholic educational system at the parochial level. If the means were new, the end was a very old one: "to make religion," as Kenrick put it, "the foundation of the happiness you wish to secure for those you love so tenderly." "Listen not," he concluded, "to those who would persuade you that religion can be separated from secular instruction."

That Kenrick was chosen to write the pastoral was appropriate, for by the 1850s the Midwestern prelates had taken the clear initiative in promoting Catholic education. As early as 1846 a group of Western clergy, in preparing for the Sixth Provincial Council of Baltimore, recommended that "schools

13. Francis Kenrick, "Religion the Basis of all Sound Education," in *Concilium Plenarium Totius Americae Septentrionalis Foederatae, Baltimori Habitum Anno 1852* (Baltimore: John Murphy, 1853), quoted in Meiring, *Educational Aspects*, 132–35.

be established in *every congregation* [italics mine] through the province."[14] It is perhaps an exaggeration to claim that the Germans were the real founders of the parochial school system in the United States. They certainly played a prominent role in shaping the conciliar legislation regarding education from the 1850s on. The dioceses in the so-called German Triangle between Saint Louis, Milwaukee, and Cincinnati led the way in establishing parochial schools. For the Germans education and the preservation of their language and culture were integral to the preservation of faith. As they put it, "language saves faith."

Cincinnati, under John Baptist Purcell for nearly a half century from 1833 to 1879, was a pacesetter in the growth of education during these years. Purcell brought in the Jesuits, the Sisters of Notre dame de Namur, the Marist Brothers, and the Holy Cross Fathers to conduct colleges and schools in his diocese. At the First Provincial Council of Cincinnati, held in 1855, the bishops declared that their goal was to have a school in every parish. That goal had already been virtually realized in Cincinnati. As the region and the diocese grew in the 1850s and 1860s, the parochial system kept pace. There were sixty-one schools in 1860, one hundred and three in 1870.

Religious orders, particularly those of women, were a key to such growth. Harold Buetow notes that between 1829 and 1884, forty-four nondiocesan communities of religious women and eleven teaching brotherhoods were established in the United States. The Midwestern dioceses attracted a disproportionate number of them for their schools.[15]

That Catholics were going their separate way in education provided additional fuel for nativist charges that Catholics were truly alien. "We bid them welcome," Horace Bushnell wrote in 1853, "and open to their free possession, all the rights of our American citizenship. They, in return, forbid their children to be Americans, pen them as foreigners to keep them so. . . . And then, to complete the affront, they come to our legislatures demanding" a share of public funds for "the purpose of keeping their children from being Americans." "Take your place with us in our common schools, and consent to be Americans, or else go back to Turkey, where Mohammedans, Greeks, Armenians, Jews are walled up by the laws themselves."[16] If that was the tone

14. Responses to Question 8, 6th Provincial Council, 1846, AAB A-R-8, AASMSU.

15. See Harold A. Buetow, *Of Singular Benefit: The Story of Catholic Education in the United States* (New York and London: Macmillan, 1970).

16. Horace Bushnell, *A Discourse on the Modifications Demanded by the Roman Catholics Delivered in*

of the leading Protestant theologian of the day, it becomes easy to see why Catholics found themselves such an alien minority. It also indicates what chance there was for Catholics obtaining any share of public funds.

When the Second Plenary Council of Baltimore convened in the year following the end of the Civil War, the archbishop of the premier see was a Midwesterner, Martin John Spalding, who as Bishop of Louisville had played a key role in the First Provincial Council of Cincinnati. The decrees of the council on education decried the creeping indifferentism in the public schools, the danger of mixing boys and girls in public classrooms, and the biased textbooks. In its most important decree the council prelates edged toward the Cincinnati prescription. "It seems," they declared, "that the best, or rather the only remedy that remains by which these very serious and troublesome evils [in public education] can be met is that in every diocese, next to each and every church schools be erected in which the Catholic youth may be imbued with literature and the fine arts as well as with Religion and good morals." Significantly, an attempt to exempt certain areas where satisfactory public schools existed was defeated. The only recognition of Catholics going to public schools was the call to establish catechetical schools in regions that could not establish regular schools.

The prelates of the Second Plenary Council were contemplating a comprehensive Catholic educational network that would meet the various needs of the entire Catholic community. Thus they called for the establishment of Catholic reformatories or industrial schools to provide for Catholic delinquents or orphans; they confessed the need for a Catholic university, although they admitted that the resources of the American Catholic community might make such an undertaking premature.

James McMaster, Rome, and the Instruction of 1875

"That we are to have schools and colleges of our own," the convert Orestes Brownson wrote in 1862, we take it is a 'fixed fact.'" What concerned Brownson was the quality of those schools. But having accepted them as inevitable in the circumstances, he urged his fellow Catholics to make the system worthy of the great tradition of Catholic education. One way to improve the schools, of course, was through public aid. Hopes of obtaining such aid

---

the North Church, Hartford, on the Day of the Late Fast, March 25 1853 (Hartford: 1853), 10, in Meiring, *Educational Aspects*, 161.

in most areas were weakening. Those who clung to the declining prospect of public support for parochial education increasingly invested their hopes in an arrangement that had been worked out between Church and public authorities in several cities that had in effect created "public" Catholic schools. The first such arrangement appears to have been in Lowell, Massachusetts, in 1823–24 for the children of Irish immigrants working in the textile mills of the town. The town paid the salary of the Catholic teachers and supplied the textbooks. In exchange the teachers had to meet public standards. This "public school" in Lowell lasted until 1852, when a pastor's attempt to staff the school with religious sisters caused town officials to terminate its funding. Other similar arrangements were worked out in Savannah, Hartford, New Haven, and Poughkeepsie.

The Poughkeepsie experiment was the work of Patrick McSweeny, the pastor of St. Peter's Church. The local school board paid a dollar a year for the use of the parish buildings. The teachers were hired by McSweeny, but examined and paid by the board. Religious instruction took place either before or after regular school hours. McSweeny thought that this met perfectly the nonsectarian requirement of public educational policy, while providing for the legitimate religious needs of students. If Poughkeepsie became a model, it would mean the state appointing Catholic teachers for Catholic children and Protestant teachers for Protestant children.[17]

One person who did not share McSweeny's view was James McMaster, the editor of the *New York Freeman's Journal and Catholic Register.* McMaster was a convert, a former Presbyterian in whom much Scotch rigorism survived his conversion. Converts, beginning with Elizabeth Ann Seton, have had an enormous impact upon Catholic education in the United States, but none perhaps had as much influence in shaping Catholic education as did McMaster. As editor of the leading Catholic journal in the country, he lobbied for years for Catholic education and against nonsectarian public education. Unlike McSweeny and most of the bishops, McMaster wanted no part of state aid in whatever form. In 1869 he wrote:

> The Catholic solution of this muddle about Bible or no Bible in schools is, "Hands off!: No State taxation or donation for any schools. You look to your children, and we will look to ours. We don't want to be taxed for Protestant, or for godless

17. Patrick F. McSweeny, "Christian Public Schools," *The Catholic World* 44, no. 262 (March 1887): 796, cited in Harold A. Buetow, *Of Singular Benefit*, 160.

schools. Let the public school system go to where it came from—the devil. We want Christian schools, & the state cannot tell us what Christianity is.[18]

As for McSweeny's experiment, McMaster referred to it as "The Poughkeepsie School for Betraying the Christian Faith." The bottom line in Poughkeepsie, so far as McMaster was concerned, was state control with all its predictable consequences for religious freedom.

McMaster assumed that Catholics had the wealth to build a separate school system. The success that the dioceses in the West had had in developing their parochial institutions encouraged that assumption. In the 1870s McMaster carried his lobbying efforts to Rome. There he had a very valuable ally, Ella B. Edes, another convert and a veteran newspaper woman with important connections in Rome, especially in the Congregation for the Propagation of the Faith (*Propaganda Fide*), under whose jurisdiction the Church in the United States fell. Edes was steadily reporting to Propaganda officials about the controversy over the Poughkeepsie plan, including the removal of statues and crucifixes from the classrooms. In 1874 McMaster, through Edes, sent a special report to the Roman congregation. The report portrayed the public schools in the United States as grave threats to the faith of Catholic children and asserted that virtually every parish in the country was capable of supporting a school. Propaganda officials subsequently queried the American prelates about the situation. Most of the American bishops, in their responses, claimed that McMaster was greatly exaggerating the evils of public education; in addition, it was not practicable to deny absolution to parents who sent their children to public schools rather than available Catholic ones, since attenuating circumstances were often at play in such decisions. The collective response notwithstanding, the Roman congregation found McMaster's *j'accuse* a persuasive one, thanks in no small part to Ella Edes' persistent commentary on the state of education in the United States and the need for Rome to address it. "That we will sooner or later," she wrote officials in the congregation in the fall of 1875, "have a war on the scholastic question is certain and the difficulty is that our bishops and our priests are divided in their manner of thinking on the subject. We anxiously are awaiting a decision of the Sacred Congregation of Propaganda on the question, perhaps a series of instructions which they promised to give us a year ago."[19] Two months later

18. *Freeman's Journal*, December 14, 1869.

19. *Congressi rif. nei Congressi America Centrale* 1875, vol. 26, folio 379, 380, APF, cited in "Public

Propaganda sent an instruction that became part of the guidelines for the legislation on education in the Third Plenary Council in 1884. The instruction found public schools dangerous; Catholics could not in conscience attend schools "hostile to Catholicity." It charged the American prelates to use "every means" to keep children from all contact with the public schools. Nothing more was needed, it concluded, than to have Catholic schools in every place. The instruction represented the first detailed papal statement on American education. Ironically two lay persons were responsible. A Roman congregation had given more credence to their views than to those of the American bishops, not the first and hardly the last occurrence of this sort of extracanonical influence.

Conclusion

The Third Plenary Council went beyond Rome in setting a timetable for the completion of the parochial system (a quixotic two years from the close of the council) and calling for the establishment of a Catholic university. Ironically the pastoral letter after the council said nothing about the timetable for the building of schools, perhaps one indication that there was still much disagreement about the best means of fulfilling the goal. At any rate this goal of the council of building a school system that could accommodate virtually all Catholic children was never remotely realized within two or twenty years of the 1884 decree. In 1898 only one-third of the Catholic children in New York City were in parochial schools. One half of the parishes were still without schools. The Archdiocese of Boston, with a Catholic population of 610,000, had but sixty-one parochial schools for 39,000 students. By contrast, the Western archdioceses of Cincinnati, Saint Louis, and Milwaukee had a much greater proportion of their Catholic children in parochial schools.[20] Only eight dioceses, virtually all in the Midwest, had set up school boards in compliance with the decrees. The great period of growth would not come until

---

Schools versus Catholic Schools and James McMaster," by Thomas T. McAvoy, C.S.C., *Review of Politics* 28 (January 1966): 27.

20. Cincinnati had 100 parochial schools for 26,472 students in a Catholic population of but 190,000; the comparable figures for Saint Louis were 138 for 24,430 students in a Catholic population of 212,338; for Milwaukee, 150 for 27,703 students and a population of 237,900. Figures are from *The Catholic Directory, Almanac and Clergy List for 1900* (Milwaukee: Bruce Publishing, 1900), in *In Hoc Signo?: A Brief History of Catholic Parochial Education in America*, by Glen Gabert (Port Washington, N.Y: Kennikat, 1973), 128.

the second and third quarters of the twentieth century, when second and third generations of American Catholics began to move into the middle class of American society. For scores of millions a Catholic parochial education would become part of that passage. By 1965 roughly half of American Catholic students would be in parochial schools. That would mark the highwater mark of the Catholic ghetto that the Third Plenary Council had sanctioned, a ghetto that in that decade began to collapse under the pressure of developments within the Church and the larger society.

The year 1884 can be said to have marked the point when separate educational institutions became a vital part of the American Catholic community. The parochial schools were integral components of the ethnic networks that were spanning Catholic America. In much of this development, Church leaders had little choice. Conscious of the minority status of Catholics in an alien Protestant-dominated culture, they had to provide for the needs and growth of their people as best they could. By 1884 they had decided, however reluctantly, as had John Carroll, that a separate school system was the best way in which American Catholics could preserve their religious heritage within this pluralistic society.

Chapter 10

The Church in the Public Square

Archbishop Corrigan and the Crusade against Roman-Sanctioned Liberalism in the 1890s

WITH JOHN HUGHES' establishment, if ever so reluctantly, of the model of a separate parochial school system to answer the educational needs of Catholics, and James McMaster's relentless campaign to make such a system universal within Catholic America, New York had played a major role in bringing about the decree of the Third Plenary Council, which mandated a Catholic school for every parish in the country. In the course of the next decade another New York figure emerged as the principal defender and promoter of Catholic primary education that would be completely separate, completely free of the state in every respect. To do that would paradoxically force Archbishop Michael Corrigan to resort to utilizing political connections and waging a surreptitious campaign in the press that came to jeopardize his own position as leader of New York's Catholics. The following chapter draws upon two previous pieces. A portion was published as part of "Conservative Thought and Strategy in the School Controversy, 1891–93," *Notre Dame Journal of Education* 7 (Spring 1976): 44–62. Another portion comes from an unpublished paper presented at the annual meeting of the American Historical Association in New York City in 1997 under the title "Michael Augustine Corrigan and American Catholicism in the Gilded Age: The Satolli Conspiracy and the Church-Tammany Connection."

The Question of Catholic Public Schools

The mandate of the Third Plenary Council in 1884 for every diocese to establish schools in every parish would seem to have settled the matter of the direction the Church in America would take regarding the primary education of Catholics. As it soon became clear, that matter was still an open question. Not only had most dioceses failed to come remotely close to meeting the quixotic goal of having parochial schools in every parish within two years, but the separate, privately financed school system that John Hughes had reluctantly adopted and James McMaster enthusiastically promoted was not, as it turned out, a settled course for the Church in America. What diverse forms these schools could take was still an open matter. In 1890 the issue unexpectedly rose to challenge those who assumed that the decree of the council had left no room for any further discussion. The catalyst was an address given by Archbishop John Ireland of St. Paul at a convention of the National Education Association held in his city. The state, Ireland proclaimed, shared the parents' duty to educate children and rightly imposed laws to enforce it. Unfortunately, he went on, Catholics could not in conscience accept the existing state school as ideal, because it excluded religion from its curriculum. Nor could they continue to bear the burden that denominational schools entailed. Hence they were demanding the "Christian State School." Ireland offered two plans by which this could become a reality. The state could simply underwrite the secular education given in denominational schools or it could adopt the model that Catholic authorities had adopted in such places as Poughkeepsie, New York, in which the local school board rented the parish buildings during class hours, supplied texts, paid the teachers' salaries, and conducted the examinations of the pupils. Religion was taught only outside of formal school hours, and there was a tacit understanding that the Catholic teachers (mostly nuns) would be retained by the school board so long as they passed the normal examinations.[1] A year later Ireland put the Poughkeepsie Plan into operation in two parish schools in Faribault and Stillwater.

Ireland was attempting to find a solution to a problem that had been vexing American education for the past half century. Since the abrasive fight between John Hughes and the New York Public School Society, American Cath-

1. John Ireland, "State Schools and Parish Schools," in *The Church and Modern Society*, 2 vols. (St. Paul: Pioneer Press, 1905), 217–32.

olics had been almost totally stymied in seeking funds for their schools. One of the consequences of the Third Plenary Council's decree was a renewal of the effort to obtain state aid. Monsignor Thomas Preston, Archbishop Corrigan's vicar-general, had taken to the pages of the *Forum* to show why such funding was essential so that Catholics "could practice their religion with the full freedom which the Constitution . . . guarantees them."[2] What Preston was proposing was essentially what Ireland had in mind. Ireland's plan, as the latter pointed out, was already in operation in Poughkeepsie, Albany, and Milwaukee, among other places. But there were some important presuppositions that divided Ireland and Preston. Preston did not concede that the state shared responsibility with the parent in the education of the child. To concede this for many conservatives was to facilitate the same tendency toward socialism that they had found in Edward McGlynn's denial of private property rights.[3] And the implicit judgment of Preston's essay, reflecting the conservative position, was that the public schools represented a proximate danger to the faith and morals of Catholic schools.

Complaints began to pour into Rome about Ireland's address. Prominent among the plaintiffs were German American prelates who saw in Ireland's defense of the state's right to provide for the education of its citizens an endorsement of the controversial legislation that had been enacted in the Wisconsin legislature in 1890. That legislation had required that English be the language of instruction in all the schools of the state, a blow to the German parochial schools, which had been founded on the principle that "language saves faith."[4] Cardinal James Gibbons of Baltimore also had recourse to the Vatican, but his appeal to Rome was that it would take no action that would put into serious doubt the compatibility of Catholicism with American principles and institutions. When the Vatican left the issue unresolved, Gibbons himself attempted to settle the controversy by having Thomas Bouquillon, a

2. Monsignor Thomas Preston, "What the Roman Catholics Want," *Forum* 1 (April 1886), 161–71.

3. Archbishop William Elder of Cincinnati, for instance, wrote Bishop Richard Gilmour of Cleveland in January 1890 that he thought "it is very important that Catholics associate themselves with all their fellow citizens who are disposed to maintain parental control over education & to check the march toward socialism"; Elder to Gilmour, Cincinnati, January 27, 1890, Archives of the Diocese of Cleveland.

4. For the background of the Bennett Law, as well as of the school controversy in general, see Daniel F. Reilly, O.P., *The School Controversy, 1891–1893* (Washington, D.C.: The Catholic University of America Press, 1943).

professor of moral theology at the Catholic University of America, publicly lay out the rights and duties of education. In a thirty-nine-page pamphlet entitled *Education: To Whom Does It Belong?* (Baltimore: John Murphy, 1891), Bouquillon asserted that it was the exclusive property of neither individual, family, state, nor church; all four shared in the educational process. Heads of church and state had the obligation to find some "practical application" of these complementary responsibilities that would best serve the common good.[5]

Archbishop Corrigan responded in kind. Less than two weeks after Bouquillon's pamphlet appeared in November 1891, a rebuttal was in print. Rene Holaind, S.J., a moral theologian at Georgetown University, evidently at Corrigan's request, brought out *The Parent First* (New York: Benziger Brothers, 1891), which denied any such rights in education to a non-Christian state like the United States.[6] The controversy continued to heat up through the winter of 1891–92. Bouquillon and Holaind resumed their debate through additional pamphlets, with others getting into the controversy as well. Ireland gave a lengthy interview to the New York *Herald* in which he defended his plan and attacked the critics of Bouquillon. The foreign press took up the issue, with the *Civiltà Cattolica* being the chief organ of the conservatives and *Moniteur de Rome* becoming the main channel for the liberals. Ireland, who had gone to Rome to defend his plan, asserted there that the American archbishops, at their annual meeting in St. Louis, had endorsed his Stillwater-Faribault plan when he had presented it to them.

Corrigan denied that they had done any such thing. As he had earlier explained to the cardinal prefect of Propaganda, what bothered him about Ireland's experiment in his diocese were not so much the actual operations at the two parishes, but the ideological claims the plan was inspiring in its defenders. To Corrigan parochial schools were an absolute necessity in the United States. This conviction, he reminded the congregation officials, was

5. This marked the first time that an American Catholic theologian had granted the state such rights in education, even that of providing compulsory education when the parents failed to do their duty.

6. Holaind had been helping Corrigan to prepare for a meeting of the country's archbishops in St. Louis when the Bouquillon essay appeared. Corrigan paid for the printing of Holaind's pamphlet; Corrigan to Holaind, New York, October 22, 1891, Archives of Georgetown University 190–5. Alphonse Magnien, a Sulpician confidant of Gibbons, claimed that Holaind admitted that Corrigan had asked him to answer Bouquillon; Magnien to Ireland, Baltimore, March 31, 1892, Archives of the Diocese of Richmond (hereafter ADRi), microfilm copy in The Catholic University of America Archives.

the reason the Third Plenary Council had passed its decree on education. Funding those schools was the province of American Catholics alone. Happily, the remarkable record of school building that had taken place since the council, the archbishop claimed, was proof of Catholics' willingness to bear that burden, even though they were already paying taxes for state schools. For the most part, those schools could hold their own against any public schools in the areas of the quality of the buildings, the capability of the teachers, and the rigor of the education. Despite this success, some were attempting to foist upon Catholics "a certain new and foreign theory; that state schools best suited the needs of our times" and no harm would come to children handed over by their parents to the government for their education. He had little doubt that those, like John Ireland, who were resorting to such arguments, were led to such straits "by too great a love of American institutions," and while such a position might win much public favor, it was actually undermining the future of Catholicism in the United States.[7]

Corrigan subsequently circulated among eleven of the thirteen archbishops in the country, Gibbons and Ireland being the two not included, a statement that declared the primary obligation of family and Church to educate and the necessity of Catholic schools "if the welfare of the rising generation is to be secured." The Faribault and Stillwater experiment had merely been mentioned at the last archbishops' meeting. No judgment from the prelates had been expected, the statement concluded, much less "an approval of the secularization of those schools."[8] Seven of the archbishops signed it, and Corrigan forwarded it to Roman officials.

A Roman Judgment

Corrigan's Roman sources subsequently assured him that the Vatican would soon condemn the principles that Bouquillon had laid out in his pamphlet. A special committee of five cardinals had indeed been charged with examining Ireland's plan and its implications for parochial education in America. In late April 1892 the committee, without ever seeing the statement of the archbishops sent by Corrigan, issued a report that concluded that the Stillwater-Faribault experiment could be tolerated "taking into consideration

7. Corrigan to Giovanni Simeoni, [January] 1892, copy, AANY.

8. [Archbishops] to [Salvador Brandi], Director of the *Civiltà Cattolica*, n.d., copy, AANY, unclassified.

all the circumstances." Worse still, from the conservatives' stance, the committee commended Ireland for providing "in the best manner possible" for the spiritual welfare of the children of his archdiocese. The pope approved the decision.[9] "It is a triumph," an elated John Keane, rector of The Catholic University, told Ireland, "which marks an epoch. It opens up a future of harmonious relations between America and the Church."[10]

There ensued between the two sides in America a struggle to define the meaning of "tolerari potest." Michael Corrigan seized the occasion of a banquet in honor of the consecration of a New York bishop to stun the gathering with the announcement that a cable he had just received "from someone in high authority in the Vatican" declared that "Faribault has been condemned. Local case tolerated." The cable sender was Salvatore Brandi, the editor of *Civiltà Cattolica*, who was working overtime in Rome to reverse the committee's decision. The New York Province bishops penned a letter to the pontiff in which they expressed their deep concern about the well-being of parochial education amid the current confusion about Rome's position toward it. The letter also denied there was any foundation for Archbishop Ireland's apocalyptic insinuation that a persecution of American Catholics would likely follow a Roman decision against the Faribault-Stillwater plan.[11] Their concern only deepened when Leo responded by claiming that Ireland had raised no such alarms and by counseling the New York prelates to do their utmost to get the government to provide religious schools that would relieve Catholics of their present financial burdens.[12]

9. Ledochowski to Ireland, Rome, April 30, 1892, in Reilly, *School Controversy*, 160–62.

10. Keane to Ireland, Washington, D.C., April 29, 1892, Archives of the Diocese of Richmond. Leo XIII's biographer, Count Eduardo Soderini, claimed that the pope hoped that the United States would eventually support Catholic schools, since the Church represented the strongest force for nurturing law-abiding citizens. Soderini believed that Leo intended the toleration of Ireland's experiment to be seen as close as possible to official approval to assure the American government that Rome was not opposed to democratic institutions; Eduardo Soderini, "Leo XIII and the U.S. of America," unpublished manuscript, n. 88, AUND. There is no direct evidence that Ireland or his associates attempted to convince Leo that the Faribault-Stillwater system would lead to confessional schools supported by the state. Corrigan's conservative allies in Rome strongly suspected that Ireland had told Leo that, if the Holy See favored his position, the U.S. government would eventually take the Catholic Church under its protection and subsidize church schools in general. One does not need to scrutinize too deeply between the lines of the liberals' strategy and arguments to discern the inference that the American Church under their leadership could obtain a favored place.

11. Corrigan to Cardinal Parocchi, June 9, 1892, copy, AANY.

12. Leo XIII to New York ordinaries, Rome, May 24, 1892, AANY.

Corrigan was undeterred in his efforts to overturn the committee's work. To the pope's vicar-general the archbishop quoted from letters penned by Ireland and Gibbons (that, thanks to his Roman allies, had come into Corrigan's possession) to prove that they indeed raised the specter of persecution. More to the point, he addressed the major consequence of "tolerari potest," should Ireland's interpretation of it be allowed to stand: "a total revolution in Catholic education" whereby Catholic parents would feel justified in seeking a government alternative to a costly parochial school system. The liberals, Corrigan concluded, were sabotaging the strong tradition of episcopal authority in America by their insistence on downgrading all that the episcopacy had been urging in the area of Catholic education since 1875.[13] His conservative allies in the episcopacy pressed him to continue his sharp resistance. "We must be bold, strong, impulsive in our dealings with Rome," Bishop Otto Zardetti of St. Cloud wrote him while in the Eternal City. "That is the way I[reland] carried his point. This is the only way we can obtain something. I[reland] has felt the two weak points of the Roman curia: yielding to 1) money, and 2) terrorizing." The key to counteracting the liberals, Zardetti stressed, lay in collective action, with Corrigan and Archbishop Frederick Katzer of Milwaukee leading the campaign.[14]

A Delegate from Rome

The conservatives saw the upcoming meeting of the archbishops in the fall of 1892 as a crucial opportunity to reverse the liberal momentum supporting public Catholic schools. When the meeting was postponed to mid-November, Corrigan read this as strengthening his party's hand by giving it more time to prepare its strategy. "Already the tide is beginning to turn in our favor in Rome," he wrote McQuaid at the end of August.[15] Archbishop Patrick Ryan of Philadelphia saw a possibly darker consequence in the postponement. If the Republicans were successful in the upcoming November elections and held the White House, Ryan cautioned Corrigan, Ireland would be sure to "endeavour to get some kind of promise from the administration

13. Corrigan to Parocchi, New York, June 9, 1892, copy, AANY. At this same time, Corrigan had begun a correspondence with the former pastor of the parish in Stillwater to attempt to show that Ireland was not justified in claiming that the parishioners were incapable of sustaining a parochial school; Corrigan to Rev. M. E. Murphy, Mt. St. Vincent's, July 6, 1892, AANY, C-18.

14. Zardetti to Corrrigan, Rome, June 6, 1892, AANY, C-44.

15. Corrigan to McQuaid, New York, August 31, 1892, ADR.

to favor a Faribault plan"[16] The Vatican, it turned out, had a very high estimation of Ireland's power within the party of Lincoln. A month later, in early October, Ella Edes wrote Corrigan that Vatican officials were convinced "that Mgr. Ireland holds the Government in the hollow of his hand."[17] That impression was no doubt reinforced when the archbishop arranged to have a United States vessel provide an official escort into New York harbor for the official delegate that Pope Leo had sent to settle the school question.

The Archbishop of New York and his conservative colleagues were wary of the delegate Francisco Satolli, a professor of dogma at the Propaganda College, even before Ireland's ploy in New York Harbor. Satolli had, after all, in the previous spring been a strong character witness when the St. Paul prelate was making his case to Vatican officials. When Satolli proceeded to spend most of his first month in America at Ireland's residence in St. Paul, the outlook for the conservatives darkened even more. Suddenly the archbishops' November meeting in New York looked anything but promising.

The cardinal prefect of Propaganda had instructed the archbishops to take up the question of providing for Catholic children in public schools. Ireland wanted to limit their discussion of education to that one topic. The conservatives were not about to abandon their hopes of changing the policy regarding parochial and public education, even though the environment was clearly against them. On the first day of the four-day meeting in New York City, Archbishop Satolli informed the assembled prelates that the pope had commissioned him to speak on the school question and proceeded to introduce to them "in the name of the Pope" fourteen propositions intended to settle the controversy. Several of the propositions repeated, in language consistent with a liberal interpretation, the legislation of the Third Plenary Council, including the commitment to erect quality Catholic schools and the prohibition against denying the sacraments to parents who chose to send their children to public schools. Other propositions explicitly upheld Ireland's school plan and the state's right to educate.[18] In fact, unbeknownst to most of the prelates

16. Ryan to Corrigan, September 3, 1892, AANY, C-44.

17. Edes to Corrigan, Rome, October 6, 1892, in "Private Record of the Case of Rev. Edward J. McGlynn," 275–81, AANY, L-3.

18. For instance, the conciliar prohibition against pastors refusing the sacraments to parents of public school children applied, not in a general way as Satolli's proposition had it, but only when the parents had the approval of the ordinary to send their children to public schools; *Abstract of the Minutes of the Third Annual Conference of the Most Rev. Archbishops of the United States* (Baltimore: John Murphy, 1892).

at the meeting, the propositions had been prepared by a liberal colleague of Ireland's, Denis O'Connell, rector of the American College in Rome.[19]

When Satolli closed his statement by asking the archbishops to show their acceptance of the pope's will in the matter by affixing their names to the propositions, the stunned prelates refused to consider approving them without certain changes. The ablegate agreed to do so.[20] Corrigan wrote a hasty note to Satolli in which he conveyed evidence that Ireland really wanted to make his system the norm for Catholic education. He pleaded that Satolli not allow Ireland to "impose his fantasies upon the entire American episcopacy. It is a question on which millions of souls hang."[21]

Three days later, on the final day of the meeting, Satolli represented the propositions, having made some incidental modifications. Corrigan raised further objections, at which point the ablegate stormed out of the room. Archbishop Ireland subsequently worked out an agreement whereby the propositions remained unsigned by the prelates, but bore a notation by Satolli: "all these were read and considered at the archbishops' meeting, the difficulties answered, and the requisite alterations made, November 17, 1892." In addition, there would be no publication of them until the prelates had had the opportunity to write to Rome.[22] Meanwhile, the conservatives had gotten their own "propositions" adopted by a majority of the prelates at the meeting. Among them was a renewed call for the erection of Catholic schools "so that there may be accommodation in them for more and, if possible, for all our Catholic children." Another declared that "the decision of the Holy See as to the Faribault plan does not affect these decrees [of the Third Plenary Council], except to strengthen them. Parochial schools are the rule. Plans of various kinds the tolerated exceptions where the rule cannot be carried out." That proposition, on its face, was irreconcilable with several of Satolli's propositions, especially Proposition VII, which stated that "[t]he Catholic Church . . . and especially the Holy See, far from condemning or treating with indifference the public schools, desires rather that, by the joint action of civil

19. Gerald P. Fogarty, S.J., *The Vatican and the Americanist Crisis: Denis J. O'Connell, American Agent in Rome, 1885–1903* (Rome: Università Gregoriana Editrice, 1973), 214.

20. There are no extensive minutes of the four-day meeting. The best accounts are in a letter from Ryan to Gibbons, December 5, 1892, cited in John Tracy Ellis, *The Life of James Cardinal Gibbons, 1834–1921* (Milwaukee: Bruce Publishing, 1952), l:695–96, and in an unpublished account, "The School Question in America," by James Conway, S.J., MPA, GULSC.

21. Corrigan to Satolli, November 17, 1892, copy, AANY.

22. Conway, "The School Question," MPA, GULSC.

and ecclesiastical authorities, there should be public schools in every state, according as the circumstances of the people require, for the cultivation of the useful arts and natural sciences."

In an apparent move to preserve some semblance of unity, the prelates decided not to release the conservatives' resolution on the Faribault plan. When, despite Satolli's promise, the American press soon printed his entire statement and began to report that the propositions represented a decisive victory for Ireland, Corrigan decided that he needed to work the same medium that was becoming such a vital instrument in shaping public opinion in the last decade of the nineteenth century. On December 11 the New York *Herald* carried the startling news that John Ireland had been the only prelate at the meeting to have accepted Satolli's propositions. Corrigan was the likely source for the story.[23]

Events over the next two months precipitated an escalation of the conservatives' resistance to the ablegate and his liberal prodders. Corrigan received scores of letters from bishops, clergy, and laity about the demoralizing effects of Satolli's pamphlet upon grassroots support for the parochial system. Then, a month after the archbishops' meeting, Satolli restored Edward McGlynn to good standing within the Church without even consulting Corrigan, McGlynn's ordinary. Other clerical dissidents soon began finding Satolli a responsive court of appeals against their bishops. Finally, in early January, the announcement came that Pope Leo had appointed Satolli to be the permanent apostolic delegate to the United States. By whatever measure, the liberal triumphs were devastating to the conservatives. Ireland's victories in the school controversy were breaching the solid front among clergy and laity that the hierarchy had been wielding together for the past quarter century and calling into question the conservative conviction that American Catholics were inescapably a people apart. McGlynn's dubious restoration seemed to sanction the defiance of episcopal authority that McGlynn had come to incarnate. Worst of all, Rome had finally done what the hierarchy had been trying to avoid for decades: send a special delegate to America; and the consequences—for the conservatives—had matched their worst fears.

23. Three weeks before the story appeared Corrigan had informed a *Herald* reporter that the archbishops as a group were displeased at the distorted way in which the school question was being aired in the Catholic press. At the end of November Archbishop Katzer, angry at the release of the propositions, asked Corrigan: "Are we not justified to come out before the Public and state that we refused our Consent!"; Katzer to Corrigan, Milwaukee, November 28, 1892, AANY, C-44.

The official confirmation or rejection of Ireland's school plan as a norm for the future was a matter that was in Rome's hands. But the conservatives knew that a massive slippage in Catholic schools would make the acceptance of the Faribault system an accomplished fact that edicts from Rome would little affect. Thus Archbishop Corrigan and the conservatives began to attack it in the public fora, wherever it was vulnerable. The sense of crisis and the need to resort to bolder and more devious means seem to have accelerated sharply with the confluence of events that began with the archbishops' meeting in New York. Stopping Satolli from his seeming onslaught against the cherished institutions the conservatives had been strengthening for the past decades, such as parochial education and episcopal authority, became unquestioned ends that would sanction some very dubious means, especially where they were convinced that liberals were resorting to some very illicit methods themselves to promote their program in the form of false information or bribery of Vatican officials or fabricated cables.

Ecclesiastical Conspiracy

On January 8, 1893, the Chicago *Sunday Post* published an article charging the Archbishop of New York, Michael Corrigan, with conducting an international conspiracy to "discredit and disgrace Archbishop Ireland and Mgr. Satolli, the papal ablegate to America." The *Post* specifically charged that Corrigan and priests at his Cathedral residence had organized and directed the outpouring of letters and articles against Ireland and Satolli that had been appearing in newspapers across the country since the previous November. The *Post* offered as evidence a letter from Corrigan to a Chicago layman in which he asked his help in publishing an article that a friend of his supposedly wished to publish. A few days later an unsigned article had appeared that purported to be a conversation between a Philadelphia priest and a layman criticizing Archbishop Ireland's attempt to get Vatican support for his controversial school system. Even more damning in the *Post* article were several letters allegedly written by Michael Lavelle, the rector of Corrigan's cathedral parish, to several Midwestern laymen, urging them to use their influence to have newspapers print articles or letters protesting Ireland's influence in Rome and Satolli's "offensive and annoying" influence in American Catholic affairs. "The battle cry of 'No force bill,'" Lavelle reportedly said in an allusion to the abortive attempt of Congress to pass legislation to enforce the civil rights of African Americans in the South, "won the late election. We must have such a cry in order to alarm the pope and force him to recall Mgr. Satolli." As additional evidence of the New York–inspired conspiracy, the *Post* cited anti-Ireland pamphlets that had recently been published in France and Italy that were really authored by persons close to the Archbishop of New York. It also claimed that Ella Edes, a correspondent of the Archbishop's in Rome, was fabricating cables from that city designed to strengthen Corrigan's position.

The priest editor of St. Paul's diocesan paper, the *Northwestern Chronicle*, summed up the evidence in the *Post*'s article: "It is a conspiracy against the Church, a conspiracy against the Pope, Archbishop Satolli, honest men, an enlightened policy, and a conspiracy against the spirit and harmony of the United States."[24]

Archbishop Satolli, for one, believed the story and called Corrigan's vicar-general, Monsignor John Farley, to Washington to convey personally to his superior his angry reaction to Corrigan's recent behavior, including Corrigan's responsibility for the critical newspaper items and the fabricated cables from Rome.[25] Indeed the story was essentially true, as Archbishop Corrigan admitted to Bishop Bernard McQuaid of Rochester. "The traitor in Chicago is Lahiffe," Corrigan wrote McQuaid. Edward Lahiffe was a journalist whose services Corrigan had utilized when Lahiffe had been a reporter for the New York *World* to get his views a favorable public hearing. In August 1892 Lahiffe had accepted a position with a Chicago paper, the *Herald*. Before leaving, he had suggested to Archbishop Corrigan the advantages of printing in Chicago the entire memorial that Ireland had presented to the pope earlier in the year. From Chicago the Associated Press could carry it across the country while hiding the source of the disclosure.[26] Shortly before Christmas of 1892 Corrigan took up Lahiffe's offer and sent the letter with the material that found its way to the *Post*. Why Lahiffe suddenly turned against the archbishop is not clear. Corrigan himself later was inclined to believe that Lahiffe had been "in the pay of the other side" all along and had been setting him up.[27] But there is evidence that Lahiffe was generally repelled by the nature of the article that Corrigan sent. For whatever reason, Lahiffe broached the matter with his pastor in Chicago, who got in touch with Archbishop Ireland. Ireland took himself to Chicago and persuaded Lahiffe to surrender the letter and other

24. New York *Evening Sun*, January 11, 1893.

25. Corrigan to Satolli, New York, January 23, 1893, "Private Record," AANY, L-3.

26. Lahiffe to McQuaid, New York, August 20, 1892, ADR.

27. Corrigan to McQuaid, New York, January 12, 1893, ADR.

documents to him. Friends of Ireland apparently worked up the subsequent exposure for the *Post*.

The *Post* article climaxed an increasing number of news stories discussing the campaign that Corrigan was inspiring among his followers against Satolli and Ireland. The press subsequently began to report efforts being made to depose Archbishop Corrigan. Archbishop Ireland was himself keeping his peace, but privately had forwarded to Cardinal Rampolla charges that Corrigan was making devious efforts to undermine Satolli.[28] Corrigan was not taking the deposition threats lightly. Rumors began to spread that the archbishop would be forced to resign or accept a coadjutor. On January 13, five days after the Chicago *Post* article, Corrigan denied in a letter to Cardinal Rampolla that he had conspired in any way against the Holy See, including the inspiration of any of the letters or articles that had appeared against the delegate or [McGlynn].[29] Strictly speaking, this was correct. The "Philadelphia article" had primarily attacked Ireland rather than Satolli. There is no evidence that Archbishop Corrigan strictly advised anyone to write a specific letter or article against Satolli. Others like Joseph Daley and Thomas Addis Emmet readily came forward to absolve the archbishop of any attempt to work up protests against Satolli's appointment or McGlynn's restoration.[30] But the archbishop was being disingenuous in trying to establish the image of someone who was somehow above all the attacks taking place in the press and elsewhere. Some of the closest friends of the archbishop were making some of the loudest noise about Satolli's policies. Frederick Coudert and George Bliss, two prominent New York Catholics, were writing letters to newspapers under thinly veiled pen names. Every week Corrigan was getting advance copies of the *Catholic Herald*, which was very involved in the campaign. It is fairly obvious, indeed, that the archbishop or his assistants were supplying anonymous or pen name–using writers with materials and arguments to use in their attacks against Ireland and Satolli. The archbishop pleaded that he could not control the press, but it is clear he was very ready to intervene when he saw fit with the Catholic press in his archdiocese, as he had with *The Catholic World* on more than one occasion. One has to conclude that he took no active steps to discourage the Lavelles and Couderts simply because they substantially echoed his own sentiments.

28. Burtsell Diary, vol. 9, January 25, 1893, AANY.

29. Corrigan to Rampolla, New York, January 13, 1893, copy, AANY, I-41.

30. Daley to Corrigan, January 25, 1893, AANY, G-12; Emmet to Corrigan, New York, January 22, 1893, AANY, G-13.

In fact the archbishop was writing anonymously against Ireland's plan and Satolli's support of it. The "Philadelphia article" cited in the *Post* exposé has every appearance of being from his pen. He wrote at least one lengthy letter to the New York *Sun* under a pseudonym. On December 30, 1892, the *Sun* printed a letter from a "D.J." of Staten Island that laid out in detail the financial statement of St. Michael's parish in Stillwater to prove that the parish, notwithstanding Ireland's claims, was quite capable of supporting a parochial school. Corrigan had been in correspondence with the retired pastor of St. Michael's to obtain this information. The letter closed:

> Now if Mgr. Satolli will assure us of his delight in all this, in beautiful Latin, and tell us that he expresses the mind of the Holy Father, I for one, will come to the conclusion that there is no connection between theology and financiering, and that there is at least one memorial in the history of the Church in America that gave signs of having been written by a great man whose memory had failed him.[31]

The style is quintessential Corrigan.

Nor was the archbishop confining his attempts to discredit Ireland and Satolli to newspaper articles written by himself or others. On January 15, 1893, the New York *Herald* reported that the enemies of Ireland and Satolli had been spying on Ireland, Keane, O'Connell, and Archbishop Riordan of San Francisco for the past month, and that a large number of their letters had been stolen. That very week Corrigan had entered into a correspondence with a C. A. Doeing, the owner of the Catholic Publishing Company in San Francisco and editor of the *Western Witness*, to obtain some letters written to Archbishop Riordan from Ireland, Gibbons, and O'Connell, which had somehow fallen into Doeing's hands. Doeing claimed that the letters proved that there existed "in this country and in Rome a *conspiracy*" against Corrigan, "Rome itself, and the German American Episcopate." Since the editor claimed that he had already sent a protest to Propaganda about the substance of the letters, he professed reluctance to send copies of them to Corrigan until he heard further from Rome. A month later the archbishop obtained notarized copies of the letters. They confirmed the liberals' attempt to put liberal prelates in key sees, specifically Milwaukee and Omaha, discussed the German threat and the school question, and contained some very embarrassing language about Corrigan, but hardly constituted a basis upon which anyone could have built a conspiracy case.

Despite his disastrous experience with Lahiffe and the Chicago *Sunday*

31. New York *Sun*, December 30, 1892.

Post, Corrigan persisted in his propaganda campaign against Ireland's plan and the delegate. In March 1893 he asked Sebastian Messmer for a list of the leading German papers, especially in the West, to which Corrigan intended to send copies of a new pamphlet attacking Ireland. Messmer refused the request on the grounds that such strategy would only compound the accusations about Corrigan's conspiracy against Ireland and Satolli. Corrigan, the Milwaukee archbishop suggested, was so identified with the Germans that any such pamphlet appearing simultaneously in various German periodicals would only point suspicion toward New York. Instead he proposed that Corrigan plant it in a few reviews like the Philadelphia-based *American Catholic Quarterly* and the *Catholic World*. Once there he was sure that the German American Catholic press would "jump at it."[32]

A year later, in April 1894, the New York *Herald* published a story that closely paralleled the 1893 *Sunday Post* story. The apostolic delegate, the *Herald* story reported, was preparing a formal accusation against Corrigan for plotting to destroy his influence. According to the *Herald*,

> Among the charges which are to be made against Archbishop Corrigan . . . is . . . that he employed the editor of a Catholic newspaper, published in this city to carry on the literary part of the warfare. This editor has been called the "press agent" of the Archbishop. He is a devoted Catholic and is said to have been convinced that he owed a higher duty to Rome than to the Archbishop. He is said to have furnished all the facts in his possession to the Apostolic Delegate.[33]

The editor, of course, was Michael Walsh of the *Catholic Herald*, who had given Satolli evidence of his work for Corrigan, including portions of letters from the archbishop himself. Ireland, having seen the purported letters, was convinced that they irrefutably connected the New York archbishop "with the diabolical war waged against the delegation. . . . The question now is: Who goes down C[orrigan] or S[atolli]? . . . I am told . . . that C. is just now quite frightened. . . . He knows that W[alsh] holds the key to the situation."[34]

Walsh was working both sides of the street. At the very time he was passing on the letters to Ireland and Satolli, he was self-righteously denying publicly that he was the source of the new accusations against the archbishop.

32. Messmer to Corrigan, Green Bay, March 13, 1893, AANY, G-4.

33. New York *Herald*, April 19, 1894.

34. Ireland to O'Connell [New York], April 29, 1894, ADRi. It is unclear whether Satolli or Ireland saw the actual letters. The portions quoted by Ireland seem a mixture of Corrigan and Walsh.

Indeed he pleaded with Corrigan that the latter make a public statement denying that Walsh was his public advocate. The archbishop refused, and Walsh continued his secret denunciations to prelates in America and Rome.

Walsh had for a long time passed on his articles to the archbishop for prepublication approval. In addition he passed on confidential information gathered from sources at home and abroad. Corrigan at the same time used Walsh as a chief channel of his views and those of conservatives. The falling-out seems to have been precipitated by Walsh's desire for greater income. In 1892 the editor had asked Corrigan to use his influence with John Crimmins, a prominent New York contractor and Democratic park commissioner, to secure for the *Herald* the commission of publishing legal notices for the city. For whatever reason, Walsh got no city commission. A year and a half later, in January 1894, Walsh sought Corrigan's aid to be named a collector of Internal Revenue in the city. Corrigan expressed interest in the editor's application, but there is no evidence that he did anything to secure it.[35] Four months after the New York *Herald*'s story, the archbishop wrote Walsh that he had "no further use" for the *Catholic Herald* and asked him to submit a bill for the services he had rendered. Walsh submitted a figure of $6,750 for his services.

Corrigan refused to pay the sum, and stories began to circulate that Walsh was attempting to blackmail the archbishop. Publicly Walsh denied the rumor, but privately he warned the archbishop that he might have cause to regret his failure to pay. According to Walsh, Archbishop Satolli himself had urged him not to publish the book that Walsh claimed to have written under the title "The Three Years' Crisis," but Walsh insisted that he had no choice, since the book already had more than 1,000 subscribers, mostly clergy and prelates.[36] The editor now wanted $9,000 from the archbishop for withholding from print his book, which contained his inside knowledge of Corrigan's crusade against Ireland and Satolli since 1891. Satolli himself had seen the manuscript and suggested that Corrigan would be wise to meet Walsh's price. There is no evidence that Corrigan complied, but the book was never published.[37]

Richard Burtsell, still in Rome when Satolli and Walsh began sending the

35. Walsh to Corrigan, New York, June 16, 1892, AANY, C-43; Walsh to Corrigan, New York, July 17, 1892, AANY, C-43; Walsh to Corrigan, New York, January 22, 1894, AANY, G-8; Walsh to Corrigan, New York, January 27, 1894, AANY, G-8.

36. Walsh to Corrigan, New York, December 10, 1894, AANY; Corrigan memorandum, 1894, AANY, G-8.

37. Corrigan memoranda, 1894, AANY.

evidence to Secretary of State Rampolla, thought that the compromising letters would surely result in some action against his ordinary. To abet such an outcome, Burtsell had given Rampolla a lengthy resumé of the role Burtsell thought Corrigan had been playing in frustrating Rome's American policy during the past decade. This document also found its way into print in the New York *World* on September 25, 1894, with the by now familiar evidence pointing to Archbishop Corrigan as the center of a conspiracy against Satolli, with Walsh as his chief instrument. Much of the evidence had obviously been supplied by Walsh.

The article itself was probably the result of Burtsell's frustration that Rome had taken no action against the Archbishop of New York. It is certainly revealing to compare the reaction of Satolli to the original conspiracy charge in the Chicago *Post* in January 1893 with these later stories, which had a good deal more evidence behind them. In 1893 the delegate denounced the alleged attempts to subvert Ireland and himself; a year and a half later he was expressing outrage at the stories themselves. He called the *Herald* story of April absolutely false, even while he was forwarding to Rampolla copies of Corrigan's purported letters to Walsh. So too with the *World* piece, which he attributed to people "of evil disposition."[38]

By then Satolli had decided to mollify Corrigan's opposition rather than to expose it. Corrigan had gained important allies in Rome, especially in the Sacred Congregation for the Propagation of the Faith, where his opposition to Satolli, an appointee of the Secretariate of State with whom Propaganda had serious differences, had made him a natural ally. When Otto Zardetti of St. Cloud raised the matter of Corrigan's alleged conspiracy with Pope Leo XIII, the pontiff replied that "There were such accusations. But Satolli had assured him that "*Mgr. Corrigan was always loyal to the H. See.*"[39]

Archbishop Corrigan and Tammany Hall

If one threatened scandal was subsiding in the fall of 1894, another one was just beginning, or rather reviving. Another of Archbishop Corrigan's priests, Thomas Ducey, pastor of St. Leo's in New York City, was claiming to

38. New York *Evening Sun*, April 19, 1894; Satolli to Corrigan, Washington, D.C., April 19, 1894, AANY, G-9; Satolli to Corrigan, Washington, D.C., September 29, 1894, in "Private Record," 412, AANY, L-3.

39. Zardetti to Corrigan, Rome, October 19, 1894, AANY, G-9.

be the commissioned reporter of the Vatican at the Lexow Commission Investigation into the relationship between the Democratic Party and organized crime in New York City. The implication was that Vatican officials were deeply concerned about the reputed alliance between Tammany Hall and the Church in New York. There were rumors that Ducey would be called to testify on this very point. John Lancaster Spalding thought that Ducey's actions might "stir up the nastiest mess yet."[40] Ducey had seen some of the evidence that Walsh had prepared for Satolli. More than that, as Ducey told Denis O'Connell, he knew positively that "there is in the hands of some of the most representative men in the country, not Catholics, awful evidence of Abp. Corrigan's corrupt relation with corrupt Tammany Hall. . . . These gentlemen have consulted me, and I have asked them to delay the exposure, as I believe Rome will act soon and most justly and vigorously, in the interests of the Church of the United States. Should . . . Abp. Corrigan be permitted to remain in New York he becomes virtually Pope of America, supported and ruled by Tammany Hall."[41]

The "awful evidence" would seem mainly to have been the product of Ducey's desire to be the instrument of Corrigan's demise. The archbishop waited until after the November elections to forbid Ducey to attend any further sessions of the investigation. Ducey not only continued to attend the meetings as conspicuously as possible, but published a letter he had sent to his archbishop in response to the archbishop's order, in which Ducey accused Corrigan of throwing the Catholic Church "to the winds" in New York City by his involvement with a corrupt political party, and warned that he also had strong evidence "that here in the city of New York we have had the very front and citadel of organized opposition to the action and wishes of the Holy See."[42]

As one New Yorker wrote Denis O'Connell in that month, "the Catholic Church authorities in New York City was [sic] one of [Tammany's] strongest allies, upholding in every possible way Tammany Hall. So far has this gone that the Catholics themselves have frequently spoken of their church as the annex of Tammany Hall."[43] The informant pointed out that at the Church of the Sacred Heart in New York, where Corrigan's vicar-general, Joseph Moony, was pastor, the assistant priests at the masses on the Sunday before the election had urged their parishioners from the pulpit to vote the Democratic ticket.

40. Spalding to James Ryan, Peoria, December 7, 1894, Archives of the Diocese of Peoria.

41. Ducey to O'Connell, New York, July 30, 1894, ADRi.

42. New York *World*, November 23, 1894.

43. A. M. Brown to Denis O'Connell, New York, November 13, 1894, ADRi.

Since the mid-1880s, when Archbishop Corrigan suspended Edward McGlynn for his support of Henry George's mayoralty campaign, the archbishop had been accused of being in league with Tammany Hall. That charge was part of McGlynn's diatribes about the "Ecclesiastical Machine" in New York. The Sacred Heart priests' endorsement of the Democratic ticket was reminiscent of the public statement of an earlier vicar-general of the archbishop, Thomas Preston, who on the eve of the 1886 election publicly assured a Tammany leader that the Catholic Church in New York, pace Edward McGlynn, did not endorse the candidacy of Henry George; every priest he knew, Preston continued, would "deeply regret" George's election. Although Preston made clear that the Catholic authorities "never interfere directly in elections, we would not wish to be misunderstood," he concluded, "when the best interests of society may be in danger."[44] Burtsell and Ducey, among others, charged that prominent Democrats had pressured Corrigan to suspend McGlynn in 1886 to prevent him from persuading many Catholics to desert the Democratic ticket in favor of George. One Tammany leader, Bourke Cockran, took credit for convincing Corrigan of the danger of George's candidacy.[45] Corrigan admitted that many prominent Catholics, including politicians, had expressed to him their extreme displeasure over McGlynn's activities in George's behalf, but denied that any of them specifically asked him to suspend McGlynn, and there are extant letters from several politicians, such as John Crimmins, that support his denial.[46]

What were Corrigan's ties to the Democratic Party?—personal friendships with several prominent politicians, including Park Commissioner John Crimmins, Judge Joseph Daley, lawyer Frederick Coudert, and Eugene Kelly. When Coudert, along with other Democratic officials, tried to get Corrigan to endorse, even indirectly, Grover Cleveland in 1884, Corrigan was greatly annoyed: "the insinuation," he confided to Gibbons, "that Catholics belong to the Democratic party and are not at liberty to vote otherwise is . . . amusing."[47] He took offense at insinuations that he was in league with Boss Richard Croker, whom he barely knew. In regard to state aid to Catholic charitable

44. Preston to J. O'Donoghue, New York, October 25, 1886, cited in Frederick Zwierlein, *The Life and Letters of Bishop McQuaid* (Rochester: Art Print Shop, 1927) 3:6–7, quoting the Rochester *Union and Advertiser*, October 29, 1886.

45. Stephen Bell, *Rebel, Priest, and Prophet: A Biography of Dr. Edward McGlynn* (New York: Devin-Adair, 1937), 35.

46. Corrigan Memoranda, 1895, AANY; Crimmins to Corrigan, New York, January 25, 1895, AANY, G-12; Joseph Daley to Corrigan, New York, January 7, 1895, AANY, G-12.

47. Corrigan to Gibbons, New York, October 6, 1884, AAB 78-Q-11.

institutions the regular Democrats had proven to be loyal supporters over the years. He was willing to use those connections to secure positions or other favors at times.[48] In the 1892 gubernatorial elections he apparently wrote in favor of the candidacy of the Democratic candidate for Lieutenant Governor, whose brother was police commissioner in New York City, and reprimanded Michael Walsh for opposing him in the *Catholic Herald*.[49] He also was accused of pressuring several priests into supporting the candidate publicly.

The November 1894 elections were the newest occasion for assertions of Corrigan's alliance with Tammany. At issue in the election were the amendments to the state constitution passed by the Republican majority in Albany the previous summer. One of these ironically denied the use of any state funds to support private education and put in jeopardy state aid to charitable institutions, as well. Church authorities feared the loss of all subsidies and their tax exemption on Church property. Indeed Corrigan, through Frederick Coudert and George Bliss, had unsuccessfully tried to influence the delegates to defeat the amendments. As Corrigan reported to the Secretary of State, Cardinal Rampolla, what happened in New York would very well decide the future of public subsidies for Catholic institutions. "If the people, not being well enough informed about the problem," voted for the amendments, the parishes of the archdiocese were facing an annual loss of millions of dollars.[50] The Sacred Heart priests pushed the Democratic slate in order to undo the work of the Republicans. As O'Connell's New York informant saw it, "in face of this horrible corruption" revealed by the Lexow Commission, "Catholic priests from God's Holy Altars were ordering their people to vote the straight Democratic Ticket." The newspapers also noted that George Washington Plunkett was a parishioner and judged the sermons as ones that "about settles things in this district" for the election.[51] The archbishop again denied any affiliation with Tammany and claimed that he had no advance knowledge of the Sacred Heart priests' endorsement. But he took no action against the priests' offense against Church rules prohibiting clerical involvement in political matters. Interestingly, two months before the elec-

48. See Bishop Winand Wigger's notes to Corrigan in May of 1891, thanking him for his offices in securing for a friend of Wigger the position of city marshal; Wigger to Corrigan [South Orange], May 22, 1891, AANY; Wigger to Corrigan [South Orange], May 26, 1891, AANY.

49. Walsh, in his defense, claimed that he had been "assured that you took no interest in the matter"; Walsh to Corrigan, New York, February 3, 1892, AANY.

50. Corrigan to Rampolla, New York, September 14, 1894, in Soderini ms., VI, 57,copy, UND.

51. New York *Herald*, November 16, 1894.

tion, Corrigan, in a reply to Cardinal Rampolla, who had suggested that the pope might make some statement calling for the American people to foster state aid to parochial education, warned that this would have a very counter-productive consequence—the resentment of the pope trying to intervene in the independent political life of the country. But he said nothing about local ecclesiastics using their influence.[52]

Despite the clerical endorsement, the elections were a disaster for the Democrats and the anti-amendment forces. The satirical journal *Puck* celebrated the victory for reform by running a cartoon that showed the Tammany tiger on his deathbed, with Archbishop Corrigan on one side and Boss Croker on the other trying to revive the dying animal with batteries in the form of ecclesiastical and political machines, respectively. The label above the scene read: "The Tammany Tiger Executed by the People, November 6, 1894."

Archbishop Corrigan was convinced that the real corrupt alliance between Church and party was not that of the New York archdiocese with Tammany, but that between John Ireland and the Republican Party of New York State. He was incensed at the role Ireland had played in the last election in promoting Republican fortunes in New York. "Fancy... my going to St. Paul," he wrote Gibbons, "staying three weeks at the Ryan House without calling on the archbishop, then parading myself at political meetings, and giving Abp. Ireland's subjects pointed advice on the way they ought to vote!"[53] Bishop Bernard McQuaid, in a sermon at his cathedral in late November, charged that Ireland had come to New York as a paid agent of the Republican Party. McQuaid and Corrigan knew that after the election, the Republican leader, Chauncey Depew, had been responsible for raising some $50,000 to assist the St. Paul archbishop in his financial difficulties. What was unclear was whether it was a gift or a loan. Archbishop Corrigan spent months trying to clear up the mystery, presumably as evidence to use against Ireland in Rome, but the evidence he uncovered was inconclusive.[54]

52. Corrigan to Rampolla, September 14, 1894, in Soderini ms., copy, UND.

53. Corrigan to Gibbons, New York, November 15, 1894, AAB 93-M10.

54. One of the benefactors admitted to the archbishop that he considered it a gift, but others considered their subscriptions loans; Corrigan to McQuaid, New York, February 6, 1895, ADR; Corrigan to McQuaid, New York, February 28, 1895, ADR; Corrigan Memorandum, January 1895, AANY.

Triumph and the Ghetto

If Corrigan's political fortunes in his own state were being frustrated, his fortunes in Rome were vastly improving as 1894 turned to 1895. Public propagandizing had helped make the New York prelate a force in the conservative realm that greatly increased his power in the geopolitical world of the Vatican. Corrigan was able to take advantage of the tensions between Propaganda and the Secretariate of State (see chapter 8). State had been largely responsible for Satolli's appointment, but the delegate as well as the Church in America still fell under the direction of Propaganda. Corrigan's opposition to Satolli made him a natural ally of the Sacred Congregation. In supporting Corrigan, Propaganda could help check the larger strategy of the pope and Rampolla to pursue the papacy's *ralliement* policy to gain leverage against the Triple Alliance, especially Italy. This *realpolitik* forced Satolli to make peace with the New York archbishop, and a ceremony of reconciliation followed in the summer of 1893 at Saint Patrick's Cathedral between the two prelates. Thereafter Satolli began to take radically different positions on the issues that were polarizing the prelates, including that of parochial education. Not only did he praise parochial education, but began to put emphasis on promoting such education as the Catholic norm, a trend that culminated with his address to the German Americans at Pottsville, Pennsylvania, in April 1895. John Ireland's own experiment at Faribault and Stillwater had collapsed two years earlier, a victim not of opposition from conservative prelates, but of an aroused Protestant citizenry that refused to sanction even Ireland's version of a working agreement between church and state.[55] By the end of the century the conservatives had clearly won the battle over the school question. In doing so they had laid the groundwork for the development of a school system that, though serving but a minority of American Catholic students, would be unrivaled in the Catholic world. They had also aided in the consolidation of the American Catholic ghetto that the Third Plenary Council had begun, with its implicit endorsement of a Catholic subculture, with the parochial school at its center.

55. Ireland to O'Connell, St. Paul, November 14, 1893, ADRi.

Part 3

Social Justice and the Intellectual Life

Chapter 11

Confronting "The Social Question"

American Catholic Thought and the Socio-Economic Order in the Nineteenth Century

THE AMERICAN bishops as a body have not been renowned for prophetic activity. Their more recent history, however, makes clear that they are taking very seriously a prophetic function in addressing from a Christian perspective the fundamental structures of the society in which we live. In their 1983 pastoral "The Challenge of Peace" they challenged the prevailing rationale upon which our nuclear defense rests. A year and a half later they released the first draft of their pastoral on "Catholic Social Teaching and the U.S. Economy," in which they concluded that this country still falls far short of the justice that the Gospel impels us to seek in our economic and social structures. If the first pastoral made the military-industrial complex somewhat nervous about its traditional support from the Catholic community, especially its hierarchy, and led one clerical pundit to charge that the bishops had become the "Haight-Ashbury of the American Church," their second provoked angry responses that the prelates should stick to their prayers and leave business to businessmen. There was a time, of course, when bishops were regarded as being too much like businessmen in their thinking and orientation. But, if they are still reading the *Wall Street Journal*, they have gone elsewhere for their ideas about the economy.

In keeping with Catholic American tradition, the bishops had minimal recourse to their own community's intellectual past in shaping their pastorals in the 1980s. John Ryan and the Bishops Program of 1919 are cited, as are some previous pastorals in the twentieth century. The only

American mentioned who predates 1900 is the Puritan John Winthrop. The prelates draw upon Winthrop's "knit together . . . as one man" image to buttress their claim that an ethics of the common good runs deep in American history.[1] As Bruce Douglass has observed, this tradition is at the heart of the pastoral, "that the common good should be consciously willed and pursued in the design of social institutions and public policy."[2]

A prominent Catholic historian has noted that the 1983 pastoral marked a new departure for the bishops from their traditional stance of support for government policy and silence on political issues outside the realms of education and family life.[3] In the socio-economic order, the American hierarchy in the nineteenth century was equally prudent. Still, as the following chapter attempts to show, American Catholics in the course of that century did begin to recover and develop a social ethic to bring to bear upon the new complexities of urban-industrial life. To that recovery and development individuals and groups in the New York and Chesapeake regions made important contributions. This chapter first appeared as an article in *U.S. Catholic Historian* 5 (1986): 165–93.

Cosmopolitan Conformism

What David O'Brien has written about American Catholic social action holds as well for its social thought: that our heritage is "far from clear," but that it has been primarily shaped by "two sometimes conflicting forces: by the demands made on the Church to conform its values and ideals to those of American culture, demands increasingly assimilated and internalized by the Church and its leaders, and by the needs and aspirations of the Catholic people themselves."[4]

Of the 25,000 or so Catholics at the beginning of the American Revolu-

1. In his "Modell of Christian Charity," Winthrop wrote, "For this end [building a community] we must be knit together in this work as one man, we must entertain each other in brotherly affection, we must be willing to abridge ourselves of our superfluities, for the supply of others' necessities"; cited in "Catholic Social Teaching and the U.S. Economy" (First Draft), *Origins: NC Documentary Service* (November 15, 1984): 350.

2. Bruce Douglass, "At the Heart of the Letter," *America* (June 21, 1985): 360.

3. Gerald P. Fogarty, S.J., "Public Patriotism and Private Politics: The Tradition of American Catholicism," *U. S. Catholic Historian* 3 (November 1984), 1–48.

4. David O'Brien, "The American Priest and Social Action," in *The Catholic Priest in the United States: Historical Investigations*, ed. John Tracy Ellis (Collegeville, Minn.: St. John's University Press, 1971), 424, 429.

tion, a large portion was Maryland gentry and solid German Pennsylvania farmers. Despite the imposition of penal laws during the last seventy years of the Colonial period in Maryland, the Maryland gentry did not suffer economic loss as a consequence of political disability. Indeed the period from 1720 to 1750 was one of great prosperity for the leading Catholic families. Through land speculation, industrial ventures, agriculture, and commerce, Catholics like Charles Carroll of Annapolis, James Digges, and Richard Bennett accumulated considerable fortunes. At his death in 1749 Bennett was reputed to be the richest man in America. A generation later, Charles Carroll of Carrollton enjoyed the same reputation.

Except for their support of religious liberty, these Catholics were in their social attitudes "cosmopolitan conformists," alive to European intellectual currents but little inclined to challenge social or economic structures.[5] Religion tended to influence personal and family behavior, but did not influence social attitudes. Charles Carroll of Carrollton, who became the leader of the Catholic community in Maryland, came home from Europe convinced that the proprietor and the court party that had for so long been the refuge of Maryland Catholics would not be the dominant force shaping the colony's future. Eventually, of course, he cast his considerable fortune with the Patriot party, as did the majority of Catholics. The role that Catholics like the Carrolls played in the Revolution led to their being more acceptable in the larger society and tended to confirm their conservative, conformist tendencies. They were Federalists in their politics, much opposed to the social leveling they associated with the Republicans. Property was the basis of the social order. The key to preserving social peace, according to Charles Carroll, was the "example of frugality and industry to the common people" that property holders had the responsibility to give.[6] To "excite hostile feelings between the different classes of society," wrote another prominent Catholic of the early national period, was nothing less than "treason against social happiness."[7]

The separation of church and state in America encouraged Catholics to restrict religion to the private sphere. John Carroll, who wholeheartedly supported the American arrangement as a model for the world, saw the state as

5. The phrase is C. Joseph Neusse's in his study of *The Social Thought of American Catholics, 1634–1829* (Washington: The Catholic University of America Press, 1945).

6. Neusse, *Social Thought of American Catholics*, 64.

7. William Gaston, An *Address delivered before the American Whig and Cliosophic Societies off the College of New Jersey (Princeton, N.J.: R. E. Hornor, 1835)*, 21, in Neusse, *Social Thought of American Catholics*, 211.

essentially secular in nature; the success of republican government rested on its preservation of the liberty and property of its citizens. As Bishop John England told the Congress in 1826: "You have no power to interfere with my religious rights; the tribunal of the church has no power to interfere with my civil rights. It is a duty which every good man ought to discharge for his own and for the public benefit, to resist any encroachment upon either."[8] The Bishops' first Pastoral Letter (written by England) in 1829 was more explicit about this principle of noninvolvement in the social order: "Your flocks . . . [expect] from you . . . instruction for the service of God, not suggestions as to the regulation of their own temporal concerns with which you should scrupulously avoid any entanglement."[9]

The Immigrant Church

In his struggles with parish trustees, who claimed far-ranging powers toward fulfilling their duty, John Carroll had discovered within his own church the difficulty of enacting such a rigid separation of the spiritual and temporal orders. By 1830 a larger development within American Catholicism was making it increasingly impossible for Church leaders to take such a hands-off attitude toward the society in which Catholics lived. Immigration was drastically changing the profile of the Church in America. Irish Catholics, the largest group of immigrants, were the poorest people America had ever taken in since it had become a republic. Large-scale Irish immigration became, in the 1840s, a tidal wave of those fleeing famine in their homeland. The Great Hunger brought approximately a million and a half Irish to this country within less than a decade. With this enormous influx of Irish Catholics and a lesser immigration of German Catholics, the Church in America suddenly numbered more than three million by the Civil War, nearly 10 percent of the population. It had become larger than any single Protestant denomination in the country.

In 1855 a Protestant historian could observe:

> the Roman Church . . . meets only the extremes of society, especially the lowest, poorest and most uncultivated class of emigrants who form . . . its flesh and blood; embracing also . . . a larger or smaller number of influential families of the higher

8. John England, "Address before Congress," *The Works of the Right Reverent John England: First Bishop of Charleston*, ed. Sebastian G. Messmer, (Cleveland: Arthur H. Clark, 1908): 7:35.

9. Peter Guilday, *The National Pastorals of the American Hierarchy, 1792–1919* (Washington, D.C.: National Catholic Welfare Conference, 1923), 51–52.

and educated order, including many converts from the different Protestant denominations, especially the Episcopalians.[10]

This mixture of immigrants, old Catholic gentry, and converts had a profound impact on the evolution of American Catholic social thought in the next seventy years.

In the garrets and cellars of New York, Philadelphia, Baltimore, and Boston, the Irish transplanted their villages. They took such unskilled work as they could find as day laborers and domestic servants. Many fell into crime as a way of seeking the American dream. They were soon a majority of the population of the prisons and charity wards along the East Coast and in New Orleans.[11]

Native-born American Catholics, whether cradle ones or converts, were largely appalled at this development. Illiterate Irishmen in cellars and saloons were not the American Church of the Carrolls or the Setons, a sanctuary of authority and stability in the swirling sea of materialism and freedom that life in the United Sates seemed by mid-century to be to many conservative Catholics. Attempting to divert such a scrutiny of his ethnic brethren, Bishop John Hughes, an immigrant Irishman himself, contended, at the height of the Famine immigration, that the real reason for the extraordinary growth of the American Church lay not in its immigrant but its native-born members. He noted that "hundreds of thousands" of the descendants of Catholic immigrants had been lost to the Church through ignorance, isolation, or indifference. Moreover, statistics showed, he claimed, a staggering mortality rate of one-third of the current Irish immigrants because of the terrible circumstances in which they found themselves, "exposed to the accidents of life, to sickness, hardship of every kind, . . . toilsome poverty, . . . epidemics . . . of cholera, yellow fever, or anything else which decimates them."[12]

On the eve of the Great Famine, Hughes had delivered two addresses in which he had excoriated the Malthusian assumptions of the reigning political

10. Philip Schaff, *America: A Sketch of the Political, Social and Religious Character of the United States* (New York: Charles Scribner, 1855), 226, quoted in Aaron I. Abell, *American Catholicism and Social Action: A Search for Social Justice* (Notre Dame, Ind.: University of Notre Dame Press, 1960), 13.

11. Lawrence J. McCaffrey, *The Irish Diaspora in America* (Bloomington: University of Indiana Press, 1976), 68.

12. John Hughes, "Lecture on the Present Condition and Prospects of the Catholic Church in the United Sates," delivered before the Young Catholics' Friends Society, at Baltimore, January 17, 1856, in *Complete Works of the Most Reverend John Hughes*, ed. Lawrence Kehoe (New York: Catholic Publication House, 1865), 2:122–32, cited in *American Catholic Thought on Social Questions*, ed. Aaron I. Abell (Indianapolis: Bobbs-Merrill, 1968), 12.

economy that exploited labor in the name of liberty, "a mockery of freedom" in which "the starving laborer" was pitted against "bloated capitalists."[13] This indictment of economic orthodoxy was unique for a Catholic bishop in the antebellum period. But the bishop's focus was England, not the United States, which he found in 1844 to be "the most prosperous and happy land on the surface of the globe, . . . with a population among whom there are no privileged classes, among whom education and enlightened enterprise are almost universal."[14] Twelve years later Hughes was less the booster and more aware of the price that immigrants were paying to be part of this exceptional society. His consolation was that immigration seemed to be declining. He apparently still shared the national myth that the Old World social conditions had no parallel in this country.

Colonization

Others were convinced that the Irish had to be rescued from the lethal cities in which they were trapped. The colonization movement was a radical response to the urban pattern of settlement that characterized that of the overwhelming majority of Irish Catholics. Catholic colonization went back at least to the 1780s, when a group of Maryland Catholic families headed west for Kentucky. At the turn of the century Demetrius Augustine Gallitzin had established in western Pennsylvania a community in which Catholic culture could prevail. Already in 1817 the Irish Emigrant Society of New York was exploring colonization as a solution for the social problems that urban immigrants were encountering. By the 1850s interest in colonization was growing, not only as a relief for immigrants, but to defuse the charges of nativists that Catholics were overrunning the cities. A group of Catholic clergy and laity sponsored a convention in Buffalo in February 1856 to plan a colony for Catholics in Nebraska, but Hughes, the most prominent Irish American bishop, found it impractical. As bad as the Irish might have it in the cities, they were utterly unprepared for the complex husbandry that American agriculture required.[15]

13. Hughes, "A Lecture on the Importance of a Christian Basis for the Science of Political Economy, and its Application to the Affairs of Life," in *Complete Works*, ed. Kehoe, 1:521, cited in "American Catholics and the Social Question, 1865–1900," by James Edmund Roohan (Ph.D. diss., Yale University, 1952; repr. New York: Arno Press, 1976), 66.

14. John Hughes, "The Influence of Christianity on Social Servitude," *Complete Works*, 1:372, in Roohan, "American Catholics and the Social Question," 71.

15. Henry J. Browne, "Archbishop Hughes and Western Colonization," *Catholic Historical Review* (October 1950): 269–73, cited in *Documents of American Catholic History*, ed. John Tracy Ellis

In the postbellum period Catholics continued to promote colonization as an antidote for the "social problem." The most utopian idea was the "Christian reductionism" of the Louisiana lawyer and jurist T. Wharton Collens. Based on the Paraguay reductions that the seventeenth-century Jesuits had begun for the AmerIndian population, Collens' ideal was a network of colonies in the spirit of the apostolic communities, which would freely embrace poverty in opposition to "riches-and-comfort-seeking socialism," and vow themselves to obey appointed leaders. In an era of association, Collens was confident that the creation of such communities would be infectious; that replicas would quickly multiply in response to their examples.[16] Apostolic poverty and obedience would save the Catholic communes from the selfishness and anarchy that had wrecked the utopian societies in the 1840s and 1850s.

Such romantic possibilities stirred few American Catholic hearts. Poverty had less attraction for the American Irish than the land itself. Other more conventional forms of colonization were more successful. The best-known was the Irish Catholic Colonization Association of the United States, founded in 1879 under the leadership of Bishop John Ireland of St. Paul. Ireland had already founded five colonies in Minnesota. He loved to tell urban Catholics that "man made the city but God made the country."[17] The association's first president, Bishop John Lancaster Spalding, as a priest in New York City in the early 1870s had experienced first-hand the effects of urban life upon the immigrant. To promote the work of the association, Spalding published in 1880 *The Religious Mission of the Irish People*, in which he argued that colonization was the most urgent issue facing the American Church. Left "in its present floating and unsettled state" in the cities, the Irish, Spalding concluded, could have "little hope of a future in America." Only their settlement on their own farms "upon the cheap lands of our country" could protect "the sanctity of the family, preserve the purity of childhood, and promote the growth of religious character."[18]

(Chicago: Henry Regnery, 1967), 1:317–21. It may well be that Hughes' opposition was due in part to the fact that the organizers of the convention had not sought his approval beforehand. He himself had earlier explored the possibilities of a Catholic colony in Wisconsin.

16. T. Wharton Collens, "Views of the Labor Movement," *Catholic World* 10 (March 1870), reprinted in Abell, *American Catholic Thought*, 72–90.

17. Quoted in James P. Shannon, *Catholic Colonization on the Western Frontier* (New Haven: Yale University Press, 1957), ix.

18. John Lancaster Spalding, *The Religious Mission of the Irish People* (New York: Catholic Publication Society, 1880), 147–49.

Despite the backing of much of the hierarchy, Ireland and Spalding's plan for a national colonization program failed to materialize. The Irish Catholic Benevolent Union, which Ireland envisioned as a coordinating force for the movement, proved to be an organization on the decline and hopelessly divided over the issue. Even more fatal was the lack of enthusiasm of Irish workers in the East. Ireland, Spalding, and other spokesmen for the Association worked the circuits of churches and meetings halls in New York, Baltimore, Boston, and elsewhere, and raised $100,000 for colonies in Minnesota and Nebraska, but few workers accepted their offers to come west and purchase railroad land under their auspices. Those who did were largely unsuccessful.[19] Nor was it merely their lack of experience. By the 1880s Western farmers were beginning to feel the hard times that would worsen for the rest of the century. The West was no longer, if it ever had been, a safety valve for individuals or groups. Even the immigrants increasingly knew that their opportunities lay, if anywhere, in the cities.

Benevolence and Alienation

The disproportionate number of Catholics in prisons, orphanages, and other public institutions was both an embarrassment and a concern to Catholic leaders. Discriminatory rules that denied priests access to inmates in many institutions in the antebellum period brought criticism from Catholics and pressure to build their own institutions, with or without state support. Through the lead of such figures as Levi Silliman Ives, the convert bishop of the Episcopal Church, industrial schools were begun in mid-century in New York City, Baltimore, and elsewhere for juvenile delinquents. As early as 1845 the Saint Vincent de Paul Society began to provide relief to the poor in American cities. In response to criticism about the dominance of the poor rolls by the Irish, Ives retorted that:

> for a considerable proportion of these, our Protestant countrymen have made themselves responsible,—inasmuch as these paupers, or their families, have been reduced to this state, by the hardships and dangers of that kind of labor to which, through Protestant cupidity, they have been subjected; and, in which the health of some, and the lives of others, have been lavishly sacrificed.[20]

19. Shannon, *Catholic Colonization*, 265–66; Abell, *American Catholicism and Social Action: A Search for Social Justice* (Notre Dame: University of Notre Dame Press, 1963), 51.

20. Levi Silliman Ives, *Church and State Charities Compared with Special Reference to the System of New York State Charities* (New York: 1857), in Abell, *American Catholic Thought*, 98.

Charges of materialism and avarice afflicting American society were common enough from Catholics leaders, especially after the Civil War and among the foreign-born. Antoine Walburg, the German pastor-scholar, wrote in 1889 that "Money is a power everywhere, but here it is the supreme power." It was significant to the Cincinnati priest that the corruption plaguing American public life was a native product, not an import, and its practitioners were in the main the native-born.[21] For the most part Catholic authorities preached patience and respect for law.[22]

To be sure, there were a few Catholic thinkers, even before the Civil War, who went beyond moralism in their examination of the economic order. None was more committed to *laissez faire* principles than Robert Walsh, a Maryland Federalist who edited the nation's first quarterly, the *American Review of History and Politics*. To Walsh the counterpart of self-government in politics was self-reliance in social action; state protection of the poor in America would constitute "tyranny and slavery."[23] He opposed labor unions and any social legislation. In a democracy, government could not provide for the necessities of the people, since they maintain it, and not vice versa. In an essay on the poor in 1836 he saw life as essentially a lottery in which all had a chance. To attack the rich was to disturb the order that enabled the poor to rise to their level.[24] Nonetheless, like many conservatives then and since, Walsh was willing to abandon strict *laissez faire* principles to allow government to intervene through tariffs to protect industrialists, since the subsequent profits would trickle down to the masses.

21. "Who are the devotees at the shrine of mammon?" Walburg asked. "Who compose the syndicates, trusts, corporations, pools, and those huge monopolies that reach their tentacles over the nation, grinding down the poor and fattening in immense wealth? They are not Germans or Irish, but Americans"; Antoine Walburg, *The Question of Nationality in its Relation to the Catholic Church in the United States* (Cincinnati: 1889), cited in Abell, *American Catholic Thought*, 40, 42.

22. As Donna Merwick notes about the Boston clergy in the 1870s: "the only safe way for the priest to attack the situation was by pointing out the lack of virtue in the exploiters, not by attacking the system head-on. To do so was absurd. At best, it meant putting into question the clergy's Americanism. In some situations, it would result in getting the parishioners into trouble at the factory." And there was always the danger of offending rich Catholics in the pews; Merwick, *Boston Priests, 1848–1910: A Study of Social and Intellectual Change* (Cambridge, Mass.: Harvard University Press, 1973), 107.

23. Robert Walsh, *Notes on the American Constitution* (Keesville, N.Y.: 1849), cited in Neusse, *Social Thought of American Catholics*, 218.

24. Walsh, *Didactics: Social, Literary, and Political*, 2 vols. (Philadelphia: Carey, Lea and Blanchard, 1836), cited in Neusse, *Social Thought of American Catholics*, 220.

A counterpart to Walsh in Philadelphia was an Irish printer, Matthew Carey, who abhorred Adam Smith and saw the direction of economic life as a fundamental obligation of government. The growing gap between rich and poor in Philadelphia deeply disturbed him. He debunked the notion that will was the only necessity to obtain work in America. While defending charitable societies, he looked to government to help workers, especially females, obtain a living wage:

> Many citizens entertain an idea that in the present state of society in this city, every person able and willing to work, may procure employment; that all those who are thus employed, may earn a decent and comfortable support; and that if not the whole, at least the chief part of the distresses of the poor, arises from idleness, dissipation, and worthlessness. Alas! nothing can be further from the truth.[25]

Anticipating Herbert Croly by some eighty years, Carey was calling for government to promote a balance of economic interests within the society by protecting labor as well as agriculture and industry.

One of the most influential converts in shaping the intellectual life of the American Church during the nineteenth century was Orestes Brownson. During his odyssey from transcendentalism to Catholicism, Brownson wrote in 1840 one of the most radical critiques of American society to appear in the antebellum period. Like Hughes, Brownson's initial focus in "The Laboring Classes" was Great Britain, especially Thomas Carlyle's charge that the British aristocracy was responsible for the exploitation of labor. But Brownson quickly broadened his scope to include America, as well.

"No one can observe the signs of the times with much care, without perceiving that a crisis as to the relation of wealth and labor is approaching." The condition of the worker was rapidly deteriorating, even in America, where labor had previously enjoyed certain ideal conditions. The cause of this evil, he went on,

> is not merely individual in its character. It is not . . . of any one man's procuring, nor can the efforts of any one man, directed solely to his own moral and religious perfection, do aught to remove it. . . . But the evil . . . is inherent in all our social arrangement. Could we convert all men to Christianity in both theory and practice, as held by the most enlightened sect of Christians among us, the evils of the social state would remain untouched.

25. Matthew Carey, "Essays on the Public Charities of Philadelphia," *Miscellaneous Essays* (Philadelphia: 1830), cited in Roohan, "American Catholics and the Social Question," 51.

The path to reform lay through a recovery of the "true gospel of Jesus," announcing social justice as the essence of the kingdom and through government intervention that would destroy economic privilege, including inherited property. Brownson had no illusions that the rich would freely consent to such a radical reordering of society. "It will be effected," he concluded, "only by the strong arm of physical force. It will come, if it ever comes at all, only at the conclusion of war, the like of which the world as yet has never witnessed."[26]

The election of 1840, in which the Whigs showed that they had learned the value of political symbolism all too well from the Jacksonians (Tippecanoe and Tyler too!) was a severe blow to Brownson's radical faith. Four years later he entered the Catholic Church. Tracing Brownson's social thought over his thirty-some years as a Catholic is no exercise in logical development. At times he extolled poverty as an antidote to the dominant acquisitive spirit of Americans. At others he sounded like the Brownson of "the Laboring Classes." "The men of wealth," he declared in 1866,

> the business men, manufacturers and merchants, bankers and brokers, are the men who exert the worst influence on government in every country, for they always strive to use it as an instrument of advancing their own private interests. They act on the beautiful maxim, "Let government take care of the rich, and the rich will take care of the poor," instead of the far safer maxim, "Let government take care of the weak, the strong can take care of themselves."[27]

The Church he saw as a moral guide consoling "the poor with the assurance, that if they bear their poverty with resignation, for Christ's sake, theirs is the kingdom of heaven" and admonishing the rich to use their wealth as stewards.[28] Catholicism's belief in the goodness of human nature and its organic view of society, in Brownson's view, gave it a superior claim to this role over Protestantism's individualism and darker understanding of man. Through the maddening ideological shifts he gradually lost the conviction that democracy and Catholicism were compatible. By 1868 he confessed to

26. Orestes Brownson, "The Laboring Classes," *The Boston Quarterly Review* (July 1840), reprinted in *The Transcendentalists*, ed. Perry Miller (Cambridge, Mass.: Harvard University Press, 1950), 436–46.

27. Brownson, *The American Republic: Its Constitution, Tendencies, and Destiny* (New York: 1866), 383, cited in Roohan, "American Catholics and the Social Question," 134.

28. Brownson, "Mission of America," *Brownson's Quarterly Review* (October 1856), excerpted in Abell, *American Catholic Thought*, 34.

his fellow convert Isaac Hecker that he had become a convert to the encyclical *Quanta Cura*, including its Syllabus of Errors, "and am almost beginning to despair of the success of the American experiment. I never had the spine of real radicalism in my composition, and all my radicalism was always . . . spasmodic. . . . I think I am turning Paddy."[29] Brownson continued to excoriate capitalism, but had lost any hope in government as a remedy, since business now controlled government as well as labor. By the 1870s he was preaching colonization and a return to rural values and decentralization.

For all the zigzagging of his social thought, Brownson, as James Roohan has observed, "put iron in Catholic spines, made [them] more outspoken in defense of their religion and less hesitant in their criticism of American society."[30] One person deeply influenced by Brownson was the Boston priest John T. Roddan. Roddan, the editor of *The Pilot* from 1848 to 1858, early in his tenure defended local tailors against their employers. "In a republic like this," he editorialized in 1849, "the press must naturally "give the workers a fair opportunity for effecting a revolution of their own."[31] As Brownson became more conservative and social strife increased in Boston, Roddan changed his attitude toward workers. By 1853 he was denouncing strikes as the products of the mutual selfishness of labor and business.

Temperance

Conscious of their alien status in American society and wanting very much to be accepted as Americans, most Catholic leaders made little or no effort to connect poverty to social or economic causes, even though the majority of the poor in most cities were Catholic. The president of the Vincent de Paul Society in 1865 was probably typical in his belief that "Where there is health, temperance and industry, there cannot be poverty in this country. . . . Intemperance is the great evil we have to overcome; it is the source of the misery for at least three fourths of the families we are called upon to visit and relieve."[32]

Catholic temperance societies had begun in the United States in the 1840s with an endorsement from the bishops at the Fourth Provincial Council of

29. March 10, 1866, in *The Brownson-Hecker Correspondence*, ed. Joseph Gower and Richard Leliaert (Notre Dame, Ind.: University of Notre Dame Press, 1979), 242.

30. Roohan, "American Catholics and the Social Question," 154.

31. *The Pilot*, September 15, 1849, cited in Merwick, *Boston Priests*, 26.

32. *Report of the Supreme Court of New York, 1864–1865* (New York: 1866), cited in Abell, *American Catholicism*, 29.

Baltimore. Theodore Mathew, the Irish Capuchin, inspired hundreds of thousands of American Catholics to take the pledge during his tour of the country at mid-century. Depression and Civil War thinned the ranks of the movement, but it revived after Appomattox, thanks, in part, to the missions or Catholic revivals that the Paulists, Passionists, and Jesuits were preaching. One of their themes was the need for Catholics to abstain from intoxicating drinks to reform their lives.[33] The pastoral letter from the bishops following the Second Plenary Council of Baltimore in 1866 also highlighted the enormous damage alcohol was doing to Catholic families and the reputation of the Church. Five years later James Roosevelt Bayley, the Bishop of Newark, founded the Catholic Total Abstinence Union of America, but it was John Ireland ("the Father Mathew of the West") who more than anyone else put his stamp on the movement. Although the Union was formally committed to a policy of moral suasion in promoting temperance, many individual leaders, including Ireland, and many local branches pursued prohibition through legislation. John Keane, the rector of The Catholic University, defended this approach: "Moral suasion with its spiritual sanctions, and civil authority with its coercive helps, must be united in every human social system."[34]

The Union's biographer, Joan Bland, has noted that "it was the incarnation of Archbishop Ireland's ideal of a prosperous, civic-minded, Americanized Catholicism." Certainly the teetotaling and sabbatarianism that the Union championed were more in tune with nineteenth-century evangelicalism than traditional Catholicism, a point that German American Catholics were especially quick to make. Sebastian Messmer, the Bishop of Green Bay, contended that such extreme policies "had done more to render the word 'Temperance' odious among thousands of temperate and intemperate Catholics immigrated here from continental Europe" than anyone could imagine.[35]

The union's peak decade was the 1890s, during which it doubled its membership and attempted to pressure Catholic saloon keepers and liquor dealers by having them expelled from Catholic societies. One bishop, John A. Watterson of Columbus, even forbade his priests to absolve those who trafficked in liquor. When the Germans protested, the apostolic delegate, Fran-

33. Joan Bland, SND, *Hibernian Crusade: The Story of the Catholic Total Abstinence Union of America* (Washington, D.C.: The Catholic University of America Press, 1951), 44–49.

34. Bland, *Hibernian Crusade*, 154.

35. Sebastian G. Messmer, "A Catholic Temperance League," *Ecclesiastical Review* 11 (December 1894): 416, cited in Bland, *Hibernian Crusade*, 191–92.

cisco Satolli, sustained the bishop. The total abstinence forces even managed to close down a Benedictine brewery in Pennsylvania. But growing support for prohibition within the union and opposition to it within the general Catholic population spelled decline for the organization by the turn of the century.

The CTAU was essentially a middle-class organization. Although it distributed over a million tracts, it is questionable how deeply its appeals to sobriety, respectability, and other domestic virtues touched Catholic workingmen. For the latter the saloon was many things: social center, political club, refuge. Drink may have been a menace to soul and family; it was certainly not the root of the workingman's problems.

Social Earthquakes and the Labor Movement

Henry May has noted that it took the triple earthquake of labor strife in 1877, 1886, and 1892–94 to shake Protestants from their complacent social thought.[36] By the mid-1880s some were even beginning to fear that permanent class divisions were developing that were threatening the very republic itself. Since a majority of Catholics were working-class, the shock was not quite the same in the Catholic community. Nonetheless the strikes of the late nineteenth century played a crucial role in shaping Catholic attitudes toward social issues in industrial America.

Even before the first strikes of 1877, Catholic America had been rocked by the Molly Maguire killings in the coalfields of Pennsylvania in the early 1870s. Apparently the Mollies were a particularly violent form of Irish terrorism or Whiteboyism transplanted to America. In an industry brutally opposed to labor organization, secret societies were a necessity. The Ancient Order of Hibernians was strong in Pottsville and the other mining towns in northeastern Pennsylvania. The Mollies were an extreme element within the AOH. In 1876–77 twenty Irish Catholics, all members of the AOH, were tried, convicted, and hanged for various murders in the region.[37] Catholics were quick to denounce the murderers. James Wood, the convert bishop of Philadelphia, had condemned the Molly Maguires as early as 1864; in 1875, he extended his condemnation to the AOH itself and cooperated with the president of the Reading Railroad in infiltrating and prosecuting the Mollies. A few editorial voices saw a deeper issue in the sensational crimes. George Dering Wolff, the editor of

36. Henry F. May, *Protestant Churches and Industrial America* (New York: Harper, 1949).

37. For the best account of the affair and the Church's involvement, see Wayne G. Broehl, Jr., *The Molly Maguires* (Cambridge, Mass.: Harvard University Press, 1964).

the Philadelphia *Catholic Standard* and, like Wood, a conservative convert, saw a parallel between the violence in Ireland and its offshoot in Pennsylvania:

> in both cases the outrages themselves were utterly unjustifiable, either morally or legally, but in both cases those outrages grew out of desperation caused by previous oppression. . . . Do justice to the miners. Let them be honestly, fairly dealt with, and the desperate unprincipled men who have perpetrated the horrible crime . . . will no longer be able to find sympathizers or abettors.[38]

As shocking as the Molly Maguires' story was, it was a local affair. In contrast the railroad strikes in the summer of 1877 leapfrogged across the country, spreading violence and fears of class warfare. When the Bishop of Pittsburgh, John Tuigg, attempted to pacify the rioters, presumably mostly Catholic, he was stoned for his efforts.[39] Much of the Catholic press deplored the violence, but blamed corporate industry for the conditions that had precipitated the strikes. None was more blunt than the immigrant John Boyle O'Reilly of *The Pilot*, who reminded his readers that workers did not commit violence "without deep cause," and that "corporations have large pockets but no souls." Indeed O'Reilly charged that the corporations had been using the excuse of the Panic of 1873 to cut wages to "starvation level":

> The Corporations of Pennsylvania first drove the miners into Molly Maguirism and murder; and then virtuously hounded them to the scaffold. The same corporations have caused the present strikes, and have dragged down on themselves the fire of their burning wealth and the blood of many victims.[40]

O'Reilly called for compulsory arbitration to avert future outbreaks and secure justice for labor.[41]

Few Catholic editors or clergymen shared O'Reilly's reading of the strike or his enthusiasm for arbitration. But fewer still could any longer ignore "The Social Question." As the New York *Catholic Review* commented, "The Old World no longer faces alone the labor problem. It is here and it presses for a solution."[42]

38. *Catholic Standard*, June 30, 1877, cited in Roohan, "American Catholics and the Social Question," 177.

39. Roohan, "American Catholics and the Social Question," 189–90.

40. *The Pilot*, July 28, August 25, 1877, cited in Roohan, "American Catholics and the Social Question," 198.

41. *The Pilot*, August 4, 1877.

42. *Catholic Review*, August 11, 1877, cited in Roohan, "American Catholics and the Social Question," 206.

In the 1880s the labor movement dominated Catholic social thought. At the Third Plenary Council of Baltimore in 1884 the prelates confined their social planning to a call to Catholics to band together in all significant activities of their social and religious lives. Although the bishops here laid the groundwork for the Catholic ghetto that would set Catholics apart from American society in general well into the next century, they had no intention of creating Catholic labor unions. In a sermon on the Church's "moral and social mission," Patrick J. Ryan, Archbishop of Philadelphia, recommended "Christian kindness to the poor and the working men and women and the inculcation of patience in poverty, after the example of Our Lord" as "the best securities against the communism and anarchy that seem to threaten society."[43] In their pastoral letter the bishops condemned the abuse of Sunday work as a violation of "the poor man's day of rest" and a symptom of the social discontent in the country.[44] They warned the faithful against joining secret societies, but did not specifically mention labor unions.

The question of labor unions did come up during the council. The Knights of Labor, the largest American labor union, a majority of whose members were Catholic, had already been judged a prohibited society by Propaganda Fide, the Roman Congregation that had jurisdiction over the American Church. The complication was that this judgment had been rendered about the Knights in Canada. It was unclear whether it extended to the United States, as well. A committee of bishops, headed by Archbishop Michael Corrigan of New York, prepared a report on prohibited societies for the council in which they proposed that associations be considered forbidden "which are unjustly prepared to prevent craftsmen or workers from exercising their industry or labor for others, or contracting for their own, and this especially if violence is added to injustice."[45] Corrigan had no doubt that the Knights were as condemned in New York as they were in Quebec. The majority of the council prelates, however, deferred any action by appointing another committee to deal with the status of particular suspect societies.

For most Catholic leaders, secret societies suggested Masonry, anti-clericalism, deism, liberalism. In the case of labor unions one could add socialism.

43. Abell, *American Catholicism*, 53.

44. Guilday, *National Pastorals of the American Hierarchy*, 253.

45. *Relationes eorum qui disceptata fuerunt ab illmis ac revmis metropolitis cum suis suffraganeis in suis singulis provinciis super schema futuri councilii praesertim vero super capita cuique commissa* (Baltimore: John Murphy, 1884), 32.

Archbishop James Bayley of Baltimore, for instance, found labor unions even worse than secret societies, since their very essence was "communistic and no Catholic worth any idea of the spirit of his religion will encourage them."[46] They seemed a threat to the rights of private property and the freedom of the individual. Then, too, there was the violence that they seemed to breed. Still, the Second Plenary Council in 1866 had cautiously approved them.

Between the end of the Third Plenary Council in December 1884 and the spring of 1886 the Knights' membership mushroomed from 100,000 to more than 700,000, culminating in a series of successful strikes. A subsidiary group, the Federation of Organized Trades, called for a general strike on May 1, which nearly 200,000 workers heeded. Three nights later someone threw a bomb into a squadron of Chicago police as they were moving in to break up a protest meeting called by a group of anarchists at Haymarket Square. When one of the leaders proved to be a former Knight, organized labor was condemned for making an alliance with anarchy and radicalism.

Terrence Powderly, the Grand Master Workman of the Knights of Labor and a Catholic, had been making every effort to avert a condemnation of the organization by the Church. Two months before the general strike he had denounced precipitous strikes and boycotts and urged his members not to participate in the general strike.[47] When he first assumed leadership of the Knights in 1879, Powderly had eliminated most of its elements of secrecy. In 1884 he had even proposed to Archbishop Patrick Ryan of Philadelphia that the Plenary Council of the Bishops examine the constitution of the Knights and indicate what changes they should make in order to be acceptable to the Church.[48]

In October 1886 the archbishops met as a committee to consider the status of the Knights. Despite the May turmoil, six of the nine metropolitans voted against condemnation. The majority were assured that the Knights opposed boycotts and closed shops.[49] Since the vote was not unanimous, the final decision had to be referred to Rome.

46. Abell, *American Catholicism*, 46.

47. "I am ashamed," Powderly wrote, "to meet with clergymen and others to tell them our order is composed of law-abiding, intelligent men, while the next dispatch brings news of some petty boycott or strike"; Henry Browne, *The Catholic Church and the Knights of Labor* (Washington, D.C.: The Catholic University of America Press, 1949), 153–54.

48. Powderly to Ryan, October 24, 1884, copy, Powderly Papers, Archives of the Catholic University of America (hereafter ACUA).

49. Archbishop Corrigan, who abstained on the vote about the Knights, had reason to

To ensure that Propaganda would not overturn the vote of the majority of the archbishops, in the late winter of 1887 the Cardinal Archbishop of Baltimore, James Gibbons, took their case with him to Rome, where he had gone to receive his red hat. Gibbons argued that the Knights did not deserve condemnation under the conditions Rome had established for judging secret societies. Their secrecy was the minimal required to protect them as a labor organization. They were not opposed to religion; many were Catholics. Indeed, Gibbons gave the impression that the Knights were essentially a Catholic organization to which Protestants were admitted. In America, he pointed out, it made no sense to segregate Catholic laborers under the direction of their own clergy within a separate organization.[50] Although much of Gibbons' argument was prudential citing of the consequences the Church would suffer from a condemnation of the Knights, the cardinal's support for labor's right and need to organize was unmistakable:

> That there exist among us, as in all other countries, grave and threatening social evils, public injustices which call for strong resistance and legal remedy, is a fact which no one dares to deny—a fact already acknowledged by the Congress and the President of the United States.... [T]hat the heartless avarice which, through greed of gain, pitilessly grinds not only the men, but even the women and children in various employments, make it clear to all who love humanity and justice that it is not only the right of the laboring classes to protect themselves, but the duty of the whole people to aid them in finding a remedy against the dangers with which both civilization and social order are menaced by avarice, oppression and corruption.

It was clear to Gibbons that labor could protect itself and remedy these evils only through organization. "[I]n such a struggle," he concluded,

> of the great masses of the people against the mail-clad power, which...often refuses them the simple rights of humanity and justice, it is vain to expect that every error and every act of violence can be avoided; and to dream that this struggle can be

---

question their position on closed shops. As he wrote Gibbons in April 1887, "we have 150 men working steadily in our cemetery, and receiving larger wages than are given in any other Cemetery in the neighborhood, but these Knights have not only asked me...to raise these wages still higher, but they also insist that we must neither employ nor discharge a single workman without their previous knowledge and consent"; Corrigan to Gibbons, New York, April 12, 1887, AAB.

50. Bishop England had instituted the Brotherhood of San Marina, an organization for immigrant laborers under Catholic auspices, in Charleston in the 1830s, but like many of England's ideas it hardly spread beyond his diocese. Some conservative Catholics in the late nineteenth century, such as Thomas Preston, the vicar-general of the Archdiocese of New York, were still advocating clerical-controlled workingmen's societies as a counterweight to the Knights, but they had little support.

hindered, or that we can deter the multitudes from organizing, which is their only hope of success; would be to ignore the nature and forces of human society in times like ours.

He reminded his Roman readers what Cardinal Manning had observed about that society, that "[t]he church has no longer to deal with Parliaments and princes, but with the masses and with the people. Whether we will or no this is our work; we need a new spirit and a new law of life."[51]

John Ireland and John Keane provided Gibbons the ideas and much of the rhetoric for the memorial. They may well have written more than they intended in attempting to resist a catastrophic condemnation of an organization that was already showing signs of collapse.[52] Whatever their intent, the document not only accomplished their objective, but more importantly put the American hierarchy squarely behind the labor movement as an indispensable means for achieving social justice in America.

Henry George and Edward McGlynn

In 1880, in his first address to the General Assembly of the Knights of Labor, Powderly had condemned the wage system as a "pernicious system which leaves one man at the mercy of another." Until it was abolished, "labor and capital [will] be at war, and no strike can deliver a blow sufficiently hard to break the hold with which unproductive capital today grasps labor by the throat." In its place Powderly urged an economy of cooperation that alone could "give the laborer a fair proportion of the products of his toil." The eventual goal, however, was "a system of colonization" in which men and women might "band together for the purpose of securing the greatest good to the greatest number, and place the man who is willing to toil upon his own homestead."[53] As we have seen, colonization had little appeal to

51. Abell, *American Catholic Thought*, 147–61.

52. Ireland became increasingly complacent about the industrial capitalism that he considered the very foundation of American democracy. By the turn of the century his basic message to labor was to trust capital and avoid strikes. "The country suffers too much from strikes," he told a Labor Day crowd in St. Paul; "it has grown tired of them; it will not tolerate them." As for the bloated fortunes of plutocrats, Ireland took consolation from the fact that they usually broke up in two or three generations. Even in the conspicuous consumption that Thorstein Veblen and other critics of the new order were attacking, Ireland found the hidden benefit of an indirect distribution of wealth; John Ireland, "Labor and Capital," in *The Church and Modern Society: Lectures and Addresses* (St. Paul: Pioneer Press, 1905), 2:341–75.

53. Quoted in Powderly, *The Path I Trod: The Autobiography of Terrence V. Powderly*, ed. Harry J.

Eastern workers, but land reform and a simpler economy had much support among Irish American labor in the 1880s as the key to the social problem, both in Ireland and America.[54]

To Powderly and many Irish American leaders, Henry George was a natural prophet. George's *Progress and Poverty* identified land monopolization as the primary source of economic inequity and proposed a single tax on the unearned increment that land speculation produced as the medium through which such monopolies could be broken up and opportunity for individual enterprise recreated for all. When George became the candidate of the United Labor Party for mayor of New York in 1886, Powderly was a highly visible supporter.

Another prominent proponent of George was Father Edward McGlynn, who had established within his New York City parish a network of benevolent operations that made it an institutional model for the urban Church. By the 1880s, however, McGlynn had concluded that "You may go on forever with hospitals and orphan asylums and St. Vincent de Paul societies. But with them you can't cure the trouble. They relieve, not eradicate."[55] He had also discovered that George's doctrines were "good gospel, not only for Ireland, but for . . . America, too."[56]

Henry George was no socialist. He admitted the right of private property, but denied that land could lose its basic communal character. Perhaps because of this ambiguous stance, in 1886 as a candidate for mayor of New York, he was supported by both the Knights of Labor and the Socialist Labor Party, among others. As noted in chapter 8, when McGlynn publicly campaigned for George, Archbishop Corrigan suspended him from his priestly ministry and demanded that he retract his support for George's land theories. McGlynn adamantly insisted that he would continue to teach that "private ownership of land is against natural justice, no matter what civil or ecclesiastical laws it may be sanctioned," and that, given the opportunity, he would confiscate without compensation all private property in land.[57] "All men," he de-

---

Carman, Henry David, and Paul N. Guthrie (New York: Columbia University Press, 1940), 268–70).

54. John L. Thomas, *Alternative America: Henry George, Edward Bellamy, Henry Demarest Lloyd and the Adversary Tradition* (Cambridge, Mass., and London: Harvard University Press, 1983), 184.

55. New York *Tribune*, November 26, 1886.

56. Stephen Bell, *Rebel, Priest and Prophet: A Biography of Dr. Edward McGlynn* (New York: Devin-Adair, 1937), 26–27.

57. McGlynn to Corrigan, New York, December 20, 1886, AANY.

clared in his most famous address, "The Cross of a New Crusade," "inalienably, always, everywhere, have a common right to all the general bounties of nature; and this is in perfect and beautiful keeping with the other law of labor that every mouth has two hands with which to feed itself, a necessary corollary of which is that these hands must have equal direct or indirect access to the general bounties of nature out of which to make a living."[58]

McGlynn's excommunication in the summer of 1887 for his refusal to go to Rome to explain his position only intensified the controversy that one contemporary remembered as having brought New York City to near anarchy with "all the furies let loose."[59] Scores of thousands marched in protest in New York against the archbishop, and mass demonstrations were held in Chicago and elsewhere in support of McGlynn. Many of his strongest and most persistent supporters seemed to find in McGlynn not so much a spokesman for economic reform as a defender of individual conscience against the abuses of ecclesiastical power. Powderly himself soon broke with both McGlynn and George over ideological and personal issues.[60]

Catholic conservatives in America and Rome were convinced that the Church needed to condemn not merely McGlynn, but the Georgian doctrine he was preaching. At their behest Archbishop Corrigan formally petitioned Pope Leo XIII that the Congregation of the Index examine *Progress and Poverty*. In return several American prelates counseled against any such condemnation. Gibbons again took the lead, arguing that the relationship of the state to the right of ownership of land was a "very complex question, very much subject to the diverse circumstances of time and place, and not yet ready to be resolved by a decisive judgment."[61] At any rate, Gibbons thought that George's influence, like the Knights, was on the wane.

Despite the coordinated appeals from Gibbons and others against a pre-

58. McGlynn, "The Cross of a New Crusade" (April 2, 1887), in Abell, *American Catholic Thought*, 167.

59. Maurice Francis Egan, *Recollections of a Happy Life* (New York: George H. Doran, 1924), 133.

60. Thomas, *Alternative America*, 230–33.

61. John Tracy Ellis, ed., *Documents of American Catholic History*, 2:458–60. Even a conservative prelate like Richard Gilmour of Cleveland thought a condemnation inopportune. "To condemn the book," he wrote a fellow prelate, "would be but to make George a martyr & create bitter hostility towards the church by the working men & the poor who are getting *edged* enough as it is. . . . Here in America we are drifting with a large, large stream into the ranks of wealth & when we speak it is timidly in the face of capital"; Gilmour to William Henry Elder, Cleveland, April 17, 1888, AAC.

mature condemnation, the Holy Office in the spring of 1889 officially condemned George's book, but refused to allow the condemnation to be made public "in light of the peculiar circumstances."[62] In response Corrigan pleaded for some explicit declaration regarding the right of private property to combat the socialistic theories he saw spreading in the United States. Two years after the condemnation of George's writings, Leo issued *Rerum Novarum*, in which he declared that private property was in accord with the natural law and condemned "certain obsolete opinions" that denied any individual ownership of land. The conservatives naturally felt themselves vindicated against McGlynn and George, but Rome had not spoken the last word on the McGlynn case.[63] In December 1892 the apostolic ablegate, Archbishop Francisco Satolli, restored McGlynn to good standing within the Church after four professors at The Catholic University of America had judged there was nothing in McGlynn's teaching about property that was contrary to Catholic doctrine.[64] If the suspension and excommunication of McGlynn had seemed an indication of the Church's allying itself with the propertied classes, his restoration, even though six years later, was a reverse signal to the working class. If McGlynn added nothing to the permanent body of Catholic social thought in this country, he was nonetheless important as a symbol of the Church's concern for social justice and the working class.

Conclusion

Rerum Novarum of course had been more than an indirect analysis of George's ideas. As two historians of social reform in late-nineteenth-century America have judged, it was "the Magna Carta of Catholic social policy."[65] While upholding the "inviolability" of private property, it also affirmed that "the blessings of nature and the gifts of grace belong to the whole human

62. Simeoni to Corrigan, April 9, 1889, printed, AANY.

63. George himself bitterly shared Corrigan's judgment about the encyclical's treatment of his ideas about land.

64. In a statement submitted to the four examiners, McGlynn had distinguished between "the exclusive private possession" of land, which McGlynn conceded was necessary for the full realization by the individual of the fruits of his industry, and the strict ownership of land, which McGlynn maintained the community could never surrender to any individual; Frederick J. Zwierlein, *The Life and Letters of Bishop McQuaid, Prefaced with The History of Catholic Rochester Before His Episcopate* (Rochester: Art Print Shop, 1927), 3:75–79.

65. Ronald C. White, Jr., and C. Howard Hopkins, *The Social Gospel: Religion and Reform in Changing America* (Philadelphia: Temple University Press, 1976), 218.

race in common."[66] The responsibility of government was not merely to defend property rights, but to provide for the common good of its citizens. As the Church desired that all people "should rise above poverty and wretchedness, and better their condition in life" and had in her history intervened "directly in behalf of the poor" through benevolent associations, so too "all human agencies," including the state, should do likewise in providing "for the welfare and the comfort of the working classes."[67] "Whenever the general interest or any particular class suffers," Leo concluded, "or is threatened with harm, which can in no other way be met or prevented, the public authority must step in to deal with it."[68]

John Ryan later recalled the impact of the encyclical upon him as a seminarian in the 1890s: "to American Catholics, who, like their fellow Americans had been indoctrinated with theories of nonintervention which were not far removed from *laissez faire*, the declarations of Pope Leo on the regulatory functions of the state over industry were new and, indeed, startling."[69] Not only did the pope legitimize the state as a promoter of social justice in behalf of the weaker classes, but he also recognized the right of laborers to organize and to receive a living wage. It would be another generation before Ryan, William Kerby, and other Catholic social leaders would begin to put flesh on the bones of Catholic thought regarding capital and labor that Leo had enunciated in 1891. If Leo had condemned both economic liberalism and socialism, American Catholics in the 1890s continued to combat the latter rather than the former. Liberal prelates like John Ireland were still too committed to the prevailing economic theory to encourage a serious critique of the system or proposals for reforming it. Even the labor movement, with the growth of the American Federation of Labor in the wake of the demise of the Knights of Labor, continued to look toward self-help rather than state intervention.

Individuals such as Phineas of the Boston *Pilot*, Peter L. Foy, John Brisbane Walker, and George Dering Wolff called for such measures as compulsory arbitration, income tax, public ownership of transportation and communication networks, and social security legislation to meet the social problems that the depression and strikes of the early 1890s once again brought to public

66. Etienne Gilson, ed., *The Church Speaks to the Modern World: The Social Teachings of Leo XIII* (Garden City, N.Y.: Image Books, 1954), 219.

67. Gilson, *The Church Speaks*, 223.

68. Gilson, *The Church Speaks*, 224–25.

69. John A. Ryan, *Social Doctrine in Action: A Personal History* (New York: Harper, 1941), 44.

attention. The Catholic congresses held in Baltimore in 1889 and 1893 promised to provide a periodic forum for the Catholic response to social questions, but the conservative trend of the latter 1890s in Catholic circles halted the congresses as well as other forms of American Catholic democracy.

If the American Church still shared too much in the complacency that marked society in the United States at the turn of the century, nonetheless it had come a good way from the cosmopolitan conformism of the early nineteenth century. It had renounced *laissez faire* principles; it had endorsed the labor movement; it had slowly come to recognize the problems that an urban industrial economy had brought to America. That it had been so slow to address those problems was understandable, given its minority position, its peculiar composition, and the radically new world of the nineteenth century. As William Kerby wrote at the beginning of 1900:

> the social system in which we live has not had a fair trial; we have seen its worst and not its best. Economic forces were turned loose a century and a quarter ago when the industrial revolution came. Political philosophy cleared away all legal barriers, and the disintegration of religion weakened the moral forces of society. The economic development carried all before it, and our social problem is the result.

There was, Kerby was saying, a profound intellectual lag that the Church had to address in its service to society. In such a situation the Church had the obligation to use its energies to regenerate society as she found it. But revelation, Kerby warned, although indispensable, would not be enough. What was also crucial was a "philosophical and scientific" knowledge of society, the kind that came from detailed research and complex reasoning. And it had to be impartial, "free from professional bias and party spirit." Only by training up individuals to pursue such knowledge through the inspiration of revelation could the Church, according to Kerby, have a message for the age.[70]

Kerby and John Ryan would both embody that commitment at The Catholic University of America over the first half of the twentieth century. If it reflected a progressive trust in the "exaltation of will and the accumulation of data" to solve social problems, it also marked an important point of passage for Catholic social thought in America.

70. William Kerby, "The Priesthood and the Social Movement," *Catholic University Bulletin* 6 (January 1900): 18–28, in Abell, *American Catholic Thought*, 266–77.

Chapter 12

Vying to Be the Intellectual Center

Catholic Higher Education in New York and Washington, 1884–1914

THE LATTER HALF of the nineteenth century saw the emergence of the modern American university. It also marked the rise of the university as the perceived nucleus of intellectual life in any community in which it took root. In a society increasingly organized and professionalized along discrete lines of behavior and knowledge, the university organized intellectual life along segmented lines of specialized knowledge. Within the Catholic community, the quest to develop a national university of its own inevitably touched off a competition between the historically two most important regions within Catholic America—New York and the Chesapeake—to locate such an institution of higher learning within their own boundaries.

The Catholic University of America

Orestes Brownson, the eccentric convert who was so instrumental in shaping the intellectual life of the Church in the nineteenth century, was perhaps the first to raise the need for a national Catholic university when, writing in 1857, he called on the American episcopate to establish an institution of higher education that would act as a catalyst for the American Catholic community, assuming "the commanding position in the modern world" through its intellectual leadership.[1] The first prelate to take up the cause of

1. Orestes Brownson, "Present Catholic Dangers," *Brownson's Quarterly Review*, New York Series 2 (July 1857): 362, cited in C. Joseph Nuesse, *The Catholic University of America: A Centennial History* (Washington, D.C.: The Catholic University of America Press, 1990), 9.

a national Catholic university was Martin John Spalding, the Archbishop of Baltimore, who wrote a fellow bishop in 1865: "Why should we not have a Catholic University? It would be a great thing, if we could only agree as to the location and arrangement."[2] The following year Spalding raised the question at the Second Plenary Council of Baltimore; the prelates decided to postpone the matter until a later meeting. That postponement proved to be nearly two decades. By the time the bishops reassembled in Baltimore for the Third Plenary Council in 1884, not only had the idea of a university been given flesh in the founding of Cornell and Johns Hopkins, as well as in developments at Harvard, Columbia, and Michigan, but voices across the Catholic community, especially Isaac Hecker and John Lancaster Spalding, the archbishop's nephew, were calling upon Catholics to incarnate their own university idea. Indeed the younger Spalding (his uncle had died in 1872) became the moving force behind the establishment of a university that would "consolidate our educational forces so far as the higher mental culture is concerned" and serve as the "crown of all other [Catholic] institutions of learning."[3]

In a sermon delivered at the Cathedral of the Assumption Spalding told the prelates assembled for the council that "enlightened men" could not but favor "an American Catholic university." The only question, he pointed out, was whether it was feasible to do so.[4] The question was rhetorical. Three days earlier, Mary Gwendoline Caldwell, a twenty-one-year-old New York heiress and family acquaintance of the Peoria bishop, had announced an offer, no doubt prepared by Spalding, to provide $300,000 for the founding, under the control of the episcopacy, of a "National Catholic School of Philosophy and Theology," toward the eventual end of forming a Catholic university.[5] A delegated committee of prelates reported to the plenary body in early December 1884 that they favored the erection of a seminary, such as "Louvain in Belgium," from which as "a seed the University is to grow."[6] Surely most of the prelates who had voted to begin the institution had very limited notions of what a Catholic university ought to be; they clearly thought of the institution

2. Martin John Spalding to John Timon, C.M., August 23, 1865, Martin John Spalding Papers, Letterpress, 150, AAB, cited in Nuesse, *The Catholic University of America*, 10.

3. Quoted in Neusse, *The Catholic University of America*, 23.

4. John Lancaster Spalding, *University Education Considered in Its Bearing on the Higher Education of Priests* (Baltimore: John Murphy, 1884), 32.

5. Gibbons Papers, AAB 78-T-6, cited in Nuesse, *The Catholic University of America*, 28–29.

6. *Acta et Decreta Concilii Plenarii Baltimorensis Tertii* (Baltimore: 1884), lxxix, trans. *ibid.* 110, in Nuesse, *The Catholic University of America*, 30.

as primarily a higher seminary for the more effective training of clergy. But they had committed themselves to the establishment of a center of learning that potentially had a very high ceiling for intellectual achievement and outreach.

Having decided in favor of a university, the prelates of the council formed a second episcopal committee composed of Spalding, Archbishop James Gibbons of Baltimore, Archbishop John Ireland of St. Paul, Archbishop Michael Corrigan of New York, and three others to carry out the decision to establish a university. Corrigan had been a member of the original committee (as had Spalding, Gibbons, and Ireland), where he had played a passive role; he had merely reported to his superior, Cardinal John McCloskey, that the committee had voted favorably on the "acceptance of Miss Caldwell's gift, and the beginning of a nucleus of a future university."[7] He apparently was of the belief that any national Catholic university would be established at Seton Hall, in South Orange, New Jersey, across the Hudson River from New York. Caldwell herself indicated as much when she told a New York reporter in December 1884 that, despite her preference for a Southern location (she, like Spalding, was originally from Kentucky), she had been won over to the view that the best site would be near a major Northern city.[8] The matter seemed a closed issue in January 1885, when the executor of the Caldwell estate proposed to the new episcopal committee that they purchase Seton Hall College, which the Bishop of Newark, Winand Wigger, was offering to sell. Not willing to act without Mary Gwendoline Caldwell's approval, Corrigan, Spalding, and Ireland, on behalf of the committee, approached her about the proposal to acquire Seton Hall. To their surprise (at least Corrigan's and Ireland's), Caldwell, whether on her own initiative or Spalding's, now wanted them to consider an alternate site, Brookland, within the District of Columbia. A month later, Spalding publicly declared his preference for the Southern location. When Bishop Wigger changed his mind about selling the college, Brookland remained the only option on the bishops' table.[9]

Archbishop Gibbons himself had not been among the promoters of

7. Corrigan to McCloskey, Baltimore, November 1884, AANY, quoted in John Tracy Ellis, *The Formative Years of the Catholic University* (Washington, D.C.: The Catholic University of America Press, 1946), 110.

8. New York Sun, December 11, 1884, in Ellis, *Formative Years*, 116.

9. Gibbons to Corrigan, Baltimore, March 24, 1885, AANY, C-2; Corrigan to Gibbons, New York, March 25, 1885, AAB 79-H3-1.

the Catholic University of America, much less of locating it in Washington, within his own archdiocese. With Caldwell in effect insisting on the national capital as the site and with Ireland, John J. Keane, Bishop of Richmond, and Denis J. O'Connell, a priest friend of Gibbons, prodding the cardinal, he acquiesced on placing the university within the boundaries of his see.[10] Corrigan, who claimed he had no stake in locating the university either in New York or its environs, nonetheless opposed the Washington site, particularly since Caldwell, whose relationship with Spalding was a cause of concern for the New York archbishop as well as for other prelates, was bent on determining it.[11] Corrigan advised Gibbons in writing that the committee should take no action whatever until they had the money in hand from Caldwell.[12] Gibbons replied that he was still hoping that Wigger would change his mind and make the Seton Hall site available. A month later, on May 7, 1885, the committee met in Baltimore. Spalding read a letter from Caldwell assuring them that, no matter what their choice of site, she would still provide the $300,000. A majority of the committee subsequently voted to place the university in Washington, the four yea votes presumably coming from Spalding, Ireland, Archbishop John Williams of Boston, and Gibbons, and the three negative ones from Corrigan, Archbishop Patrick Ryan of Philadelphia, and John Farley, Cardinal McCloskey's secretary. The entire committee signed letters to the pope and officials of the Congregation for the Propagation of the Faith requesting permission to establish a university in Washington, D.C.[13]

Bishop Bernard McQuaid of Rochester was in shock that the "Grand American Catholic University" would be in the South.[14] Other prelates shared McQuaid's distress, but the die had been cast. Or perhaps not. The cardinal prefect of Propaganda in September 1886, having heard, very likely from Ella Edes, the veteran American newswoman who was Corrigan's main contact in Rome and a confidante of the prefect, that there was opposition to the proposed university, solicited the New York archbishop's candid opinion about the issue. Corrigan responded that many of the bishops of the United States now regretted their hasty approval of the idea at the Third Plenary Council. On further reflection they thought that American Catholics were in no finan-

10. Thomas W. Spalding, *The Premier See: A History of the Archdiocese of Baltimore, 1789–1989* (Baltimore and London: Johns Hopkins University Press, 1989), 252–53.

11. Corrigan to William Henry Elder, New York, March 23, 1885, AAC.

12. Corrigan to Gibbons, New York, March 25, 1885, AAB 79-H3.1.

13. Ellis, *Formative Years*, 147–48.

14. McQuaid to Corrigan, Rochester, June 20, 1885, AANY, C-3.

cial position to support an institution for which they had no real need. Corrigan added that the expenses in putting together an appropriate faculty would be prohibitive, that there was no market of students from which to populate it, and that even if there were need for such a university, Washington, being the "corrupt, political center" that it was, was a terrible place to locate it.[15]

When John Keane, chosen to be the first rector of the university, arrived in Rome shortly afterward to secure formal approval for its plans, Propaganda officials shocked him with the disclosure that, despite the claim of unanimous support among the prelates for the university, at least some of the American hierarchy, specifically the Archbishop of New York, among others, opposed it.[16] Gibbons, who arrived in Rome in early 1887 to be elevated to the cardinalate, was so taken back by the revelation that Corrigan was the major source of opposition (until that point he had given Gibbons every reason to believe he was in favor of the university) that the soon-to-be cardinal was ready to abandon the project and let the responsibility for its failure fall upon those who had undermined it. Keane was willing to defer to Gibbons' judgment. John Ireland, who had accompanied Keane to Rome, would hear no talk of surrender, and prevailed upon the others in pushing forward to secure full Roman approval. Gibbons delivered to Propaganda a response to Corrigan's objections, in which he suggested that the matter of the location of the institution be reopened for the American bishops to decide. In April they received the pope's formal approval of the university.[17] Gibbons, back in America, polled his fellow prelates on their preference for its site. Washington won by a large majority, New York being a distant second.[18]

In November Archbishop Corrigan submitted his resignation from the episcopal governing board of the university. He had sought McQuaid's advice about the matter. The bishop predictably urged him to sever all connections with the institution. "Have nothing to do with it, and especially do not permit it to be placed in your diocese. They will only come down to that when they see they have no hope of success. They would throw the odium on you of the predestined failure. . . . We do not want to have anything to do with a Southern seminary."[19] Despite Gibbons' plea that the archbishop's resignation would

15. Corrigan to McQuaid, New York, October 9, 1886, ADR.

16. John Keane, "Chronicles of the Catholic University from 1885," 11–12, ACUA.

17. Keane, "Chronicles," 19–20.

18. Washington received 33 votes, New York 7; Keane, "Chronicles," 20.

19. McQuaid to Corrigan, June 23, 1887, AANY, C-16.

be "disastrous" at this critical phase of the formation of the university, Corrigan persisted.[20] The university lost not only the presence on its board of the leader of the largest Catholic community in the country, but the financial support of the richest, as well.

Joseph Havens Richards and Georgetown's Quest

A year and a half later, in the spring of 1889, Joseph Havens Richards, president of Georgetown University, delivered an address of welcome to John Keane, recently returned from another Roman visit. Richards, in his comments, pointed to "the confusion existing at present in our Catholic educational system," a confusion that he attributed to the "want of concentration and want of organization." What was needed was a Catholic university that would provide the matrix for such intellectual concentration. The new university, he went on, would do that, indeed was already doing it in the "able and admirable" professors that Keane had attracted to its faculty. "And what spot so suitable for this collection of eminent men, for the focus of light and learning, as our own city of Washington, the nation's capital. Here the Science, the wit, the literature, the art of our country is slowly but surely concentrating."[21] Keane later complimented Richards that his remarks were the best he had ever heard on the topic of the Catholic university. What Keane did not realize was that the university Richardson had in mind was not the one that was just beginning, new papal charter in hand, but one that was celebrating its centennial and had possessed a papal charter for over half a century.

Richards' plan was to transform Georgetown into nothing less than a modern university: a comprehensive institution that would bring together all the arts and sciences, provide a broad but elastic liberal education for undergraduates, attract and develop specialists to do research, especially in the sciences and medical profession, and serve as an intellectual center for the community, Church, and nation. He intended to revive the university's observatory as a research facility and to open a scientific school that would embrace instruction and investigation in physics, chemistry, biology, and engineering. He intended to build a hospital where a first-rate clinical staff would have the wherewithal to give superior clinical training and do cutting-edge

20. Gibbons to Corrigan, Baltimore, December 3, 1887, AANY, C-15.

21. Richards, "Address of Welcome to Bishop John J. Keane," Other Colleges, Box 1, folder CUA 1890–99, GUA, GULSC.

research. He also was determined to reclaim the Jesuit theologate or divinity school that Jesuit officials had transferred in 1869 from Georgetown to Woodstock, Maryland. "Situated as we are in the nation's Capital," Richards later commented, "we have an admirable field for development into one of the greatest, perhaps the greatest institutions of the country."[22]

His first goal was to secure a cadre of specialists in the rapidly proliferating disciplines of knowledge in the late nineteenth century. As John Keane did in reaching beyond America to obtain his professors, so Richards set his sights on the international academic community in procuring his faculty; unlike Keane, Richards' search was not limited to the fields of theology and philosophy, but encompassed the sciences and humanities. His first recruit was the Austrian astronomer John Hagen, whom Richards brought to Georgetown to direct its observatory. Beyond Hagen, however, his searches brought scant results, and those virtually all in the natural sciences, in which Richards himself had been trained at Harvard. At the local level he was much more successful in bringing in government scientists at the Smithsonian Institution and elsewhere in Washington to staff the graduate studies, which he formally began in 1891. His efforts to establish a scientific school proved fruitless when he failed to raise the funds to support the project. For the medical school Richards expanded their facilities, ended the school's tradition as a "sundown college," standardized the curriculum, increased the course of studies from three to four years, and constructed a hospital, which opened in 1898.

Woodstock College

During Richards' entire presidency (1888–1898) he fought an uphill struggle to reclaim the theological school from the rural site fifteen miles west of Baltimore that had housed it since 1869. By the late 1880s there was general agreement in Jesuit circles, from Rome to America, that the move to Maryland had been a serious mistake; that the theologate should be in an urban setting. Joseph Havens Richards, seizing the opportunity to recapture it for Georgetown University, sought the superior general's approval for returning the theological college to its original home in Washington. Others were seeking alternate urban sites for it. In April 1891 the provincial superior, a New Yorker, petitioned Anton Anderledy, the general of the Society, for

22. General Lefevre, September 21, 1894, Richards Letterbooks, vol. 9, 717–20, GUA.

permission to convert Fordham into a day college and to prepare to transfer Woodstock to the Bronx.[23] Anderledy preferred to put the matter to the will of officials and senior members of the province. Richards thought such a test "worse than useless in fact.... Will not factional and sectional feuding be aroused"?[24] True to Richards' prediction, the ensuing polling revealed in full play the regional rivalry within the province. The majority of Jesuits hailing from or connected with the northern portion of the province strongly preferred transferring Woodstock College to New York and Fordham College, despite the fact that the latter had no professional schools and a weak undergraduate program with a declining enrollment. New York, so the thinking of the majority went, was the cultural and intellectual hub of the nation, as well as being heavily Catholic, and the ecclesiastical authorities there looked favorably upon such a development. Georgetown, on the other hand, was located in a city that was merely the political center of the country, with but a tenth of the Catholic population that New York had; moreover, Washington was the home of the pontifical Catholic University of America, whose ecclesiastical patrons in Rome and America would surely resent the introduction of a competing institution in the higher studies of philosophy and theology.[25]

Havens Richards was not one to go quietly into the night. By virtually any measure—age, reputation, development, and site—Georgetown, Richards had earlier informed the general, had the best claim as an urban home for the theologate. "This city daily grows as the center and sun of the entire intellectual life of this republic." There was a rapidly growing intellectual infrastructure in the form of museums and libraries, scientific institutes, and the Cosmos Club, and Georgetown was rapidly establishing working relationships with the people involved with them. As for the Catholic University, its rector had himself expressed his hope that all the religious orders in the United States would locate their houses of studies in its vicinity. If the Catholic University proceeded to flourish as an institution, it would be important to have Jesuit theologians and philosophers at Georgetown as a countervailing weight to the pontifical faculty across town. If it failed, "which already seems probable to many lay people—it behooves us to be here to take it over."[26] In brief, Richards argued, Georgetown in its present development was "far in advance of

23. Edward Boursaud to Anderledy, New York, April 28, 1891, MD 12-XXIV-19, ARSI.

24. Richards to James Doonan, May 11, 1892, Letterbooks, 867–70, GUA.

25. Campbell to Anderledy, Frederick, June 3, 1890, MD 12-XXIX-18, ARSI.

26. Richards to Anderledy, Georgetown, March 16, 1890, MD 12-XXIV-3, ARSI.

any other Catholic educational institution in the United States." With the addition of the theological and philosophical faculties, "we should *ipso facto* be possessed of *a fully developed University which could not be equaled in its present condition by any other institution, no matter how much money they might possess, for the next thirty or forty years.*"[27]

Richards' arguments, however, swayed few, the general not among them. The provincial superior in 1892 officially forwarded to Rome the request of the Maryland–New York Province that Fordham be designated the new home of the theologate. Death, however, had claimed the superior general, Anton Anderledy. His successor, Luis Martín, alluding to the "practical politics" involved in the potential move, denied the request.[28] One element of those politics was the opposition of Archbishop Corrigan, who had no intention of hosting another theological seminary when he was just in the process of opening his own. Another was Cardinal Gibbons, who insisted that the theologate remain in the Archdiocese of Baltimore.[29] He strongly favored its transfer to Georgetown, which was then part of the See of Baltimore, and assured Jesuit officials that they had no need to fear any ill consequences from Catholic University officials, should they make the move.[30] The Jesuit Roman curia, it turned out, had deep fears of the backlash from the Vatican that they might experience as a consequence of appearing to compete with a pontifical university. Richards' plan to bolster the university as an intellectual center by reclaiming its school of divinity fell victim to provincial politics and Roman caution.[31]

27. Richards to [?], [1891], MD 12-XXIV-26, ARSI.

28. Edward Purbrick to Martín, May 15, 1899, MD 13-I-40, ARSI.

29. Richards, for one, made sure that Rome understood the full implications of Gibbons' opposition to the move to New York. "You already know," he reminded the new superior general, "of the animosity of many bishops, in particular that of the Cardinal of Baltimore toward the Archbishop of New York. Should we move the scholasticate to New York the suspicion will easily arise that we are taking the Archbishop's side and opposing the Cardinal"; Richards to Martín, Georgetown, January 9, 1893, MD 12-X-11, ARSI.

30. Purbrick to Martin, April 14, 1898, MD 13-I-20, ARSI. After meeting with the cardinal, Purbrick had sought out the rector of the Catholic University, Thomas Conaty, to confirm what Gibbons had told him about the sentiments of CUA officials. Conaty assured him that there would "no objections to our H[ouse] of S[tudies] being at G'town. He was very hearty and from all I know & hear of him very sincere. As your Paternity, however, said to me, the danger may be in Italy rather than in the States"; Purbrick to Martín, June 19, 1898, MD 13-I-26, ARSI.

31. Purbrick to Martín, New York, March 11, 1899, MD 13-I-36, ARSI.

The Monthly Review

While Richards was waging his campaign to bring the theologate to Georgetown, he seized upon another development in Jesuit America to enhance his university as an intellectual center. Jesuit officials in 1890 had approved in concept the establishment of a monthly review of religion, science, and the intellectual life, something on the order of the *North American Review.* Richards was keenly aware that universities had begun to be the base for scholarly publications in the 1880s, such as Johns Hopkins' *American Chemical Journal* (1879), Columbia's *Political Science Quarterly* (1886), and Harvard's *Quarterly Journal of Economics* (1886). He himself had already set up a virtual university press for the publication of books by the faculty in various academic fields. "Concentration at Georgetown," Richards remarked to his predecessor, James Doonan, "is now the only watchword that will lead us to a high standing before the world. . . . The review will be the greatest engine for 'booming' a college, in the line of dignified and able intellectual work that has ever been in the possession of the province." And Washington itself was the natural home for such a journal. "[W]hat is most important to consider, [is] all [of Washington's] advantages in the line of scientific collections, libraries, &c. &c must always continue to increase with ever accelerating rapidity" as the government inevitably expanded its intellectual concentration and other academic institutions sprang up.[32]

Apparently the initial intention of province officials was to house the journal at Georgetown; at least Richardson felt encouraged enough to begin negotiations with a local printer about publishing the periodical. But New York's centripetal forces within the Society soon prevailed, and by the end of 1890 a team of six editors, drawn from the provinces of the United States and Canada, had set up headquarters at St. Francis Xavier College in that city. The following spring, Richardson, in a final attempt to pull the "Review" out of the New York fire, persuaded Peter Collier, the New York publisher whose son, Robert, was at Georgetown, to approach the regional provincial with an offer to publish the periodical, including the assumption of its costs. One can only surmise that Richards had alerted Collier to the project, presumably with the hope of using him as a lever to secure the journal for Georgetown. Whatever Collier's full intentions, the publisher and the province never reached an agreement, as the provincial became frustrated over the former's growing specifications

32. Doonan, August 24, 1889, 460–62, Richards Letterbooks, vol. 4, GUA, GULSC.

about the project and had second thoughts about securing enough Jesuit contributors to provide the articles that would be needed for a monthly review. In the end neither New York nor Washington secured the review. In the late fall of 1891 the provincial superior reluctantly dropped the project.[33]

Attempted Annexation of Georgetown's Professional Schools

Concern about the latent competition between Georgetown University and the Catholic University of America to be, in fact, what the latter institution claimed in its title led to a Roman initiative in 1893 to incorporate Georgetown's law and medical schools within the new university. The Vatican's new apostolic delegate to the United States, Francisco Satolli, saw this as a solution to any possible conflict between the two Catholic institutions of higher education within Washington. Without professional schools Georgetown would no longer be a university.[34] Luis Martín, the superior general of the Jesuits, mortally concerned that the Vatican might actually order the suppression of Georgetown in order to prevent competition with the pontifical university across town, had already given his approval to the proposed annexation. Richards himself was at first inclined to consent to Satolli's proposal to transfer the two schools to the Catholic University, so long as Catholic paid Georgetown a sufficient amount of money ($75,000 to $150,000) to cover its prior investment in the professional schools, and gave the university the first rights toward reclaiming them, should the Catholic University of America not survive. Its short-term failure was something that Richards indeed saw on the horizon. "Our consent," he explained to the provincial superior, "would show a disinterested desire on our part to do whatever the Holy Father may think best for Catholic education in this country, and at the same time would open the way for the [Catholic] University itself to be transferred to us at some future time."[35]

Fortunately for Georgetown's own educational future, the law and medi-

33. Campbell to Robert Whitty, New York, June 5, 1891, *MD* 11-III-8, *ARSI*; Thomas Hughes to Whitty, New York, June 2, 1891, *MD* 11-III-6, *ARSI*; Campbell to Anderledy, New York, August 17, 1891, *MD* 11-III-12, *ARSI*; Consultors' Minutes, November 10, 1891, Maryland Province Archives at Roland Park; Campbell to Anderledy, New York, November 11, 1891, *MD* 11-III-17, *ARSI*; Whitty to Richards, Fiesole, December 30, 1891, Law 1889-91, GUA, GULSC.

34. Patrick Henry Ahern, *The Catholic University of America 1887–1896: The Rectorship of John Keane* (Washington, D.C.: The Catholic University of America Press, 1948), 100–3.

35. Father Provincial [Pardow], November 24, 1893, Richard Letterbooks, Society of Jesus, vol. 2, 177–82, GUA, GULSC.

cal faculties rebelled against the proposal and threatened, if forced to it, to set up an independent university, free from any outside control, ecclesiastical or other. That threat ended the matter. By the following year no one at the Catholic University of America claimed to have ever been in favor of the transfer. In 1895 it opened departments not only in law, but in engineering, philosophy, and letters. Within a year it had 115 graduate students in the new departments. A recruiting war for graduate students broke out between the two institutions, both offering scholarships to graduates of Catholic colleges to lure them to their respective programs.

Fordham as the American Louvain

In 1906 Franz Wernz became Superior General of the Society of Jesus. Among the new general's goals was that of creating a great Jesuit university in the United States, on the order of the ones the Society had in Rome and Louvain. The place for such a university, sadly for Georgetown, was not Washington, but New York, the intellectual center of the nation. Wernz wanted Fordham to become "a great center of studies and publications," housing the Society's periodicals in the United States, as well as a full range of graduate faculties, including professional schools as well as the theologate.[36] Fordham had been struggling to survive as a college since the late nineteenth century, but had a few years earlier incorporated itself as a university when it had begun law and medical schools (a move it had taken in the face of a rumored threat of The Catholic University of America to locate its professional schools in New York City).[37]

Wernz immediately began to take steps to fulfill his vision for the Society's intellectual apostolate in New York. In 1907 he relocated the *Messenger of the Sacred Heart*, which had been housed at Woodstock, in New York. The editor of the *Messenger*, John J. Wynne, S.J., proposed the establishment of a new weekly journal of opinion, which would include articles, editorials, and reviews of art and literature. It was the "Review" *revividus*. Wernz readily approved, and in 1909 *America*, as the journal was named, made its first appearance in 1909, with its offices established in New York City.[38]

36. Wernz to John Wynne, Mondragone, August 12, 1907, Register of Responses, Maryland Province, 1900–1911, 209, ARSI.

37. Gannon to Martín, New York, June 23, 1904, MD 13-II-30, ARSI; Gannon to Martín, New York, July 9, 1905, MD 13-II-38, ARSI.

38. Thomas H. Stahel, S.J., "America," in *The Encyclopedia of American Catholic History*, ed.

One of the first actions Wernz took as superior general was to order the Maryland–New York provincial superior, Joseph Hanselman, to take the necessary steps to relocate the theologate to Fordham.[39] Securing the blessing of Cardinal Gibbons, who had thwarted the attempted move in the 1890s, was essential to realize the change. Cardinal Gibbons, when approached about the possible move, was "grieved and pained," but indicated he would no longer stand in the way.[40] Nor did the Archbishop of New York, now John Farley, any longer oppose the move.[41] "He was very much pleased with everything," the Fordham president reported to Wernz. "[H]e promised me to do all that he could to help Fordham to become the greatest Catholic University in the country."[42] Fordham itself now became the main roadblock. The new university (it had become one in 1907) opposed the imposition of the theologate upon its campus. Provincial officials, for their part, had come to the conclusion that implanting Woodstock upon Fordham would be a bad thing for several reasons, including the fear of the clericalization of the university through the additional presence of several hundred seminarians and priests.[43]

Despite prodding from the superior general that the province implement the move to New York, matters dragged along, with province and university negotiating a property settlement that neither really wanted to make. Finally in 1911 provincial officials persuaded Wernz to abandon Fordham as a site for the theologate. In its stead they acquired a fifty-four acre estate in Yonkers, just above the city.[44] As the provincial explained to the superior general, the property was "practically in New York City now and will certainly be so in a few years."[45] Having a house of theological studies five miles from the Fordham campus, the provincial superior observed to Wernz, "would serve sufficiently well for a centralization of [intellectual] activities" as the present location of the Fordham law school downtown, an equidistance from the Bronx campus.[46]

Michael Glazier and Thomas J. Shelley (Collegeville, Minn.: Liturgical Press, 1997), 21–22; Wernz to Hanselman, Rome, March 4, 1909, Register, 325–26, ARSI; Wernz to Hanselman, July 30, 1909, Register, 359–63.

39. Wernz to Hanselman, May 21, 1907, Register, 199–201, ARSI.

40. Hanselman to Wernz, New York, Sept 14, 1907, MD 14-I-21, ARSI.

41. Hanselman to Wernz, New York, July 8, 1908, MD 14-VII-4, ARSI.

42. Thomas J. McCluskey to Wernz, New York, April 3, 1912, MD 15-IX-11, ARSI.

43. Hanselman to Wernz, New York, March 25, 1911, MD 14-V-11, ARSI.

44. Wernz to Hanselman, Rome, April 12, 1911, Register, 457, ARSI.

45. Hanselman to Wernz, New York March 25, 1911, MD 14-V-11, ARSI.

46. Hanselman to Wernz, New York March 25, 1911, MD 14-V-11, ARSI.

But opposition to the new site quickly developed, particularly in the Chesapeake portion of the province. Many considered the site to be an inconvenient one and its cost prohibitive. As one senior member of the province wrote to superior general Wernz: it was "an ideal spot for a rich gentleman's country-seat,—but [not for a house of studies] . . . it is a crime to saddle the Province with a debt that threatens bankruptcy."[47] At a provincial congregation in 1915 a majority of the delegates petitioned the superior general that the Yonkers site be abandoned as the home of the theologate. A clearly exasperated Hanselman reported to Wernz:

> I am afraid that some, if not many of the members of the Congregation, were not without strong preconceived notions on the subject . . . the sentiment expressed was to the effect that the transfer of the scholasticate from Woodstock to Yonkers was to be prevented at all costs.
>
> . . . [Some were opposed simply because, being old, they oppose any change.] There are those who originally belonged to the old Maryland Province who are bent on keeping Woodstock in the south. The feeling actuating them dates back to the early part of the last century when Fr. Neale wished to keep the centre of influence in Maryland (in the South), and Fr. Kohlmann, more far-sighted, wished to have it in New York. That spirit has never completely died out. And yet the center of influence, progress and development, is now in New York & in the North, and not in Maryland or in the South. [Some others favored Fordham as the site. And there were those] who wish to have the scholasticate in the woods, as it is now. . . .
>
> [B]y no means and under no consideration should we part with our site at Yonkers. We shall never get a like opportunity. It is a site so advantageously situated, that we shall never be compelled by the progress of the city of New York, or for other reasons, to abandon it.[48]

Events, however, were moving against Hanselman: not only the growing opposition within the province, but the outbreak of a soon-to-be world war in Europe, and the death, three weeks later, of Franz Wernz, who had been such an advocate of making New York the intellectual center for the Jesuits in the Eastern United States. Woodstock would eventually move to the City, but not until more than a half century later.

47. The purchase of the Lillienthal estate had cost the province $750,000. Many felt they had paid far too much for it, a conviction that could only have been hardened by an assessment of the property the following year that put its value at $326,000, or less than half of what they had paid; E. I. Devitt to Wernz, Washington, D.C., Sept 1, 1913, *MD* 16-I-25, *ARSI*; Zwinge to Gannon, Baltimore, Oct 3, 1915, *MD* 16-XXVIII-2, *ARSI*.

48. Hanselman to Wernz, Woodstock, August 26, 1913, *MD* 16-XXVI-3, *ARSI*.

Pascendi Dominici Gregis and an End to Vying

In the very New York suburb where the Jesuits were seeking to move their theologate, there was already a seminary that, but a few years previously, was becoming an intellectual force within the Church in America. Dunwoodie Seminary possessed, by the beginning of the new century, an outstanding faculty, including Francis E. Gigot, the leading Catholic Scripture scholar in the country, Joseph Bruneau, professor of dogmatic theology, and James F. Driscoll, professor of Semitic languages. In 1905, under the lead of Driscoll, the rector of the seminary, Dunwoodie became the home of the first scientific Catholic theological review in America. Its purpose, its editor, Driscoll, explained in the initial edition, was to interpret with becoming care and reverence the old truths in the light of the new science."[49] In articles written by faculty members as well as by European Catholic scholars, the *New York Review* made available to an American public the latest developments in Scripture studies, philosophy, and theology. Sadly its history was a very brief one. In 1908 it ceased publication, a victim of the intellectual repression that set in after *Pascendi Dominici Gregis* (1907), Pope Pius X's encyclical that formally condemned Modernism, including its use of historical criticism, evolutionary philosophy, and literary exegesis in the interpretation of theology and Scripture.[50] The chill of the papal condemnation and of the oath against Modernism that every theological professor now had to take effectively silenced the faculty; Driscoll himself was transferred to a parish.

Neither the Catholic University of America nor Georgetown fared well in the new climate. The Catholic University proved to be an early victim of the conservative reaction that gathered force from the middle 1890s on. John Farley eventually coaxed Corrigan back onto its board of trustees, but financial support from New York continued to be minimal, at best, and student enrollment from the city practically nonexistent, a pattern that prevailed among conservative dioceses whose prelates resented the liberal bent that the university faculty, under Keane, quickly took in the area of curriculum and of issues related to education and political economy. In 1896 John Keane was forced to resign, one of the first prizes conservatives garnered in their counterattack.

49. Michael V. Gannon, "Before and After Modernism: The Intellectual Isolation of the American Priest," in *The Catholic Priest in the United States: Historical Investigations*, ed. John Tracy Ellis (Collegeville, Minn.: St. John's University Press, 1971), 334.

50. See Thomas J. Shelley, "John Cardinal Farley and Modernism in New York," *Church History* 61 (September 1992): 350–61.

Then followed the dual condemnations of Americanism and Modernism in 1899 and 1907, respectively. A purge of liberal faculty ensued, most notably that of Henry Poels, a professor of Scripture, in 1910. Its weak finances, the result of small graduate enrollments and lack of support from the hierarchy, got desperately worse when the reckless real estate investments of its treasurer led to the disastrous loss of sixty percent of the university's endowment. To meet the crisis, the university in 1904 introduced undergraduate education to its courses of study. By 1915 the Catholic University of America had become primarily an undergraduate institution. Significantly, by the nineteen teens the National Shrine of the Immaculate Conception, under construction on the campus, was absorbing more of the attention of the rector than the university itself.

At Georgetown the steps that Havens Richards had taken toward making Georgetown a true university were either not pursued or discontinued. One of Superior General Wernz's first actions toward the concentration of intellectual resources at Fordham was to advise Georgetown to discontinue its graduate program. For all practical purposes it did so.[51] Graduate studies virtually disappeared after 1906. The law and medical schools once again operated in their own spheres. Rectors after Richards tended to concern themselves mainly with the college and undergraduate activities. Richards' immediate successor became best known as the chief recruiter and cheerleader of the football and baseball teams.

Such was the intellectual state of the Catholic institutions of higher learning in the New York and Chesapeake areas on the eve of America's entry into the First World War. Neither area came close to producing, or even setting on the road to, a Catholic university that would fully justify its name. Those Catholic leaders in the 1880s with the grand dreams and visions, the promise of an intellectual flowering, would have found little in those institutions in 1915 in which to take satisfaction, their efforts to elevate them to positions of intellectual prominence having gone largely to waste. They were just portions of a larger American Catholic institutional landscape beset with intellectual stagnation—a mental rigor mortis that bred complacency, inertia, and isolation.

51. By 1912 a Georgetown president would lament that relations between his university and the Catholic University of America would be fine if only the latter would confine itself "to their original purpose of doing graduate work only"; Donlon to Wernz, Washington, D.C., July 23, 1912, MD 15-X-13, ARSI. Havens Richards' vision of graduate studies becoming the core element of Georgetown's educational mission had long since vanished.

Bibliography

Primary Sources

Archives

Archives of the Archdiocese of Cincinnati
Archives of the Archdiocese of New York
Archives of The Catholic University of America
Archives of the Diocese of Cleveland
Archives of the Diocese of Peoria
Archives of the Diocese of Richmond
Archives of the Diocese of Rochester
Archives of the University of Notre Dame
Archivo Di Propaganda Fide
- *Atti*
- *Congregationi Particulari*
- *Lettere e Decreti*
- *Letteri della S. Congregatione*
- *Scritture riferte nei congressi, America Centrale*

Archivum Provinciae Belgicae Septemtrionalis Societatis Jesu
Archivum Romanum Societatis Jesu
- *Epistolae Vicarum Generalium in Russia,* 1809–1814
- *Liber Litterarum Generalis* (Register of the Letters of the General of the Society of Jesus)
- *Litterae Annuales Provinciae Marylandiae*
- *Marylandia*

Associated Archives at Saint Mary's Seminary and University
Archives of the Archdiocese of Baltimore
- John Carroll Papers
- Samuel Eccleston Papers
- James Gibbons Papers
- Ambrose Maréchal Papers

Sulpician Archives, Baltimore
Carmelite Monastery Archives, Baltimore
English Province Archives
- Foreign Correspondence, 1776–1859

Georgetown University Libraries Special Collections
- American Catholic Sermon Collection
- Catholic Historical Manuscript Collection
- Diary of Stephen Dubuisson, S.J.
- Diary of James Levins, S.J.
- Diary of Thomas Lilly, S.J.
- Diary of John McElroy, S.J.
- Diary of Joseph Mobberly, S.J.
- Thomas Hughes, S.J. Papers
- "History of the Society of Jesus in North America: Text III," unpublished redaction of 1933
- Georgetown University Archives
- Thomas Mulledy, S.J., Papers
- Joseph Havens Richards, S.J., Papers
- Joseph Havens Richards, S.J., Letterbooks, 1888–1898
- Maryland Province Archives of the Society of Jesus
- Catalogues
- Proceedings of the Corporation of the Roman Catholic Clergymen

Georgetown Visitation Archives
Maryland Province Archives of the Society of Jesus at Roland Park
National Archives and Records Administration
New York Province Archives of the Society of Jesus
The Catholic University of America Archives

Newspapers/Journals

America	*New York Daily Tribune*	*New York World*
Catholic World	*New York Evening Sun*	*The Pilot*
Forum	*New York Herald*	*Washington Daily National*
Freeman's Journal	*New York Sun*	*Journal*
National Intelligencer	*New York Times*	*Woodstock Letters*

Additional Primary Sources

Abell, Aaron I., ed. *American Catholic Thought on Social Questions.* Indianapolis: Bobbs-Merrill, 1968.

Abstract of the Minutes of the Third Annual Conference of the Most Rev. Archbishops of the United States. Baltimore: John Murphy, 1892.

Baxter, Roger. *The Most Important Tenets of the Roman Catholic Church Fairly Explained.* Washington, D.C.: 1820.

Bouquillon, Thomas. *Education: To Whom Does It Belong?* Baltimore: John Murphy, 1891.

Brownson, Orestes. "The Laboring Classes." *Boston Quarterly Review* (July 1840). Reprinted in *The Transcendentalists*, edited by Perry Miller, 436–46. Cambridge, Mass.: Harvard University Press, 1950.

———. "Mission of America." *Brownson's Quarterly Review* (October 1856). Excerpted in *American Catholic Thought on Social Questions*, edited by Aaron I. Abell, 34. Indianapolis: Bobbs-Merrill, 1968.

———. "Present Catholic Dangers." *Brownson's Quarterly Review.* New York Series 2 (July 1857): 362.

———. *The American Republic: Its Constitution, Tendencies, and Destiny.* New York: P. O'Shea, 1866.

——— "The Church and Monarchy." *Catholic World* 4, no. 23 (February 1867): 638.

Burtsell, Richard. *Canonical Status of Priests in the United States.* New York: John J. O'Brien, 1887.

Bushnell, Horace. *A Discourse on the Modifications Demanded by the Roman Catholics Delivered in the North Church, Hartford, on the Day of the Late Fast, March 25 1853.* Hartford: 1853.

Butler, Frederick. *A Catechetical Compendium of General History.* Hartford: 1818.

Callahan, Nelson J., ed. *The Diary of Richard L. Burtsell, Priest of New York: The Early Years, 1865–1868.* New York: Arno, 1978.

Carey, Matthew. "Essays on the Public Charities of Philadelphia." In *Miscellaneous Essays.* Philadelphia: Carey and Hart, 1830.

Catalogus Provinciae Marylandiae Societatis Jesu Ineunte Anno MDCCLI. Georgetown: 1851.

Catholic Directory, Almanac and Clergy List for 1900. Milwaukee: Bruce Publishing, 1900. In *In Hoc Signo? A Brief History of Catholic Parochial Education in America*, by Glen Gabert, 128. Port Washington, N.Y: Kennikat, 1973.

A Collection of Affidavits and Certificates, Relative to the Wonderful Cure of Mrs. Ann Mattingly. Washington, D.C.: 1824.

Collens, T. Wharton. "Views of the Labor Movement." *Catholic World* 10 (March 1870). Reprinted in *American Catholic Thought on Social Questions*, edited by Aaron I. Abell, 72–90. Indianapolis: Bobbs-Merrill, 1968.

Concilia Provincialia, Baltimorei Habita Ab Anno 1829 usque ad annum 1849, Editio Altera. Baltimore: John Murphy, 1851.

Curran, Robert Emmett, ed. *American Jesuit Spirituality: The Maryland Tradition, 1634–1900*. New York and Mahwah, N.J.: Paulist Press, 1988.

Denziger, Henricus. *Enchiridion Symbolorum Definitionum et Declarationum: De Rebus Fidei et Morum*, ed. Karl Rahner. Freiburg: Herder, 1955.

Egan, Maurice Francis. *Recollections of a Happy Life*. New York: George H. Doran, 1924.

Ellis, John Tracy, ed. *Documents of American Catholic History*. Chicago: Henry Regnery, 1967. Later 3-vol. edition Wilmington, Del.: Michael Glazier, 1987.

England, John. *Letters to the Honorable John Forsyth on the Subject of Domestic Slavery*. Baltimore: John Murphy, 1844.

———. "Address before Congress." In *The Works of the Right Reverent John England: First Bishop of Charleston*, edited by Sebastian G. Messmer, 7:35. Cleveland: Arthur H. Clark, 1908.

An Examination of a Protestant's Objections to the Popish Miracle Lately Wrought in America. London: 1824.

Gilson, Etienne, ed. *The Church Speaks to the Modern World: The Social Teachings of Leo XIII*. Garden City, N.Y.: Image Books, 1954.

Goodrich, S. G. *The Child's Second Book of History*. Boston: 1836.

Gower, Joseph, and Richard Leliaert, eds. *The Brownson-Hecker Correspondence*. Notre Dame, Ind.: University of Notre Dame Press, 1979.

Grassi, Giovanni. *Notizie varie sullo stato presente della repubblica degli Stati Uniti dell' America settentrionale scritte al principio del 1818*. Milano: 1819.

Guilday, Peter. *The National Pastorals of the American Hierarchy, 1792–1919*. Washington, D.C.: The Catholic University of America Press, 1923.

Hanley, Thomas O'Brien, ed. *The John Carroll Papers*. 3 vols. Notre Dame: University of Notre Dame Press, 1976.

Holaind, Rene, S.J. The Parent First. New York: Benziger Brothers, 1891.

Hughes, Thomas, S.J. *History of the Society of Jesus in North America: Colonial and Federal*. Text. 2 vols. London: Longmans, Green, 1908, 1917.

———. *History of the Society of Jesus in North America*. Documents. 2 Parts. London: Longmans, Green, 1908, 1910.

———. "Reminiscences." *Woodstock Letters* 51 (1922).

Ireland, John, *The Church and Modern Society*. St. Paul: Pioneer Press, 1905.

Ives, Levi Silliman. *Church and State Charities Compared with Special Reference to the System of New York*

State Charities. New York: 1857. Reprinted in *American Catholic Thought on Social Questions*, edited by Aaron I. Abell, 98. Indianapolis: Bobbs-Merrill, 1968.

Kehoe, Lawrence, ed. *Complete Works of the Most Reverend John Hughes*. New York: Catholic Publication House, 1865.

Kerby, William. "The Priesthood and the Social Movement." *Catholic University Bulletin* 6 (January 1900): 18–28. Reprinted in *American Catholic Thought on Social Questions*, edited by Aaron I. Abell, 266–77. Indianapolis: Bobbs-Merrill, 1968.

Letters and Notices 12 (1878–79), 171–75.

McCloskey, Neil G. S.J., ed. *Catholic Education in America: A Documentary History*. New York: Teachers College, Columbia University, 1965.

McCulloch, John. *Epitome of Workman's Geography*. Philadelphia: 1816.

McElroy, John, S.J. "Chaplain for the Mexican War." *Woodstock Letters* 16 (1887): 226.

McGlynn, Edward. "The Results of Cardinal Satolli's Mission." *The Forum* 22 (February 1897): 695–705.

McSweeny, Patrick F. "Christian Public Schools." *The Catholic World* 44, no. 262 (March 1887): 796.

Messmer, Sebastian G. "A Catholic Temperance League." *Ecclesiastical Review* 11 (December 1894): 416.

———, ed. *The Works of the Right Reverend John England: First Bishop of Charleston*. Cleveland: Arthur H. Clark, 1908.

Miller, Perry, ed. *The Transcendentalists*. Cambridge, Mass.: Harvard University Press, 1950.

Morse, Samuel B. *Imminent Dangers to the Free Institutions of the United States Through Foreign Immigrations*. New York: 1835.

Narrative of Two Wonderful Cures Wrought in the Monastery of the Visitation at Georgetown in the District of Columbia in the Month of January 1831. Baltimore: 1831.

Powderly, Terrence V. *The Path I Trod: The Autobiography of Terrence V. Powderly*, edited by Harry J. Carman, Henry David, and Paul N. Guthrie. New York: Columbia University Press, 1940.

Preston, Monsignor Thomas. "What the Roman Catholics Want." *Forum* 1 (April 1886): 161–71.

Read, E. George, ed. *Letters of the late Bishop England to the Hon John Forsyth, on the Subject of Domestic Slavery*. Baltimore: John Murphy, 1844.

Relationes eorum qui disceptata fuerunt ab illmis ac revmis metropolitis cum suis suffraganeis in suis singulis provinciis super schema futuri councilii praesertim vero super capita cuique commissa. Baltimore: John Murphy, 1884.

Report of the Supreme Court of New York, 1864–1865. New York: 1866.

Ryan, John A. *Social Doctrine in Action: A Personal History*. New York: Harper, 1941.

Schaff, Philip. *America: A Sketch of the Political, Social and Religious Character of the United States*. New York: Charles Scribner, 1855.

Smith, Sebastian. *Notes on the Second Plenary Council*. New York: P. O'Shea, 1874.

Smyth, Patrick. *The Present State of the Catholic Mission, Conducted by the Ex-Jesuits in North America.* Dublin: P. Byrne, 1788.

Spalding, John Lancaster. *The Religious Mission of the Irish People.* New York: Catholic Publication Society, 1880.

———. *University Education Considered in Its Bearing on the Higher Education of Priests.* Baltimore: John Murphy, 1884.

Spalding, Thomas W. *John Carroll Recovered: Abstracts of Letters and Other Documents Not Found in the John Carroll Papers.* Baltimore: Cathedral Foundation Press, 2000.

Walburg, Antoine. *The Question of Nationality in Its Relation to the Catholic Church in the United States.* Cincinnati: 1889. Reprinted in *American Catholic Thought on Social Questions*, edited by Aaron I. Abell, 40, 42. Indianapolis: Bobbs-Merrill, 1968.

Walsh, Robert. *Didactics: Social, Literary, and Political*, 2 vols. Philadelphia: Carey, Lea and Blanchard, 1836.

———. *Notes on the American Constitution.* Keesville, N.Y.: 1849.

The Washington Miracle Refuted: Or, a Review of the Rev. Mr. Matthew's Pamphlet. Georgetown, 1824.

Woodbridge, William C. *A System of Universal Geography.* Hartford: 1835.

Secondary Sources

Abell, Aaron I. *American Catholicism and Social Action: A Search for Social Justice* (Notre Dame, Ind.: University of Notre Dame Press, 1963.

Ahern, Patrick Henry. *The Catholic University of America 1887–1896: The Rectorship of John Keane.* Washington, D.C.: The Catholic University of America Press, 1948.

Alvarez, David J. "The Papacy in the Diplomacy of the American Civil War." *Catholic Historical Review* 69 (April 1983): 233–34.

Andreassi, Anthony D. "'The Cunning Leader of a Dangerous Clique'? The Burtsell Affair and Archbishop Michael Augustine Corrigan." *Catholic Historical Review* 86 (October 2000), 620–39.

Baker, Jean H. *Ambivalent Americans: The Know-Nothing Party in Maryland.* Baltimore and London: Johns Hopkins University Press, 1977.

Barker, Charles. *Henry George.* New York: Oxford University Press, 1955.

Bell, Stephen. *Rebel, Priest and Prophet: A Biography of Dr. Edward McGlynn.* New York: Devin-Adair, 1937.

Berlin, Ira. *Slaves Without Masters: The Free Negro in the Antebellum South.* New York: Pantheon Books, 1974.

Bevan, Thomas R. *220 Years . . . A History of the Catholic Community of the Frederick Valley.* Frederick: Da-Mark Associates, 1977.

Binzley, Ronald A. "Ganganelli's Disaffected Children: The Ex-Jesuits and the Shaping of Early American Catholicism, 1773–1790." *U.S. Catholic Historian* 26 (Spring 2008): 47–77.

Bland, Joan, SND. *Hibernian Crusade: The Story of the Catholic Total Abstinence Union of America.* Washington, D.C.: The Catholic University of America Press, 1951.

Brackett, Jeffrey. *The Negro in Maryland: A Study of the Institution of Slavery.* Baltimore: Johns Hopkins University Press, 1889.

Broehl, Wayne G., Jr. *The Molly Maguires.* Cambridge, Mass.: Harvard University Press, 1964.

Brown, Dorothy M., and Elizabeth McKeown. *The Poor Belong to Us: Catholic Charities and American Welfare.* Cambridge, Mass.: Harvard University Press, 1997.

Brown, Thomas N. *Irish-American Nationalism, 1870–1890.* Philadelphia and New York: J. P. Lippincott, 1966.

Browne, Henry J. *The Catholic Church and the Knights of Labor.* Washington, D.C.: The Catholic University of America Press, 1949.

———. "Archbishop Hughes and Western Colonization." *Catholic Historical Review* (October 1950): 269–73.

Buetow, Harold A. *Of Singular Benefit: The Story of Catholic Education in the United States.* New York and London: Macmillan, 1970.

Burton, David H., and Frank Gerrity. *St. Joseph's College: A Family Portrait, 1851–1976.* Philadelphia: St. Joseph's College, 1976.

Callahan, Nelson J. *A Case for Due Process in the Church: Father Eugene O'Callaghan, American Pioneer of Dissent.* Staten Island, N.Y.: Alba, 1971.

"Catholic Social Teaching and the U.S. Economy" (First Draft). *Origins: NC Documentary Service* (November 15, 1984): 350.

Chinnici, Joseph, OFM. "American Catholics and Religious Pluralism, 1775–1820." *Journal of Ecumenical Studies* 16 (Fall 1979): 742–43.

———. "Politics and Theology: From Enlightenment Catholicism to the Condemnation of Americanism." Working Papers Series. Center for the Study of American Catholicism, Spring 1981.

Cline, Ruth Harwood. "Bridging Two Worlds: Stephen Larigaudelle Dubisson, Émigré Missionary." *Catholic Historical Review* 90 (October 2004): 675–96.

Codignola, Luca. "Roman Catholic Conservatism in a New North Atlantic World, 1760–1829." *The William and Mary Quarterly* 64 (October 2007): 717–56.

Contosta, David R. *Saint Joseph's: Philadelphia's Jesuit University—150 Years.* Philadelphia: St. Joseph's University, 2000.

Curran, Francis X., S.J. *The Return of the Jesuits: Chapters in the History of the Society of Jesus in the Ninteenth Century.* Chicago: Loyola University Press, 1964.

Curran, Robert Emmett. "Conservative Thought and Strategy in the School Controversy, 1891–93." *Notre Dame Journal of Education* 7 (Spring 1976): 44–62.

———. *Michael Augustine Corrigan and the Shaping of Conservative Catholicism in America, 1878–1902.* New York: Arno Press, 1978.

———. *The Bicentennial History of Georgetown*. Vol. 1, *From Academy to University, 1789–1889*. Washington, D.C.: Georgetown University Press, 1993.

———. *A History of Georgetown University*. 3 vols. Washington, D.C.: Georgetown University Press, 2010.

Dignan, Patrick J. *A History of the Legal Incorporation of Catholic Church Property in the United States: 1784–1932*. Washington, D.C.: The Catholic University of America Press, 1933.

Dolan, Jay P. *The Immigrant Church: New York's Irish and German Catholics, 1815–1865*. Baltimore: Johns Hopkins University Press, 1975.

———. *The American Catholic Experience: A History from Colonial Times to the Present*. New York: Doubleday, 1985.

Dooley, Patrick J. "Woodstock and Its Makers." *Woodstock Letters* 56 (1927).

Douglass, Bruce. "At the Heart of the Letter." *America* (June 21, 1985): 360.

Dunigan, David R., S.J. *A History of Boston College*. Milwaukee: Bruce Publishing, 1947.

Durkin, Joseph, S.J. *Georgetown University: The Middle Years*. Washington, D.C.: Georgetown University Press, 1963.

Durkin, Joseph, Gerald Fogarty, and Robert Emmett Curran. *The Maryland Jesuits, 1634–1833*. Baltimore: Corporation of the Roman Catholic Clergymen, 1976.

Ellis, John Tracy. *The Formative Years of the Catholic University*. Washington, D.C.: The Catholic University of America Press, 1946.

———. *The Life of James Cardinal Gibbons, 1834–1921*. 2 vols. Milwaukee: Bruce Publishing, 1952.

———. *Catholics in Colonial America*. Baltimore: Helicon, 1965.

———. ed. *The Catholic Priest in the United States: Historical Investigations*. Collegeville, Minn.: St. John's University Press, 1971.

Ewens, Mary, O.P. "Removing the Veil: The Liberated American Nun in the Nineteenth Century." Working Papers Series. Spring 1978.

Faherty, William B., S.J. *Better the Dream: St. Louis University and Community, 1818–1968*. St. Louis: St. Louis University Press, 1968.

Fields, Barbara Jeanne. *Slavery and Freedom on the Middle Ground: Maryland During the Nineteenth Century*. New Haven and London: Yale University Press, 1988.

Finn, Peter, "The Slaves of the Jesuits in Maryland." Master's thesis, Georgetown University, 1974.

Fogarty, Gerald P, S.J. *The Vatican and the Americanist Crisis: Denis J. O'Connell, American Agent in Rome, 1885–1903*. Rome: Università Gregoriana Editrice, 1973.

———. "Public Patriotism and Private Politics: The Tradition of American Catholicism." *U. S. Catholic Historian* 3 (November 1984): 1–48.

Gannon, Michael. *Rebel Bishop: The Life and Era of Augustine Verot*. Milwaukee: Bruce Publishing, 1964.

———. "Before and After Modernism: The Intellectual Isolation of the American Priest." In *The Catholic Priest in the United States: Historical Investigations*, edited by John Tracy Ellis, 311–34. Collegeville, Minn.: St. John's University Press, 1971.

Gabert, Glen. *In Hoc Signo? A Brief History of Catholic Parochial Education in America*. Port Washington, N.Y: Kennikat, 1973.

Gaston, William. An *Address delivered before the American Whig and Cliosophic Societies off the College of New Jersey*. Princeton, N.J.: R. E. Hornor, 1835. In *The Social Thought of American Catholics, 1634–1829*, by Joseph C. Neusse. Washington, D.C.: The Catholic University of America Press, 1945.

Glazier, Michael, and Thomas J. Shelley, eds. *The Encyclopedia of American Catholic History*. Collegeville, Minn.: The Liturgical Press, 1997.

Gleason, Philip. "'The Main Sheet Anchor': John Carroll and Catholic Higher Education." *The Review of Politics* 38 (October 1976): 576–613.

———. *Keeping the Faith: American Catholicism Past and Present*. Notre Dame: University of Notre Dame Press, 1987.

———. *Contending With Modernity: Catholic Higher Education in the Twentieth Century*. New York and Oxford: Oxford University Press, 1995.

Green, James Jeremiah. "The Impact of Henry George's Theories on American Catholics." Ph.D. diss., University of Notre Dame, 1956.

Guilday, Peter. *The Life and Times of John Carroll, Archbishop of Baltimore (1735–1815)*. 2 vols. New York: Encyclopedia Press, 1922.

Hennesey, James, S.J. *American Catholics: A History of the Roman Catholic Community in the United States*. New York and Oxford: Oxford University Press, 1981.

———. "Catholicism in the English Colonies." In *Encyclopedia of the American Religious Experience*, edited by Charles H. Lippy and Peter W. Williams, 1:354. New York: Charles Scribner's Sons, 1988.

Isaccsson, Alfred, O.Carm. *The Determined Doctor: The Story of Edward McGlynn*. Tarrytown, New York: n.d.

Johnson, Whittington B. "The Origins and Nature of African Slavery in Seventeenth-Century Maryland." *Maryland Historical Magazine* 73 (1978): 236–45.

Kaiser, M. Laurina, O.S.B. *The Development of the Concept and Function of the Catholic Elementary School in the American Parish*. Washington, D.C.: The Catholic University of America Press, 1955.

Kenrick, Francis. *A Vindication of The Catholic Church*. Baltimore: John Murphy, 1855.

———. "Religion the Basis of all Sound Education." In *Concilium Plenarium Totius Americae Septentrionalis Foederatae, Baltimori Habitum Anno 1852*. Baltimore: John Murphy, 1853.

Kolchin, Peter. "In Defense of Servitude: American Proslavery and Russian Proserfdom Arguments, 1760–1860." *American Historical Review* 85 (October 1980): 809–27.

Kselman, Thomas A. *Miracles and Prophecies in Nineteenth-Century France*. New Brunswick, N.J.: Rutgers University Press, 1982.

Kupke, Raymond J., ed. *American Catholic Preaching and Piety in the Time of John Carroll*. Lanham, Md.: University Press of America, 1991.

Kuzniewski, Anthony J., S.J. "Francis Dzierozynski and the Jesuit Restoration in the United States." *Catholic Historical Review* 78 (January 1992): 51–73.

———. *Thy Honored Name: A History of The College of the Holy Cross, 1843–1994*. Washington, D.C.: The Catholic University of America Press, 1999.

Lalli, Anthony B., S.X., and Thomas H. O'Connor. "Roman Views on the American Civil War." *Catholic Historical Review* 57 (April 1971): 34.

Lapomardi, Vincent A., S.J. *The Jesuit Heritage in New England*. Worcester, Mass.: Holy Cross College, 1977.

Larkin, Emmet. *The Roman Catholic Church and the Creation of the Modern Irish State: 1878–1886*. Philadelphia: American Philosophical Society, 1975.

Leahy, William P., S.J. *Adapting to America: Catholics, Jesuits, and Higher Education in the Twentieth Century*. Washington, D.C.: Georgetown University Press, 1991.

Light, Dale B. *Rome and the New Republic: Conflict and Community in Philadelphia Catholicism between the Revolution and the Civil War*. Notre Dame and London: University of Notre Dame Press, 1996.

Lippy, Charles H., and Peter W. Williams, eds. *Encyclopedia of the American Religious Experience*. 3 vols. New York: Charles Scribner's Sons, 1988.

Mannard, Joseph G. "The 1839 Baltimore Nunnery Riot: An Episode in Jacksonian Nativism and Social Violence." *The Maryland Historian* 11 (Spring 1980): 13–27.

Maxwell, John Francis. *Slavery and the Catholic Church: The History of Catholic Teaching Concerning the Moral Legitimacy of the Institution of Slavery*. Chichester and London: Barry Rose Publishers, 1975.

May, Henry F. *Protestant Churches and Industrial America*. New York: Harper, 1949.

McAvoy, Thomas T., C.S.C. "Public Schools versus Catholic Schools and James McMaster." *Review of Politics* 28 (January 1966): 19–46.

McCaffrey, Lawrence J. *The Irish Diaspora in America*. Bloomington: Indiana University Press, 1976.

Meagher, Walter J., S.J., and William Grattan. *The Spires of Fenwick: The History of the College of The Holy Cross, 1843–1963*. New York: Vantage Press, 1966.

Meiring, Bernard Julius. *Educational Aspects of the Legislation of the Councils of Baltimore, 1829–1884*. New York: Arno Press, 1978.

Melville, Annabelle M. *John Carroll of Baltimore, Founder of the American Catholic Hierarchy*. New York: Charles Scribner's Sons, 1955.

Merwick, Donna. *Boston Priests, 1848–1910: A Study of Social and Intellectual Change*. Cambridge, Mass.: Harvard University Press, 1973.

Minnich, Nelson H., et al., eds. *Studies in Catholic History in Honor of John Tracy Ellis*. Wilmington, Del.: Michael Glazier, 1985.

Morris, Charles R. *American Catholic: The Saints and Sinners Who Built America's Most Powerful Church*. New York: Random House, 1997.

Morrissey, Thomas, S.J. *"As One Sent": Peter Kenney, S.J., 1779–1841*. Washington, D.C.: The Catholic University of America Press, 1996.

Murphy, Thomas, S.J. *Jesuit Slaveholding in Maryland, 1717–1838*. New York and London: Routledge, 2001.

Murtha, Ronin John, O.S.B. "The Life of the Most Reverend Ambrose Maréchal, Third Archbishop of Baltimore, 1768–1828." Ph.D. diss., The Catholic University of America, 1965.

Neusse, C. Joseph. *The Social Thought of American Catholics, 1634–1829*. Washington, D.C.: The Catholic University of America Press, 1945.

———. *The Catholic University of America: A Centennial History*. Washington, D.C.: The Catholic University of America Press, 1990.

Noonan, John T., Jr. "The Catholic Justices of the United States Supreme Court." *Catholic Historical Review* 67 (July 1981): 369–85.

O'Brien, David. "The American Priest and Social Action." In *The Catholic Priest in the United States: Historical Investigations*, edited by John Tracy Ellis, 424, 429. Collegeville, Minn.: 1971.

O'Connor, Thomas H. *The Boston Irish: A Political History*. Boston: Back Bay Books, 1995.

———. *Boston Catholics: A History of the Church and Its People*. Boston: Northeastern University Press, 1998.

Osofsky, Gilbert. "Abolitionists, Irish Immigrants, and the Dilemmas of Romantic Nationalism." *American Historical Review* 80 (October 1975): 889–912.

Pastor, Ludwig. *History of the Popes from the Close of the Middle Ages*. Vol. 8. St. Louis: 1908.

Power, Edward J. *Catholic Higher Education in America: A History*. New York: Appleton-Century, Crofts, 1972.

Quinn, John E. "'Three Cheers for the Abolitionist Pope!' American Reaction to Gregory XVI's Condemnation of the Slave Trade, 1840–1860." *Catholic Historical Review* 90 (January 2004): 67–93.

Reilly, Daniel F. O.P. *The School Controversy, 1891–1893*. Washington, D.C.: The Catholic University of America Press, 1943.

Rice, Madeleine Hooke. *American Catholic Opinion in the Slavery Controversy*. New York: Columbia University Press, 1944.

Roohan, James. *American Catholics and the Social Question, 1865–1900*. New York: Arno Press, 1976.

Ryan, Edmund. "An Academic History of Woodstock College in Maryland, 1869–1944: The First Jesuit Seminary in North America." Ph.D. diss., The Catholic University of America, 1963.

Schroth, Raymond A., S.J. *Fordham: A History and Memoir*. Chicago: Loyola University Press, 2002.

———. *The American Jesuits: A History*. New York: New York University Press, 2007.

Schultz, Nancy Lusignan. "Prince Hohenlohe's Miraculous Meddlings: Transatlantic Intercessions in Washington, D.C. and Charlestown, Massachusetts." *U.S. Catholic Historian* 20 (Winter 2002): 1–19.

Shelley, Thomas J. *The Archdiocese of New York: The Bicentennial History (1808–2008)*. Strasbourg: Editions du Signe, 2007.

Shratz, Sabine. *Das Gift Des Alten Europe Und Die Arbeiter Der Neuen Welt: Zum amerikanischen Hintergrund der Enzyklika* Rerum Novarum *(1891)*. Paderhorn-Munich-Vienna-Zurich: 2011.

Shannon, James P. *Catholic Colonization on the Western Frontier*. New Haven: Yale University Press, 1957.

Shannon, William V. *The American Irish*. New York: Macmillan, 1966.

Shaw, Richard. *John DuBois: The Founding Father*. Yonkers, N.Y.: United States Catholic Historical Society, 1983.

Shea, John Gilmary. *History of the Catholic Church in the United States*. Vol. 3. New York: John G. Shea, 1890.

Shelley, Thomas J. "John Cardinal Farley and Modernism in New York." *Church History* 61 (September 1992): 350–61.

Spalding, David [Thomas W.], C.F.X., ed. "Martin John Spalding's 'Dissertation on the American Civil War.'" *Catholic Historical Review* 52 (April 1966): 66–85.

Spalding, Thomas W. *The Premier See: A History of the Archdiocese of Baltimore, 1789–1989*. Baltimore and London: Johns Hopkins University Press, 1989.

———. "The Maryland Tradition." *U.S. Catholic Historian* 8 (Fall 1989): 51–58.

Talbot, Francis X., S.J. *Jesuit Education in Philadelphia: Saint Joseph's College, 1851–1926*. Philadelphia: St. Joseph's College, 1927.

Taves, Ann. "Context and Meaning: Roman Catholic Devotion to the Blessed Sacrament in Mid-Nineteenth-Century America." *Church History* 54 (December 1985): 482–95.

Thomas, John L. *Alternative America: Henry George, Edward Bellamy, Henry Demarest Lloyd and the Adversary Tradition*. Cambridge, Mass., and London: Harvard University Press, 1983.

Tonsor, Stephen J. "Lord Acton on Dölliger's Historical Theology," *Journal of the History of Ideas* 20 (1959): 329–52.

Trisco, Robert. "Bishops and Their Priests in the United States." In *The Catholic Priests in the United States: Historical Investigations*, edited by John Tracy Ellis, 111–292. Collegeville, Minn.: St. John's University Press, 1971.

Turner, Thomas Reed. *Beware the People Weeping: Public Opinion and the Assassination of Abraham Lincoln*. Baton Rouge: Louisiana State University, 1982.

Varga, Nicholas. *Baltimore's Loyola, Loyola's Baltimore, 1851–1986*. Baltimore: Maryland Historical Society, 1990.

White, Ronald C., Jr., and C. Howard Hopkins. *The Social Gospel: Religion and Reform in Changing America*. Philadelphia: Temple University Press, 1976.

Zwierlein, Frederick J. *The Life and Letters of Bishop McQuaid, Prefaced with The History of Catholic Rochester Before His Episcopate*. 3 vols. Rochester: Art Print Shop, 1927.

Zwinge, Joseph, S.J. "The Jesuit Farms in Maryland." *Woodstock Letters* 39–44 (1910–1915).

Index

Shaping American Catholicism: Maryland and New York, 1805–1915 was designed in Quadraat and typeset by Kachergis Book Design of Pittsboro, North Carolina. It was printed on 60-pound Natures Natural and bound by Thomson-Shore of Dexter, Michigan.